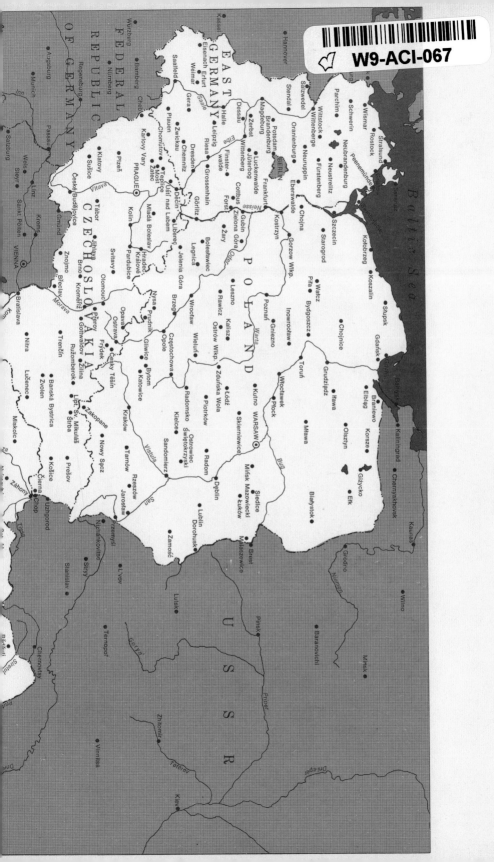

HOOVER INSTITUTION PUBLICATIONS

THE COMMUNIST REGIMES IN EASTERN EUROPE

The Communist Regimes
In Eastern Europe:
An Introduction

By **RICHARD F. STAAR**

The Hoover Institution on War, Revolution and Peace
Stanford University, Stanford, California

© 1967 by the Board of Trustees of the
Leland Stanford Junior University
All rights reserved

Library of Congress Catalog Card Number: 67-24367

Printed in the United States of America

FOR JADWIGA, MONICA AND CHRISTINA

Preface

THE IDEA for this book originated during the 1963–1964 academic year, while I occupied the Chester W. Nimitz Chair of Social and Political Philosophy at the United States Naval War College in Newport, Rhode Island. In the course of the foreign area studies program, in seminars devoted to Eastern Europe, and in discussions with senior field grade officers from all branches of the Armed Forces, as well as civilian students of comparable rank from various government agencies, the need for an introductory textbook became obvious. To this outstanding class at the Naval War College go my thanks for the inspiration and intellectual stimulus to embark on a difficult task.

Since that time, two or three books have been published specifically on the changing face of Eastern Europe during the past decade. Comprising either edited versions of lectures or symposia to which several authors have contributed individual chapters, they were found to be unsatisfactory as texts in a classroom situation. On the other hand, several excellent monographs do exist, but these deal with single countries and not the entire area. Hence there appears to be a definite need for one volume which would present an introduction to East European governments and politics for the university student, both civilian and military.

As this manuscript was being completed in draft form, two scholarly and erudite books appeared: James F. Brown, *The New Eastern Europe* (New York, 1966), and H. Gordon Skilling, *The Governments of Communist Eastern Europe* (New York, 1966). Both approach their subject functionally, Mr. Brown giving an across-the-board survey of political, economic, and cultural developments, as well as nationalism and relations between the area and outside powers. Professor Skilling provides more historical depth by discussing political traditions, the process of government, the elites that rule, how decisions are implemented, and what the future may hold. These two volumes, written by a Britisher and a Canadian respectively, may be too complex for the beginning student.

The present work attempts to fill the vacuum with a monograph which can serve both as a basic textbook and as an introduction to the source materials that are available in this difficult field. Much of the data has been extracted from articles and books in the original East European languages. In many instances—especially Albanian, Hungarian, and Romanian—I have used translations. This is indicated in the footnotes. Reports of monitored East European radio broadcasts also proved most useful. These were obtained from tapes which had been transcribed verbatim at Schleissheim, West Germany.

Materials from the research files of Radio Free Europe (RFE), in Munich, West Germany, and from its *Situation Reports* and other publications are cited throughout the study. Two visits to RFE, in March and August-September 1966, helped to bring up to date certain of the charts and tables. I am specifically grateful for the courtesy shown me by Messrs. John Kalo of London, England (on Bulgaria); Hanuš Hajek and Ladislav Niznansky (on Czechoslovakia); Miss Dorothy Miller (on East Germany); Wojciech Krzyżanowski and Kazimierz Zamorski (on Poland). They were most helpful in responding to a series of written questions during the research stage of this project. Mr. Zdenko Antič of Munich offered valuable comments on Yugoslavia.

This book is organized into eleven chapters. The first eight treat individually the countries of Eastern Europe now under communist regimes. Each describes the government structure, including constitutional framework and elections; the ruling party, which is variously designated as a workers' or a socialist or a communist movement; domestic policies; and foreign relations. No uniform outline has been adopted, in order to avoid repetition that might prove tedious for the student. The last three chapters incorporate an area-wide approach, in that they discuss military and economic integration through the Warsaw Treaty Organization and the Council for Mutual Economic Assistance as well as the development of polycentrism. Chapter 12 is a brief epilogue.

Although errors in fact and interpretation are my own, I wish to acknowledge with gratitude the reading of separate draft chapters by the following scholars: Messrs. Ivanko Gabensky, Sandor Kiss, Pavel Korbel, Dan Neculce, and Jerzy Ptakowski (all national editors of *East Europe* magazine in New York); Mr. Emery S. Kobor, Dr. Stanisław Skrzypek, and Dr. Emilia Wilder (Washington, D.C.); Professors L. A. D. Dellin (University of Vermont), Ernst C. Helmreich (Bowdoin College), and Edward Taborsky (University of Texas). The Bundesministerium für gesamtdeutsche Fragen, in Bonn, filled in the gaps concerning some of the information for the chapter on East Germany. Finally, the Office of External Research in the U.S. Department of State proved most cooperative in supplying scholarly data in response to specific queries as well as up-to-date directories.

Mr. Jesse M. Phillips did more than is expected of an editor by questioning various points in the manuscript which had been presented in an elliptic form. His meticulous editing transformed the book into a readable volume, and for his conscientious efforts I am immensely grateful.

Last, but not least, I would like to acknowledge with thanks the financial assistance without which this book would not have been possible: Emory University for repeated grants from its Research Committee which subsidized trips to the Library of Congress, Washington, and the final typing of the manuscript; the Relm Foundation in Ann Arbor, Michigan, for an award which allowed me to spend an entire summer on research instead of teaching and enabled me to make a trip to search for materials in West European libraries; and The Hoover Institution on War, Revolution and Peace at Stanford University, where a rough draft of this book was completed on a generous visiting scholar grant.

Permission to use extracts and other data from articles written by me since 1962 has been given by the *Journal of Central European Affairs*, the *Revista de Estudios Políticos, Current History*, the *Journal of Public Law, Die Wehrkunde, East Europe, United States Naval Institute Proceedings, Il Politico, Naval War College Review, Communist Affairs*, and *Moderne Welt*. The Foreign Policy Research Institute at the University of Pennsylvania has given permission for similar use of material in a study I prepared on the Warsaw Treaty Organization.

RICHARD F. STAAR

Washington, D.C.
August 1967

Contents

List of Tables

List of Abbreviations

ÁVH   State Security Authority (Államvédelmi Hivatal). Secret police in Hungary, detached in December 1949 from the Interior Ministry and made into a special department.

BKP   Bulgarian Communist Party (Bulgarskata Komunisticheska Partiya). The ruling party in the Bulgarian People's Republic.

CMEA   Council for Mutual Economic Assistance (Sovet Ekonomicheskoi Vzaimopomoshchi). Established in 1949 at Moscow to coordinate economic activities in Eastern Europe. Also known as CMEA or COMECON.

CPSU   Communist Party of the Soviet Union (Kommunisticheskaya Partiya Sovetskogo Soyuza). Designation since October 1952, before which it was called the All-Union Communist Party (Bolshevik).

ČSM   Czechoslovak Youth Union (Československý Svaz Mládeže). The only youth organization allowed in the Czechoslovak Socialist Republic.

DDR   German Democratic Republic (Deutsche Demokratische Republik). The name of East Germany since 1949, when it was given "sovereignty" by the Soviet Union.

DKMS   Dmitrov Communist Youth Union (Dimitrovski Komunisticheski Mladezhki Soyuz). The only youth organization allowed in Bulgaria; named after Georgi Dimitrov.

DOSAAF   Voluntary Society for Cooperation with the Army, Air Force, and Navy (Dobrovolnoe Obshchestvo Sodeistviya Armii, Aviatsii, i Flota). Paramilitary organization, established in 1927 by the Soviet Union.

FDGB	Free German Trade-Union Alliance (Freie Deutsche Gewerkschaftsbund). Consolidated labor movement in East Germany.
FDJ	Free German Youth (Freie Deutsche Jugend). The only youth organization allowed in East Germany.
GDR	German (East) Democratic Republic. See DDR.
KGB	Committee for State Security (Komitet Gosudarstvennoi Bezopasnosti). Attached to the U.S.S.R. Council of Ministers. Current name for the secret police.
KISZ	Communist Youth League (Kommunista Ifjusági Szövetség). The only youth organization allowed in Hungary.
KPD	Communist Party of Germany (Kommunistische Partei Deutschlands). Designation for the clandestine communist party in the Federal Republic of (West) Germany. For the East German equivalent, see SED, below.
KSČ	Communist Party of Czechoslovakia (Komunistická Strana Československa). Ruling party in the Czechoslovak Socialist Republic. See also KSS.
KSS	Communist Party of Slovakia (Komunistická Strana Slovenska). Separate communist movement in Slovakia since 1939 and the German occupation, although subordinate to the KSČ.
LPG	Agricultural Producers' Cooperatives (Landwirtschaftliche Produktionsgenossenschaften). Designation for collective farms in East Germany.
MSZMP	Hungarian Socialist Workers' Party (Magyar Szocialista Munkáspárt). Name of the communist party in Hungary, as reorganized in November 1956 by János Kádár, following the abortive revolution.
NKVD	People's Commissariat for Internal Affairs (Narodnyi Komissariat Vnutrënnykh Del). Name of the Soviet secret police until 1946, when redesignated MVD. For current name, see KGB.

PZPR   Polish United Workers' Party (Polska Zjednoczona Partia Robotnicza). Name of the communist party in Poland since December 1948, when the communist Polish Workers' Party absorbed the left wing of the Polish Socialist Party.

ROH   Revolutionary Trade-Union Movement (Revoluční Odborové Hnutí). Unified labor-union organization in Czechoslovakia.

SAG   Soviet Joint Stock Company (Sowjetische Aktiengesellschaft). Established in East Germany at the end of the Second World War and still in existence for such raw materials as uranium.

SED   Socialist Unity Party of Germany (Sozialistische Einheitspartei Deutschlands). The communist party in East Germany, established during April 1946 as a compulsory fusion between the KPD (see above) and the Social Democratic Party in the Soviet occupation zone.

SKJ   League of Communists of Yugoslavia (Savez Komunista Jugoslavije). Since 1958 this has been the designation for the communist party in Yugoslavia.

SSJ   League of Yugoslav Trade Unions (Savez Sindikata Jugoslavije). Consolidated labor-union movement in Yugoslavia.

SSRN   Socialist Alliance of Working People (Socijalistički Savez Radnog Naroda). National front organization in Yugoslavia.

SVAZARM   Union for Cooperation with the Army (Svaz pro Spolupráci s Armádou). Paramilitary organization in the Czechoslovak Socialist Republic equivalent to DOSAAF in the U.S.S.R.

UTM   Union of Working Youth (Uniunea Tineretulni Muncitor). Only youth organization allowed in Romania. Renamed the Communist Youth Union.

WTO   Warsaw Treaty Organization (Organizatsiya Varshavskogo Dogovora). Established in 1955. Military alliance system which officially includes the U.S.S.R. and all East European states except Yugoslavia.

The Communist Regimes in Eastern Europe

Chapter 1 / ALBANIA:
Land of Mountaineers

STILL a thorn in the flank of Yugoslavia, a shadow on a formerly Soviet sphere of influence, Albania provides a window into Europe for the Chinese communists. The region now known as the People's Republic of Albania, bordering on Yugoslavia and Greece as well as the Adriatic Sea, has an area of about 11,000 square miles and a population of only 1.8 million. Yet this small, poor, and unproductive land of mountaineers, no larger in area than the state of Maryland, plays a significant role in communist international politics. From the days of the Greek and Roman empires, when traders plied its coasts, Albania remained aloof and detached from world affairs well into modern times.[1] It was ruled by the Ottomans for nearly four hundred years, commencing in 1468 with the defeat of the Albanian national patriot Skanderbeg, who had defended the country against the Turkish army for almost a quarter of a century with his rugged mountain warriors.

Although the people of Albania have usually stood aside from affairs outside their borders, they found themselves overrun and engulfed by events of the Second World War. A little-known schoolteacher and later self-appointed army general, Enver Hoxha, organized a clandestine movement which became known as the National Liberation Front. As the Italians and Germans withdrew in 1944, Hoxha and his communist-dominated "democratic front" succeeded in liquidating most of the Albanian anticommunist organizations, such as the Nationalist Front (Balli Kombëtar) and the Legality (Legaliteti) movement.[2]

In the absence of any other effective opposition, Hoxha and his associates on November 29, 1944, established a new, revolutionary

1

government at Tirana.[3] Up to this time the Albanian communists had been directed and led by Josip Broz-Tito's Yugoslav communist party. Although the Albanian communists could claim only 4 to 5 percent of the population as supporters, the spurious democratic front received 91.8 percent of the votes cast to elect a constituent assembly, which in January 1946 declared Albania to be a people's republic. The new dictatorial regime, supported by neighboring Yugoslavia, strengthened communist influence within the country not only through the physical liquidation of the more notable non-communists, but also by application of ruthless purges to its own party.

Seemingly unimportant to the world—except for the Soviet Union, which was looking for a foothold on the Mediterranean—Albania began to move closer to Moscow. Afraid of impending annexation by his Yugoslav mentors, Hoxha broke off relations with Tito [4] in July 1948, but continued to maintain close ties with the U.S.S.R. until the 1956 denunciation of the deceased Stalin which led to the public break in 1961. Left without a strong protector in Europe, Hoxha turned to the Chinese communists, who readily answered his request for assistance in the ideological dispute with the Soviet Union.

THE COMMUNIST PARTY OF ALBANIA

Sympathy for Marxist ideology among certain Albanians dates back to June-December 1924, the period of the revolutionary government under Premier Bishop Fan Stylian Noli.[5] An earlier affinity for Russia became evident after Soviet communists revealed the secret treaty of London (1915), which provided for the partition of Albania. Lenin was considered a hero by some in that country, since he allegedly had saved it from partition. Five minutes of silence was observed by the Albanian parliament in tribute to the leader of the Bolshevik Revolution upon his death in January 1924. Although a communist party was not founded until 1941, Albanian communists and fellow travelers were supported by the Comintern in the late 1920's and the 1930's while they continued to agitate as a minority group within Albania and from exile.

During the years 1924-1939, King Zog I maintained an authoritarian regime. For twenty years after 1924 there were no legal political parties in Albania except the fascist movement, organized under the 1939 Italian occupation. The Albanian communist party was established secretly at Tirana in November 1941 under the supervision of two Yugoslav emissaries, Miladin Popovič and Dušan Mugoša, who directed the party until the end of the Second World War.[6]

The postwar communist system in Albania came into being without the assistance or presence of Soviet troops. Local communists organized and achieved power under the decisive leadership of their Yugoslav mentors, who followed directives from Tito. The leaders chosen by the Yugoslavs to head the party in Albania included the intellectual Enver Hoxha—the first and, as of this writing, the only head of the Albanian communist party—and the proletarian Koci Xoxe, who was executed in 1949 as an "enemy of the people." [7]

ORGANIZATION. The structure of the party was defined and sanctioned in 1948 at its first congress. A name was also selected: the Albanian Workers' party. The statute adopted at this congress based the organizational hierarchy on the principle of democratic centralism, wherein full and free discussion theoretically is permitted and, after a unanimous or majority vote, the minority submits to the majority. The 1950 constitution of Albania recognized the special status of the party.[8] The Albanian Workers' party is organized according to the country's territorial subdivisions, with a central apparatus in Tirana.

The highest organ, according to the 1948 statute, is the party congress, which is expected to meet every four years. This supreme body is made up of delegates nominally elected by district, regional, and city conferences. Its functions include ratification of reports submitted by the Central Committee and other main organs, review and amendment of the party program and statutes, determination of party tactics regarding current policy, and election of members to the Central Committee. In practice, the principal role of the congress remains that of giving the impression of democratic party rule and providing an opportunity for deserving members to be elected as delegates.

The Central Committee, according to the statute, directs all party activities in the periods between congresses. It supervises lower-ranking party organizations, elects members to central party organs, administers party funds, and represents the party in its relations with communist parties and mass organizations in other countries. In reality, the Central Committee has little authority and power, owing to its size and the fact that it is not in continuous session. The day-to-day functions of this committee are delegated to the Politburo and the Secretariat, both composed of persons elected by the Central Committee from among its own membership.

The real locus of power is the Politburo, the policy-formulating body of the party. In 1967 it consisted of eleven full members and five candidate members.[9] Through placement of these persons in top government offices and in the leadership of mass organizations, the Politburo can formulate policy that is certain to be carried out. Having Politburo members serve as premier and deputy premiers is a constant feature of party policy, and this procedure assures continuity in power and control over the government. The system can be described as one of interlocking directorates, and it still remains patterned directly after that of the U.S.S.R. despite the suspension of relations between the two countries.

Regardless of this basic pattern, the Albanian communists have emulated the Chinese by assigning at least twelve high-ranking bureaucrats (including five Politburo members) to additional duties at the city or district level. This may have been connected with preparation for a new party congress, which should have convened after four years according to the statute. Additional suggestions of preparation appeared in an "Open Letter" released by the Central Committee to all party members on March 4, 1966. This communication admitted that there was a chasm between the bureaucracy and the masses.[10] It probably was disseminated down to the lowest organizational units.

The lowest level in the party hierarchy is the basic cell, which corresponds to the primary party organization in the Communist Party of the Soviet Union. There are 2,000 cells, scattered in factories, transport and construction centers, various institutions, towns, and villages. They are formed only in places where at least three party members work, and they comprise a link between the masses and the governing organs of the party. Their functions include recruitment of new members, administration of local party affairs, and close surveillance over every group of persons living in the community or work center. The cell acts as an arm of the police state, but it remains subordinate in turn to local party committees which are formed successively at city, regional, and district levels.

Local committees meet once a month and are controlled by an executive agency, called the bureau, consisting of not more than eleven members. The bureau includes a first secretary and an additional two or more secretaries, all of whom must be approved by the Central Committee. The first secretary is the overall political boss of the committee and is a trusted member of the party. The functions of the committees are to assure fulfillment of party directives, supervise the implementation of these directives, administer the party's fiscal affairs, and approve the enrollment of new members.

MEMBERSHIP AND COMPOSITION. The paucity of information available concerning the membership and social composition of the Albanian Workers' party precludes more than a cursory and uncertain coverage of this subject. According to one author, who cites an official source, party membership in 1943 totaled about 700 persons. The regime newspaper twenty-three years later provided a figure of more than 66,000 members. (See table 1.)

TABLE 1

GROWTH OF THE ALBANIAN WORKERS' PARTY, 1943-1966

Year	Occasion	Membership
1943		700
1944		2,800
1948	First Congress (November)	29,137
1952	Second Congress (March-April)	44,418
1955	Third Congress (May-June)	48,644
1961	Fourth Congress (February)	ca. 53,000
1963		53,659
1966	Fifth Congress (November)	66,326

SOURCES: *Zëri i popullit,* March 24, 1954, as cited in Jani I. Dilo, *The Communist Party Leadership in Albania* (Washington, D.C., 1961), p. 10; Radio Free Europe (report by J. F. Brown), "Background Notes to Albania's Party Congress," February 2, 1961 (57 pp.), at pp. 17, 19; U.S. Department of State, Bureau of Intelligence and Research, *World Strength of the Communist Party Organizations* (Washington, D.C., 1967), p. 49; *Zëri i popullit,* November 10, 1963; Radio Tirana, November 1, 1966.

The data concerning the social composition of the party are similarly of somewhat dubious validity. In 1952 the membership could be subdivided as 74.1 percent poorer class (probably from rural areas for the most part), 22.2 percent middle class, and 3.7 percent former wealthy classes. In the words of one expert, "the Albanian Communist Party is fundamentally a party of poor peasants." [11] More recent statistics indicate that the percentage of industrial workers in the party had increased at the time of the February 1961 congress. The social composition then appeared in terms of new categories, namely, about 30 percent industrial workers, about 24 percent peasants on collective farms, about 42 percent white-collar workers and government employees, and only 3 percent private-entrepreneur farmers.[12]

The communist party of Albania resembles that of the Soviet Union in many ways besides organizational structure. The policies and activities of both have included widespread purges and intra-party rivalry. In Albania, as in any other communist totalitarian state, the party is run by one man, the first secretary. Numerous front organizations are operated to implement policies of the party and the government.

CONSTITUTION AND GOVERNMENT

The People's Republic of Albania is currently functioning under a fundamental law known as the 1950 constitution.[13] This is the second Soviet-type document adopted since power was seized by the communists, and it is the eighth constitution since Albania won independence in 1912 from Turkey. The first postwar constitution was adopted in March 1946. Because the Albanian communists at that time were an adjunct of the Yugoslav communist party, the new constitution was not difficult to draft. Its verbiage strikes the reader as an almost direct translation from the then newly promulgated Yugoslav document, which, in turn, was based on the 1936 "Stalin" constitution of the Soviet Union.

The major difference between the Albanian and Yugoslav texts was that the single legislative chamber known as the People's Assembly in Albania had as its counterpart in Yugoslavia, owing to the federal structure of that state, an assembly composed of two chambers. Other differences included the omission of any reference to the political supremacy of the Albanian Workers' party, which already represented the locus of power. References to a regime monopoly over domestic trade and the socialist development of agriculture also were lacking. These deficiencies, however, were remedied in the version adopted in July 1950. The changes apparently involved the intention to bring Albanian basic law into close conformity with the constitutions of the other East European states.

PRINCIPAL FEATURES OF THE 1950 CONSTITUTION. This document is divided into three parts. The first contains fundamental principles defining the People's Republic of Albania, the state's avowed social and economic goals, and the rights and duties of the citizen. The second treats the structure of the state—which includes the People's Assembly and its presidium, the Council of Ministers, the judiciary, the People's Councils, and the armed forces. The third describes the flag and state seal, and confirms Tirana as the capital city.[14]

The People's Republic of Albania is defined as having all its powers derived from and belonging to the population, which rules through the People's Councils (that is, the organs of local self-government) and the People's Assembly or national legislature. These bodies allegedly are elected by the citizens on the basis of a universal, equal, direct, and secret ballot. Social and economic measures are stressed in the Albanian constitution as in the corresponding documents of other communist-ruled countries. Control over natural resources and over industry and other means of production is placed in the hands of the state. Private property is guaranteed protection, but can be limited in its amount or expropriated if it is used to the detriment of the state. The rights and duties of citizens resemble those affirmed by other East European countries. In fact, the outside observer may be led to believe that the constitution includes Western democratic principles which guarantee certain inalienable rights vis-à-vis the state. In reality, however, the constitution is based upon the dictatorship of the proletariat or, rather, its vanguard, which is the communist party. Unrestricted authority of the state is upheld, and the rights of the citizen may be curtailed at any time.

According to the constitution, the 240-member People's Assembly is the highest and most important organ in the governmental structure. The Assembly is "elected" every four years by all of the citizens eligible to vote. It meets twice a year, at which times the deputies are expected to approve all items on the agenda. Since the party selects all of the candidates for the Assembly and presents them to the voters on a single-slate ballot for election, the People's Assembly is merely a rubber stamp for approving decisions by the party. Political rights as known in Western democracies are nonexistent in present-day Albania. (See table 2 for official election returns.)

TABLE 2

OFFICIAL ALBANIAN ELECTION RETURNS, 1958-1966

Date	Registered voters	Votes for regime	Percent	Votes against regime
June 1, 1958	780,061	779,935	99.80	126
June 3, 1962	889,875	889,868	99.98	7
July 10, 1966	978,161	978,154	99.99	3

SOURCES: *ACEN, Survey of Developments in the Captive Countries,* V (March-October, 1958), 6, and XII (January-June, 1962), 53. Radio Tirana, July 11, 1966.

NOTE: Votes against the regime have been computed. In 1966, four persons did not cast their ballot; forty votes were declared to be not valid. *Zëri i popullit,* July 12, 1966.

The People's Assembly elects fifteen of its members to form a legislative presidium, and the powers of the Assembly are exercised between its sessions by this small group.[15] The presidium interprets and makes decisions concerning the constitutionality of laws, ratifies international agreements, appoints and recalls diplomatic envoys, issues decrees, and promulgates laws passed by the Assembly. It also creates governmental commissions, proclaims elections, and convenes the Assembly. Yet the presidium is said to be responsible to the Assembly, which in theory may recall, replace, or dismiss any or all of its members.

The Council of Ministers is considered to be the supreme executive and administrative agency. It is formally appointed by the People's Assembly. The powers assigned by the constitution to the Council of Ministers include supervision over all social, economic, and cultural activities of the country. In reality, the premier, his three deputies, and the various ministers [16] comprising the Council are selected by the Political Bureau of the party. Their main function is to ensure that all party decisions are translated into action and carried out.

The local government organs consist of the People's Councils at district, regional, and city levels. These units are evolved by the people through direct elections for terms of three years. They have authority over administrative, economic, and cultural matters within their own geographic areas. Additionally, they maintain order, enforce the laws of the state, and are supposed to uphold the rights of the citizen.

According to the constitution, the highest judicial organ is the Supreme Court, whose membership is elected by secret ballot in the People's Assembly. Courts at the various lower levels are formed similarly by the corresponding People's Councils and thus allegedly represent the "will of the citizens."

The Office of the Prosecutor General is another agency, supposedly controlled by the People's Assembly. It supervises the implementation of laws by the ministries, other administrative bodies, and all public officials and citizens.

GOVERNMENT. The typical Soviet-style relationship between party and government is well established in Albania. The constitution of 1950 recognized the privileged and controlling position of the Albanian Workers' party, as already mentioned. Enver Hoxha, first secretary of the Central Committee, holds the top party position.[17] He effectively controls the government from this office, even though the titular head of state is the chairman of the Assembly presidium, Haxhi Lleshi. Table 3 lists the Politburo members and indicates their related positions in the government. The government is definitely subordinate to the party, and available information would indicate that the communists are well entrenched. Hoxha (b. 1908) and his fellow party leaders in top positions are relatively young, and it is not likely that these men will retire from the political scene in the near future.

If free elections were to be held in Albania today, the communists probably would not poll a majority. Such elections cannot be expected, however, because the communists will not permit them.[18] Neither is it to be anticipated that Albania will supply strong enough indigenous leadership to bring the country out from under communist control, but some writers think the future is not totally without hope for recovering this satellite from the influence of Peking.

DOMESTIC AFFAIRS

Economic and social transformation has come slowly and only recently to Albania, owing to its historic isolation from the mainstream of West European affairs. More than two decades of communist rule, however, have brought greater changes than occurred during all the preceding four centuries of Ottoman domination and the sixty years of influence to a varying degree by European powers. Progress in modernization is very considerable, in relation to past backwardness, but it still leaves Albania far behind the other nations of Europe, both east and west.[19]

TABLE 3
ALBANIA'S INTERLOCKING DIRECTORATE, 1967

Politburo	Secretariat (and responsibility)	City or district organization	Council of Ministers (and portfolio)	Other position
FULL MEMBERS				
Çarçani, Adil			Deputy premier	
Balluku, Beqir			Deputy premier and Defense minister	
Hoxha, Enver	Leader			
Nushi, Gogo		Berat		
Toska, Haki			Deputy premier	
Kapo, Hysni	Cadres			
Myftiu, Manush		Tirana		
Shehu, Mehmet			Premier	
Alia, Ramiz	Ideology			
Marko, Rita		Durrës		
Koleka, Spiro			Chairman, State Planning Commission	
CANDIDATE MEMBERS				
Këllezi, Abdyl				Chairman, Sino-Albanian Friendship Society
Hazbiu, Kadri			Internal Affairs minister	
Theodhosi, Koço			Industry and Mining minister	
Dume, Petrit				Chief of staff, armed forces
Peristeri, Pilo				Director, Tractor Spare Parts Factory (Tirana)

SOURCES: U.S. Department of State, Bureau of Intelligence and Research, *Directory of Albanian Officials* (Washington, D.C., November 1966), 60 p., for Council of Ministers and other positions. Radio Tirana, November 8, 1966, for new Politburo and Secretariat elected that day. Order given, as broadcast by this source.

NOTE: Three of the four members of the Secretariat are listed above. The fourth is Xhafer Spahiu, the party secretary for industry. He is not listed because he is not a Politburo member.

TRADITION. Despite the communist philosophy of subordinating the individual to the state through contrived mass uniformity, the Albanian population apparently has changed little and clings to its prewar ethnic customs. In rural areas clan or feudal relationships still persist and, as is usual in such sociological groupings, the traditional norms can be altered very slowly. Although the clan may now be organized into a village People's Council, there would appear to be some question as to whether this is a fiction of communist terminology or a genuine sovietization of organizational forms. While the past two decades have brought change in established mores and institutions, these differences cannot be attributed exclusively to the nature of the government. To a certain extent they remain in consonance with the social phenomena accompanying the modernization of any traditional society. The communist regime, of course, has done its utmost to mold and adapt these changes to the Stalinist model.

Prewar Albania essentially comprised a two-class society of large landowners and peasant farmers. The smaller groups of artisans, government employees, and teachers could be classified as the nucleus of a middle class, though their limited numbers rendered them insignificant from the point of view of influence. Under the present regime this basic social stratification still exists; only the occupations of the elite have changed. Party members immediately assumed the role formerly held by the *beys,* or landed aristocracy, to form what Milovan Djilas called the "new class" in neighboring Yugoslavia.

Industrial progress and the rise of a government bureaucracy have fostered social mobility, and the Albanian new class (not recognized as such by communist definition) is increasing in size. Within this group, rejection of tradition is most pronounced. While in one sense this break is designed under state guidance to lead into the patterns of a Marxist utopia, in another sense it creates the basis for a modicum of political objectivity.

Migration of labor, under government control, from agrarian pursuits to the industrial complexes of the city represents another significant factor in the gradual diminution of Albanian traditionalism. During 1960 some 70 percent of the population still lived in rural areas and, therefore, probably was employed in agriculture.[20] More recent statistics indicate that this percentage is declining. While the urbanization of transposed peasants under a communist regime might seem to represent a potential source of unrest within the country, in actual fact it has created few problems. The inequity of living conditions, totalitarian rule, long working hours, and low pay of the industrial worker are merely a continuation of his former agrarian existence. The substitution of local party leadership for the elders of his feudal clan remains the essential difference. The degree to which acceptance of this change has taken place is the great unknown.

The social and cultural objectives of the party include the substitution of ersatz Marxist concepts for traditional values stemming from the Albanian inheritance of Ottoman, Greek, and Western culture. For achievement of this goal, the government attempts to shape the functions of religion, culture, and education. Where they cannot be molded by influence, force is used to attain conformity.

RELIGION. Since communist regimes have been unable to eliminate religion, they try to "nationalize" it as a compromise expedient of control and a step toward its eventual destruction.[21] In Albania this is being carried out with limited opposition owing to the division into sects of the Moslem believers, who comprise some 70 percent of the population. These are divided into Sunni, Bektashi, and other orders which have been recognized by the regime as independent religious communities. The rest of the population, about 20 percent Orthodox and 10 percent Roman Catholic, is insufficient numerically to register serious opposition. A temporary accord with the faithful is provided for officially in the constitution of 1950, which states that freedom of religious practice is guaranteed so long as the church is not utilized as a political vehicle. Due to the basic intransigence of the Catholic Church vis-à-vis the tenets of communism, all ties with the Vatican were severed in 1951 and a "National Albanian Catholic Church" was established.[22]

While the state has brought religion and even church officials under strict control, of necessity a more tolerant view has been taken toward personal religious beliefs. Again, this represents an expedient rather than a relaxation of ideological imperatives. The principal tactic employed by the party is a subtle campaign to degrade religion to the level of superstition and slowly to eliminate places of worship. The thought seems to be that without the substance of organization and ceremony, the credence given to religious concepts will gradually erode. Western observers tend to discount the effect of this approach; their views, however, may reflect wishful thinking.

CULTURE. Literature, the theater, music, and art are controlled by the party through various cultural organizations, such as the Union of Writers and Artists, the Union of Albanian Women, and the Committee for Arts and Culture. Under the influence of the Chinese communists, Albania in 1966 launched a cultural revolution of its own which called for the production of a "national" culture and the rejection of classical works.

Intellectual "revisionism" of the type appearing in Poland, Hungary, or Czechoslovakia is almost nonexistent.[23] While the controls of the Hoxha regime are more than adequate for suppressing any artistic "deviations" into nonconformity, it is probably a dearth of intellectuals rather than the repressive regime that accounts for the absence of substantial dissident sentiment after more than two decades of communist rule.

In September 1966 an article entitled "Let Us Turn the Basic Party Organizations into True Revolutionary Cells" appeared in the monthly theoretical journal *Rruga e Partisë*.[24] It was written by Manush Myftiu, a Politburo member and the first secretary of the District Committee for Tirana. He complained about two categories of negative reaction, one that openly opposes the party and even slanders it, and another, acting from behind the scene and slow to make fundamental changes, that questions the politics of the party.

EDUCATION. The objectives of the Albanian educational system vary little from those pursued by the standard communist thought-control pattern: development of technical skills, popular acceptance of Marxist ideology, and formation of a politically reliable intellectual elite. As with certain of the less developed East European countries, the initial emphasis has been on the creation of technical skills in both vocational and engineering fields. Each government ministry is responsible for vocational training through *teknikums* (vocational schools). In 1957 a university was established, but until the end of 1961 the preponderance of higher education was accomplished by sending students to Russia and other East European countries.

Illiteracy represented the fundamental problem to be overcome by the communist government. By 1963 the prewar (1938) illiteracy rate of 90 percent reportedly had been all but eliminated in the population group up to the age of forty years. A statement by Hoxha, as quoted in an American periodical, indicates that in 1964 it was planned that one out of every 4.6 persons should be attending some school.[25] The goal by 1970 is to have eight years of compulsory education for all children. Claims by the regime as to the effectiveness of its educational institutions are somewhat offset by frequent reforms of the system. In an elaborate description of a recent such reorganization appearing in the Albanian publication *Ylli* it was noted that the new system would offer a fresh incentive to the graduate of a secondary school: a diploma qualifying him as a "worker."

Training in communist doctrine is conducted at all levels and within all schools. Adult education in such matters takes place through the medium of local party organizations. Outside observers indicate that the people have little interest in such efforts, and the benefits supposed to be derived from the process are more than countered by the day-to-day experiences of Stalinist communism in action.

The rift with the Soviet Union had an immediate effect on the quality of advanced education. Even the contribution of the Chinese cannot be expected to fill the vacuum left by the Russians. It is probably for this reason that Albania is attempting to resume closer relations with other East European states. On the other hand, in early 1966 Warsaw declared Tirana's ambassador *persona non grata* [26] after accusing him of smuggling an enemy of the Polish regime out of the country on an Albanian passport.

SECURITY CONTROLS. By democratic standards, Albania is unquestionably a police state. The leaders maintain themselves in power through an all-pervasive and powerful security organization. The effectiveness of the police may have created a conviction among the population regarding the invincibility of the regime. The hostility of the Albanian people toward the government, in whatever degree this may occur, stems from a basic dislike for the communist system and the failure of the regime to fulfill its promises of "freedom, bread, and land." [27]

It would be an error, however, to postulate that the communist nature of the regime, per se, is the only reason for this hostility. The Albanians have a long history of dislike for central authority, particularly when it stems from an alien system. Control over popular disaffection and acts of protest, either passive or active, is vested with the police and security forces under the Interior ministry.[28] These forces include: the directorate of state security, which is called the Sigúrimi, or secret police; the border guards; and the regular uniformed police.

The secret police employ the standard communist methods of controlling the population through the use of personal documentation, surveillance, and censorship. Paid or unpaid informants remain the principal source of information on antistate activities or sentiments. There is no apparent organized resistance to the government, and most instances of arrest or liquidation seem to result not from anticommunist activities but from disagreement with the Hoxha regime.[29]

The border guards, primarily operating to protect the frontiers against infiltration, serve equally well to prevent Albanians from clandestinely leaving the country. If one is so inclined, however, ingress and egress across the mountain borders should not represent any substantial problem for the indigenous population. The regular police are charged with the more conventional tasks of maintaining public order and safety.[30] Close collaboration is maintained with the directorate of state security by the border guards and the uniformed police.

NEWS. Daily papers and other media of mass communication are state or party controlled. The official newspapers—*Zëri i popullit,* which is the Albanian communist party organ, and the democratic front's *Bashkimi*—are used as political instruments. Radio Tirana functions as the broadcasting equivalent. Despite Russian claims to the contrary, there seems to be no jamming of foreign broadcasts. One observer has attributed this more to the technical inability of the Albanians to effect jamming than to any disregard for the effect of transmissions from abroad. A single experimental television broadcasting station operates in Albania. Citizens prosperous enough to purchase imported TV sets, of which there are about 300 in Tirana, can receive Italian stations, whose broadcasts they are said to prefer to local programs.

ECONOMIC AND MILITARY AFFAIRS

By any standard, Albania is the least developed country in Eastern Europe. Modernization and industrialization are the long-range objectives of the government, with principal emphasis on the extraction of mineral resources, agriculture, and light manufactured goods.[31] Under the communist regime substantial gains have been made in all economic areas, as indicated by the selected figures in table 4. Although industrial production has expanded much more rapidly than agricultural development, the difference remains relative.[32] Industrialization by Western standards has just begun, and agriculture and mining contribute most to the national product.

TABLE 4

SELECTED ECONOMIC INDICATORS IN ALBANIA, 1950-1970

Commodity	Unit	1950	1955	1960	1966	1970 (planned)
Electricity	million KWH	21.1	85.3	194.3	389.9	700
Petroleum	thousand metric tons	131.8	208.1	725.5	855.8	1,200
Coal	"	40.9	194.6	290.6	385.2	650
Cement	"	15.9	44.5	72.9	139.1	—
Bread	"	51.0	79.0	138.3	—	—
Sugar	"	0.6	7.1	13.3	—	—
Olive butter . . .	metric tons	1,342.0	2,735.0	2,169.0	—	—
Fresh fish.	"	1,493.0	2,581.0	2,599.0	—	—
Cheese	"	771.0	1,024.0	2,418.0	—	—
Sausage	"	139.0	73.0	244.0	—	—

SOURCES: L. N. Tolkunov (ed.), *Sotsialisticheskii lager* (Moscow, 1962), pp. 41-42. Harilla Papajorgii, *The Development of Industry and Its Prospects in the People's Republic of Albania* (Tirana, 1964), p. 47. Radio Tirana, June 15, 1966. *New York Times,* December 18, 1966.

NOTE: The 1965 statistical yearbook gives only value in leks and percentage increase over the 1938 base year. [Albania], *Vjetari Statistikor i Republika Popullore e Shqipërisë, 1965* (Tirana, 1965).

Economic policies are formulated by the Politburo of the party, and specific production goals are established by the State Planning Commission. This latter agency coordinates the plans of national and local government enterprises, cooperatives, and individual producers. With the exception of a few small businesses and some farms, all economic activity is state owned and operated.[33]

In 1949 Albania became a member of the Council for Mutual Economic Assistance (CMEA). Since the openly avowed rift with Moscow in October 1961, however, it has not actively participated in Council affairs and has not sent representatives to meetings. The U.S.S.R. was the principal trading partner of Albania from 1948 to 1961, accounting for more than half of exports and imports. During this period a consistently adverse foreign trade balance of payments had to be financed with Soviet, other East European, and Chinese credits. These reportedly amounted to almost 2.2 billion rubles, as shown in table 5. Since the Albanian-Soviet rift, China has assumed

TABLE 5

SINO-SOVIET BLOC CREDITS TO ALBANIA, 1945-1965
(In millions of rubles)

Country	Amount	Country	Amount
U.S.S.R.	948	Poland	85
Czechoslovakia	222	Hungary	80
East Germany	152	Bulgaria	62
China	555	Total	2,196
Romania	92		

SOURCES: Ranko Banovič, *Posleratni razvoj privrede u Albaniji* (Belgrade, 1959), p. 14. Presseausschnitte und Radioberichte aus den Osteuropaeischen Laendern, *Albanien und seine "Protektoren"* (Munich, August 17, 1966), pp. 10-11.
NOTE: The ruble is exchanged officially at the rate of $1.11 each.

a major part of the trade formerly conducted by the U.S.S.R. In 1950 Tirana's deficit amounted to 779 million leks, and has increased since then, amounting in 1955 to 1,491 million, in 1960 to 1,613 million, and in 1964 to 1,910 million.[34]

INDUSTRY. The industrial sector of the Albanian economy comprises limited extraction of basic raw materials, processing industries, and food and textile plants, but little else. The government has stressed the development of production in mining, petroleum, and building materials. Only limited attempts have been made to establish other heavy industries, due to the small market within Albania and the lack of technical expertise.

Communist industrial policy can be divided chronologically into two basic phases. The years 1944-1947 saw the reconstruction of industries destroyed by war and the simultaneous nationalizing of sources of production. From 1947 to the present the industrial sector has been guided by the original Stalinist model and a succession of economic plans. The first plans were drawn up on an annual basis, followed by a two-year plan for 1949-1950.

By 1951 sufficient progress had been made to allow for reasonable planning over five-year intervals. This first *pyatiletka* followed the Stalinist line of increasing heavy industrial output at the expense of agriculture and consumers' goods.[35] With a great deal of Soviet technical aid, the objectives of this plan allegedly could be reached. It has been asserted that before the break with Moscow a fifteen-year (1961-1975) perspective plan was worked out to coordinate Albanian economic development with that of other East European countries.[36]

During the second five-year plan (1956-1960), industrial output again reportedly increased. Certain authors have cited Albanian government sources as claiming that the most recent five-year plan (1961-1965) necessitated a growth of 51 percent in industrial output.[37]

This third five-year plan was proclaimed in advance as being relatively successful, despite minor setbacks ensuing from the disagreement with the U.S.S.R. Official reports indicate that substantial economic difficulties, postulated by Western observers as resulting from the withdrawal of Soviet economic assistance, have not materialized, thanks primarily to the substitution of Chinese aid. One problem stemmed from the lack of spare parts for machinery of Soviet origin. The Chinese, through extensive copying, have been able either to provide the necessary parts or to replace the basic equipment.

Economic agreements with France, Italy, Austria, and Romania [38] should lead to significant (by Albanian standards) technical and material aid for Tirana's industrial efforts. While achievement of current five-year plan goals will still leave the industrial sector far behind the rest of Eastern Europe, the gains made on a relative basis serve as evidence that a communist government can create rapid economic progress through totalitarian means over a limited period of time.

AGRICULTURE. In common with many other East European countries, Albania suffers from the fact that agriculture has not kept pace with industrial gains. While this can be attributed to a number of factors, it would appear that the difficulty lies essentially in the ideological foundation of Marxism. The millennium for the proletariat is a condition which did not embrace the working peasantry initially. Albanian or any other standard communist doctrine in regard to collectivization [39] fails to recognize the traditional independence of the farmer and his attachment to the land. The factory worker, having once been deprived of his traditional orientations, can in some instances be molded according to the socialist form; the peasant possesses different psychological characteristics and is less likely to adapt.

Albania's drive to collectivize the agrarian sector has gone through the customary cycles. Unlike the "revisionist" policies in Poland and Yugoslavia, the immediate objective had been full collectivization.[40] In June 1963 Hoxha reported to the Central Committee that 86 percent of all arable land had come into the possession of collective farms and that the peasantry had slowly begun to change its way of life by embracing a "new culture." Notable by its absence was a comparison of the output between this high percentage and the remaining 14 percent, still almost all independently owned at that time. The total value of all agricultural production in 1962 amounted to 28.4 billion leks, allegedly 117 percent above any figure attained before the Second World War. In the most recent comprehensive book on Albania, published in 1956, it was noted that despite collectivization the independent farmer grew an overwhelming part (some 94 percent) of all agricultural products.[41] The years 1955-1957 seem to have been the time of greatest pressure by the regime, because collectivization increased from 18 percent of the arable land to 57 percent during that period.[42]

Policies of soil reclamation and the cultivation of marginal lands have helped to raise agricultural production. Although programs for expanding the amount of arable land are limited by topography, the present emphasis is on increasing the area under cultivation by 89,000 hectares to a total of 540,000 hectares by 1970. State farms seem to play a very insignificant role, since only thirty-one existed in 1964, seven years after the first was established.[43] They concentrate on animal husbandry, olive growing, and seed production. The data in table 6 suggest that some success is being achieved in animal husbandry.

Students of East European affairs have observed that communism does not appeal to the peasant and that, almost without exception, this element of the population is hostile to government policies. This unquestionably is true, yet the very independence that engenders such hostility precludes any action in unison against the government. Consequently, it can be somewhat misleading to assume that the peasantry poses a substantial threat to any communist regime. The danger, if any, is indirect and stems from the dissatisfaction created among the more cohesive elements of the population when food is not in ample supply. In Albania this indirect threat is of less importance than in the more advanced East European countries, for the average Albanian has never been exposed to any but a harsh and limited diet.

TABLE 6

DOMESTIC ANIMALS IN ALBANIA, 1950-1964
(In thousands)

Year	Cows	Horses	Sheep	Hogs	Domestic fowl
1950	114.0	50.5	1,707.0	46.7	660
1955	112.0	48.7	1,734.0	85.9	1,201
1960	146.3	49.0	1,548.5	130.4	1,580
1964	157.1	44.2	1,682.2	146.6	1,607

SOURCES: L. N. Tolkunov (ed.), *Sotsialisticheskii lager* (Moscow, 1962), p. 46; [Albania], *Vjetari Statistikor i Republika Popullore e Shqipërisë, 1965* (Tirana, 1965), p. 234.

LABOR. The workers of Albania have been strictly regimented, and rigid labor legislation provides penalties for those who do not fulfill state norms or who fail to appear for work. The work force [44] is controlled partly by the Directorate of Labor and partly by the trade-unions, whose organization is divided into three basic sub-elements, for (1) industrial workers, (2) administration, public health, and educational-cultural employees, and (3) agricultural laborers.

Compulsory work, freezing of personnel in their jobs, and state control over mobility proceed along Stalinist lines. The principal difficulties involve a shortage of trained industrial workers and lack of sufficient incentive to increase output. Stakhanovite and "shock-worker" methods have been copied from the Soviet system, but have met with greater resistance than in the U.S.S.R.[45] The Albanian still tends to regard factory work as "unmanly," and only by intense indoctrination of the younger generation through contrived "youth action" programs is this belief slowly being dispelled.

ARMED FORCES. The armed forces of Albania are relatively insignificant by East European standards and consist of approximately 39,000 men. They are organized along conventional lines. The Chinese have replaced the Russians as advisers, although on a much smaller scale. An indication of Peking's influence appeared in the decision by the Sixteenth Plenum of the Central Committee, in Tirana on March 4, 1966, to abolish all military ranks and reintroduce political commissars.

The departure of Soviet naval forces from the base at Valona and the island of Sasseno marked the end of Moscow's influence. One source has reported that the Albanians refused to allow the U.S.S.R. to withdraw some of its submarines and equipment after the Tirana-Moscow break.[46] Allegedly, an actual armed engagement of limited scope took place between Soviet and Albanian personnel. Subsequent negotiations resulted in the Soviets' leaving four Class W submarines at Valona, along with support equipment. The Albanian armed forces pose little threat to either the North Atlantic Treaty Organization (NATO) or to Eastern Europe. In combination with internal security forces they do comprise an effective element of control over the country.[47] (See chap. ix, on the Warsaw Treaty Organization.)

FOREIGN AFFAIRS

While the postwar history of Albania's friendship and differences with the outside world has been shaded to a degree by overtones of political doctrine, there is little to indicate that ideological differences, per se, have predominantly influenced Albanian actions. As one expert has phrased it: "In the Communist world, conflicts have to take an ideological form even when the real motives may be the interests of individuals or groups or the power politics of countries." [48]

YUGOSLAVIA. Relations between Albania and Yugoslavia traditionally have been hostile, stemming from ethnic differences, territorial disputes, and the very nature of Balkan politics. During the Second World War, common interests were generated by Axis occupation and the Marxist orientation of guerrilla groups in both countries, leading to a postwar rapprochement between their governments.[49] This collaboration became increasingly unilateral, in favor of Belgrade, and by 1947 it appeared that Tito's vision of Balkan unity involved less of an independent federation of Balkan states and more of a Greater Yugoslavia.[50] The link between Belgrade and Tirana paralleled the master-satellite relationship of the Soviet Union vis-à-vis the other countries of Eastern Europe. The political opportunity for a break came with the Cominform expulsion of the Yugoslav communist party. Beginning in July 1948, the Soviet Union replaced Yugoslavia as the protector of Albania.

During the remaining years of Stalin's life, Albania supplied a prominent voice in the Soviet-inspired campaign of East European vituperation against Belgrade. Traditional animosities and the existence of the Kosmet (Kosovo and Metohija) enclave, where about 900,000 Albanians resided within Yugoslavia, made it not difficult for the Tirana regime to maintain the attitude that close cooperation with the Soviet Union remained a necessity for the preservation of Albanian independence.[51] The U.S.S.R. in turn benefited from the arrangement both through the propaganda advantage and through access to a military bastion on the Adriatic.

After the death of Stalin and the subsequent modification in Soviet policy toward Yugoslavia, the advantages of close cooperation with the U.S.S.R. became more economic than military. The attempt by Tito to exert influence on the politics of Eastern Europe, coupled with the geographic proximity of Belgrade to Tirana, created a threat to the party leadership in Albania. This danger, while not necessarily directed at territorial integrity, was sufficiently grave to cause concern among Hoxha and his followers for their personal security. It was apparent that, for them to remain in control, the repressive methods of Stalinism had to be continued.

THE SOVIET-ALBANIAN RIFT. In 1957, in a speech to a plenum of his Central Committee in defense of Stalin, Hoxha injected the ideological basis for the subsequent rift between Albania and the U.S.S.R. During the period 1957-1960 the charges and countercharges of Marxist deviation were relatively subdued, being conducted on a highly esoteric level.[52] Soviet military and economic aid to Albania continued, but ties between Tirana and Peking already were forming. The staff of the Chinese embassy in Albania was enlarged, and translation of articles from *Pravda* gradually were replaced with those from *Jen Min Jih Pao,* the Chinese communist party newspaper.

In 1960 the extent of discord between Albania and the U.S.S.R. became more apparent to the Western world. The absence of Hoxha and Mehmet Shehu from the East European summit meeting at Bucharest, the purging in September 1960 of Politburo member Liri Belishova and Audit Commission chairman Koço Tashko from the

Albanian communist party,[53] and the ever increasing shrillness of the academic debate on "revisionism" indicated that a serious split was developing. These events became compounded by the growing divergence of views between the U.S.S.R. and Communist China.

Tirana did not receive an invitation to the Twenty-second Congress of the Soviet communist party in October 1961, an event of considerable significance for international communism. At this party congress the Albanian leadership was bitterly attacked by Khrushchëv. Chou En-lai, chief representative of the Chinese communists, departed from Moscow soon thereafter, but not before indicating his support for Albania and his condemnation of certain Soviet policies. During the year 1961 it was alleged by Albania that a Khrushchëv-sponsored *coup* had attempted to overthrow the Hoxha regime. With words now reportedly transmitted into action, the split was all but complete. By December 1961 the U.S.S.R. had stopped all aid to Tirana and had even suspended diplomatic relations.

While Albania represents little current economic or military value to the Soviet Union, the fact of its successful defiance, its position as an amplifier of internal discord within the communist bloc, and its use by the Chinese as an actual rather than theoretical platform for influence in East European affairs does appear important.

COMMUNIST CHINA. With the disappearance of Soviet influence from Tirana, Peking has assumed the role of protector.[54] Initially, the ability of distant China to support a European protégé was questionable. It may be that Moscow felt this might soon become obvious to the Albanians and that an accord would again be reached. Such has not happened, if for no other reason than China's surprisingly effective program of assistance. Chinese aid, which amounted to $123 million as a loan during 1961-1965, does not approach in magnitude or quality the previous Soviet effort, but the very impetus earlier given Albania by the U.S.S.R. seems to have created a base sufficient for Chinese support to be adequate. The foreign trade of Albania has shown a surprising increase, as indicated in table 7. During 1966 China was committed to supplying machinery for nitrogen and thermal-power plants at Fier, a textile factory in Berat, and the Elbasan steel and cement works.[55]

ATTITUDE TO THE WEST. Despite hostility toward the United States, based to a large extent on ideology, the Albanian regime maintains varying degrees of diplomatic and economic relations with other major Western powers. France and Italy have become increasingly active in its foreign trade. Britain has indicated willingness to resume diplomatic relations, subject to some compensation for damage sustained by two British warships which in 1946 struck mines in the Corfu Channel.[56]

TABLE 7

ALBANIA'S FOREIGN TRADE, 1950-1964
(In millions of leks)

	1950	1955	1960	1964
Exports	324	650	2.441	2,996
Imports	1,103	2,141	4,054	4,906
Total	1,427	2,791	6,495	7,902

SOURCES: L. N. Tolkunov (ed.), *Sotsialisticheskii lager* (Moscow, 1962), p. 47. [Albania], *Vjetari Statistikor i Republika Popullore e Shqipërisë, 1965*, p. 313.

NOTE: The current official rate of exchange is five leks to one U.S. dollar. The figures in the table reflect the old rate of fifty leks to the dollar, i.e., the pre-August 1965 exchange.

Differences with Greece, stemming from the latter's claims to part of southern Albania (Epirus), the abduction into Albania of some 25,000 Greek nationals by the communist-insurgent ELAS at the termination of the civil war in Greece, and the support given ELAS by Albania during the conflict are being gradually forgotten.[57] Informal discussions were undertaken toward an initial rapprochement and in March 1966 a two-million-dollar trade agreement was signed in Paris, the first between Athens and Tirana since the Second World War.

OTHER COUNTRIES. Most probably due to the common tie provided by their Moslem background, the Albanians have maintained friendly relations with the United Arab Republic and Algeria. Trade with the U.A.R. increased by 50 percent during 1966, compared with the previous year. Since the break with Moscow, even Albanian-Turkish contacts have improved.

There is some significance in the fact that several of the communist-ruled countries (while otherwise following the U.S.S.R.) have resumed economic relations with Albania, which they had severed after 1961. That they have done so may mean that Moscow has had second thoughts on the usefulness of a total economic blockade. These states include North Vietnam, North Korea, Cuba, and Romania.

There are indications that the Albanians would be favorably disposed toward some type of trade with the United States. So long as China remains the principal benefactor of Tirana, however, it is not likely that the Albanian regime would jeopardize its position by any agreement with Washington. Typical of the vituperative commentary in Tirana is the following:

> [U.S. President Lyndon B.] Johnson has openly declared that violence will go before reason. . . . All this shows the aggressive and fascist character of the Johnson Doctrine which, in its barbaric actions, surpasses even the Hitlerite predecessors. . . .[58]

Albania is a member of the United Nations, admitted in 1955 through the device of a trade-off and an American voting abstention. One source states that Albania is no longer a member of CMEA. In any case, the exact status of its relationship with that organization is not known. Although Albania has not participated in Warsaw Pact matters since 1961, its membership in this treaty organization presumably remains only in suspension. Hoxha did not receive an invitation to the pact meeting of July 4-6, 1966, at Bucharest.[59]

There was one school of thought which contended that the verbal friction between the Soviet Union and Albania had evolved into a personal vendetta between Khrushchëv and Hoxha. From this followed the conclusion that with the passing of one or both of these leaders from the political scene Albania and the Soviet Union might again be brought together. While this outcome is well within the realm of possibility (Khrushchëv was deposed in mid-October 1964), the events of the past several years suggest that a rapprochement is likely only if it involves an advantage to the leadership in Tirana [60] which outweighs significantly what can be obtained from China.

NOTES

1 For a good historical introduction see Stavro Skendi (ed.), *Albania* (New York, 1956), pp. 1-30.

2 The chairman of this last organization in exile, Dr. Nuci Kotta, died at New York. See *ACEN News*, No. 119 (September-October 1965), p. 29, and [Albania], *Twenty Years of Socialism in Albania* (Tirana, 1964), p. 12.

3 For names and offices in this ten-man regime see Free Europe Committee, Inc., *A Chronology of Events in Albania, 1944-1952* (New York, 1955), p. 1; hereafter cited as *Chronology of Events*.

4 On the eve of the Stalin-Tito break, Stalin suggested that Yugoslavia absorb Albania. Milovan Djilas, *Conversations with Stalin* (New York, 1962), p. 143. For the aid that Belgrade gave Tirana before that time see Harry Hamm, *Albania: China's Beachhead in Europe* (London, 1963), p. 50.

5 An exile since December 1924, Noli died in the United States. It is interesting to note that the U.S.S.R. posthumously hailed his political and literary activity, stressing his efforts for Albania's independence. Radio Moscow, March 18, 1965.

6 Vladimir Dedijer, *Jugoslovensko-Albanski odnoši, 1939-1948* (Belgrade, 1949), p. 5. It has the distinction of being the youngest communist party which holds power today.

7 Jani I. Dilo, *The Communist Party Leadership in Albania* (Washington, D.C., 1961), pp. 7-8, provides names of others purged before and after Xoxe.

8 Article 21, as given in V. N. Durdenevskii (ed.), *Konstitutsii evropeiskikh stran narodnoi demokratii* (Moscow, 1954), p. 112.

9 Radio Free Europe, *Communist Party-Government Line-Up* (Munich, July 1967), p. 1; hereafter cited as *Line-Up*. Seven characteristics shared by the Politburo members are listed in Dilo, *op. cit.*, pp. 5-6, 19-20.

10 Radio Tirana, February 10, 1966; *Neue Zürcher Zeitung,* March 15, 1966.

11 Skendi, *op. cit.*, pp. 84-85.

12 U.S. Department of State, Bureau of Intelligence and Research, *World Strength of the Communist Party Organizations* (Washington, D.C., 1967), p. 49, gives rounded-off figures; hereafter cited as *World Strength*. See also "Maverick in the Balkans," *East Europe,* X, No. 4 (April 1961), p. 5.

13 For the text and a discussion see N. Ya. Kurpits, *Konstitutsiya i osnovnye zakonodatelnye akty Respubliki Albanii* (Moscow, 1951).

14 *Ibid.* Only the 1946 constitution appears in English in Amos J. Peaslee (ed.), *Constitutions of Nations* (2 vols.; Concord, N.H., 1950), I, 35-50. The second edition (1956) does not carry the 1950 constitution either.

15 The chairman of this People's Assembly presidium, his three deputies, and the secretary are identified in *Line-Up,* p. 2.

16 Article 69 of the constitution enumerates ten ministries. Durdenevskii, *op. cit.*, pp. 121-122. There exist, however, thirteen such offices. *Line-Up,* p. 2, provides the names of incumbents.

17 For a glorified description of this man's wartime exploits see Edward Karłowicz, *Wolność przyszła z gór* (Warsaw, 1956), pp. 96-157.

18 In this connection a Soviet broadcast stated: "The leaders of the Albanian Workers' party have established in their country a system of censorship which is the most severe in the entire world." Radio Moscow, September 16, 1964.

19 For this implication see N. D. Smirnova, *Obrazovanie Narodnoi Respublii Albanii* (Moscow, 1960), pp. 187-188.

20 E. B. Valev, *Albaniya* (Moscow, 1960), p. 21. The plan for 1965 called for a drop to 67 percent. Harilla Papajorgje, *The Development of Socialist Industry and Its Prospects in the People's Republic of Albania* (Tirana, 1964), p. 138.

21 Kemal Vokopola, "Church and State in Albania," in U.S. Senate, Committee on the Judiciary, *The Church and State under Communism* (Washington, D.C., 1965), II, 33-47.

22 Skendi, *op. cit.*, pp. 293-296, indicates that the Roman Catholic Church is directly persecuted. Severance of relations occurred in August 1951, allegedly on the initiative of the Catholic Church in Albania. *Chronology of Events*, p. 125. See also *L'Osservatore Romano*, July 11, 1967; cited in the *New York Times* the following day, which reports that the last churches were closed by Red Guards, depriving 130,000 Catholics of public places to worship.

23 Note, however, the discussion of art in the weekly organ of the Writers' and Artists' Union, *Drita*, September 12, 1966, which criticized a modern art exhibit.

24 Cited in Radio Free Europe report, "Opposition to the Albanian Cultural Revolution," September 22, 1966 (7 pp.). Radio Free Europe is hereafter cited as RFE.

25 "Albania," *East Europe*, XII, No. 7 (July 1963), p. 35. In 1963, Albania had thirteen professors, sixty-four "candidates in sciences," and sixty-eight assistant professors. *Twenty Years of Socialism*, p. 101. Tirana University reportedly enrolls 7,000 students. *New York Times*, October 30, 1966.

26 RFE, *Situation Report*, February 28, 1966, p. 2.

27 An alleged transcript for an espionage trial would indicate that at least four organizations as late as 1950 opposed the communists: the Nationalist Front, the Legality movement, the Independent Bloc, and the Agrarian party. *Le Procès des Espions Parachutés en Albanie* (Paris, 1950), p. 23. See also the article by Rahman Parllaku in *Bashkimi*, October 26, 1966, p. 3.

28 A United Nations survey indicated that some 80,000 persons from the 1.7 million population (or 3 percent) were held in concentration camps during 1945-1956 and that more than 16,000 had died there.

29 The harsh penal code, as amended, has been translated in M. A. Gelfer (ed.), *Narodnaya Respublika Albaniya* (Moscow, 1961), pp. 157.

30 James Cameron, "Albania: The Last Marxist Paradise," *The Atlantic*, CCXI, No. 6 (June 1963), p. 48.

31 See "Albania," *British Survey* (October 1964), pp. 1-20.

32 The total wheat requirements of Albania have been estimated at 240,000 tons per year. Most of the deficit, or about 50,000 tons annually, has been coming from China. RFE reports, "Sino-Soviet Dispute and Albanian Agricultural Yields," September 9, 1964 (4 pp.), and "Renewed Importance of Agriculture for Albania," September 19, 1966 (4 pp.).

33 The regime has been discussing economic decentralization as well as studying supply and demand, according to *Zëri i popullit*, May 21, 1965. *Ekonomia popullore*, May-June 1965, revealed that certain enterprises were being transferred from national to local industry—that is, to control by the respective People's Councils.

34 V. I. Zolotarev, *Vneshnyaya torgovlya sotsialisticheskikh stran* (Moscow, 1964), p. 141; [Albania.] *Vjetari statistikor i Republika Popullore e Shqipërisë 1965* (Tirana, 1965), p. 313.

35 During 1965 a 50 percent increase for investment in heavy industry was announced. RFE report, "Albania Pushes Heavy Industry," March 25, 1965 (3 pp.). In the 1966-1970 period heavy industry is scheduled to increase twice as rapidly as consumers' goods production. *New York Times*, December 18, 1966.

36 Valev, *op. cit.*, pp. 30-31.

37 Capital investment for industry during the first two five-year plans involved percentages of 48.4 and 44.1 of the totals, respectively. L. V. Tyagunenko, *Development of the Albanian Economy* (Washington, D.C., 1961), p. 11; translated from the Russian.

38 Speech by Premier Mehmet Shehu, as cited in *East Europe*, XV, No. 11 (November 1966), p. 37.

39 See the commentary in RFE report, "Yugoslavia Attacks 'State Collectives' in Albania," October 2, 1964, p. 2, which makes the point that "the

land following collectivization, as the principal means of production, has for all practical purposes become the property of the state."

40 For basic documents see N. D. Kazantsev (ed.), *Osnovnye zakonodatelnye akty po agrarnym preobrazovaniyam v zarubezhnykh sotsialisticheskikh stranakh* (4th ed., Moscow, 1958), pp. 5-60 on Albania.

41 Skendi, *op. cit.*, p. 170.

42 Tyagunenko, *op. cit.*, p. 42. Figures for 1964 indicate that 10 percent of the arable land is still in private hands plus an additional 7 percent of the collective farms in the form of garden plots. *Vjetari statistikor . . . 1965*, p. 180. Twenty percent of the peasants have not been collectivized as yet, according to Premier Mehmet Shehu. *New York Times*, December 18, 1966.

43 *Twenty Years of Socialism*, p. 64.

44 For details on the average wages of twenty-five to thirty dollars monthly for skilled workers and the prices of food as well as other necessities see Athanas Gegaj and Rexhep Krasniqi, *Albania* (New York, 1964), p. 36.

45 Another standard technique to wipe out the savings of the population has been the currency reform. In August 1965 ten old leks were exchanged for one new lek. Announced in advance by Radio Tirana, July 15, 1965.

46 Leo Heiman, "Peking's Adriatic Stronghold," *East Europe*, XIII, No. 4 (April 1964), pp. 15-17. Eight submarines and a modern Soviet supply ship reportedly did leave Albania in June 1961. Hamm, *op. cit.*, p. 23.

47 Beqir Balloukou [Balluku], *Discours Prononcé à la Réunion Solennelle Consacrée au 20e Anniversaire de la Fondation de l'Armée Populaire* (Tirana, 1963), p. 51. See also RFE report, "Hoxha Creates an Ascetic Military Organization," August 30, 1966 (3 pp.).

48 Stavro Skendi, "Albania and the Sino-Soviet Conflict," *Foreign Affairs*, XL, No. 3 (April 1962), p. 474.

49 Dedijer, *op. cit.*, pp. 198-209, lists Yugoslav assistance.

50 Yet the Albanian communist party's Central Committee reportedly met in February 1948 to discuss incorpora-

tion of the country by Yugoslavia. Skendi, *Albania*, p. 24.

51 See also Gegaj and Krasniqi, *op. cit.*, p. 29. Albanian-Yugoslav trade during 1966 amounted to five million dollars. *Borba*, December 29, 1966.

52 Hamm, *op. cit.*, pp. 11-23.

53 Dilo, *op. cit.*, p. 8.

54 See Peter S. H. Tang, *The Twenty-second Congress of the Communist Party of the Soviet Union and Moscow-Tirana-Peking Relations* (Washington, D.C., 1962), pp. 76-90. Note also Mao Tse-tung's message to the Fifth Congress of the Albanian Workers' party, as cited in the *New York Times*, November 3, 1966.

55 Deputy trade minister Vasil Kati in *Zëri i popullit*, March 19, 1966; as cited in RFE report, "Albania Looks for More Expansive Foreign Trade," April 4, 1966 (6 pp.). See also *Albanien und Seine "Protektoren"* (Munich, 1966), pp. 7-8, for other new projects during 1966-1970.

56 Il Yung Chung, *Legal Problems Involved in the Corfu Channel Incident* (Geneva, 1959), 287 pp.

57 Although the population is 95 percent Albanian, there is a Greek minority, the largest in the country, which numbers about 30,000. Karłowicz, *op. cit.*, p. 13.

58 Radio Tirana, October 7, 1965. U.S. restrictions on travel to Albania were lifted March 15, 1967.

59 An invitation from Poland to attend the January 19-20, 1965, meeting of the Pact's political-consultative committee at Warsaw was rejected by Albania. *Zëri i popullit*, February 2, 1965, as cited in *East Europe*, XIV, No. 3 (March 1965), p. 34. A note concerning the Bucharest meeting revealed that Albania was "not invited." *Zëri i popullit*, July 20, 1966.

60 Hoxha's position is strong because he has purged 13 of the 14 original resistance commanders, 14 of the 31 postwar Central Committee members (1944-1948), and 79 of the 109 deputies to the first National Assembly. Tang, *op. cit.*, p. 134, n. 3. See also Anton Logoreci, "Albania and China," *Current History*, LII, No. 308 (April 1967), pp. 227-231, 245.

Chapter 2 / BULGARIA:
Prussia of the Balkans

In a geographical sense, Bulgaria occupies a rather special position in the communist bloc of Eastern Europe. Anchored on the southern flank of the former satellite belt, it is unique in having just one other bloc neighbor (Romania to the north) and in being the only country to border on more than two non-bloc states (Turkey and Greece to the south, Yugoslavia to the west).[1] Also, Bulgaria shares with East Germany the distinction of remaining under Soviet influence without being contiguous with the U.S.S.R.

Bulgaria, slightly smaller than New York State, encompasses 42,818 square miles within its dimensions of roughly 250 by 150 miles. Significant topographical features include the Danubian table-land across the north; the Balkan mountains in the center; the Thracian plains to the south; and mountains in the southwest. The national language is Slavic but shows the influence of Turkish and Greek. The population, composed of about 91 percent ethnic Bulgarians and 6 percent Turks, was estimated at the end of 1965 to be 8.2 million, of which roughly 3.8 million were classified as urban (43.9 percent) and 4.4 million as rural (53.6 percent).[2]

HISTORY

For five hundred years Bulgaria was under Turkish rule, with the decline of which came oppression, all the less tolerable because of the new standards and aspirations resulting from the penetration of modern ideas from Western Europe.[3]

By the early nineteenth century a national liberation movement had begun to develop from the writings of a monk named Paissi of Hilender, who recalled heroic deeds of the glorious past and inspired

29

the people to fight for spiritual and political liberation. During that century the Bulgarians suffered setbacks in several minor revolts but finally initiated in 1876 a major and widespread uprising. It failed also and resulted in the massacre of about 30,000 men, women, and children.

Yet this uprising generated an international protest over the Turkish atrocities, evoked considerable sympathy for the Bulgarians, and eventually led to Russia's taking up arms against Turkey. The following year, a Russian army crossed the Danube and, joined by Bulgarian volunteers, defeated the Turks. The terms of the peace treaty, signed in 1878 at the town of San Stefano near Constantinople, provided for an autonomous Bulgarian state encompassing a considerable territory which included most of Macedonia and had access to the Aegean. This, however, proved to be unacceptable to Great Britain and Austria-Hungary. When the terms of peace were renegotiated under the Treaty of Berlin that same year the country's proposed size was reduced by two-thirds.

In the course of the First World War the Bulgarian government entered into a secret alliance with the Central Powers and subsequently declared war on neighboring Serbia. Being on the losing side cost Bulgaria the loss of part of Western Thrace to Greece and part of the western frontier area to Yugoslavia.[4] When the Second World War broke out, Bulgaria repeated the mistake and in 1941 became an ally of Germany for the purpose of getting the territories envisaged at San Stefano. Initially things went well and, with the Germans, Bulgaria occupied parts of Greece and Yugoslavia to which it felt it had legitimate claims. By 1944, defeat appeared inevitable and Bulgaria sought to break from the alliance. Its plea for an armistice with the Western Powers was delayed by the U.S.S.R., which, although not then at war with Bulgaria, proceeded to declare war and occupy the country. Under the eventual armistice terms, Bulgaria was forced to evacuate the territories gained in Greece and Yugoslavia.[5]

THE TIRNOVO CONSTITUTION. Both treaties of 1878 at San Stefano and Berlin provided for the convocation of a Bulgarian Assembly to elect a prince and to institutionalize a future government. The initial draft of the Bulgarian constitution, prepared by the temporary Russian governor, was worked over by a Russian professor of constitutional law explicitly to include the principles of a parliamentary monarchy. But the Assembly, when it convened the following year at the ancient capital of Tirnovo, went even further:

> [It] adopted the principles of extreme liberalism with the framework of a parliamentary form of government. Parliament was to be unicameral, elected on the basis of universal suffrage, and controlling the executive. Absolute political and civil liberty was explicitly guaranteed. Thus, the pure and spontaneous democratism of the Bulgarian people gave them what was then referred to as "one of the most democratic constitutions in the world." [6]

During the sixty-five years of its existence, the Tirnovo constitution was frequently violated, owing to impulsive actions and personal ambitions. Probably some blame can be attributed to lack of experience and a general absence of tradition in self-government. Nevertheless, this constitution represented one of the most advanced and democratic among fundamental laws in the world at that time. It explicitly guaranteed broad political, civil, and social liberties. Significantly, "the Tirnovo constitution has remained the symbol of free government for all democratic Bulgarians" and, possibly with this in mind, the communists, when they usurped power in the Second World War, disarmingly professed a return to its principles. [7]

THE 1947 DIMITROV CONSTITUTION. After the communist-inspired Fatherland Front seized the government and the Red Army occupied Bulgaria, in 1944, the communists methodically undertook to consolidate their rule. [8] Initially holding only the governmental agencies for Interior (including the police) and Justice, they conducted widespread purges and trials in order to eliminate the opposition. As their control became more nearly absolute, an attack was launched on the old Tirnovo constitution, and "popular requests" were trumped up for a new one. In September 1946 the results of a plebiscite eliminated the monarchy and declared Bulgaria to be a republic. [9] The following month, elections were held for a Grand National Assembly (*Sobranje*) which would enact a new constitution. After the new legislature convened in November, Georgi Dimitrov formed his government.

Since he was so closely associated with it, the new fundamental law of the People's Republic of Bulgaria is commonly called the Dimitrov constitution. Born in 1882 of a working-class Protestant family, as a young man he became active, through the trade-unions, in the "narrow" socialist movement and was instrumental in its transformation (1919) into the Bulgarian communist party.[10] During 1920-1921 Dimitrov served as delegate to the second and third congresses of the Comintern at Moscow and subsequently was a member of its executive committee. In 1923 he fled Bulgaria after an unsuccessful *coup*. Ten years later he was arrested in Germany for alleged complicity in the Reichstag fire.

Through the intervention of the Soviet Union, Dimitrov was released and deported to the U.S.S.R., where he became a Soviet citizen. From 1935 to 1943 he held the post of secretary-general of the Comintern. He initiated the Fatherland Front and returned to Bulgaria, still as a Soviet citizen, in November 1945 to become the leading communist in the country, holding power at various times as chairman (later secretary-general) of the Central Committee, chairman of the Politburo, and premier. Dimitrov went to the Soviet Union for "medical treatment" at the beginning of 1949 and died in July of that year at a sanatorium near Moscow.[11]

Although the initial draft of the Dimitrov constitution, as prepared by a committee of the Assembly, was somewhat similar to the Tirnovo document, it later underwent revision by a special group and when promulgated closely resembled the "Stalin constitution" of the U.S.S.R. It seems more than coincidental that during the interim between drafts, the legal opposition within the Assembly had been silenced. Moreover, the signing of a peace treaty eliminated further necessity for the Tirnovo façade. The new version [12] received formal approval by the Grand National Assembly on December 4, 1947, the eleventh anniversary of the Stalin constitution.

The eleven chapters and 101 articles of the constitution cover practically all facets of life within the People's Republic. They define collective ownership of the means of production (by the state or cooperatives); indicate that the regime can nationalize any and all industrial, trade, transport, or credit enterprises; proclaim that the right of ownership cannot be detrimental to the public interest; and mention that private property is subject to compulsory restrictions and expropriation.[13] Furthermore, it is laid down that all economic activity is to be directed by the government on the basis of national economic plans which make participation compulsory.

The constitution defines the unicameral National Assembly as the "supreme organ of state power" and stipulates that its members,[14] elected to four-year terms on the basis of one representative for every 30,000 people, shall meet twice yearly (in November and February). Theoretically, the Assembly elects its presidium, the judges of the Supreme Court, and the State Prosecutor; appoints the Council of Ministers; amends the constitution; and performs a number of other legislative functions. The eighteen-member presidium of the Assembly [15] combines legislative and executive authority. Theoretically, it exercises the prerogatives of a collective head of state by representing the country externally, legislating by decree, interpreting laws, and calling elections.

The Council of Ministers is defined by the constitution as the "supreme executive and administrative organ of the state," and in 1967 consisted of a chairman or premier, a first-deputy chairman, five deputy chairmen, ten Bureau of the Council members (with some overlapping), and twenty-six ministers or heads of various committees.[16] This body is responsible for the general administration of the country. The present premier, Todor Zhivkov, is also the first secretary of the Bulgarian communist party (and thereby a member of its Central Committee), a deputy in the Assembly, and a national councilman of the Fatherland Front.[17]

Local government is administered by People's Councils elected to three-year terms and primarily responsible for the implementation of economic, social, and cultural policies laid down by superior organs of the state. These councils are equivalent to the soviets in the U.S.S.R. and exist at the district (*okrug*) and commune (*obshtina*) levels, with a vertical and horizontal system of responsibility typical of communist government. This provides for a dual system of control.

The judicial organ at the highest level is the Supreme Court, supported by 12 regional and 93 district courts. The courts are "composed of judges and lay assessors who are generally elected by the citizens, by the People's Council, or by the National Assembly." [18] Exceptional power is held by the State Prosecutor in controlling observance of the law by government organs and officials as well as by all citizens. He is charged specifically

> to attend to the prosecution and punishment of crimes which affect the state, national, and economic interests of the People's Republic, and crimes and actions detrimental to the independence and state sovereignty of the country.[19]

The longest chapter in the constitution deals with guarantees over a wide range of civil liberties and economic and social rights. As in the equivalent Soviet document, almost every imaginable and desirable right is spelled out: equality before the law; individual liberty; inviolability of domicile; freedom of religion, speech, press, assembly. There is the qualification, however, that these rights may be exercised only in the interests of the working people.

It would seem on the surface that the Dimitrov constitution provides Bulgaria with a democratically representative form of government. While it does not adhere to the principle of separation of powers, it nevertheless indicates a theoretical degree of responsibility. Against the objection that it is strongly flavored with the dominance of the state over the individual, the communists argue that the state represents the people who elect the government and that guarantees of individual rights and liberties are abundantly enumerated.

CONSTITUTION AND GOVERNMENT IN PRACTICE. Theory remains far removed from practice in Bulgaria, where the literal provisions of the constitution bear little resemblance to the actual operation of governing the country. Basically, the constitution amounts to little more than a façade behind which the communist party wields tight control over national power. Thus, the constitution is merely an instrument that can be used or abused as the need dictates. Bulgaria today is a dictatorship of the proletariat (meaning, the communist party) and, in Lenin's definition, "a power limited by nothing, by no law, directly based on violence." [20]

In practice, the constitutional provisions for a representative government remain a farce, since only the views of the communist leadership can become policy and law. Only those persons ultimately approved by the party can be nominated or may participate in administering the government.[21] Deputies to the Assembly are previously approved and then "elected" without opposition. They convene twice a year for periods of one to three days and rubber-stamp the proposals of the Assembly presidium, the Council of Ministers, or the Central Committee of the party. The same electoral process applies to the judiciary. In all cases, officeholders who fail to adhere to the party line can be recalled. Despite the assertion of individual liberties and human rights in the basic law, it is obvious from many examples that freedom of speech, assembly, and press is permitted only when its exercise is consonant with party policies. Deviation from the dictates and will of the party simply is not permitted.

In their own words, communist leaders have refuted the existence of any law or institution superior to the controlling power of the party. For example, Vulko Chervenkov, prime minister until 1956, stated that

> No institution, organization, or person can be above the Politburo and the Central Committee. All important issues of the government of the country must be decided by the Politburo and Central Committee. Those guilty of deviation from this Bolshevik rule must be held responsible and punished.[22]

Thus the government of Bulgaria remains in a practical sense merely a transmission belt behind which a dictatorship of the Bulgarian communist party operates the controls.

THE COMMUNIST PARTY OF BULGARIA

Dimitar Blagoyev, born in Macedonia and educated in Russia, introduced communist ideas into Bulgaria toward the end of the nineteenth century. The socialist movement that thus received its inspiration failed to grow in its early years owing to a split into "narrow" and "broad" groups. Apart from the lack of a substantial urban proletariat, the peasants on their small holdings were not susceptible to easy organization. The "narrow" faction advocated communist policies based on an industrialized economy, while the "broad" group felt more realistically that the almost wholly agrarian economy in Bulgaria would not support the classical Marxist approach. The communist party failed to work its way into the government until the end of the Second World War.[23]

After the war, defeated Bulgaria could not oppose the plans of the Soviet Union. The so-called Fatherland Front, including the communists, the Zveno group, left-wing agrarians, and left-wing social democrats, was put into power by the entry of the Red Army and by a military *coup,* with the result that Kimon Georghiev of the Zveno group was installed as premier. The new cabinet had four Zvenos, four communists,[24] four agrarians, two socialists, and two independents. Stalinization took hold with perhaps more aggressiveness than in any other East European satellite. In 1944 large numbers of persons considered to be a threat to the regime were tried as "fascists" and "traitors" and summarily executed.[25] This terror was renewed during 1945-1947, when the opposition party managed to hold one-third of the vote despite adverse conditions.

In a broadcast to the Bulgarian people in September 1946, the communist party leader Georgi Dimitrov proclaimed:

> . . . Bulgaria will be a People's Republic, a factor for Slav unity and fraternity against any possible aggression. It will not grease the axle of any anti-Slav or anti-Soviet policy leading to enmity between the peoples. Bulgaria will be a People's Republic which, together with other democratic and freedom-loving peoples, will represent a strong element of peace and democracy in the Balkans and Europe and not a tool for military adventures and aggressive wars.[26]

In a speech at the Fifth Congress of the Bulgarian communist party, two years later, Dimitrov stated that the foundation of the government involved collaboration and friendship with the Soviet Union and that Bulgaria belonged to the anti-imperialist camp.

Along with the purges, Dimitrov created 30 trade-unions, replaced the former police organization with his own militia, and appointed trusted individuals from his party to positions of authority. The general election held in November 1945 to choose members of the new Grand National Assembly was anything but free. Yet the Fatherland Front seated only 364 members to 101 for the noncommunist opposition. Of those in the Front, 277 were communists, who thus held an absolute majority.

Dimitrov, after some vacillation (especially in his views on a Balkan federation), supported the Moscow line in opposition to the nationalists, who felt that Bulgarian interests should come first. After Dimitrov died in July 1949, Vulko Chervenkov assumed control of the party and promptly eliminated the nationalist group. The orthodox Bulgarian communists were so anxious to imitate the policies of the U.S.S.R. that they found themselves making the same mistakes, long after the Soviets had taken a new approach and attempted to rectify their errors.

Purges within the party had been so thoroughgoing that they left few people of stature who were willing or able to offer any effective opposition to Moscow directives. Stalin was suspicious of all Bulgarian communists who had spent the war inside their own country and not in the U.S.S.R.—the more so after Tito of Yugoslavia came into conflict with Cominform policies. Traicho Kostov, who had been the most obvious successor to Dimitrov, was sent to the gallows as a Titoist. Chervenkov soon became the little Stalin of Bulgaria.[27]

After Stalin's death in 1953 the Chervenkov group would have preferred to continue the hard line, but was held in check by the milder "new course" in the Soviet Union. At one time Chervenkov even perceived something worth emulating in Red China's views, particularly regarding the communes. It was not that Chervenkov refused to support the Soviet position, for he always remained loyal; however, and perhaps from habit, he wanted to continue the hard Stalinist policies.

During this man's six years of rule about 100,000 persons were purged from the communist party's membership of about 460,000. Chervenkov had enjoyed a privileged position in the communist organization since the early days of the Comintern, but his removal from the highest position in the party, in 1954, was ordered by Moscow; he continued to hold office as premier for two years longer. In 1962 Chervenkov, his successor and former premier Anton Yugov, and other high officials, including the Interior minister Georgi Tsankov, were dismissed from all party and government posts.[28] The departure of Chervenkov, added to previous purges, left a dearth of communist leadership in the country. Todor Zhivkov, who eventually entered the party leadership in 1952 (becoming first secretary in 1954) and the premiership in 1962, has been unable to fill the vacuum. It is not surprising that the Bulgarian communists do the bidding of Moscow, even while other East European leaders are attempting—at least, in domestic affairs—to gain more freedom to make their own decisions.

Zhivkov's victory was assured when he obtained the support of the majority on the then nine-man Politburo and the enlarged Central Committee. (In 1962 the enlarged committee consisted of 101 full members and 67 nonvoting candidates. The party's Ninth Congress, in 1966, elected 137 full members and no candidates.) He began to reorganize the party and government along the Khrushchëv pattern. The ten-year effort to eliminate Chervenkov came successfully to an end in 1962, but the police and Soviet support are still needed to maintain control. No real improvement in the living conditions of the people has occurred, although early in his period of rule Zhivkov reduced the terror and eased the economic hardships somewhat. He has used the familiar charge of excesses and errors during the "period of the personality cult" [29] against opponents, owing in part to the necessity of finding a scapegoat for failings in the economic field.

The current party leadership under Zhivkov shows a tendency toward calm and unity. It consists of mediocre individuals completely devoted to the desires of Moscow. There are no groups or individuals of sufficient strength to suggest an independent course of action in the near future. In 1965, however, the Soviet secret police (KGB) allegedly uncovered a plot to overthrow the Bulgarian regime. Of the ten men implicated, one committed suicide and the others were sentenced to prison terms.[30] About half of this group consisted of army officers who had fought in guerrilla detachments inside Bulgaria during the war and may therefore have resented Soviet domination.

There has been no indication of such disloyalty among the rank-and-file of the party, which in July 1966 numbered 607,458 members and candidates.[31] This represents an increase of well over 100,000 since 1958, with bureaucrats accounting for most of it. Party membership within the group below twenty-eight years of age has gone from a high of 20 percent down to 15 percent, and admission of rural young people has practically ceased. Women comprise 17 percent of the party membership. The intelligentsia seems frustrated by party controls and the younger generation is apathetic toward them; the family remains unreceptive to regime indoctrination; and the peasants are hostile to programs imposed by the government. The Ninth Congress of the party met during November 14-19, 1966, and discussed some of these problems.

Party members and candidates constitute only 7 percent of the country's population. Workers still maintained in 1966 the largest bloc within the party (almost 40 percent), although not an absolute majority, and the largest share of new members. The proportion of collective farmers in the party is relatively high, constituting 29.2 percent. White collar and intelligentsia membership is increasing and has reached 28.4 percent.[32] (See table 8.)

On the other hand, the main party newspaper has complained that "the low [level of] education of a large number of party members does not correspond to the growing requirements for competent leadership of the people's economy" and termed it "a serious hindrance to the command of technology." This editorial contained specific information on the Politburo's decision to improve the party:

> . . . in the next two or three years the percentage of communists directly engaged in material output, about 49 percent of the total number of party members to date, should increase. . . . Only 7 percent of building workers in Sofia are communists [while] about 42 percent of those newly accepted as candidate members of the party belong to ordinary administrative-office type personnel. [Also] many party organizations fill their ranks with people with a low level of education, even with semiliterates . . .[33]

TABLE 8

COMPOSITION OF THE BULGARIAN COMMUNIST PARTY, 1954-1966
(In numbers of members and percents of total)

Occupational class	March 1954 (Sixth Congress)	June 1958 (Seventh Congress)	November 1962 (Eighth Congress)	November 1966 (Ninth Congress)
Workers	155,021 (34.1)	174,816 (36.1)	196,449 (37.2)	234,693 (38.4)
Peasants	180,998 (39.8)	165,615 (34.2)	169,601 (34.2)	178,464 (29.2)
Intelligentsia	81,664 (17.9)	105,083 (21.7)	124,587 (23.5) ⎫	198,022 (32.4)
Other	37,508 (8.2)	38,741 (8.0)	38,037 (7.2) ⎭	
Total	455,251	484,255	528,674	611,179
	(Including 87,109 candidates)	(Including 16,709 candidates)	(Including 22,413 candidates)	(Including 40,174 candidates)

SOURCES: *Rabotnichesko delo,* February 26, 1954; June 3, 1958; November 6, 1962. Radio Free Europe report, "Zhivkov's Party Congress Report—(II) The Party," November 25, 1966 (7 pp.), at p. 2.

Even though police pressure may have eased against the non-communist population under the new policy, the machinery of the Interior ministry has been streamlined and its new head, General Diko Dikov, whose agency since July 1965 has controlled only uniformed police and fire department personnel, has boasted that his employees "are constantly studying the experience of our brothers, the glorious Soviet Chekists and public security organs [and] striking blow after blow at enemies and criminals." [34] Security provisions remain, and their enforcement will vary with the policy in effect at any particular time.

The people realize this, and that is probably why they vote. In the elections of February 27, 1966, it was claimed that 99.85 percent of the adult population went to the polls. According to official figures, 99.9 percent of the qualified electorate cast ballots for candidates of the Fatherland Front. Despite the pressure to register an affirmative vote for the single candidate in each constituency, a total of 2,087 persons marked their ballots against the regime and the ballots of another 6,467 probably had been mutilated in protest as they were judged to be invalid.[35] (See table 9.)

TABLE 9

COMPOSITION OF THE BULGARIAN NATIONAL ASSEMBLY, 1957-1966

	Number of representatives		
Party	1957	1962	1966
Bulgarian communist party..................	160	197	280
Bulgarian National Agrarian Union [a]..........	65	80	99
Nonparty	28	44	37
Total......	253	321	416 [b]

SOURCES: L. N. Tolkunov (ed.), *Sotsialisticheskii lager* (Moscow, 1962), p. 56. *Rabotnichesko delo,* February 26, 1962. Radio Sofia, February 28, 1966.

[a] The Bulgarian National Agrarian Union, a separate political party in name only, is maintained by the communists as a control device in the villages because of its past importance and for foreign propaganda.

[b] All 416 candidates, including those labeled "nonparty," ran on the Fatherland Front ticket without any opposition. Radio Free Europe, *Situation Report,* February 8, 1966.

The role of propaganda, apart from elections, permeates every field: the education of adults and young people, trade-unions, book publication and distribution, even dress and conduct. The regime attempts to mold completely the mind of every Bulgarian. Admittedly and openly

> the party is the guiding political force in socialist [Bulgarian] society. As for public opinion, on the one hand the party plays a guiding role in the creation of the conditions and forms which are necessary premises for the normal and efficient functioning of public opinion; on the other, it is the guiding subjective force in the formation of public opinion itself. . . .[36]

According to an editorial in an official party publication: "Self-education becomes the basic method of Marxist-Leninist training of the cadres [and] depends most of all on the qualifications of the propagandist, who must have a thorough knowledge of the subject he will teach." [37] The Central Committee has called on Bulgarian women to treat friendship with the U.S.S.R. as a sacred legacy and "to watch over that friendship as over the apple of their eye, convey it to their children with their mother's milk, and bequeath it from generation to generation as the dearest heritage." [38]

The centralized control over and manipulation of public opinion was illustrated in December 1963 during the trial of Ivan-Asen Khristov Georgiev, who had been accused of spying for the Central Intelligence Agency. Organized mobs attacked the United States legation building, breaking all windows facing the street, and capsized four automobiles owned by American foreign service personnel. The police stood by without taking any action to disperse the mob until the damage was completed. There could be no doubt that the Bulgarian regime engineered this demonstration. Another attack of this type occurred in February 1965 and led to a high-level protest by U.S. Secretary of State Dean Rusk.[39]

Although it may be difficult to expose the party's role in the government, it is obvious from the interlocking directorate that all major plans, programs, and policies of the government originate with the party. (See table 10.) The party retains control in all important functions. The implementation of the communist program, however, is another matter and has come up against several problems.

First of all, Bulgaria is a farming country with doubtful resources upon which to base an industrialized economy. The emphasis on heavy industry has been supported by credits from the Soviet Union [40] and by capital extracted through forced collectivization of the peasants. While it is true that considerable gains have been made in heavy industry, neglect of consumers' goods and agricultural improvements has left the Bulgarians without the ability to raise their standards above the basic necessities of life. The results of this policy are visible, and the peasants have shown no desire to produce for the government. Even according to official data, the number of cattle and sheep has changed little over the past two decades. A tribute to personal initiative can be seen, where the peasants with their "acre and a cow" private plots, occupying less than 10 percent of the arable land, produce 40 percent of the meat and at least three times as much grain per acre as do the collectivized farms.[41]

TABLE 10

BULGARIAN PARTY-GOVERNMENT DIRECTORATE, 1967

Politburo [a]	Secretariat (and responsibility) [a]	Council of Ministers (and portfolios)	Other Positions
FULL MEMBERS	SECRETARIES		
Balgaranov, Boyan (71)	Balgaranov, Boyan (Armed Forces)		Chairman, Fatherland Front
Velchev, Boris (53)	Velchev, Boris (Cadres)		
Zhivko, Zhivkov (52)		First deputy premier (Economy)	
Mihailov, Ivan (70)		Deputy premier (Social Affairs)	
*Popov, Ivan (61)		Chairman, Science and Technology Progress Committee	
**Kubadinski, Pencho (49)		Deputy premier (Transport and Communications)	
Todorov, Stanko (47)	*Todorov, Stanko		
**Tsolov, Tano (51)		Deputy premier (CMEA representative)	
Zhivkov, Todor (56)	Zhivkov, Todor (Leader)	Premier	
*Pavlov, Todor (77)			Honorary Chairman, Academy of Sciences
	*Kotsev, Venelin (41) (Culture and Arts)		
*Dragoycheva, Tsola (69)	Pramov, Ivan (46) (Agriculture)		Chairman, National Committee for Bulgarian-Soviet Friendship

CANDIDATE MEMBERS

Dimov, Dimitar (64) .... Chairman, Presidium of the
National Assembly

MEMBERS OF THE SECRETARIAT

*Avramov, Lachezar (45) .... Deputy premier (Foreign Trade)

*Bonev, Vladimir (50)
(Fatherland Front)

*Takov, Peko (58) .... Internal Trade minister

*Gyurov, Stoyan (52)
(Trade-Unions)

*Tsanev, Angel (55) .... Lieutenant General,
State Security Service
*Vassilev, Stefan (48)   (Head, Military Department,
(Science and Education)   BCP Central Committee)

*Gyaurov, Kostadin (43) .... First Secretary,
Plovdiv District BCP

*Trichkov, Krastyu (44) .... First Secretary,
Blagoevgrad District BCP

*Abadzhiev, Ivan (37) .... First Secretary,
Sliven District BCP

SOURCES: Politburo and Secretariat, elected at Ninth Congress of the party, were announced by Radio Sofia, November 19, 1966; other identification came from Radio Free Europe report, "New Politburo and Secretariat," November 24, 1966 (11 pp.); Radio Sofia, May 17, 1967.

ᵃ Numbers in parentheses indicate years of age.   * Newly elected.
BCP = Bulgarian communist party.   ** Promoted from candidate status.

Second, the U.S.S.R. has taken advantage of Bulgaria in the price structuring of imports and exports. Discrimination, in which the Soviets inflate the charges for their exports to Bulgaria by some 44.6 percent and deflate the cost of Bulgarian exports by some 36.4 percent,[12] has retarded the economy and jeopardized further economic development. (Soviet dominance over Bulgaria's foreign trade is discussed later in this chapter.)

Third, the workers' indifference and lack of enthusiasm has made it necessary to decree harsh amendments to the labor codes. If an employee is absent without authorization for three consecutive days or for five days in any calendar year, he loses the standard increments of pay, all leave in excess of fourteen days, and all indemnities for invalidism or sickness and retirement. Work contracts must be signed for a specific period of time, which the employee is not allowed to break except with the consent of the management. If he leaves without permission, he cannot be hired by another enterprise and is still subject to the penalties for absence; [43] in addition, he must move out of government housing within one month.

Finally, lack of discipline among the young is mentioned time after time, indicating a problem of major proportions. Party leaders specify an absence of conscience, bad upbringing, lack of proper guidance at home and school, a negative attitude toward the state, formalism and banalities in lecture programs, poor Komsomol curriculum and organization,[44] the degenerate influence of bourgeois culture, consumption of alcohol, decadent music, vulgarity in dances, and the desire for cars and travel outside of Bulgaria as some of the reasons for juvenile delinquency.

The party leaders have committed the people to full support of the Soviet Union, with a concomitant restriction on freedom and initiative. The party's authority is absolute within itself, and it is supported completely by the proximity of U.S.S.R. military power. There does not appear to be much likelihood of an overthrow of the regime in the near future, although disenchantment with the leadership seems widespread even among the middle party echelons. In view of the October 1964 palace *coup* against Khrushchëv in Moscow and the abortive conspiracy of April 1965 at Sofia, the possibility of a successful attempt cannot be discounted completely.

DOMESTIC AND FOREIGN RELATIONS

Communist rule is firmly entrenched in Bulgaria. Although there has long existed a nationalistic spirit, the Soviet Union tries to capitalize on this even while attempting to create a positive image of itself. From the time of the entry of the Red Army and Dimitrov's return to the country, Bulgaria constantly has followed the Soviet example, whether it be in the destalinization program or the rift with China. Apart from Albania, it is the only country in Eastern Europe that actually envies the U.S.S.R. standard of living. Agricultural collectivization, proceeding more rapidly here than in any of the others, has been accompanied by a dismal farm production record. Bulgaria has been an ardent supporter of CMEA and consistently espouses the Soviet line in that organization, although the CMEA specialization blueprint would turn the country into an agricultural appendage. Literacy has been increased considerably and a degree of industrialization has been achieved, yet life remains somber and the level of individual creature comforts is low. The ratio of human gains to human costs speaks poorly for the socioeconomic system.

CHURCH-STATE RELATIONS. The communist regime has been able to gain substantial control over religious life. This was accomplished in several distinct phases.[45] The minority faiths (Moslem, Jewish, Protestant, and Roman Catholic) were each handled separately, but with great effectiveness. The majority of the people belong to the Bulgarian Orthodox Church, and the communist regime has capitalized upon this fact:

> The Communists have patronized the Church as the traditional national church of Bulgaria, not only to obtain support from the Church devotees, but also to unify national Orthodox Churches under the aegis of the Soviet-controlled Russian Orthodox Church. [The new Patriarch] Kiril clearly demonstrated his attitude . . . when he thanked the regime for the reestablishment of the Bulgarian Patriarchate and called on all the faithful to support the Government in its policies.[46]

Control over the Bulgarian Orthodox Church and the other churches was greatly facilitated by the 1949 statute on religious denominations, whereby all denominations were required to register with the Committee for Religious Affairs, attached to the Council of Ministers, and obtain approval for their bylaws. The statute also specified that the leadership of all religious organizations "must be responsible to the state" and that religious functionaries could not "take office or be dismissed or transferred without the approval of the Committee." [47] Religious organizations are authorized to operate schools if state permission is obtained, but they are not allowed the right to engage in secular education. These restrictions have curtailed virtually all religious freedom and have converted religious leaders into spokesmen for the state.

Moslems of Turkish descent form the largest minority religious group and have fared less well than the Bulgarian Orthodox faithful. Approximately 150,000 of the Turkish Moslems were forcibly expelled during 1950-1951, and the remaining 700,000 have been organized into communities numbering just over a thousand.[48] The Grand Mufti repeatedly has expressed his appreciation for the consideration shown the Turkish minority; he undoubtedly retains his position under conditions that forbid any but favorable statements concerning the regime and the welfare of his group. Boris Nikolov, who was first party secretary for the area at the time, had this to say about propaganda work in the Moslem-inhabited Targovishte region:

> Dissemination of scientific-popular knowledge . . . helps the Turkish population to get rid of the chains of the Islamic religion. . . . For two years in succession, we have applied seven-day courses for all Turkish intellectuals in the region. . . . [49]

The position of yet another religious group is even worse. Today, no Roman Catholic churches remain open in Bulgaria, in contrast with the situation at the end of the Second World War, when three dioceses existed and were headed by Bishop Bosilkov. In September 1952 forty leading Catholics were tried at Sofia on the charge of spying. All of the defendants were executed, imprisoned, or expelled from the country. This action and the subsequent banishment of less important personnel sufficed to obliterate the church hierarchy in Bulgaria. The country still has about 56,000 persons of the Roman Catholic faith, but no church buildings or priests to conduct religious services for them.[50]

The Protestants have suffered a somewhat similar fate, although their denominations are still active to a limited degree. Five separate groups were forcibly combined into one United Evangelical Church. All Protestant schools were closed, however, and many clergymen were placed on trial for espionage. On March 8, 1949, fifteen pastors were sentenced to imprisonment and heavy fines for alleged spying on behalf of the United States and Great Britain. Protestant churches in Bulgaria exerted a strong influence on the educated class before the war, but now these churches are under tight state control.

Another religious mniority group consists of approximately 6,000 persons of the Jewish faith. The Grand Rabbi apparently has subordinated himself completely to the dictates of the regime.[51] This was to be expected, since leaders of all recognized religious bodies have tenure which remains dependent upon the will of the communist government. The regime has allowed an unlimited number of Jews to emigrate to Israel. Some 45,000 have done so, mostly during the 1949-1950 period.[52] Fourteen synagogues still exist in Bulgaria for worship.

What effect the control exercised by the regime over the churches has had on the younger minds is impossible to judge. Religion still remains a stronghold of anticommunist feelings, however, and it is connected with a desire for genuine national independence.

FOREIGN TRADE. Bulgaria became one of the original members of the CMEA in 1949, when that organization was formed. Table 11 shows trade with the other East European states and the Soviet Union. By 1962 the bloc accounted for some 82 percent of Bulgaria's imports and exports.[53] The extent to which the U.S.S.R. will continue to press for mandatory compliance with CMEA policies is open to question. Recent bilateral trade agreements among bloc countries have given cause for doubt as to the success of this economic organization. The East European states may now form temporary alliances or even sub-blocs within the CMEA, and there is evidence that such arrangements had already occurred some time ago.[54] Without the use of its former main weapon, the threat of force, the U.S.S.R. is at a disadvantage in persuading compliance with its policies. On the other hand, the trade agreement for the period 1966-1970 calls for transactions amounting to seven billion rubles and is expected to increase Soviet-Bulgarian trade by 70 percent.

The commodity protocol for 1967 amounts to 1.26 billion rubles, 17 percent above the preceding year.[55]

Recent events indicate a lessening in the overall direction which the CMEA exercises over the individual East European economies. By 1965, for example, only some 1,500 items had been agreed upon for specialization within the bloc. The degree of specific increase

TABLE 11

BULGARIA-BLOC TRADE, 1963 AND 1964

| Country | 1963 | | 1964 (percent) of total |
| | Imports | Exports | |
	(millions of leva)		
Albania	2.5	0.7	n. a.
Czechoslovakia	95.2	82.0	6.7
East Germany	113.7	94.5	8.5
Hungary	20.8	19.1	2.0
Poland	39.6	38.4	3.3
Romania	13.4	16.3	n. a.
U.S.S.R.	585.5	521.5	53.2
Total	870.7	772.5	73.7
All foreign trade	1,091.1	975.8	100.0

SOURCES: Central Board of Statistics, *Statistical Manual of the People's Republic of Bulgaria 1964* (Sofia, 1965), pp. 108-109. [Bulgaria], *Statistichesky godishnik na Narodna Republika Bulgariya* (Sofia, 1965), p. 298.

NOTE: One U.S. dollar equals 1.17 *leva* at the official exchange, less than half the black market rate. n. a. = not available.

or decrease in future years is very difficult to predict, although the cooperation that the Bulgarian communists will offer is not.[56] Their regime is highly sensitive to the desires of the Soviet Union and can be expected to support the economic policies sponsored by it. The bilateral agreements between Sofia and Moscow have integrated entire branches of industry.

RELATIONS WITH BORDER COUNTRIES. Bulgaria is touched on the north by Romania, the west by Yugoslavia, and the south by Greece and Turkey. The country has not had particularly good relations with its neighbors, including the communist-dominated ones. Its foreign affairs, however, are predicated upon satisfying the Soviet Union and in this respect have been conducted quite successfully. Zhivkov himself is considered to be a protégé of the current Soviet leadership. During a discussion of the April

1965 conspiracy he stated: "I am known for being bound to the Soviet Union in life and death." [57]

Bulgaria has a friendship and mutual aid treaty as well as a cultural cooperation treaty with Romania, both dating from the late 1940's. Yet at a time when some 86 percent of Bulgarian foreign trade was with the bloc nations only 1.5 percent involved Romania.[58] Sofia undoubtedly attempts to avoid public airing of any intra-bloc differences, yet not too long ago Boris Stefanov Matveyev, a Bulgarian citizen but also a disgraced early leader of the Romanian communist party, was given his country's highest award, the Order of Dimitrov.[59]

Relations between Greece and Bulgaria have been hindered by the latter's failure to pay reparations of 45 million dollars, assigned by the 1947 peace treaty. Also, the communist Greek insurgents were given sanctuary in Bulgaria during the ensuing civil war. The spring of 1964, however, saw talks held in an attempt to establish full diplomatic relations between the two countries. An agreement in July provided for the payment of seven million dollars in reparations as well as the establishment of communications by telephone and air.[60] A railroad line linking Koulata in Bulgaria with the port of Salonika in Greece was scheduled for completion in 1965, as an alternative to the port of Rijeka in Yugoslavia.

Relations with Turkey have never been especially good, stemming in part from the fact that the Ottomans were the occupying power for about five centuries. Bulgaria and Turkey long have had agreements for the mutual repatriation of nationals. During 1950-1951, as mentioned above, approximately 150,000 Turks were forcibly expelled from Bulgaria. The nearly complete disregard for human and property rights shown then almost caused a break in diplomatic relations. In 1952 the Bulgarians announced that henceforth no members of the Turkish minority would be given permission to leave the country.[61] (For a census of Turkish and other nationality groups see table 12.)

Bulgaria's relations with Yugoslavia have been determined primarily by the degree of warmth or coolness between the Soviet Union and the latter country. The status of the province of Macedonia in Yugoslavia has been a prime concern and might become of increasing importance if Bulgaria should ever break out from under the control of the Soviet Union. This border region is inhabited by 1.4

million persons who, according to the director of the Ethnographic Museum in the Bulgarian Academy of Sciences, B. Bozhikov, are "very close to the Bulgarians in language and culture," and whose Macedonian language is "midway between the Bulgarian language and Serbo-Croatian," spoken in Yugoslavia. The same source further

TABLE 12

NATIONALITIES IN BULGARIA, 1965

Nationality	Number of persons (in thousands)	Percent of total
Bulgarians	7,033.7	85.5
Turks	707.4	8.6
Gypsies	213.9	2.6
Macedonians	205.7	2.5
Armenians	24.7	0.3
Russians	8.2	0.1
Other	32.9	0.4
Total	8,226.5	100.0

SOURCES: Bulgarian Telegraphic Agency, December 31, 1965, as cited by Radio Free Europe, *Situation Report,* January 4, 1966, pp. 2-3, for the total population, and L. N. Tolkunov (ed.), *Sotsialisticheskii lager* (Moscow, 1962), p. 62, for percentages, which were used to compute absolute numbers.

NOTE: The Turks are called Moslems elsewhere in the text; i.e., they are designated by religion, although they often feel themselves to be Turks. This is especially true of the 160,000 Pomaks in the group.

contends that in Bulgaria "Macedonians, as a separate nationality, do not exist." [62] On the other hand, Todor Zhivkov in 1965 told an American reporter that Bulgaria had abandoned all claims to Macedonia. He added that his regime no longer covets anyone's territory and that Bulgaria's borders are regarded as permanent and satisfactory.[63]

COLLECTIVIZATION. Agricultural collectives have expanded at a more rapid pace in Bulgaria than in any of the other East European countries. Collectivization policy has moved through several distinct phases. The first of these involved persuasion, during the time when the communists were consolidating their power. It was followed, commencing in 1948, by a most aggressive policy. Only two years later, some 43 percent of all land had been collectivized; by 1960 it was claimed that 97.4 percent was either in this status or in use by agricultural enterprises directly operated by the state.[64]

The Bulgarian constitution claims that "the land belongs to those who till it," but it goes on to admit that "the law determines how much land private persons may own." [65] As in the Soviet Union, the eventual desire of the Bulgarian communists probably is to bring all agricultural land into *sovkhozes* (state farms), although at present the greater part is in *kolkhozes* (collectives). Todor Zhivkov has ordered complete collectivization in Bulgaria, despite the sometimes discouraging results obtained by collectives, as in 1963 when it was necessary to import some 100,000 tons of wheat from Canada and a certain amount of food rationing had to be introduced.[66] Although almost total collectivization is pointed to with pride and declared to be irrevocable by officials, in practice measures are being taken to encourage production on private plots, which is more efficient. (See table 13.) Bulgarian agriculture is not producing foodstuffs in

TABLE 13

AGRICULTURE IN BULGARIA, 1965

Type of Unit	Number	Area (hectares)	Percentage of total area	Percentage of production
Collective farms	1,000	3,677,600	76.0	64.8
State farms	90 ⎫		8.3	7.0
Farms of government and cooperatives	n. a. ⎭	700,000	3.1	3.7
Garden plots on collectives	n. a. ⎫		10.0	20.2
Garden plots of government employees	n. a. ⎬	422,400	2.0	3.9
Private farms	n. a. ⎭		0.6	0.4
Total		4,800,000	100.0	100.0

SOURCES: *Kooperativno selo,* March 2, 1965, as cited in RFE, *Situation Report,* March 18, 1965, pp. 1-3. *Statistichesky godishnik na Narodna Republika Bulgariya* (Sofia, 1965), pp. 175, 181.

n. a. = not available.

sufficient quantity to supply the population adequately. Hence, some compromise must be reached between production and collectivization if the country is ever to deliver more than the basic necessities.

THE ECONOMY. Since the end of the Second World War, Bulgaria has imposed currency reforms on three different occasions, in 1947, 1952, and 1962. Each time, the revaluation was imposed to drain off excess purchasing power, curb existing inflation, and redistribute income. Since the currency reform of 1962, the low average wage had been the main reason for the depressed standard of living. To remedy this situation, all wages and salaries were to be raised from 12 to 20 percent in the course of three phases between July 1966 and January 1967.[67]

Forced industrialization, almost complete socialization of the land, and heavy reinvestment also have caused the standard of living to suffer. The perspective plan for the period 1961-1980, adopted by the Eighth Party Congress, envisages an investment rate of 27 percent. This long-range plan is intended to raise the annual national income to approximately 20 billion leva, about five times the 1960 level.[68]

As late as 1965 the regime admitted the existence of bread queues. Certain products, such as meat and eggs, are either not obtainable at all or obtainable only at rare intervals.[69] In an obvious attempt to correct some of the serious deficiencies within the economy, Bulgaria has begun a reorganization of both the government and the economy away from previous centralized lines. The so-called New Economic System was unveiled April 26-28, 1966, at a plenary session of the Central Committee.[70] Considering the low standard of living and the general disillusionment persisting within the country, it can be assumed that serious adjustments will have to be made.

Bulgaria presents an outstanding example of the fallacy of communist doctrine, both in the economic sense and in the type of society it provides. Regime leaders have imitated the Soviet Union in nearly every respect, and this has produced little of a positive nature aside from a degree of industrialization. The price the Bulgarian people have paid for this achievement is a high one. Bulgaria, once a wheat exporter, now must import grain. The western world remembers food rationing as something in the dim past; the Bulgarians view it as an existing situation.[71]

NOTES

1 Central Board of Statistics, *Statistical Manual of the People's Republic of Bulgaria* (Sofia, 1965), p. 3.

2 RFE, *Situation Report,* January 4, 1966, pp. 2-3.

3 L. A. D. Dellin (ed.), *Bulgaria* (New York, 1957), pp. 6-7; hereafter cited as Dellin (ed.), *Bulgaria.*

4 For a useful summary of these events during the First World War see, *ibid.,* pp. 16-17.

5 Nicholas Halasz, *In the Shadow of Russia* (New York, 1959), pp. 92-94.

6 Dellin (ed.), *Bulgaria,* p. 85.

7 *Ibid.,* pp. 86, 88-89, 118.

8 The Fatherland Front (*Otechestven Front*) was a communist-inspired coalition established secretly in 1942. The communists later eliminated all noncommunist opposition within the Front and assumed complete control.

For an example of recent use of the front as a "transmission belt" see the letter from its Executive Committee in Tinko Vodenicharov (comp.), *Spravochnik na aktivista* (Sofia, 1961), pp. 1031-37.

The Fatherland Front today numbers 3.5 million persons, including all trade-unions and the communist youth movement as collective members and the communist party, the subordinate Bulgarian national agricultural union, and private citizens as individual members. Article by N. Stolpov in *Kommunist vooruzhënnykh sil,* XLVI, No. 4 (April 1966), Part II, 71.

9 Robert Lee Wolff, "Bulgaria," in Stephen D. Kertesz (ed.), *The Fate of East Central Europe* (Notre Dame, Ind., 1956), p. 282. King Simeon and his mother went into exile.

10 He should not be confused with Dr. Georgi M. Dimitrov (nicknamed "Gemeto"), who served as secretary general of the Agrarian party, resigned under communist pressure, and was succeeded by Nikola Petkov. The communists arrested and hanged Petkov in September 1947. *Ibid.,* pp. 279-283.

11 Dellin (ed.), *Bulgaria,* pp. 390-391. This source also mentions rumors that Dimitrov's death was not due to illness and that he was murdered because of deviation from the Kremlin line by favoring in 1948 the creation of a Balkan federation with Yugoslavia.

12 V. N. Durdenevskii, *Konstitutsii evropeiskikh stran narodnoi demokratii* (Moscow, 1954), pp. 5-26, gives the text in Russian.

13 For the translation into English, as amended, see Zdravko Stankov (transl.), *Constitution of the People's Republic of Bulgaria* (Sofia, 1964).

14 The Assembly in 1965 numbered 321 members. U.S. Department of State, Bureau of Intelligence and Research, *Directory of Bulgarian Officials* (Washington, D.C., August 1965), pp. 26-28, lists the deputies; hereafter cited as *Directory.*

15 *Directory,* p. 25, gives the names.

16 *Line-Up,* pp. 3-4. There is some overlapping in the bureau, which in 1967 included the premier, all deputy premiers, and four ministers or committee heads. The bureau operates like an inner cabinet.

17 *Directory,* pp. 1, 28, 34, 35, 48.

18 Dellin (ed.), *Bulgaria,* p. 94.

19 *Ibid.* In addition, the regime has mobilized "volunteer" units of workers to preserve social order. *Izvestiya na Prezidiuma na Narodnoto Sobranie,* No. 22 (March 15, 1960), translated into Russian in M. A. Gelfer (ed.), *Narodnaya Respublika Bolgariya* (Moscow, 1961), pp. 179-190.

20 Quoted in Dellin (ed.), *Bulgaria,* p. 95.

21 Admitted by implication in Boris Spasov and A. Angelov, *Gosudarstvennoe pravo Narodnoi Respubliki Bolgarii* (Moscow, 1962), pp. 82-83.

22 *Rabotnichesko delo,* February 4, 1950, quoted in Dellin (ed.), *Bulgaria,* p. 136.

23 The war period is covered in the Soviet version of the party history, L. Bidinskaya (ed.), *Istoriya Bolgarskoi*

Kommunisticheskoi Partii (Moscow, 1960), pp. 345-383.

24 The communists had only 25,000 members at this time and because of their weakness were forced to establish a coalition regime. For the subsequent growth of the party see the proceedings of the Eighth Congress of the Bulgarian party, in a translation attributed to the Polish United Workers' party, *VIII Zjazd Bułgarskiej Partii Komunistycznej* (Warsaw, 1963), p. 293.

25 An official statement issued in March 1945 admitted to 2,138 executions, 1,940 prison sentences of twenty years, and 1,689 sentences of ten to fifteen years. See Stanley G. Evans, *A Short History of Bulgaria* (London, 1960), p. 189.

26 *Ibid.,* p. 184.

27 Having become an "unperson" in the 1960's, Chervenkov was not mentioned in a party history covering this period. Cf. Pavel Kostov, Minka Trifonova, and Mircho St. Dimitrov (eds.), *Materiali po istoriya na Bulgarskata Komunisticheska Partiya, 1944-1960* (Sofia, 1961), pp. 87-98.

28 *New York Times,* December 8, 1962. Note that only Chervenkov was expelled also from the party at this time. The others merely lost their seats on the Central Committee.

29 It appears that only the leader can mention an unperson by name. Thus, Zhivkov in his report to the party's Eighth Congress stated that "the personality cult of Vulko Chervenkov" had led to "incorrect, anti-Leninist methods of work and leadership." Bulgarskata Komunisticheska Partiya, *Osmi Kongres: stenografski protokol* (Sofia, 1963), p. 125.

30 Bulgarian Telegraphic Agency dispatch, June 19, 1965, cited in RFE report. "Sentences of Bulgarians in April Conspiracy," June 24, 1965, pp. 2-4. See also RFE, *Colonel Tykociński's Revelations* (Munich, 1966), pp. 44-45.

31 Figures on party membership are from *Pogled,* August 15, 1966, as cited in RFE, *Situation Report,* August 23, 1966, p. 3.

32 *World Strength,* p. 50.

33 *Rabotnichesko delo,* January 17, 1964, as translated in *Bulgarian Press Survey,* January 29, 1964; hereafter cited as *BPS.* Almost half (46.7 percent) of the factory managers do not even possess a secondary education, according to *Novo vreme,* May 1965, cited in *BPS,* June 24, 1965.

34 Speech over Radio Sofia, September 15, 1965. For laws and their practical application see Nikola D. Tsvetkovski (ed.), *Nakazatelen Kodeks: tekst, literatura, sudebna praktika* (Sofia, 1961), pp. 169-199. A new penal code was being drafted, according to *Rabotnichesko delo,* July 31, 1965. The Committee for Public Security became a new ministry the following year. See *Rabotnichesko delo,* March 13, 1966.

35 Radio Sofia, February 28, 1966. See also the discussion of elections in Spasov and Angelov, *op. cit.,* pp. 567-596.

36 *Novo vreme,* January 1964, in *BPS,* February 20, 1964.

37 *Partiyen zhivot* (December 1963).

38 Radio Sofia, March 5, 1964.

39 RFE, *Situation Report,* February 18, 1965, p. 2. Despite these attacks, the United States raised its diplomatic mission at Sofia from legation to embassy level. *New York Times,* November 29, 1966.

40 *Izvestiya,* March 18, 1965, claimed that the total over the preceding seventeen years amounted to 1.5 billion rubles. This included 530 million rubles granted in 1964 to be used as capital investment during the 1966-1970 five-year plan. Some of it may be repaid in the future with manganese, of which deposits totaling several hundred million tons have been discovered recently near Varna. Radio Sofia, August 25, 1965.

41 L. A. D. Dellin, "Bulgaria Under Soviet Leadership," *Current History,* XLIV, No. 261 (May 1963), 385.

42 Alexander Kutt, "Exploitation in Soviet-Bloc Trade," *East Europe,* XI, No. 5 (May 1962), 24; see also the same author's pamphlet, *East-West Trade and Industrial Trends in the Soviet Area* (New York, August 1965).

43 *Darzhaven vestnik,* November 29, 1963, as cited in RFE report, "Stringent Amendments to Bulgarian Labor and Wage Codes," February 7, 1964 (5 pp.).

44 See the unsigned article on the party and youth in *Rabotnichesko delo,* July 9, 1965, which indicates that Komsomol membership decreased during 1964 by 2,139 persons. The Komsomol or communist youth organization in Bulgaria is named after Georgi Dimitrov. In 1962 the membership was somewhat under one million.

45 On the techniques used see Zhivko Oshavkov, *et al.* (eds.), *Izgrazhdane i razvitie na sotsialisticheskoto obshchestvo v Bulgariya* (Sofia, 1962), pp. 266-276.

46 Dellin (ed.), *Bulgaria,* p. 187.

47 *Ibid.,* p. 189. See also Dr. Ivan Sipkov, "Church and State in Bulgaria," in U.S. Senate, Committee on the Judiciary, *The Church and State under Communism* (Washington, D.C., 1965), II, 21-32.

48 Joseph B. Schectman, *Postwar Population Transfers in Europe, 1945-1955* (Philadelphia, 1962), pp. 345-354. More recent data give the number of Moslems as between 700,000 and 800,000 or 13.4 percent of the population. Veselin Khadzhinikolov (ed.), *Materiali po osnovi na nauchniya ateizm* (Sofia, 1965), p. 239.

49 Radio Sofia, September 4, 1965.

50 All priests, monks, and nuns were forced to leave the country in 1952, according to Sipkov, *op. cit.,* pp. 29, 32.

51 Dellin (ed.), *Bulgaria,* p. 192; Sipkov, *op. cit.,* p. 32.

52 Heinz Siegert, *Bulgarien Heute: Rotes Land am Schwarzen Meer* (Vienna, 1964), p. 130.

53 V. Aperyan, *Narodnaya Respublika Bolgariya* (Moscow, 1963), p. 30. For the past decade, between 52 and 53.5 percent of all trade has involved the U.S.S.R. The agreement for 1967 envisages a 16 percent increase over the preceding year. RFE, *Situation Report,* November 10, 1966, p. 1.

54 RFE report (by Harry Trend), "Soviet Economic Relations with COMECON," October 24, 1966 (5 pp.).

55 See *Pravda,* November 10, 1966, for figures on Soviet-Bulgarian trade. See also Zhivkov's servile comments regarding the U.S.S.R. in his closing speech to the Ninth Congress of the party. *Krasnaya zvezda,* November 22, 1966, pp. 1, 3.

56 *New York Times,* October 17, 1965.

57 Quoted by *Neues Österreich* (Vienna), July 17, 1965, from an interview with five Austrian newsmen at Sofia; cited in RFE report, "Zhivkov Interview Reviewed," July 23, 1965 (9 pp.), at p. 3.

58 Imports of Romanian oil dropped from 200,000 tons in 1955 to slightly more than 58,000 in 1963; imports from the U.S.S.R. in the same years were 117,000 and 1.6 million tons. RFE, *Situation Report,* August 26, 1965, p. 2.

59 *New York Times,* September 8, 1963.

60 See "A New Era in the Balkans?" *East Europe,* XIV, No. 4 (April 1965), 3. Deputy premiers Todorov and Kubadinski visited Athens "unofficially." *Neue Zürcher Zeitung,* August 31, 1966. Bulgaria's military and naval attaché was declared *persona non grata* after being apprehended receiving information from a Greek citizen. RFE, *Situation Report,* November 8, 1966, pp. 2-3.

61 Schectman, *op. cit.,* pp. 346, 353.

62 *Istoricheski pregled,* No. 5 (May 1965), as quoted in *BPS,* February 16, 1966, p. 3.

63 *New York Times,* October 17, 1965. Note also the claim by Yugoslav Macedonians that they have minorities in western Bulgaria and northern Greece. *Ibid.,* November 20, 1966.

64 See S. D. Sergeev and A. F. Dobrokhotov, *Narodnaya Respublika Bolgariya: ekonomika i vneshnyaya torgovlya* (Moscow, 1962), p. 236.

65 Article 11, as given in Durdenevskii, *op. cit.,* p. 7. See also N. D. Kazantsev (ed.), *Agrarnoe zakonodatelstvo zarubezhnykh sotsialisticheskikh stran* (Moscow, 1958), pp. 63-142.

66 Radio Sofia, February 15, 1965, reported that queues in front of bread shops were an ordinary sight, espe-

cially on weekends. For some of the problems related to collectivization see Kiril Lazarov, *Ekonomicheskoe razvitie Narodnoi Respubliki Bolgarii* (Moscow, 1963), pp. 141-159.

67 RFE, *Situation Report,* October 4, 1966, pp. 2-3. Another aspect involves compulsory savings in more than eight million accounts, or almost as many as there are people. Statement of Finance minister, Dimitar Popov, quoted in RFE, *Situation Report,* November 2, 1965, p. 4.

68 Todor Zhivkov, *Otchëtnyi doklad* (Moscow, 1963), pp. 95-96. It is hoped that the new economic system, on which almost half the industrial production is based, will assist in meeting these targets. *Rabotnichesko delo,* September 3, 1966, carries a message to the Bulgarian people on this subject.

69 Radio Sofia, February 15, 1965. Despite this situation, credits are being extended to certain underdeveloped countries, where about 2,000 Bulgarian specialists are now working. Aperyan, *op. cit.,* p. 44; Radio Sofia, February 10, 1966.

70 See RFE report, "Zhivkov's Report on Bulgaria's New Economic System," May 18, 1966 (pamphlet, 17 pp.).

71 Party leader Todor Zhivkov, speaking at the party congress in November 1966, claimed that bread grain production fully covered domestic needs at that time; he stated that fodder grain remained inadequate. His announced target for both types is 7.2 million metric tons by 1970, or more than two million above what could be produced in 1965. RFE report, "Zhivkov's Party Congress Report—(II) Internal Situation," November 25, 1966 (10 pp.), at p. 6. Despite the above boast concerning 1966, bread lines were a familiar sight in Sofia the following year. See Damian Obreshkov's article on "Sunshine Without Fog" in *Pogled,* January 30, 1967, translated in *BPS,* February 20, 1967.

Chapter 3 / CZECHOSLOVAKIA:
The Land in Between

BEFORE the Second World War, Czechoslovakia was the most prosperous and most democratic country in Eastern Europe. The government was based on a Western-style constitution, adopted in 1920. Two successive presidents, Tomáš Masaryk and Eduard Beneš, guarded and nurtured the democratic principles laid down in the constitution. Although much of the world appeared not apprehensive regarding Nazi Germany, the absorption of Austria by the Reich in early 1938 and mounting claims by Germany to border territory within Czechoslovakia gave the government in Prague considerable reason for alarm. In September came the betrayal at Munich which countenanced the transfer of the border terrritory to Nazi rule and was the beginning of the end for free Czechoslovakia. The peace which the British prime minister thought he had purchased at Munich lasted only six months, and the remainder of Czechoslovakia fell under Nazi domination, to remain so until near the end of the Second World War.

From the moment that the Red Army entered Czechoslovakia, in October 1944, the indigenous communists began to move into key positions from which to take control over the country. The Italian and French comrades were also making rapid gains, however, and Stalin probably did not wish to alert the West by an open seizure of power in Czechoslovakia. As a result, the communists used political means to fulfill one of their long-standing ambitions: the taking control of a country through a coalition government.[1] This process took time and provided a brief respite for Czechoslovak freedom which lasted until February 1948, when the communists executed a bloodless *coup* and established a people's democracy.

CONSTITUTIONAL FRAMEWORK

Superficially the new regime, based on a constitution adopted in May 1948 was similar to that in other Soviet satellites, since it combined Marxism with several features of the old "bourgeois" regime. There were many reasons for this decision. The constitution was designed to mask the true character of communist rule by providing a façade of democratic respectability.[2] The existence of a coalition government and President Beneš in office were also factors, because many of the provisions in the constitution had been formulated before the communists seized power.

THE CONSTITUTION OF 1960. A draft of the constitution now in force was first made public only after it had been sanctioned by the Central Committee of the Czechoslovak communist party. It then received approval in July 1960 from the National Assembly or legislature.[3] Any attempt to explain why the party chose this particular time to adopt a new basic law would be difficult. The rationale behind the step is much clearer. The first and probably main reason was ideological in nature. The 1948 document had become out of date in the current political context. By adopting a new "socialist" constitution the party may have hoped to strengthen its position. The document seems also to have been intended to show that Czechoslovakia had successfully laid the foundations of socialism and thus to justify the policies which the communists had followed since gaining control.[4]

Although the 1960 constitution has no more real meaning than its predecessor, it does have propaganda value among other communist regimes in Eastern Europe. The party could proclaim that Czechoslovakia was the second country in the world to have achieved socialism. The document summarizes various claimed achievements in legal form and outlines a program for the transition from socialism to communism. The preamble states that "people's democracy, as a way to socialism, has fully proved itself" and has brought Czechoslovakia "to the victory of socialism." [5] The country is allegedly "proceeding toward the construction of an advanced socialist society and gathering strength for the transition to communism." Although this document was not a copy of the Soviet model, "its substance and semantics were borrowed from the 1936 constitution of the Union of Soviet Socialist Republics." [6]

The formulations in the 1960 basic law of Czechoslovakia are more general than those used in that of the U.S.S.R. It does not establish in detail the composition of the Council of Ministers or the structure of state administration. Although shorter than the Soviet document, it is still quite lengthy (9 parts, 112 articles). A brief synopsis of the most significant features follows.

Article 2 establishes the theoretical locus of authority by stating that "all power in the Czechoslovak Socialist Republic shall belong to the working people." Article 4, however, defines the real power center by describing the Communist Party of Czechoslovakia as the "vanguard of the working class" and as "the guiding force in society and in the state."

Article 8 lays the basis for eliminating private enterprise (permitted under the 1948 constitution) by defining socialist property as having two basic forms: "state ownership, which is ownership by the people . . . and cooperative ownership." Article 10 further clarifies this point by restricting private property to "articles of personal and domestic use, family houses, [and] savings derived from labor." Article 9 allows small private enterprise, but only when it is based on the work of the owner himself.

THE GOVERNMENT. Czechoslovakia is typical among communist-dominated states in that it has a real government (the communist party) and a formal government. The latter is a façade that carries out administration for the party, which alone makes policy. The formal government performs three functions: executive, legislative, and judicial. This represents an artificial division for discussion purposes only, because no actual separation of powers exists. Nor is there any genuine system of checks and balances which might prevent arbitrary abuse of governmental authority, which is subject only to party controls. This point was made quite clear by President Antonín Novotný when he stated that there are "no remnants of the liberal, pseudo-democratic principles of the separation of powers among the various state institutions." [7]

The executive branch of the formal government consists of the President of the Republic and the cabinet. The president is "elected by the National Assembly as the representative of state power [and is] accountable to the National Assembly" (Article 61). After East Germany followed other satellites in installing a collective head of state, Czechoslovakia became unique in the Soviet bloc. Its constitution provides for a president who exercises real executive functions.

The Czechoslovak communists apparently decided to retain the one-man presidency, rather than to adopt the standard presidium, for two reasons. First, the party was trying to capitalize on the prestige and stature which the office had acquired under Presidents Masaryk (1918-1935) and Beneš (1935-1948). Second, the office represented a valuable political asset. Each of the three communist presidents (Klement Gottwald, 1948-1953; Antonín Zápotocký, 1953-1957; and Antonín Novotný, 1957-   ) was eager to occupy Hradčany Castle, cloak himself with the mantle of respectability, and exploit the office to help solidify his own position.[8] Attempts to abolish the presidency have also been complicated by the fact that the office has been occupied by the leader of the communist party.

The duties of the Czechoslovak president include most of those discharged by chiefs of states which have a parliamentary system of government. He must sign all laws enacted by the legislature, but may not veto legislation. He can declare a session of the National Assembly ended, although he has no authority to dissolve it. The power to appoint and recall the cabinet does not include the authority to dismiss a minister. The president represents the state in foreign relations, negotiates and ratifies treaties, and appoints and receives envoys. He has the right but not an obligation to submit a "state of the republic" message and recommend courses of action. He is the supreme commander of the armed forces. In addition, the president is given flexible powers, since he is entitled to "exercise authority which is not explicitly reserved to him in the constitution if a law so provides" (Article 62).

The president is "elected" for a term of five years, and there is no provision for impeachment. In theory he is responsible to the National Assembly for the conduct of his office. There is no provision, however, for enforcing this accountability. In practice each communist president has been a dictator, although his power and prestige are derived not from his office but from his position in the ruling party. In 1964 Novotný was reelected to a second five-year term.[9]

The cabinet is composed of the premier, an unspecified number of deputy premiers, and the ministers. It is defined as "the supreme executive organ of state power" and is responsible only to the National Assembly (Article 66). The president has the right to appoint the cabinet, and the National Assembly the theoretical power to vote it out of office (collectively or individually). The cabinet is organized into three distinct levels of authority: first, the premier; second, the government presidium, which is not mentioned in the constitution and consequently has no legal basis; and, third, the Council of Ministers.

The cabinet safeguards the fulfillment of state tasks, directs and controls the work of ministries and other central organs of administration, and issues binding resolutions and ordinances which are based on laws and implement the latter. The ministers issue binding regulations also on the strength of government ordinances (Articles 68, 72). As can be seen, the constitution seemingly has assigned to the cabinet a decisive executive role. In practice, however, this organ is nothing more than a body of routine administrators. Issues of importance are decided in advance by the presidium of the communist party before they are even considered by the cabinet.[10]

If the cabinet really exercised the authority granted it by the constitution, the premier would hold more political power than the president. As matters stand, the premiership is assigned to a second- or third-ranking communist, whose actual power is directly connected with his position in the party oligarchy.[11] It is apparent that the premier never will attain the same importance that other communist premiers enjoy, as long as the presidency is filled by the number one communist. The government presidium, composed of the premier and (at present) four deputy premiers, is empowered to control the activities of the various ministries and agencies and to direct and control the entire work of the cabinet.

The Council of Ministers patterns itself after the Soviet model. In 1967 it had twenty-six members. The cabinet has never exercised the role of supreme policy-maker assigned to it by the constitution. The ministers have so little real importance that the trend has been to appoint mediocrities to many of the cabinet posts. This also provides a supply of expendable scapegoats, who can be sacrificed when difficulties develop.[12]

THE LEGISLATIVE BRANCH. According to the constitution, the National Assembly is "the supreme organ of state power" and the "sole state-wide legislative body" (Article 39). In theory, this gives it a law-making monopoly and, thus, considerable influence over all other central government agencies. The powers of the National Assembly would seem to be almost unlimited, since only it has the power to amend the constitution, from which it draws its authority.

The theoretical authority of the National Assembly includes: resolution of basic questions, both for internal and for external policies of the state; adoption of laws; ratification of international treaties; election of the president; control over other organs of the government; election of the Supreme Court and recall of its members; establishment of ministries; and declaration of war (Articles 40-49). In actual practice, the National Assembly is a legislative rubber stamp for party decisions. Owing to its theoretical and potential importance, however, an examination of its organization is necessary.

The National Assembly is headed by a chairman. He and two deputy chairmen are elected by the members for terms of four years. The chairman presides over the Assembly and its presidium, signs all laws and legislative measures, and reports to the Assembly on any action taken by the presidium while the full body was not in session. What looks like an "inner presidium" represents the second level of authority. It comprises the chairman of the National Assembly and the deputy chairmen. This inner group handles all important matters and probably is the directing organ of the Assembly. It disposes of current business, drafts the Assembly's agenda, and controls the work of all committees. The full presidium of the National Assembly is composed of the chairman and his two deputies, the chairmen of permanent legislative committees (which vary in number), and twenty-six other members. Election to this body is by the Assembly and again for terms of four years. It is charged with the task of directing the work of the National Assembly and has the power to enact laws when the Assembly is not in session. It is explicitly accountable to the Assembly.[13] This is the group that would act as the collective head of state in a typical communist government.

The Assembly comprises 300 members who represent their constituencies during four-year terms after direct election. Membership and participation in the Assembly is basically an honorary function, and members hold other positions as a means of livelihood.[14] The Assembly normally meets in March for one session and in October for another, although more than two sessions may convene annually (for example, a four-day meeting was held in June 1965). The near-perfect attendance record at these sessions is surpassed only by the habit of unanimity. Between 1948 and 1960 there was never so much as one dissenting vote and no amendment of any type was offered from the floor. Thanks to this harmony, the Assembly has been able to enact legislation with amazing speed. The only incidents which slow down the proceedings are the "spontaneous outbursts of enthusiasm" and "stormy applause"—carefully graduated according to the speaker's importance—that greet even such dry reports as the one on the annual budget.[15]

THE JUDICIARY. The prewar judicial system in Czechoslovakia was not unlike that of other Western parliamentary democracies. Judges were appointed to life tenure by the President of the Republic or the cabinet, and their independence was guaranteed. Law represented the foundation of the judicial system, and justice was its goal.

The present organization bears no resemblance to the former one. It is a miniature copy of the Soviet model, specifically designed to serve the will of the party and allegedly intended to "protect the socialist state, its social order, and the rights and true interests of its citizens and of the organizations of the working people" (Article 97). Courts are also assigned the task of educating citizens so that they will be devoted and "loyal to their country and the cause of socialism" and will observe the "laws and the rules of socialist conduct" (ibid.). These principles include respect for socialist property, labor discipline, meeting production quotas, informing about hostile acts, and fulfilling obligations imposed by the state.

Judicial bodies are arranged in four tiers. The Supreme Court, at the top, is followed in descending order by the regional, district, and local or people's courts. Each higher level has supervisory and directive powers over the courts below. Besides the review of cases, these powers include the right to interpret the law for lower levels and even to withdraw cases from their jurisdiction.

Professional and lay judges in the local courts have equal status, and both are selected for terms of two years at meetings of the population; they are chosen by acclamation and not in general elections. Members of the Supreme Court are chosen by the National Assembly; of the regional court, by the appropriate regional National Committee; and of district courts, by the citizens in direct elections (Article 99). Qualifications for a judgeship include being at least twenty-three years of age and being known for devotion to the "people's democratic system." [16] Professional judgeships have the added requirement of legal training. Article 102 directs judges to interpret the laws and regulations in accordance with the "socialist legal spirit." This means that civil and criminal cases are basically political in nature and must be decided accordingly. Judges are accountable for their actions and are subject to recall.[17] Article 101 provided for the creation of local courts to "ensure increased participation of the working people in the work of the judiciary activities." This provision was implemented by a June 1961 law which created the local courts. The real reason for establishing these low-level bodies was to reduce the burden of petty cases on the judicial system. In these "people's courts" there is only one judge, an unpaid layman who must be at least twenty-one years old; he is elected for a two-year term.[18]

The traditional roles of judge, public prosecutor, and attorney are not applicable to Czechoslovak courts. The defense lawyer must place the interests of society above those of his client, and lawyer-client communications are no longer privileged. Many of the powers formerly held by judges have been transferred to the prosecutor, who is in effect a direct representative of the party.

The Office of the Procurator General exercises "supervision of the precise fulfillment and observance of laws and other legal regulations" (Article 104). Primary duties include enforcement and strengthening of socialist legality, implementation of party policies, and educating the people in socialism. The Procurator General is appointed by the President. He is responsible only to the National Assembly (Article 105) and probably has more power than any court in Czechoslovakia. The following constitutional provision eliminates any possible misunderstanding with regard to the role and responsibility of the Procurator: "The organs of the Procurator's office shall be subordinated to the Procurator General only and shall discharge their functions independently of local organs" (Article 106).

LOCAL GOVERNMENT. The units of local government are organized on three levels: regional (10 units), district (108), and local (14,000). The city of Prague forms an additional territorial unit, with regional status, and is subdivided into ten districts. The local administrative agencies, known as National Committees, are defined as "the organs of state power and administration in regions, districts, and localities" (Article 86). Each Committee will have from nine to 150 members, depending upon the level and the population of the area. Members serve terms of four years, after direct elections. The organization on each tier is identical. The executive organ for any Committee is a council composed of a chairman, his deputy or deputies, a secretary, and a varying number of members.[19]

These local councils, although nominally chosen by the committeemen and responsible to them, are indirectly subordinate to the central government. Councils perform most of a Committee's legislative functions by issuing decrees and ordinances. The local councils are assisted by commissions, elected or appointed by the Committee, which are responsible for the operation of various administrative activities at the local level.

The National Committees gradually have been given more administrative authority, but they are not permitted to make policy. Their task is to organize and direct all economic, social, and cultural construction in the specific area. Regional and district administrations are organized into functional departments for planning, finance, agriculture, transportation, and so on. There is no mandatory departmentalization for the local levels, which are permitted to organize, with the approval of the next higher level, as the particular needs of the area dictate. Most of the effort expended by local government is devoted to the fulfillment of the state economic plan from indigenous resources and to strengthening the political system. As generally in East European countries, increasing agricultural production and protecting socialist property are two of the priorities.

Local administrations, despite the extensive theoretical power which they exercise in areas ranging from national defense to recreation programs, do little more than carry out the directives of higher authority and have no self-government in the true sense. The principle of democratic centralism, with each level subject to the absolute authority of the next higher level, is strictly enforced. Members of the party dominate all levels of government and ensure that the party remains in fact "the leading force in the state and society."

The Slovak National Council, once a powerful organ of local government, enjoyed unique autonomy under the 1948 constitution.

(For a listing of national minorities see table 14.) Today the Council is described as "the national organ of state power and administration in Slovakia" (Article 73). Its legislative and executive actions may be repealed by the National Assembly. This loss of autonomy has generated many problems for President Novotný and caused much resentment among Slovak communists and noncommunists alike.

TABLE 14

NATIONALITY COMPOSITION OF CZECHOSLOVAKIA, 1964

Nationality	Population	Percent of total
Czechs	9,158,000	65.4
Slovaks	3,994,000	28.5
Hungarians	546,000	3.9
Germans	136,000	1.0
Poles	69,000	0.5
Ukrainians and Russians	56,000	0.4
Other and unidentified	45,000	0.3
Total	14,004,000	100.0

SOURCE: Ústřední Komise Lidové Kontroly a Statistiký, *Statistický Ročenka ČSSR 1965* (Prague, 1965), p. 87.

NOTE: Unlisted above are some 150,000 gypsies, many of whom live in eastern Slovakia. *Predvoj,* August 19, 1965, translated in *Czechoslovak Press Survey,* September 2, 1965.

By 1966 the total population had increased only to 14,240,000, of which 4,414,000 lived in Slovakia. *Rudé právo,* July 28, 1966. This is due in part to the 105,800 legal abortions compared with 231,000 live births during 1965. *New York Times,* September 4, 1966 (from official figures).

It is entirely possible that this dissatisfaction precipitated the May 1964 party resolution enlarging the number of commissioners and reviving Council departments which now exercise at least some measure of executive power.[20] That this process will be slow can be seen from the fact that it was March 31, 1966, before the Slovak National Council for the first time submitted a bill on its own initiative to the National Assembly in Prague.

THE ELECTORAL SYSTEM. Voting in Czechoslovakia is direct, universal, and allegedly secret. Elections are held every four years to send representatives to all levels of the government. The "democratic" character of these elections is ensured by procedures which are typical throughout the communist bloc. There is only one candidate per seat, and no write-in names are permitted. Only those who are hostile to the regime, it is claimed, would exercise the right to cast a secret ballot. The communist-dominated National Front has complete control over the conduct of elections and tallying of ballots. It nominates the members of the electoral commissions on all levels from among the party faithful. As a final measure of control, the National Front is given the right to recall any "unworthy members" who might be elected.

In past elections the National Front has held the exclusive right to nominate candidates for the electoral list. This reportedly is to be changed. A law passed in February 1964 permits one or more candidates to be proposed for each electoral district. The right to nominate candidates now extends to political parties, meetings of workers, social organizations, and like groups. A newspaper in Bratislava explained at the time that under the new law preparation for the election would be divided into three stages:

> In the first stage (February 1 to March 23) candidates will be selected and proposed. The second stage (March 25 to May 14) will give the voters opportunity to "unite themselves" on a candidate, who will then be registered. The last stage (May 14 to June 12) will allow the voters to get acquainted personally with their selected candidate.[21]

It is doubtful that the voters have really been given a greater choice as to who "represents" them, since only one final candidate from each district can appear on the ballot, as before. That candidate must be acceptable to the National Front—and thus, in reality, to the communist party.

The party in Czechoslovakia shares the passion for unanimity that prevails throughout the communist world. Although there is no legal obligation to vote, the force of the party and governmental apparatus is brought to bear on the individual so that the "will of the people" shall be properly expressed in support of the regime. According to official statistics, which the communists have made public, there has been almost perfect success in getting out the vote. In the most recent national elections, it is claimed, more than 9,400,000 persons, or 99.94 percent of those eligible, cast their ballots for the National Front.[22]

GOVERNMENT CONTROLS. Tight controls are the essence

of most totalitarian states which seek to maintain the masses in submission, and Czechoslovakia represents no exception. The communist party, of course, is in absolute command. It has followed the Soviet model in establishing a firm grip on the administrative apparatus.

Perhaps the decisive power in Czechoslovakia is still external. The Soviet Union can influence the communist leaders in Prague via official channels. This method might be likened to the surface current of a stream. The real power is in the invisible undercurrent which is represented by Moscow's network of native and Soviet agents. This network has proven to be an efficient device for keeping the native Czechoslovak rulers and party in line, without the overt threat of force.

The police provide the most effective internal control device, and it is the secret, not the uniformed, police that generate fear in those who might be tempted to deviate. Secret agents have been infiltrated into every organization of the Czechoslovak Socialist Republic. The efforts of police functionaries are augmented by the extensive use of informers. The role of the Procurator General's office has already been discussed and requires little further amplification, except to note that it is in a position to accuse and is supported by its power of judicial prosecution.

The Central Commission of People's Control and Statistics is yet another powerful organization. It, too, has considerable independence and the authority to probe without restriction. This agency may investigate, recommend corrective action, and take disciplinary measures that include initiation of criminal prosecution. Specifically, it has the authority to maintain "strict control over the custody, receipts, and expenditures of state, cooperative, and other monetary funds and material values"; to check on "the execution of the laws, ordinances, and decisions of the government"; to give its "opinion on the report of the Finance Ministry on the fulfillment of the state budget"; and to handle the "complaints of the working people and take appropriate measures." [23]

The state economic plan at one time represented yet another very effective control device. It worked as a yardstick by which all persons were measured. Fulfillment of a goal or a quota used to be of the utmost importance to the individual since, in the communist world, results were taken as an indication of his personal effort and intent.

Failure, regardless of the cause, could and did have dire consequences for the person responsible for it. This led, among other things, to falsified reports. There has been a gradual introduction of a new system for economic management based in part on the law of value, the relationship between supply and demand, and certain principles of a traditional market economy.[24]

PROBLEMS OF ADMINISTRATION. Czechoslovakia is experiencing the same administrative difficulties which plague most of the communist bloc: bureaucratism, disloyalty, incompetence, and dishonesty. The hard core of the communist party was small in 1945, and many opportunists were inducted during the rapid expansion which followed. The initial shortage of trustworthy communists was compounded by the rapid growth of governmental machinery brought about by extensive nationalization.

Although the communists obtained the necessary manpower, the government continued to be filled with former middle-class people. After the purging of these "bourgeois" individuals, incompetent and frequently untrustworthy communists were put in to fill the vacancies. Further cycles of purge and reorganization have followed, but inefficiency and apathy still prevail. The average educational level in high government positions is quite low. For example, among all leading officials in the state administration, some 61 percent have only an elementary school education, about 10 percent attended lower special school, and about 9 percent completed their secondary education, while only about 9 percent are university graduates.[25]

A cumbersome administrative machinery has resulted in overlapping and poorly defined areas of responsibility. This is advantageous for the average communist bureaucrat, who prefers to remain anonymous and escape responsibility. An organization which accepts no excuse for failure makes experimentation dangerous. It is easy to understand, thus, why initiative has been stifled. A massive bureaucracy is also an ideal breeding place for corruption, and the spoils system has flourished. Stealing from the state seems to be an accepted practice in most communist countries.[26]

In an effort to alleviate some of the discontent resulting from such difficulties, President Novotný was forced to dismiss Premier Viliam Široký [27] and agree to the removal of two other old Stalinists (Karol Bacílek and Július Ďuriš) from high positions. There can be little doubt that one of the factors contributing to these changes was pressure by younger liberals who wanted to modernize the system and reverse the trend toward deterioration. The reorganization of the government, however, does not seem to have satisfied the liberal elements, and probably it has raised their hopes for more freedom and a higher standard of living. They have been maintaining pressure on the regime, and the Stalinist leadership has repeatedly had to give way.

In 1964 the Central Committee of the party rehabilitated a number of prominent Slovak writers and former government officials, all of whom were communists. They had been condemned for "bourgeois nationalism" and other "political mistakes." It was admitted that they had been made scapegoats—obviously for failures in the high party leadership.[28] In 1966, for the first time, noncommunists were being rehabilitated.

At present there seems to be a stalemate in the struggle between the entrenched bureaucracy and the liberals, with each side maneuvering behind the scenes to gain support for its own views. In view of the Czechoslovak leadership's cautious attitude in the past and the country's physical proximity to the U.S.S.R., no moves toward a truly democratic form of government are to be expected. The current trend suggests that Czechoslovakia is being brought into line with bloc-wide developments. Any "liberal" government that might be installed in Czechoslovakia would still be a communist government.

THE COMMUNIST PARTY, ORIGIN AND ACTIVITIES

Czechoslovakia, known formerly for its political democracy, has been since 1948 a communist one-party state. This reversal of political, social, and economic orientation resulted from international developments and domestic conditions which culminated in the February 1948 *coup*. Because this reversal took place while Soviet armed forces were not present in the country, a fundamental question arises. What were the contributing factors that enabled the Communist Party of Czechoslovakia (*Komunistická Strana Československa—KSČ*) to seize and maintain control?

The First World War and the resultant independence of Czechoslovakia had an important effect on the realignment of political parties in that territory. The outward appearance of communist party growth and legality provided a façade behind which doctrinal struggles took place. In the aftermath of severe criticism in 1928 of KSČ leadership by Moscow at the Sixth Congress of the Comintern, Klement Gottwald became the general secretary of the Czechoslovak party.[29] Immediately upon taking office he instituted a large-scale purge.

From 1930 until 1938 Gottwald concentrated on the bolshevization of the party and the recruitment of young unskilled workers. This program, however, was not successful in producing a mass party. Official figures indicate that KSČ strength never exceeded 75,000 members before the war. After the Munich crisis, the party was banned from all political activity. By the time the Germans completed their occupation of Czechoslovakia, in March 1939, the majority of the KSČ leadership had fled the country. By what "appeared to be a prearranged plan," they took refuge abroad: Gottwald, Slánský, Kopecký, and Nejedlý in Moscow; Nosek, Hodinová, and Kreibich in London; Šverma and Clementis in Paris.[30] Some communists, among them Dolanský and Zápotocký, were apprehended while trying to escape to Poland and later sent to Nazi concentration camps.

Hitler's invasion of the U.S.S.R. brought the communists into superficial cooperation with the Beneš government-in-exile. A portent of the future came with the signing of the Soviet-Czechoslovak agreement in December 1943 at Moscow. Beneš regarded the treaty as "one of the links in the postwar system of security." [31] Article 5 of the agreement precluded Czechoslovak participation in any alliances not acceptable to the U.S.S.R. For the KSČ, this was the first step toward its ultimate goal: communist control of the country.

PENETRATION TACTICS. Beneš decided to negotiate with representatives of various political parties about the establishment of a government in the liberated areas of the country. In March 1945 he arrived in Moscow from England. The talks began in an atmosphere of communist domination, with Gottwald pressing home "the tremendous psychological and political advantages accruing to them [the communists] from the Red Army's control over Czechoslovakia and the overt Soviet support of their cause." [32] Beneš accepted a plan for a "government of the National Front of Czechs and Slovaks" in which communists were assigned eight of 25 cabinet seats. The communists demanded and obtained the important government ministries of Interior, Agriculture, and Information, among others.[33]

At the national, regional, and local levels, communist-dominated National Committees were acting as organs of government. Not regularly elected, these were of a revolutionary nature, having been established under Red Army occupation and hence under communist control. From these bases the KSČ began an intense drive during which the party made rapid strides toward the attainment of political and economic power. The communist program was facilitated rather than hampered by the withdrawal of the Red Army at the end of 1945, since the action could be interpreted by many Czechs and Slovaks as evidence of Soviet nonintervention.

A historian of the KSČ has described how the political, social, and economic structure underwent a revolutionary assault. Actions included the confiscation of property; the prohibition of certain "bourgeois" political parties; and the transformation of parliament, "actuating the further development and consolidation of the revolution into a direct instrument for the socialist building of the country." [34] Meanwhile, since in order to achieve parliamentary control it was necessary for the KSČ to increase its voting base, a communist recruitment campaign strove for mass enrollment.

Opportunists saw real advantages in joining the party. Significant inducements and the lack of any ideological tests resulted in great success for the recruiting effort. At the end of the war the party had 27,000 members. A year later, just before the general election, there were 1,159,164 registered communists.[35] (See table 15 for subsequent growth.) The objective of the KSČ was to gain an absolute majority in the May 1946 voting for a Constituent Assembly to establish the postwar government. The results were a disappointment to the communists, because they polled only 38 percent during the balloting. Since the KSČ had achieved more votes than any other party, however, communist leader Gottwald became premier in a cabinet of twenty-six members, only nine of whom officially belonged to his party. The communists with 38 percent of the votes and the Social Democrats with 13 percent together obtained 153 (114 plus 39) of the 300 seats in the Constituent Assembly. Clearly, Zdeněk Fierlinger, a fellow traveler and the leader of the Social Democratic party, looked like the key to KSČ strategy.

Cooperation was encouraged by Fierlinger, but this failed in

November 1947, when he was ousted and anticommunists took control of the Social Democratic party. Other political groups employed parliamentary maneuvers to impede the KSČ programs. A communist plot to murder Deputy Premier Petr Zenkl, Foreign Minister Jan Masaryk, and Justice Minister Prokop Drtina (who had been sent packages with explosives) was discovered by organs of security

TABLE 15

CZECHOSLOVAK COMMUNIST PARTY MEMBERSHIP, 1948-1966

Date	Members	Candidates	Total
June 1948	n. a.	n. a.	2,418,199
May 1949	1,788,383	522,683	2,311,066
February 1951	1,518,144	159,299	1,677,443
June 1954	1,385,610	103,624	1,489,234
June 1958	n. a.	n. a.	1,422,100
July 1960	1,379,441	179,641	1,559,082
October 1962	1,588,589	92,230	1,680,819
July 1963	1,624,197	55,286	1,679,483
January 1964	n. a.	n. a.	1,676,509
January 1965	ca. 1,627,416	ca. 57,000	1,684,416
June 1966	n. a.	n. a.	ca. 1,700,000

SOURCES: *Rudé právo,* issues of July 2, 1949; February 23, 1951; June 12, 1954; June 22, 1958; July 8, 1960; December 5, 1962. *Život strany,* issues of October 1963, September 1964, and May 1965, Vladimír Krechler (ed.) *Příručni slovník k dějinám KSČ* (Prague, 1964), I, 325-332. Radio Free Europe report (by H. Hajek and L. Niznansky), "New Czechoslovak CP Central Committee," June 14, 1966 (4 pp.).

NOTE: No breakdown was given regarding members or candidates before 1949; at some other times, official data were not available (n. a.). The Thirteenth Congress of the KSČ abolished the candidate status and provided that by September 1966 all should be full members.

and the judiciary. In addition, the Soviet demand that Czechoslovakia withdraw from announced participation in the Marshall Plan conference at Paris had served to undermine KSČ prestige. The decline in communist strength also showed on a poll conducted by the Institute of Public Research, a branch of the KSČ-controlled Ministry of Information.[36]

SEIZURE OF CONTROL. The *coup* of February 1948 followed the resignation of twelve noncommunist members of the cabinet in protest over the replacement of several ranking police officials by communists. Under normal conditions, this action would have forced new elections. But the communists utilized key organizations, such as workers' councils, the Interior (police) and Information ministries, a workers' militia armed by the communists, and the "action committees." These last groups, which had operated clandestinely, revealed themselves and took over the direction of all government and industrial activities.[37] An incident involving such an action committee in the Justice ministry, headed by the anticommunist Drtina, has been publicized only recently:

> Drtina had excellent safeguards at the Ministry but eight Justice personnel, unknown to Drtina, were communists. One of these communists, Comrade Severa, ejected Drtina from the building on February 25. Drtina was infuriated [and] threatened him with serious sanctions. [Then] he stopped threatening; over the radio, he could hear that Beneš had accepted his resignation.[38]

Communist pressure on Beneš was severe. Demonstrations, the loss of government control to action committees, and the threat of civil war caused Beneš, a sick man, to accede to the demands presented by Gottwald. A former Czechoslovak diplomat has described the situation as follows: "Once Beneš had come to the conclusion that the only alternative to surrender was a bloody civil war, with strong likelihood of direct or indirect Soviet intervention, he was incapable of acting otherwise." [39]

In assuming control over the country, Gottwald enjoyed many advantages that had not accrued to Lenin after his seizure of power in Russia. Some of these centered on the experience that the communists had gained during active participation in the government over a three-year period prior to the *coup*. Major industries had been nationalized, and no large segment of the population offered opposition to the regime.[40]

TRANSMISSION BELTS. Six political organizations, including the two communist parties (a separate one exists for Slovakia), comprise the National Front. It actually represents a coalition of KSČ-dominated political groups and mass organizations.[41] Retention of subordinate organizations has been useful in preserving the fiction that a multiparty system and political freedom exist in Czechoslovakia. These groups also provide transmission belts to population segments which reject doctrinaire communism. Sufficiently large, their support is required for achieving communist objectives.

Even since adoption of the 1960 constitution, which proclaimed the KSČ as the leading force in society, the National Front façade has been retained. Communist control over the National Front at the highest level is exercised through the KSČ presidium. The chairman or one of the deputy chairmen of the National Front has always been a member of that body. The presence of important communist leaders assures that all party directives will be implemented.

Mass organizations also are necessary under the communist concept of population control. The communists will exploit the help of nonparty elements so long as they work for KSČ purposes and are subordinate to its leadership. Mass organizations transmit the party line in their particular sphere of activity. These groups parallel in structure the organization of the ruling party, and communist control is maintained by the appointment of important KSČ members to key positions at all levels.

From a political and an economic point of view the Revolutionary Trade-Union Movement (*Revoluční Odborové Hnutí*—ROH), with a membership of more than five million, is the most important.[42] The ROH is a symbol of the worker-KSČ alliance. It is, however, more concerned with party goals than with traditional West European trade-union objectives. There are thirteen unions in the ROH.

The Czechoslovak Youth League (*Československý Svaz Mládeže* —ČSM), like the Soviet Komsomol, serves as an apprentice organization for the party, with membership covering the age group from fifteen to twenty-six years. Its propaganda seeks to develop an early dedication to communism. Advancement in industry and higher education are practically impossible for those who fail to join. Yet, apathy and indifference, according to newspaper comments, are the hallmark of the ČSM, and total membership, at one time more than 1.5 million, has declined in recent years to about a million.[43]

The Union for Cooperation with the Army, (*Svaz pro Spolupráci s Armádou*—SVAZARM), with almost 800,000 members,[44] performs the same function as the Soviet DOSAAF in support of paramilitary training. Another organization is the Czechoslovak-Soviet Friendship League, which has numbered close to 2.5 million members.[45] It sponsors cultural and social ties with the U.S.S.R. Much of the propaganda effort emphasizes Soviet scientific and cultural achievements, together with U.S.S.R. support for Czechoslovakia; the objective, of course, is the strengthening of ties between the two countries.[46] Communist control over mass organizations from the national down to the local level is facilitated by the parallel structure of all organizations, in which both vertical and horizontal controls are utilized.

THE COMMUNIST PARTY. The KSČ or Communist Party of Czechoslovakia, comprising approximately 11.6 percent of the total population in 1966, has about 1,700,000 members and about 50,000 primary party organizations.[47] Proportionately, the KSČ is one of the largest communist organizations in the world. By comparison, the Communist Party of the Soviet Union (CPSU) has in its ranks only about 7 percent of the total U.S.S.R. population. The organizational structure of the KSČ is established by the party statute. The pyramidal system, with final authority held by a small group at the top, closely parallels that of the CPSU. In reality, the operating procedures and locus of power are entirely different from the formal structure.

The Presidium (formerly called the Politburo) of the Central Committee determines policies for the KSČ. A self-perpetuating body, formally elected by the Central Committee, insulated from rank-and-file party members by several layers, the Presidium holds supreme authority. It currently numbers ten full members and five candidates. (See table 16.) Only five of the fifteen have had substantial experience on this body: Antonín Novotný, president of Czechoslovakia and first secretary of the KSČ; Bohuslav Laštovička, chairman of the National Assembly; Jiří Hendrych, member of the Secretariat and chairman of the Central Committee's ideological commission; Otakar Šimůnek, an economic expert of the post-Stalin period and a deputy premier; and Jaromír Dolanský, who is semi-retired. The other five members and the five candidates, who have joined the Presidium since 1962, reflect the process of bringing younger blood into this policy-making organ, being between forty and just over fifty years of age.[48]

The Secretariat is allegedly the administrative arm of the Presidium, but in fact is the party organ of real authority. Its activity officially is restricted to the implementation of policy and nominally subject to review by the Presidium. The Secretariat transmits party orders from top to bottom and supervises the selection and activities of secretaries at lower party levels. Together with the secretaries of the region, district, and city committees and other full-time functionaries, its staff comprises the *apparatchiki* or backbone of the party. Three of the five secretaries at the national level (Novotný, Hendrych, and Kolder) are also Presidium members and are thus the most powerful persons in the country.

TABLE 16
CZECHOSLOVAK COMMUNIST PARTY LEADERSHIP, 1967

Name	Born	Position and responsibility	Joined Presidium or Secretariat
Presidium full members:			
Černik, Oldrich ...	1923	Deputy premier	1966
Chudík, Michal ...	1914	Chairman of Slovak National Council	1964
Dolanský, Jaromír .	1895	Chairman of KSČ Living Standard Commission	1946
Dubček, Alexander	1923	First secretary, Slovak communist party	1963
*Hendrych, Jiří	1913	Secretary (Ideology)	1958
*Kolder, Drahomír .	1925	Secretary (Economy)	1962
Laštovička, Bohuslav	1905	Chairman of National Assembly	1962
Lenárt, Josef	1923	Prime minister	1962
*Novotný, Antonín .	1904	First secretary of KSČ, president of the republic	1951
Šimůnek, Otakar ..	1908	Deputy premier and CMEA representative	1958
Presidium candidate members:			
Kapek, Antonín ..	1922	Manager of Prague Heavy Engineering Factory	1962
**Pastyrik, Miroslav .	1912	Chairman, Central Council of Trade-Unions	1966
Sabolčík, Michal ..	1924	Economic expert for Slovak communist party	1963
Sadovsky, Stefan ..	1924	Chairman of Western Slovak National Committee	1966
**Vaculík, Martin ...	1922	First secretary, Prague city KSČ	1963
Secretariat (including three secretaries indicated above by *):			
Koucký, Vladimír .	1920	Secretary (International Affairs)	1958
Strougal, Lubomir.	1924	Secretary (Agriculture)	1965
Secretariat members (including two members indicated above by **):			
Pecha, František ..	1914	First secretary, Eastern Bohemia KSČ	1966

SOURCE: Radio Free Europe report (by L. Niznansky), "The New CPCS Presidium and Secretariat," June 7, 1966 (4 pp.). RFE. *Communist Party-Government Line-Up* (Munich: March 1967), pp. 9-11.

The current Central Committee, elected at the Thirteenth Party Congress in May-June 1966, consists of 110 full members and 56 candidates.[49] Theoretically, it is the official ruling organ of the KSČ, when the party congress is not in session. In reality, its powers are in the hands of the Presidium and the Secretariat. The Central Control and Audit Commission, comprising thirty members, is responsible for making disciplinary investigations, screening KSČ members, and hearing appeals against decisions of lower party organs. Another function is to audit the records of all KSČ organizations in economic and financial matters.

The Communist Party of Slovakia (*Komunistická Strana Slovenska*—KSS) has a special position within the formal structure of the KSČ. There are about 30,000 Slovak communists, or 17.5 percent of the party membership in Czechoslovakia; in contrast, the population of Slovakia is about 30 percent of the total for the country.[50] The retention of the KSS as an "independent" organization is a concession to Slovak nationalist sentiment and tradition. The KSS presumably cherishes the fiction of its equality with the KSČ, but is definitely subordinate. Firm KSČ control is maintained by an interlocking directorate in which three full members of the seven-member KSS Presidium also are members or candidates in the Presidium of the KSČ. Utterances of Slovak communist leaders emphasize their subordination. For instance, Alexander Dubček, the KSS first secretary, has stated:

> We follow the directives of the KSČ Central Committee in full realization that it is not a one-time campaign, but a determined process in our socialist building.[51]

Connecting the top party organs with the broad base of primary units are the territorially graduated levels that correspond to the state administrative structure. Below the national level come the *kraj* (regional) organizations, each of which in turn is broken down into districts. At the city, district, and regional levels the roles of committee, bureau, and secretary have ascending importance. Orders from above, conveyed through the secretaries at the regional and district committees, who are appointed by the next higher level, outweigh the influence of the grass-roots.

The primary party units form the base of the organizational pyramid. Some 49,930 units or cells of this type exist (about 10,000 in Slovakia), mostly on an individual plant and office basis.[52] A minimum of three members is prescribed for a basic unit, and its establishment must be approved by the respective district or city committee. The essential functions of such units are to

Improve training in the fundamentals of communism;
Safeguard security of the party dictatorship;
Disseminate the party line on all aspects of domestic and foreign
    policy;
Recruit and train new party members;
Ensure that party economic goals are fulfilled and workers' morale
    is strengthened.[53]

Because of its structure the party is able to control the government's activities on all levels and to direct all its economic, social, and cultural undertaking. This very power, however, poses significant problems. It is apparent that the communists consider party discipline to be the most important factor in this process. The concept of democratic centralism is invoked to compel discipline, as in this statement by Michal Pecho, chief of the ideological department in the KSS central apparatus:

> Execution of party decisions issued by the Central Committee
> demands principled party discipline of party members. This is
> the law, and it is on this foundation that every revolutionary
> communist party is built. The extent to which the whole party
> succeeds in implementing a line, in a disciplined manner and a
> united fashion, depends on the political level and knowledge of
> life of each individual member and his identity of views as far
> as the decisions made by the party organs are concerned. The
> discussion must last until a decision is accepted.[54]

The party has difficulty in recruiting young blood.[55] This condition is reflected in the Czechoslovak Youth League, where only 5 percent (about 50,000) among the 1,000,000 members are also enrolled in the KSČ.[56] The party is getting mostly young opportunists who are ready to buy personal advantage via the youth movement. It would appear that, after almost two decades in power, the party holds little attraction for the young generation. Some evidence thereof came on May 15, 1966, when university students rioted in Prague against Novotný during their annual festival. Despite the efforts to recruit young persons the average age of KSČ membership is forty-five years, and the number of older members is increasing, while that of members under forty-five is declining. In two-thirds of the primary units in the city of Prague, the average KSČ member is sixty years old.[57] About 90 percent of the present membership, on a national scale, joined between 1945 and 1948, during a period when it was expedient to do so.

Another effort of the party is to achieve a member ratio of 60 percent industrial workers, some 20 percent collective farmers, and the remainder in the category of others. The social composition for 1962 and 1966 is shown in table 17. The party is admittedly weakest

TABLE 17

CZECHOSLOVAK COMMUNIST PARTY SOCIAL COMPOSITION, 1962 AND 1966

Occupational status	January 1, 1962		January 1, 1966	
	Number of members	Percentage of total membership	Number of members	Percentage of total membership
Industrial workers	554,054	33.4	511,917	30.2
Agricultural laborers	43,741	2.6	46,062	2.7
Collective farmers	106,373	6.4	91,109	5.4
Government officials	126,393	7.6	113,350	6.7
Public workers	31,750	1.9	27,246	1.6
Scientific workers	3,788	0.2	3,796	0.2
Engineering and technical workers	241,218	14.6	293,277	17.3
Workers in arts and culture	8,192	0.5	9,218	0.5
Teachers and professors	56,267	3.3	64,787	3.8
Students	8,044	0.5	6,372	0.4
Housewives	93,797	5.7	68,659	4.0
Pensioners	214,054	13.0	293,577	17.4
Other	170,150	10.3	168,631	9.8
Total	1,657,821	100.0	1,698,002	100.0

SOURCE: Život strany, September 1966, as reported in Czechoslovak Press Survey, October 13, 1966, p. 5.

among industrial workers, farmers, and young persons. The Slovak party newspaper divulged in 1964 that only 11.2 percent of agricultural laborers in Slovakia were party members.[58] Problems with recruitment in general have been encountered in Slovakia, for fundamental reasons. The Slovaks are a strongly Catholic people, more conservative than the Czechs, and the depredations of the Red Army are well remembered. In addition, despite the façade of unity, the Slovaks resent the traditional centralism emanating from Prague.[59]

KSČ LEADERSHIP. An excellent study [60] finds that KSČ leaders conform to a general pattern: (1) they are mainly Czech by nationality; (2) most have come from the working class; (3) they have had a minimum of formal education; (4) the majority were in their fifties at the time of the study; and (5) they are anti-intellectual.

The theme of anti-intellectualism is repeated in the party line. Antonín Novotný, speaking in the central Slovak region in 1964, stated:

> I am proud I was a worker . . . The factory, the workers' collective, and the many years of party and public work are to me, the same as to hundreds of thousands of workers who linked their whole life with the party, a real university in which we won the proud title of workers' officials.[61]

This attitude of distrust toward the intellectual is understandable because of his tendency to show originality, to deviate, and to even revolt. The admission of younger men like Lenárt, Sabolčík, Kolder, and Dubček into the KSČ presidium does not appear to be consistent with Novotný's attitude.[62] It may suggest an attempt, however, to quiet demands for further destalinization.

This phenomenon—the reaction against Stalin—has posed a serious ideological and practical problem for the party leadership. Many of the current leaders were in high positions during Stalin's life. Novotný recognizes that destalinization entails the serious risk of undermining the authority of the party and exposing his clique to undesirable public scrutiny. He stressed this point in a speech delivered early in 1964. After remarking that "Last year the KSČ Central Committee closed the books on essentially everything caused by the personality cult"—the euphemism for a Stalinist dictatorship, based on terror—he added:

> We shall never permit anyone to use the party criticism of the personality cult for promotion of his own ambitions or for undermining the authority of the Central Committee and the unity of the party.[63]

Novotný in his reference to closing the books was alluding to the removal in September 1963 of KSČ presidium members Viliam Široký and Karol Bacílek as well as others for alleged implication in the Slánský-Clementis case, indicating that all those guilty of sending these so-called national deviationists to their deaths had been punished. These remarks also covered the removal of Gottwald's mummy from its mausoleum in Prague. Himself fully implicated in the Slánský-Clementis affair, Novotný called for moderation: "Some of the people play into the hands of capitalist reaction. . . . In their false enthusiasm for rectification they completely forget the great, the enormous results which we have achieved during the period since 1948." [64]

An identical party line was stressed by Alexander Dubček, member of the KSČ presidium and first secretary of the Slovak party, during a subsequent address: "In this connection, it should be said that the rectification of past errors must not lead to the negation of everything done in the past, in the years of the first Five-Year Plan." [65] The issue of the political trials during the 1952-1954 period, which led to the execution of Slánský, Clementis, and others on false charges, continues to cause ideological problems. Evidently, KSČ control over propaganda and information media has loosened notably.

PUBLIC OPINION. The attitude of the Czechoslovaks to the current situation is reflected in their behavior. An excellent study of party propaganda methods finds that the "thoroughness of Communist indoctrination inevitably arouses apathy, for it is based on a method leading to renunciation of independent thinking." [66] Another experienced observer states that "the younger generation appears politically apathetic, unsatisfied and grumbling while mechanically executing prescribed party rituals." [67]

Perhaps the propaganda effort is more scientific than has been recognized. Indoctrination related to ties with a powerful U.S.S.R. does create apathy. This feeling is more beneficial than harmful to a dictatorship—"Working upon an apathetic populace, the regime has a better chance to consolidate than it would under conditions of intellectual ferment." [68] Perhaps the gap between the communist party and the people is to remain unbridged. The annihilating boredom that characterizes the life of the Czech and Slovak populations may be, indeed, the party objective.

DOMESTIC AND FOREIGN AFFAIRS

The party's former solid grip on the populace has loosened, but there appears to be no alternative to the communist regime at present. The population has become more critical and outspoken, however, despite the "social engineering" that has altered the class composition. (See table 18.) The Czech and Slovak domestic resistance movements against the Nazi occupation, the valor of Czechoslovak armed forces abroad in the Second World War, and the Slovak and Prague uprisings all would indicate that the people again will respond against tyranny when the time and conditions are appropriate.

TABLE 18

CLASS COMPOSITION OF CZECHOSLOVAKIA, 1930 AND 1957

Class	1930		1957	
	Number of persons	*Percent of total population*	*Number of persons*	*Percent of total population*
Workers and employees	8,601,473	61.4	10,800,000	80.5
Small and middle peasants	3,193,922	22.8 ⎫	1,577,000	11.8
Small entrepreneurs and artisans	919,970	6.6 ⎭		
Collectivized peasants	—	—	992,000	7.4
Capitalists (including kulaks) ...	1,283,132	9.2	45,000	0.3
Total	13,998,497	100.0	13,414,000	100.0

SOURCES: *Život strany,* February 1958. Article on "Development of the National Economy in Czechoslovakia," *Statisticheskii sbornik* (Moscow, 1959), p. 49, as cited in M. A. Silin, *Chekhoslovatskaya Sotsialisticheskaya Respublika: perekhodnyi period i zavershenie stroitelstva sotsializma, 1945-1961 gg.* (Moscow, 1963), pp. 144, 148.

ECONOMIC PLANNING. The Czechoslovak communist regime has encountered difficulties and found no magic formula to facilitate the execution of plans. Unforeseen circumstances forced the government to abandon its collapsing third five-year plan in 1962. An emergency one-year plan was subsequently introduced for 1963. Its goals, although eventually reported to have been attained, were admittedly met only after various adjustments. Makeshift annual plans followed until 1966.

A new five-year plan currently in operation is to guide the economy through 1970, and a different and more realistic approach may finally characterize the details.[69] Instead of a rigid quota or goal for the entire period, only twelve months at a time are to be planned in this manner. Subsequent years are supposed to have variable targets, with considerable latitude to allow for setbacks which cannot be forecast. Thus the chances for a "successful" plan may be increased and the attendant propaganda value also enhanced.

Czechoslovak economic planning until recently was under the distinct influence of doctrinaire Marxist thinking. This adherence to the classics handicapped the communists, in that they found themselves with an overabundance of heavy industrial products and a consequent shortage of consumers' goods. Nonetheless, the Czechoslovak economy proved to be beneficial for the economic growth of the Soviet Union and the other East European countries.

A stagnant population growth rate is forcing the Czechs and the Slovaks to take a closer look at their utilization of manpower.[70] The economy has reached the limit of its labor potential and further expansion will be predicated upon increased efficiency in agriculture and industrial productivity. The latter has dropped, in part because private enterprise has been thwarted by means of a continued purge over the years. In 1955 there were approximately 48,000 private entrepreneurs within the economic system. By 1959 only 9,000 remained. Since 1964, however, a very limited revival of private enterprise has been allowed. (See table 19 for national income formation.)

TABLE 19

Development of the Czechoslovak Economy, 1962-1966
(Changes compared with the preceding year in percentages)

Index	1962	1963	1964	1965	1966
Industrial production	6.2	—0.6	4.1	7.9	(8.1)[a]
Building	—3.7	—9.1	11.0	6.5	(10.9)[a]
National income (overall)	1.4	—2.2	0.9	2.5	—
National income (without agriculture)	4.1	—4.2	1.9	3.5	(4.0)[a]
Labor productivity in industry	4.0	0.0	3.9	6.2	(5.7)[b]
Average change	2.4	—3.2	4.4	5.3	9.2

Source: *Statistical Yearbook of the CSSR, 1965,* as cited in *Czechoslovak Press Survey,* July 8, 1966.

[a] Estimate on the basis of results of the first four months.

[b] Estimate on the basis of results of the first three months.

Another weakness in the Czechoslovak economy is overspecialization: a disproportionate emphasis on certain parts and a concurrent neglect of others. A prime example is found in the transportation system, wherein railroads have received the benefit of technological advances and improvements while roads and highways were neglected. The economic situation in Czechoslovakia, as in most communist countries, reflects the imbalance in planning that results from a narrow and specialized approach.

The Central Committee of the party met at Prague in 1964 to discover the reason for difficulties that had plagued the economy and also to submit proposals for improvement. The proposals were illuminating as to the causes for past failures. After two years of debate and study, the following measures were specifically scheduled for implementation in 1966:

> A great reduction in plan indices without, however, a fully objective price system to counter speculative activities by the individual enterprise;
> An incentive system based on gross receipts to replace the centrally allocated wage;
> Taxes—resulting from a compromise between plan fulfillment and net profits—which will in effect favor the less efficient enterprises;
> A price system to include large subsidies, with the increase in wholesale rates not immediately to be reflected at retail levels;
> Only limited increases in investments and foreign trade.[71]

For the year 1966 fixed prices have been introduced for 64 percent of commodity items, limited ranges for 29 percent and free fluctuation for 7 percent. Overall refiguring for 1.5 million commodities will take at least three years.[72]

INDUSTRY. Extension of communist control over the country's vast industrial complex was facilitated through the nationalization policy started in October 1945 by the Czechoslovak coalition government. After this first wave, only about 40 percent of production, and only in certain exempted industries, still remained in private hands. A second wave beginning in 1948 brought nearly every type of industry and business under state operation. The seizure of wholesale and retail businesses and all foreign trade occurred during this latter period, after which only 5 percent of industrial production and 17 percent of the physical plant continued in private hands.[73]

Although Czechoslovakia's industrial output is a significant factor within the Soviet orbit, its products have failed to regain the prestige they once enjoyed on the world scene. The former craftsmanship and skills are not apparent in the products of today. The quantity of the output is significant, but the quality has deteriorated.[74] One reason for this may be that bloc requirements were initially and are even now less stringent than those imposed by prewar customers. Another, certainly, is that the U.S.S.R. has been exploiting all East European countries by paying lower than world market prices, and inferior products help to make up for this.

The importance of Czechoslovak industry to the bloc is most evident in the supplying of certain special requirements of the other countries. Eastern Europe, including the Soviet Union, has relied heavily on Czechoslovak machinery in building up its industrial sector. Entire plants are manufactured in Czechoslovakia for shipment and installation throughout the bloc. More than three-fourths of all machinery types made in the world are available from Czechoslovakia. A considerable part of industrial production involves armaments, wherefore Czechoslovakia has often been referred to as the arsenal of Eastern Europe. Also, arms captured from insurgent forces in many of the world's trouble spots have been found to have originated there. For example, Czechoslovak arms were recently smuggled to Kurdish rebels in Iraq.[75]

AGRICULTURE. Nationalization in the agricultural sector of the economy has not been quite so thorough as in industry. Nevertheless, through expropriation of large landholdings the communists were able to exert influence and control over agriculture in a relatively easy manner. Six months before the 1948 seizure of power, private farms had already been limited to fifty hectares each. From this base, a collectivization program was initiated. When Stalin died, in 1953, it came to a temporary halt; two years later it had regained momentum.

Further to centralize control over agriculture, many of the weaker and less successful collective farms have been amalgamated into a state farm system. Behind this policy may have been the idea of more profitably applying the advantages of large-scale production and improved methods of management, as well as communist ideological considerations. Instead of a planned profit during 1965, state farms operated at a loss of 516 million crowns.[76]

In general, the agricultural economy has been beset with numerous difficulties. Output has fallen far short of established quotas and expectations. Up to the Second World War, Czechoslovakia was almost self-sufficient in food. Now it is dependent upon the Soviet

Union for large imports of wheat. During 1966, the U.S.S.R. promised to deliver 1.3 million tons, and an additional 800,000 tons were
to be purchased from Canada.[77]

Agriculture has failed to keep pace with industry in its development. A general decline in the number of persons engaged in farming also has taken place. Many of the workers, particularly the
younger people, prefer city life to the toil on the farm. Little incentive is offered the agricultural laborer; in Czechoslovakia, as
in other communist-dominated states, he has been exploited in order
to further the cause of heavy industrial expansion. The number of
farm workers has dropped from more than three million before the
war to somewhat more than one and a half million. Not quite 10
percent of the population in the Czech lands and slightly more than
15 percent in Slovakia engage in agriculture.[78] Each farmer is permitted to cultivate a private plot of land, up to an acre in size, and
he may have one cow to provide dairy products for his family. For
the distribution of agricultural land in Czechoslovakia, which is
now 92 percent nationalized, see table 20.

TABLE 20

AGRICULTURAL LAND DISTRIBUTION IN CZECHOSLOVAKIA, 1965

Type of Unit	Arable land	
	Area in hectares	Percent of total
Collective farms	5,342,858	66
State farms	1,700,000	21
Private farms [a]	647,619	8
Other (research institutes, schools, etc.)	404,762	5
Total	8,095,239	100

SOURCES: "New System of Farming Presents Special Problems," an editorial in
Prague Newsletter, May 15, 1965, a biweekly in English, as given in *Czechoslovak
Press Survey,* June 2, 1965. *Radio Prague,* June 19, 1965.

[a] Almost half of the area under private cultivation, or about 300,000 hectares, is
in Slovakia, according to Radio Bratislava, February 21, 1966.

Suggestions for improvement of the agricultural situation were
submitted by the Central Committee during its April 1965 plenary
meeting as part of the directives for control of the economy during
the fourth five-year plan, 1966-1970. A subsequent report on the
results of a national seminar indicated that 9.2 billion crowns would
be invested in agriculture during this planning period.[79] The seminar

noted two basic reasons for the unfavorable situation: (1) up to 80 percent of all agricultural buildings were incomplete installations, without proper mechanization and sufficient storage space, and (2) no full mechanization could be implemented, due to an investment cost of 1,666 crowns per hectare, for which funds were not available.

Agricultural progress in Czechoslovakia or in the other communist-dominated countries is predicated upon one of two developments. The first, and quickest, way to increase production would be to return the land to individual farmers. The private entrepreneur who owns his land and livestock is concerned about erosion, weeds, waste, and the well-being and care of his animals and equipment. Pride in ownership, which is missing from the collective, would stimulate the individual farmer into actions that rarely occur under the present system. It is to be understood, of course, that such a drastic measure is unlikely or perhaps even impossible under a firmly established communist regime. A development in this direction contradicts the very basis of Marxist philosophy and as such must be discarded as a possibility.

A second development is one that appears to be in consonance with theoretical policies in several communist states to varying degrees but would take many years to complete. It consists essentially of turning the farms into factories, with the workers being indoctrinated along the same line as their counterparts in the industrial plants. An essential prerequisite for this program is that the current generation of farm workers pass from the scene. Most of these persons are becoming old (the average age is over fifty) and have grown up on the land they are now forced to cultivate for the benefit of the state. The majority are women. Many are malcontents who long for the "good old days." The eradication of this group might lead to an atmosphere somewhat like that found in a factory. A wage system, patterned after the industrial program in theory, could provide incentives and bonuses. A scientific, technological, and impersonal approach to agriculture is envisioned, of course, under the current state farm system.[80]

CHURCH-STATE RELATIONS. Roman Catholicism has been the dominant force in Czechoslovak religious history. It is estimated that about 75 percent of the population is Roman Catholic. Unlike some of the other East Europeans, the Czechs of Bohemia as a rule have been tolerant and even indifferent toward religion. In Moravia the population has been more devout. In Slovakia the Catholic Church still plays a considerable role, especially in rural areas. Throughout the Czechoslovak state, however, all Catholic schools, religious orders, and publications have been abolished. Suppression of the clergy has alternated with intermittent relaxation, to coincide with the tactics of party leaders.

In 1952 relations with the Vatican were severed. Even before that date, the regime had imprisoned numerous high-ranking clergymen. In 1963, when the Soviet Union attempted to improve relations with the Vatican, the authorities in Prague released a number of those jailed. Yet there is no noticeable change in the basically hostile attitude toward any kind of religion.[81] The church does not appear to have much potential for active resistance to the current regime, because all of its activities are effectively controlled. Negotiations with the Vatican brought about the departure from Czechoslovakia of Archbishop (later Cardinal) Josef Beran and the appointment in February 1965 of Bishop František Tomasek as apostolic administrator. In late November 1966 Health Minister Josef Plojhar, a former priest, suggested negotiations with the Vatican in a speech to the Patriotic Priests Committee at Prague.

FOREIGN AFFAIRS

The Council for Mutual Economic Assistance (CMEA) and the Warsaw Pact provide the framework for the nature and extent of Czechoslovak activities within the Soviet sphere. Czechoslovakia was an original signatory to the statutes of both organizations and currently supports them in a comparatively wholehearted manner. The Soviet attempt at manipulating the controls of CMEA, in order that the other members shall become increasingly dependent economically on the U.S.S.R., has succeeded to some extent in the case of Czechoslovakia.

Almost all of the petroleum (91 percent) used by the country comes from the Soviet Union, as do large proportions of the iron ore (68 percent) and cotton (41 percent), together with a significant part of nonferrous metals. During 1966-1970 trade between the two countries is expected to total 80 billion crowns.[82] Consequently the U.S.S.R. is in a favorable position to exert economic pressure which should guarantee support by Czechoslovakia when and if required.

Without petroleum and iron ore, Czechoslovakia would find it difficult to operate its industries and transportation system. Strategically valuable uranium deposits also exist; [83] these, at Jachymov, have been and may still be under Soviet control and supervision.

INTRA-BLOC RELATIONS. The substantial output of complete industrial installations by Czechoslovakia has assisted the expansion of heavy industry in the Soviet Union and other communist-dominated countries. As has been mentioned, Czechoslovakia is the main supplier of machines and plants to the bloc. The specialization program of CMEA conflicts in many ways with the Czechoslovaks' new system of management. It is probable that the incompatibility will continue to grow rather than decrease.

Many of the East European communist leaders within the Soviet sphere are unhappy with CMEA owing to certain features of the program and the resulting outside interference with what these men consider to be purely domestic matters. Czechoslovakia has also expressed dissatisfaction, but for an entirely different reason. The Prague regime complains of lax enforcement procedures for CMEA decisions and seems to desire tighter control. Because of the country's heavy industrial output and contributions to CMEA, official Czechoslovak opinions must carry some weight. Still, the U.S.S.R. holds the key to future economic success, and the leadership in Prague realizes this.

Czechoslovakia has been a member of the Warsaw Pact since 1955 and apparently responds well to Soviet military directives. Unlike either Hungary or Poland (not to mention East Germany, where U.S.S.R. troops are found in division-size units), Czechoslovakia has Soviet military men on its soil only in the capacity of Warsaw Pact liaison personnel. Including security forces, the country is thought to have the equivalent of fourteen divisions available for deployment. These forces are well equipped with modern arms. The defensive capability of the Czechoslovak troops probably outweighs their offensive potential. U.S.S.R. influence throughout the armed forces may be conducted by placement of Soviet officers with Czech or Slovak names in the Prague high command. [84]

The production of arms and munitions makes Czechoslovakia a key member of the Warsaw Pact. With its industrial capacity and relatively limited manpower, Czechoslovakia becomes an "ideal" associate of the Soviet Union. It is able to make a significant material contribution to the armed forces of the Pact. Simultaneously, it poses little risk for the U.S.S.R. insofar as the development of an independent and effective war machine is concerned.

EXTRA-BLOC RELATIONS. Foreign aid to countries outside of the bloc plays an important part in Czechoslovakia's political and economic activities. In the past it has spent more than all of the other East European countries combined (except for the U.S.S.R.) on foreign aid and technical assistance. The primary beneficiaries of its aid have been the United Arab Republic, Ghana, Guinea, Ethiopia, Sudan, Mali, India, Morocco, Cuba, Brazil, and Argentina.[85] The political implications of the foreign aid and technical assistance programs repeatedly have been explained by the Czechoslovak press in order to lessen internal resentment and resistance toward the program.

The population has tended to blame the outflow of goods for the shortages experienced in certain commodities at home. Government officials have told the people that it was necessary to conduct and continue the aid program for a number of reasons, the foremost being propagation of the socialist doctrine among the neutralist or uncommitted countries by exhibiting the strength of the socialist order. Another reason given is that the West allegedly has blocked Czechoslovakia from its normal channels of trade, wherefore new markets had to be found for the export of finished products and the import of needed raw materials. In recent years, economic aid to the developing areas has decreased considerably.[86]

Czechoslovakia is attempting gradually to reinstitute those trade ties with the West which were so lucrative before the Second World War, and which were cut off almost entirely immediately after the war by communist policy. The regime has made important commercial agreements with Britain, France, Spain, the Scandinavian countries, and others. Recently, even the United States has been approached by Czechoslovak officials. During 1965 the importation of about 500,000 tons of American feed grains (corn, grain sorghum, and barley) was negotiated by the Prague government. A group of U.S. grain specialists has made a study of Czechoslovak agriculture to ascertain the potential market for future exports.[87]

NOTES

1 The basic agreement for a National Front government was announced in April 1945 at Košice. For details see Ivan Bystrzhina, *Narodnaya demokratiya v Chekhoslovakii* (translated into Russian from the original Czech; Moscow, 1961), pp. 196-205.

2 H. Gordon Skilling, "The Czechoslovak Constitution of 1960 and the Transition to Communism," *Journal of Politics,* XXIV, No. 1 (February 1963), p. 145.

3 A useful chronology of events from 1943 to early 1960 appears in M. P. Epifanov (ed.), *15 let svobodnoi Chekhoslovakii* (Moscow, 1960), pp. 186-191.

4 Skilling, *op. cit.,* p. 144.

5 [Czechoslovakia], *The Constitution of the Czechoslovak Socialist Republic* (3d ed.; Prague, 1964). Further references to the constitution apply to this edition.

6 Josef Kalvoda, "Czechoslovakia's Socialist Constitution," *Slavic Review,* XX, No. 2 (April 1961), p. 220.

7 As quoted by Kalvoda, p. 225.

8 Edward Taborsky, *Communism in Czechoslovakia, 1948-1960* (Princeton, N.J., 1961), pp. 169, 193.

9 See his official biography in Vladimír Krechler (chief ed.), *Příruční slovník k dějinám KSČ* (Prague, 1964), I, 562.

10 Taborsky, *op. cit.,* p. 200.

11 If the president also serves as first secretary of the party, the premiership is assigned to a lower-ranking communist. If the offices are separated, as was the case when Zápotocký was president and Novotný first secretary, the premier may be third in importance but not necessarily so. Jiří Hendrych, as of this writing, certainly outranks Premier Josef Lenárt.

12 Taborsky, *op. cit.,* p. 201. In 1967, however, eleven of the ministers were members of the Central Committee, as were the four deputy premiers; one minister even held a seat on the Presidium of the communist party; two ministers were candidate members of the Central Committee. *Bloc Line-Up,* pp. 9-11.

13 Skilling, *op. cit.,* p. 153. For names see U.S. Department of State, Bureau of Intelligence and Research, *Directory of Czechoslovak Officials* (Washington, D.C., September 1966), p. 41.

14 Daniel Kubat, "Communist Use of the Czechoslovak Parliament since World War II," *Slavic Review,* XX, No. 4 (December 1961), 697. Under a legislative measure of June 1960, deputies are entitled to a monthly compensation of 1,500 *koruny* (crowns).

15 Taborsky, *op. cit.,* p. 256. Both the National Assembly and the Slovak National Council reportedly have been much livelier in the recent past. See RFE report (by J. Frank), "Czechoslovakia's Parliaments: More Activity, But How Much Power?" February 12, 1966 (4 pp.).

16 Taborsky, *op. cit.,* p. 283.

17 In this connection see the "Law on the Court System" in *Sbírka zákonu ČSSR,* No. 62 (June 26, 1961), translated in M. P. Lebedev (comp.), *Chekhoslovatskaya Sotsialisticheskaya Respublika: Konstitutsiya i zakonodatelnye akty* (Moscow, 1962), pp. 341-365.

18 For the "Law on Local People's Courts," in *Sbírka zákonu ČSSR,* No. 38 (April 18, 1961), see Lebedev, *op. cit.,* pp. 366-382.

19 Taborsky, *op. cit.,* p. 317.

20 Resolution dated May 7, 1964, on "a fuller assertion of the Slovak National Council." *Rudé právo,* May 22, 1964.
   Federalism was specifically rejected in a commentary by Jan Rohač over Radio Bratislava on November 13, 1965.

21 *Večerník,* February 22, 1964, as quoted in *East Europe,* XII, No. 4 (April 1964), p. 36.

22 *World Strength,* p. 52.

23 Taborsky, *op. cit.,* p. 209, refers to the Ministry of State Control. The

commission discussed here was established in 1963, having superseded a Central Office which itself had succeeded the Ministry. A draft law on People's Control Commissions was discussed over Radio Prague, March 9, 1967.

24 Jaroslav Peszta, in an article on "Economic Experiments in Czechoslovakia," *Życie gospodarcze* (Warsaw), August 22, 1965. See also Ota Šik's interview published in *Práce,* June 4, 1966, and translated in *Czechoslovak Press Survey,* June 27, 1966; hereafter cited as *CPS.* A good analysis appears in RFE report (by Harry Trend), "General Conditions for the Czechoslovak Economic Model," October 10, 1966 (9 pp.).

25 *Kulturni tvorba,* September 9, 1965, translated in *CPS,* September 22, 1965. The remaining 11 percent presumably have not completed elementary school.

26 A round-table discussion noted that there were people in Czechoslovakia who stole "anything that's not nailed down." Radio Bratislava, September 7, 1965.

27 His biography in Krechler, *op. cit.,* II, 891, explains the dismissal in terms of insufficiencies, errors (unspecified), and poor health.

28 See "Current Developments: Czechoslovakia," *East Europe,* XIII, No. 4 (April 1964), 33 ff.

29 Josef Korbel, *The Communist Subversion of Czechoslovakia, 1938-1948* (Princeton, N.J., 1959), p. 28.

30 *Ibid.,* p. 35.

31 Edward Beneš, *Memoirs of Dr. Edward Beneš* (London, 1954), p. 258.

32 Taborsky, *op. cit.,* p. 13.

33 The separate communist parties of Czechoslovakia and Slovakia and four other political groups received three portfolios each. In addition, seven cabinet members qualified as "experts," including communists Zdeněk Nejedlý and Vladimír Clementis and the communist-leaning General Ludvík Svoboda (Defense minister). The communists also had two deputy premiers, Klement Gottwald and Viliam Široký, and the fellow-traveling premier, Zdeněk Fierlinger, who fulfilled Gottwald's directives. In this connection see Jozef Lettrich, "Czechoslovakia," in U.S. Senate, Committee on the Judiciary, *A Study of the Anatomy of Communist Takeovers* (Washington, D.C., 1966), pp. 17-25.

34 Jan Kozak, "How Parliament Can Play a Revolutionary Part in the Transition to Socialism," reprinted in U.S. House of Representatives, Committee on Un-American Activities, *The New Role of National Legislative Bodies in the Communist Conspiracy* (Washington, D.C., 1961), p. 17. See also Kozak's article on the years 1945-1948 in *Voprosy istorii KPSS,* VI, No. 4 (July-August 1962), 72-91.

35 Paul E. Zinner, *Communist Strategy and Tactics in Czechoslovakia* (New York, 1963), p. 124.

36 Taborsky, *op. cit.,* p. 19.

37 Zinner, *op. cit.,* p. 208.

38 *Pravda* (Bratislava), February 2, 1964, translated in *CPS,* April 2, 1964.

39 Edward Taborsky, "The Triumph and Disaster of Edward Beneš," *Foreign Affairs,* XXXVI, No. 4 (July 1958), 684.

40 During this initial period the communists applied the Leninist principle of *"kto kogo?"* (meaning "who [will eliminate] whom?"), according to Bystrzhina, *op. cit.,* pp. 263-264.

41 *World Strength,* p. 52. Another source, V. Chalupa, *The National Front in Czechoslovakia* (Chicago, 1958), pp. 26-30, lists the components of the National Front as the KSČ, the Slovak communist party, the four puppet Czech and Slovak political parties, the Czechoslovak Youth League, the Revolutionary Trade-Union Movement, the Czechoslovak Women's League, the Czechoslovak-Soviet Friendship League, the Union for Cooperation with the Army, and many other organizations of lesser importance, such as the Red Cross.

42 Krechler, *op. cit.,* II, 721-725. *Práce,* February 13, 1965, gives a figure of

750 delegates, each representing 6,800 members, at a national trade-union conference in Prague, which would make a total of 5.1 million.

43 ČSM membership figures given in *Mladá fronta,* April 18, 1963, and *Práce,* April 24, 1966, respectively. Only 25 percent of eligible factory youth belongs to ČSM, with an even lower ratio in rural areas. Some 6½ percent are KSČ members. RFE report (by Hajek and Niznansky), "Fifth Youth Congress," June 1967 (8 pp.).

44 *Rudé právo,* February 13, 1965.

45 *Ibid.,* August 3, 1962.

46 Vladimir Reisky de Dubnic, *Communist Propaganda Methods* (New York, 1960), pp. 64-66.

47 *Rudé právo,* July 12 and 21, 1966; *Život strany,* September 1966, translated in *CPS,* October 13, 1966, p. 6.

48 Milan Hegar (comp.), *Usnesení a dokumenty ÚV KSČ: od celostatní konference KSČ 1960 do XII Sjezdu KSČ* (Prague, 1962), pp. 689, 523. This two-volume work covers the period 1960-1962 immediately preceding the party's Twelfth Congress.

49 RFE report (by H. Hajek and L. Niznansky), "New Czechoslovak CP Central Committee," June 14, 1966 (4 pp.). Names of the new Central Committee members and candidates appeared in *Rudé právo,* June 5, 1966.

50 The KSS has been a separate organization theoretically since the 1939 Nazi occupation of Czechoslovakia, according to Krechler, *op. cit.,* I, 329-330. The RFE report cited in note 49 gives the membership figures.

51 *Pravda* (Bratislava), March 3, 1964, translated in *CPS,* April 8, 1964.

52 RFE report (by L. Niznansky), "The 15th Slovak Communist Party Congress," May 24, 1966 (9 pp.).

53 The current party rules appeared in *Rudé právo,* December 11, 1962, having been adopted at the Twelfth Congress. See also Heinrich Kuhn, *Der Kommunismus in der Tschechoslowakei* (Cologne, 1965), pp. 275-299.

54 *Pravda* (Bratislava), March 20, 1964, translated in *CPS,* April 2, 1964.

55 Jiří Kourilek, "The Key Importance of Cadre Work," *Život strany,* April 1965, translated in *CPS,* June 15, 1965.

56 This represents fewer than half of the young people eligible for membership, according to *Práce,* April 24, 1966, translated in *CPS,* May 23, 1966.

57 Radio Prague, December 9, 1965. For the total age structure, indicating that 17.4 percent of the members are over sixty, see *Rudé právo,* July 12, 1966.

58 *Pravda* (Bratislava), as reported by Radio Bratislava, March 3, 1964.

59 The communists in predominantly rural Slovakia also probably resent the allegations in the official KSČ history that the Slovak uprising against the Germans in August 1944 was started "without sufficient political preparation" and that the Communist Party of Slovakia had been penetrated by right-wingers, "which weakened the revolutionary nature of the movement." Pavel Reiman (chief ed.), *Dějiny Komunistické Strany Československa* (Prague, 1961), p. 450. Reiman is director of the KSČ History Institute. Radio Prague, September 23, 1965.

60 D. A. Tomasic, *The Communist Leadership and Nationalism in Czechoslovakia* (Washington, D.C., 1960), p. 3.

61 *Rudé právo,* April 6, 1964, translated in *CPS,* April 11, 1964, p. 9.

62 Analyses of any leadership are difficult. Among the ten full members of the KSČ presidium, three are definitely intellectuals: Jaromír Dolanský, Otakar Šimůnek, and Bohuslav Laštovička. Five others have held leading offices in the economy or the party: Jiří Hendrych, Drahomír Kolder, Alexander Dubček, Josef Lenárt, and Oldrich Černik. Perhaps the only person with worker's experience, other than Novotný, is Michal Chudik. Information courtesy of Dr. Pavel Korbel, national editor, *East Europe* magazine, New York.

See also "Czechoslovakia" in RFE, *Eastern Europe's Communist Leaders* (Munich, September 1966), Vol. IV, for biographic data on the above persons.

63 *Rudé právo*, January 31, 1964, translated in *CPS*, February 8, 1964, p. 2.

64 *Rudé právo*, March 18, 1964, translated in *CPS*, March 25, 1964, p. 2.

65 *Rudé právo*, March 27, 1964, translated in *CPS*, April 8, 1964.

66 Reisky, *op. cit.*, p. 244.

67 Ivo Ducháček, "Czechoslovakia: A Dull Drama," *Current History*, XLIV, No. 261 (May 1963), 279. See also Vaclav Mares, "Czechoslovakia's Half Century," *ibid.*, LII, No. 4 (April 1967), 200-207.

68 Quoted by Reisky, *op. cit.*, p. 243.

69 Radio Prague, May 31, 1965, gave the broad directives on this fourth five-year plan.

70 See *Rudé právo*, June 23, 1966, translated in *CPS*, July 8, 1966.

71 *Život strany*, December 1965, translated in *CPS*, February 17, 1966.

72 *Prague Newsletter*, March 19, 1966; also in *CPS*, April 22, 1966. In this connection, it was announced that wholesale prices would be increased by 20 percent on January 1, 1967. *Rudé právo*, September 24, 1966; also in *CPS*, October 7, 1966.

73 Radio Bratislava, October 28, 1965.

74 During 1965 the value of rejects totaled one billion Czechoslovak crowns. Radio Prague, January 15, 1966.

75 *New York Times*, January 24, 1966. For the clandestine shipment of arms by Czechoslovakia to the Greeks on Cyprus see, *ibid.*, December 5 and 7, 1966.

76 Radio Prague, June 19, 1965.

77 Antonín Novotný, "Toward a Further Advance of Our Socialist Society," *Rudé právo*, December 14, 1965.

78 *Svobodné slovo*, June 10, 1965.

79 Radio Bratislava, August 19, 1965. The government has approved a new model in agriculture, to go into effect on January 1, 1967. *Rudé právo*, October 27, 1966, as cited in RFE, *Situation Report*, November 2, 1966, p. 4.

80 Mikhail A. Chistyakov, *Chekhoslovatskaya Sotsialisticheskaya Respublika: ekonomika i vneshnyaya torgovlya* (Moscow, 1964), pp. 95-98, discusses the state farms and the machine tractor stations, where tractors and other farm machinery are housed in depots and repaired.

81 Since religion is "not based on science, as is the Marxist philosophy, it would be a mistake to exclude atheism from communist ideology." Radio Bratislava, September 10, 1965.

Note, however, the suggestion by Health Minister and former priest Josef Plojhar that the Czechoslovak government might begin negotiations with the Vatican. *New York Times*, November 25, 1966.

82 *Svobodné slovo*, November 21, 1965, translated in *CPS*, December 4, 1965. Also RFE report (by H. Hajek and L. Niznansky), "Czechoslovak-Soviet Relations," November 18, 1965 (8 pp.), citing *Nová mysl*, October 1965.

Czechoslovakia has been paying more than 20 rubles per ton for Soviet petroleum, whereas the U.S.S.R. sells it for 9 rubles to areas where there exists American or British competition. Václav Dubsky, "Who Is Afraid of Soviet Oil?" *Reporter* (Prague), July 16, 1966, translated in *CPS*, October 20, 1966.

83 President Novotný gave a reception at Hradčany Castle for representatives of the uranium industry and a Soviet delegation on the twentieth anniversary of the U.S.S.R.-Czechoslovak uranium treaty. RFE, *Situation Report*, November 22, 1965, pp. 1-2.

84 This has been simplified by an agreement on dual citizenship. Jan Černy and Václav Červenka (comps.), *Státní občanství ČSSR* (Prague, 1963), pp. 199-202, gives the complete text of this 1958 agreement.

85 For the period 1955-1960 see Yaroslav Shedivyi and Kveta Korzhalkova, *Vneshnyaya politika Chekhoslovatskoi Sotsialisticheskoi Respubliki v 1945-1960 gg.* (Moscow, 1960), pp. 135-145. Total assistance given by Czechoslovakia to the developing countries between 1954 and 1962

amounted to $478 million, according to an article in the quarterly *Mezinárodní vztahý*, No. 1 (1966), translated in *CPS*, October 11, 1966, pp. 5-11.

86 *Rudé právo*, May 25, 1965, explained in some detail the "limited possibilities of Czechoslovakia and the entire community of CMEA countries" in this respect.

87 U.S. Department of Agriculture, *Foreign Agriculture* (June 13, 1966), cited in RFE report, "Czechoslovak–U.S. Grain Dialogue," July 1, 1966 (3 pp.).

Whether anything will come of these talks may depend upon how the U.S. government reacts to the case of Vladimir Kazan-Komarek, an American citizen arrested on October 31, 1966, when his Aeroflot flight from Moscow to Paris made an unscheduled landing in Czechoslovakia. Sentenced to eight years in prison, he was released to the United States. *New York Times*, February 5, 1967.

Chapter 4 / EAST GERMANY:
Soviet Occupation Zone

IN BOTH East and West Germany, the initial postwar policies of the occupation forces were directed more toward reparations than rehabilitation. The U.S.S.R. pursued this goal with an almost psychotic zeal. During its two-month tenure as the sole power in Berlin, for example, the Soviet Union removed 75 percent of all capital equipment. In the first few months of occupation the physical plants of some 1,900 industrial enterprises in the U.S.S.R. zone were either partly or completely dismantled.[1] This practice, coupled with a Russian policy of taking reparations from current production, represented a violation of the letter as well as the spirit of the Yalta and Potsdam agreements. It seriously hampered the economic recovery of East Germany for many years.

Industrial holdings of "war criminals, National Socialists [Nazis], and militarists" were expropriated. These terms received broad interpretation, with the result that private enterprise was eliminated from all large and from most medium-sized industrial firms.[2] In addition, control of some 200-odd large firms whose plants were not dismantled was transferred to Soviet joint stock companies (*Sowjetische Aktiengesellschaften*—SAG). By 1948 only 8 percent of the East German industries had been socialized, but 40 percent of the total industrial output came from these socialized industries; another 25 or 30 percent was produced by SAG enterprises.

A comparison of these two figures shows clearly that only small plants and a few medium-sized enterprises, especially in the manufacture of consumption goods, like textiles, had escaped socialization.[3]

In other directions the Russians proceeded more cautiously. During 1944 and 1945 they still looked forward to the eventual reunification of Germany and the extension of "socialism" over the whole country. Thus, sovietization was accomplished under a façade of democratizing and antifascist activity designed to lull both the noncommunist East Germans and the Western powers. The following measures were taken by the Soviet Union during this initial period:

> The *Länder* or provinces were allowed legislatures, based on free elections.
> All private banks and insurance companies were suspended.
> Widespread seizure of agricultural and industrial property was justified on antifascist rather than anticapitalist grounds.
> Political activity was encouraged, and "antifascist" parties were licensed much sooner than in the Western zones.[4]

From the early days of the occupation, the Soviets encouraged formation of political parties. The German communist party (*Kommunistische Partei Deutschlands*—KPD), reestablished in June 1945 throughout East Germany, of course came first. It was followed within a month by the Christian Democrats, Liberals, and Socialists. Using the typical "people's front" tactics, which had been followed in the other satellite countries, all four parties in July 1945 joined the Antifascist Democratic Bloc, which subsequently received the name "Democratic Bloc of Parties and Mass Organizations."[5] In October 1949 this became the National Front. The communists apparently believed that they could win control over the East German government through free elections and wanted to maintain at least the pretext of separate parties.

At first many politicians regarded the Soviet reforms as a positive step. The Socialists in the summer and fall of 1945 actually suggested a merger of their party and the KPD, but were turned down by the communists.[6] By November 1945, however, the communists had come to regard the Socialist party as a serious challenge to their power, since it had a large following in the industrial areas. Despite the fact that the majority of the Socialists now opposed the move, a forced merger with the KPD was effected in April 1946 to form the Socialist Unity Party of Germany (*Sozialistische Einheitspartei Deutschlands*—SED). Ten years after the fusion, only three of the forty Socialists remain on the SED Central Committee.

In the fall of that same year, the last relatively free elections were held in East Germany. An active campaign by the SED and interference with the activities of other parties (forbidding rallies and banning candidates), still did not result in the absolute majority victory which the communists had wanted. Despite the lack of an absolute majority, the SED candidates were given key positions in all five *Länder*.[7] This was also the last time that East German voters were given any choice of candidates. All subsequent elections at the national level have presented only a single list on the ballot, and the voter has no option but to approve.

In late 1947 the SED formed from among its own membership a People's Congress (*Volkskongress*). Despite the fact that it had no popular basis, this body took upon itself the task of establishing a government for East Germany. In March 1948 the Congress named a 400-member People's Council *(Volksrat)*. This group in turn appointed a committee to draft a new constitution, which was completed by October.

To add an element of legality, national elections were held in May 1949 for representatives to the People's Congress. The ballot, however, consisted of a typical "unity list," packed with communists, and the new constitution was not mentioned during the campaign. After the election, the third People's Congress convened the end of that same month and promptly approved the constitution. The "German Democratic Republic" (*Deutsche Demokratische Republik*) thus became established. Its "capital" is Pankow, a suburb of East Berlin.

The Congress also appointed a new People's Council. In the fall, this Council declared itself to be the Provisional People's Chamber (*Provisorische Volkskammer*), or parliament, and promulgated the constitution as a fundamental law. Since the constitution envisages the *Volkskammer* as being a popularly elected representative body, this act of appointing itself gave the German Democratic Republic the unique distinction of starting with a government which had no legitimacy and was, in fact, unconstitutional.

THE CONSTITUTION

It has been noted that "a good constitution may be the backbone of a state or it may be window-dressing." [8] This comment is nowhere more true than in the case of East Germany. Its constitution provides for a strong central government based on a multiparty, parliamentary system. The power of the government is concentrated in a popularly elected representative body, the People's Chamber. The concept of separation of powers, common to the United States and most Western democracies, is lacking. In many ways the East German constitution is a remarkably liberal document and could represent the basis for a stable and representative government.[9]

> The Constitution of East Germany . . . is phrased so that, if properly implemented, a genuine democracy, in which basic rights would be preserved, could function under it. However, the wording of the Constitution also has been so framed that, once the Communists were in control, they could interpret and apply it to maintain their system of centralistic statism.[10]

It should be mentioned that this constitution was written for all of Germany, on the assumption that the East and West zones eventually would be reunited. In this respect it is similar to the Basic Law of West Germany.[11] With 17 sections and 144 articles, it is also similar in being long, thorough, and complex.

PARADOXES AND CONTRADICTIONS. Perhaps the most significant paradox in the "Constitution of the German Democratic Republic" is that its name does not describe the government which has been formed under it. The constitution was forced upon the people, without the benefit of a referendum or any other ratification. It is, thus, certainly not democratic. Since elections held in East Germany after 1946 have not been free or secret, ultimate power over the government does not reside with the people. The state is, therefore, not a republic. Finally, since the government is controlled by a communist-dominated party—the SED—it is questionable whether it should even be called "German." [12] Other contradictions are written into the constitution itself.

Article 6 states that civil rights may be suspended for the "boycott of democratic institutions or organizations," but also specifies that "the exercise of democratic rights . . . is not an incitement to boycott." This is one of the more insidious provisions, since none of the terms is clearly defined. Apparently, it has been taken to mean that the harassment of noncommunists by the government is an exercise of "democratic" rights and that any opposition, even in self-defense, is a "boycott of democratic institutions." [13]

Article 13 states that candidates for the People's Chamber may be nominated only by associations that (*a*) intend to bring about a "democratic organization of public life" and (*b*) have a nationwide organization. Obviously, any party or group which does not meet with the approval of the communist regime can be limited or banished through one or the other of these restrictive clauses.

The ownership of private property is guaranteed by Article 22. The next article, however, permits expropriation "for the benefit of the general public." Article 27 allows the socialization of private enterprises. Article 66 permits the People's Chamber to pass on the constitutionality of its own laws. According to Article 127, judges are free in the exercise of their duties and are bound only by "the constitution and the law." Article 132, however, permits the recall of judges by parliament and, thus, puts them firmly under political control.

Free elections are guaranteed both by Article 51 of the constitution and Article 1 of the electoral law. In actual practice, the voters have been presented with only a "unity list" of candidates, and the SED has had direct control of 70 percent of the names appearing on the list. Two rather interesting provisions are included in the East German electoral law. Article 47 provides that a member of the People's Chamber may be excluded, should his eligibility change. This could occur if he were to speak or vote against a government-sponsored bill.[14] Article 48 of the electoral law permits the legislature, on its own authority, to appoint new members and grant them full rights and duties. Thus, if all else fails, the People's Chamber can be filled with puppets. Although never elected, they would still vote.

THE GOVERNMENT

The regimes of East and West Germany seem, at first sight, to have much in common. Both evolved from an occupation status in 1949, both achieved formal sovereignty during 1954-1955, and both now have military forces integrated with their respective power blocs.[15] The Federal Republic of West Germany has developed into a free democratic country, whose political and economic growth has been the envy of her neighbors. The German Democratic Republic, on the other hand, still remains a Soviet-occupied territory under the one-man rule of Walter Ulbricht. To maintain this domination, many of the provisions of the East German constitution have been ignored.

Many others have been changed, with varying degrees of legality in the process.

ABOLITION OF THE LÄNDER. The provinces, or *Länder*, traditionally have been the basic units for all German governments. Evolving from the past, they have served as centers of political and social life. The constitution of the German Democratic Republic recognized this fact and established the provinces as semiautonomous entities, represented in the central government through the *Länder-kammer* or upper chamber of parliament.

In July 1952 the governments of the *Länder* and their legislative bodies were abolished by law. This action technically was unconstitutional, since Article 110 provides that any change in the territory of a *Land* requires either an amendment to the constitution or plebiscites in the *Land* concerned. The dissolved provinces were replaced by fourteen administrative areas, called districts (*Bezirke*), each containing fifteen or more counties (*Kreise*). A fifteenth district was established for East Berlin. This move completely eliminated local government as a source of even potential opposition. It also increased the strength of the central government, thus assuring greater control by the communist-dominated SED.

With the disappearance of the *Länder,* the political basis for the upper chamber of parliament was gone. It continued in existence for several years to fulfill such constitutional requirements as election of the president. In December 1958 it, too, was abolished formally. With this move, the legislative body of the German Democratic Republic became unicameral, and the last vestige of federalism disappeared.

ELIMINATION OF THE PRESIDENCY. In October 1949, two days after adoption of the constitution and the day after nominal transfer of administrative powers from the Soviet Military Administration to the East German regime, Wilhelm Pieck was elected the first and, as it has turned out, only president of the German Democratic Republic. In 1953 he was reelected, and in 1957 his tenure was extended for a third term. This last action should have been preceded by a change in the constitution, since Article 101 requires that the president be elected by a joint session of the two parliamentary chambers, but by this time the upper house had become a relatively meaningless body. It is possible that the regime considered the formality of an election too meaningless to be worth arranging.

In September 1960 President Pieck died in office. Instead of holding an election to determine his successor, the People's Chamber without debate voted to amend the constitution. The presidency became superseded by a 26-member Council of State (*Staatsrat*), elected by the People's Chamber to a four-year term of office. The new body not only assumed the duties of a chief of state, but also became empowered to issue orders and to interpret the law.[16] This step established for East Germany a collective head of state, or "collective executive," with fairly sweeping powers. Walter Ulbricht was elected by the People's Chamber as the chairman of the State Council. He thus became the chief official of the state, in which he already held supreme actual power as first secretary of the SED. This sort of arrangement, which ensures domination of a country by a single individual trusted by the communist party, has commonly prevailed both in the Soviet Union and in other East European countries.

THE NATIONAL DEFENSE COUNCIL. Called into being by legislation in February 1960, the National Defense Council (*Nationaler Verteidigungsrat*) has a chairman and at least twelve members. It remains the only leading governmental organ, the personnel of which is appointed by the Council of State although established chronologically before the latter.[17] A law in September 1961 established certain tasks for this body. Thus, it is to direct uniformly matters pertaining to the defense and security of the state. All government agencies are required to carry out regulations and orders issued by the Defense Council.

According to the January 1962 law on universal military training, the Defense Council has been authorized to issue rules implementing this legislation. These come out as regulations (*Anordnungen*) and appear in Part I of the official journal of laws (*Gesetzblatt*). The Defense minister also remains subordinate to the Defense Council, whose chairman is Walter Ulbricht. This latter man occupies the chairmanship of the Council of State as well, so perhaps the functions of the minister have been kept vague on purpose. It is possible that the Defense Council is intended to become fully operative only in time of hostilities, paralleling the Soviet organ which had a similar name during the Second World War.

GOVERNMENT ORGANIZATION AND CONTROL. According to the constitution of the East German regime, final authority rests with the people. Control is supposed to proceed upward to the various popularly elected assemblies and the councils at each level of government. In practice, this flow is reversed. Ultimate authority rests with the party control apparatus of the SED and is implemented by the councils that appear at all levels of government. Much of the important legislation takes the form of executive orders issued by the Council of State or the Council of Ministers.

The SED rules the state, and "the decisions of the [communist] party constitute the highest scientific generalizations derivable from political practice." [18] Control is applied indirectly. The Politburo makes decisions, and the Secretariat is responsible for carrying them out. Party members are detailed to governmental agencies and business enterprises, where they supervise and report. There exists also periodic review and criticism by party organs. East German political, social, and economic life is thus dominated by a single organization, whose membership constitutes approximately 10 percent of the population.

The continued existence of the communist regime in East Germany is guaranteed by the presence of approximately twenty Soviet divisions in that country. Walter Ulbricht, in an article published at Moscow in 1961, referred to the circumstances of the installation of the government in these terms:

> Protection and aid of the Soviet Union, which at that time had a military form, made it easier for the antifascist democratic forces of Germany to fulfill their historic task [and] deprived the class enemies of the possibility of resorting to measures of open violence. [19]

The facts of the situation can be discerned behind the chairman's phrases. There can still be little doubt that if the threat of Soviet military power were removed, the communist East German government would collapse.

The Soviet Union always has had a particular interest in East Germany, not only as a buffer between the other East European states and the West, but also as a source of industrial power. When the failure of the Berlin blockade stymied Soviet expansionist aims in Europe, attention turned to integrating East Germany with the

Soviet bloc. This was thought to have been accomplished, but the workers' revolt in June 1953 demonstrated that the situation had not become stabilized.

ELECTIONS. The formalities of nominating candidates and holding elections have been carried out regularly in East Germany, despite the fact that these are meaningless exercises. Through mass organizations and subordinate political parties the SED has control over most of the vote. The four subordinate parties are allowed to propose their candidates, but the choice is made in "consultation" with the SED. The communists have the power of veto over any name which may be presented.[20] All ballots until recently contained only a single "unity list," and the voters were given no opportunity for any choice. In June 1965 the SED propaganda chief Albert Norden proposed that "more candidates be nominated than the number required for election" at regional levels; no similar proposal with regard to national voting has been offered.

Article 106 of the East German constitution stipulates that elections are to be held every four years. In 1962, however, through a mere vote by the Council of Elders in the legislature, elections required by the constitution were delayed for a year. This postponement may have been due to preparations for the Sixth Congress (held in January 1963) of the SED.[21]

Meetings of "electors" take place, at which the preselected candidates are approved for inclusion on the ballot. The ballot then offers no choice to the voters, who must turn out and record approval by near unanimity (some do not vote). Ballots are constructed to give the largest bloc (59 percent, or 256 seats, in the current parliament "elected" on October 30, 1963) to members of the SED and the mass organizations. The remaining 41 percent of the seats goes to the four subordinate political groupings.

LOYALTY. The present regime in East Germany is probably more closely controlled by Moscow than that in any of the other East European countries. This influence, wielded through Walter Ulbricht and his aides, has produced the outward appearance of extreme stability. Probably the most dramatic example of East German subservience is the passive acceptance of the Oder-Neisse line as the eastern boundary of the country. In July 1950, premiers

Otto Grotewohl of East Germany and Józef Cyrankiewicz of Poland signed an agreement to accept these two rivers as the definitive Polish-East German border.

Walter Ulbricht maintains his position through "cult of personality" techniques and purges all those who disagree with him. East Germany has been called "the last stronghold of unadulterated Stalinism." Despite the divergence between his policy and that in the Soviet Union, Ulbricht's loyalty toward Moscow has never wavered. On June 12, 1964, East Germany signed an agreement with the U.S.S.R. guaranteeing the inviolability of its own frontiers [22] and subsequently pledged full support for Moscow in the present Sino-Soviet rift. So long as Walter Ulbricht stays in power, there can be no doubt that East Germany will remain fully in the Soviet camp.

AGRICULTURE. One of the earliest actions by the East German regime (based on Article 24 of the constitution) involved the confiscation of all privately owned farms of more than 100 hectares. Some of these were converted into cooperative enterprises. (*Landwirtschaftliche Produktionsgenossenschaften*—LPG), and others became state farms. More collectivization followed, and by 1959 probably about 54 percent of the arable land was in cooperative or state custody. The process was not carried any further for the time being.

In 1960 a new drive was started and toward the end of that year agriculture was 98.7 percent socialized.[23] Within three months about 340,000 farmers had been forced to join LPG's or flee to the West. In common with that of all other East European states, the German Democratic Republic's experience with collective farming has been less than satisfactory. The peasants toil unwillingly on the state farms, and production of all types of food has fallen off drastically. By 1962, with agricultural production down 40 percent, East Germany had to import more food than was planned. In 1963 the needed quantities were produced only in milk, sugar, and potatoes. The small private plots which the farmers have been allowed to own since the middle of the decade are the only bright spot in the picture.

Another serious problem is the young East Germans' leaving the farms to seek industrial employment in the cities. The average age on many of the collective farms is fifty-five years. Reportedly, fewer than one in twenty farm workers is under twenty-five. To counter this trend, Ulbricht has proposed the construction of modern farm villages, similar to the *agrogorod* suggested by Khrushchëv for the U.S.S.R. back in 1951, including multistory apartment buildings, schools, and medical facilities. To attract qualified young people, Ulbricht also stated that the farms must become "vanguards of technological machinery," using both tractors and computers.[24] The situation has deteriorated to such an extent, however, that local government agencies are permitted to declare harvest emergencies and draft workers to help with the crops.

DISAFFECTION AND INTELLECTUAL FERMENT. The most striking indicator of the disaffection of the East German people toward the communist regime was the constant stream of refugees, until the last gap in the border was sealed by the construction of the Berlin Wall. In the period from 1950 through 1961 an estimated three million persons fled from East Germany, making it one of the few countries in the world with a declining population. Since that time, in an average week about thirty East Germans manage to elude the border guards and escape to the West. During the six years since the Wall was built in 1961, fifty-eight persons are known to have been killed while trying to flee, another fifty-four wounded, and more than 2,200 caught.[25] These are signs that the popularity of the regime remains at a low level.

The German Democratic Republic has maintained close supervision over its intellectuals. There is, however, some possibility that this supervision may be relaxed. The most vocal dissident has been Robert Havemann, a professor in his sixties at Humboldt University in East Berlin. A lifelong communist, he maintained that the SED leadership was dogmatic and had replaced logic with authority and tradition. His thesis proclaimed that all mistakes and shortcomings should be publicly discussed. Professor Havemann was removed from his teaching position and ousted from the SED, because of "continued damage to the party and an outlook foreign to the party." Later he was attacked in an open letter by the Academy of Sciences president and shortly thereafter was "struck off the list of Academy members."[26]

It is perhaps rash to draw conclusions from a single isolated case, but the outlook may be encouraging. The fact that Professor Havemann could speak his mind without being executed or imprisoned indicates a change, perhaps only temporary, in basic policy. Obviously, his punishment is far greater than would have been the case in any Western country, but his continued freedom is an indication of a crack in East German totalitarianism which may grow wider.[27]

ULBRICHT'S SUCCESSOR. The ruler of East Germany, Walter Ulbricht, was seventy-four years old in June 1967, and it is high time to provide for someone who will succeed him. This person should meet two primary requirements. He must be a member of both the Central Committee's Secretariat and the SED Politburo. He should be another strong man, capable of continuing the policy that keeps East Germany within the Soviet Bloc. Two candidates may be suggested:

> ERICH HONECKER. Fifty-three years old (in 1966). Former leader of the Free German Youth (FDJ), between 1945 and 1954; full member of the Politburo; a secretary of the Central Committee, responsible for organization and security affairs.

> PAUL VERNER. Fifty-five years old. First secretary of the Berlin SED District; full member of the Politburo; a secretary of the Central Committee, supervising communist work in the West.[28]

The actual emergence of a new leader may occur only after a power struggle, when Ulbricht has died or retired.[29] (See table 21 for the party leadership as of 1967.) The possibility of a palace revolt cannot be discounted, in view of what happened during mid-October 1964 to Khrushchëv.

THE RULING PARTY

The Socialist Unity Party of Germany (*Sozialistische Einheitspartei Deutschlands*—SED), while farther geographically from Moscow than any similar bloc organization, has been characterized by the most slavish obedience to Soviet directives. During a decade of destalinization and superficial liberalization, both in the Soviet Union and to varying degrees throughout the bloc, the SED has retained its essential and original harshness.[30] It remains under the continuous unchallenged leadership of the oldest Stalinist ruler still in power, Walter Ulbricht. Functionally, the SED is something of a mirror image of the Soviet communist party, operating through similar

TABLE 21

East German Communist Party (SED) Leadership, 1967

Politburo	Age	Secretariat (and responsibility)	Other SED post	Government position
FULL MEMBERS				
Ebert, Friedrich	72			Mayor, East Berlin
Frölich, Paul	54		First secretary, Leipzig District	
Grüneberg, Gerhard	45	Secretary (agriculture)		
Hager, Kurt	54	Secretary (ideology)		
Honecker, Erich	54	Secretary (security)		
Matern, Hermann	73		Chairman, SED Control Commission	
Mittag, Günter	40	Secretary (industry)		
Mückenberger, Erich	56	First secretary, Frankfort-on-the-Oder District		
Neumann, Alfred	57			Deputy premier
Norden, Albert	62	Secretary (agitation)		
Sindermann, Horst	51	First secretary, Halle District		
Stoph, Willi	52			Premier
Ulbricht, Walter	73	First secretary, SED		Chairman, Council of State
Verner, Paul	55	Secretary (work in the West); First secretary, East Berlin District		
Warnke, Herbert	65			Chairman, Trade-Unions Council
CANDIDATE MEMBERS				
Axen, Herman	51	Secretary (international communist affairs)		
Ewald, Georg	40			Chairman, Agricultural Council
Halbritter, Walter	39			Chief, Price Control Office
Jarowinsky, Werner	39	Secretary (trade and supply)		
Kleiber, Günther	35			Chief, Electronic Data Processing
Müller, Margarete	36			Secretary, Trade-Unions Council

SOURCE: *Neues Deutschland*, April 23, 1967, p. 3.

NOTE: Among the leaders should be mentioned also Werner Lamberz (38), who is a secretary of the SED Central Committee but not on the Political Bureau. He is in charge of propaganda.

organs of control. Still, the nature of the East German people, the character of the leadership, and the conduct of the party congresses all give the SED its own peculiar form and character.

PARTY MEMBERSHIP. Of the approximately seventeen million people in East Germany, only 1,770,000 were in 1967 either full members or candidates for membership in the Socialist Unity party.[31] Like the other communist bloc parties, the SED originally assumed a mass form; this lasted from 1946 until 1948, when the order came to reorient the party into a cadre-type organization. Since that time the requirements for membership have been made much more stringent, and probably some of the opportunistic elements have been removed in the process. Membership now comes only after acceptance as a candidate and a period of trial under the careful scrutiny of party functionaries.[32] The latter come largely from the white-collar and intelligentsia classes.

Candidacy in the SED requires recommendation by other members of the party or, if the candidate is enrolled in the Free German Youth, by the local functionary. The social composition of the party (see table 22) shows a white-collar and intelligentsia plurality, as is true of most East European communist parties. Although the collectivized peasants in the German Democratic Republic number almost one million, only about 10 percent of them belong to the SED.

PARTY ORGANIZATION. The organization of the SED follows that of the Soviet communist party.[33] The smallest unit is the primary party organization, which permeates all activities on farms and in factories. The next administrative level is the town, and above this level comes the county. Superior to the county is the district organization, reporting in turn to the Central Committee. This group is elected by the party congress once every four years and, in theory, evolves from its membership a Politburo and a Secretariat. (The Seventh Congress met April 17-22, 1967.)

In actual practice, the Politburo is a self-perpetuating body. Through the Secretariat, it instructs the lower levels on the accomplishment of goals. That is, the Secretariat oversees the implementation of policy decisions made by the Politburo. Instructors are assigned by the top level to district headquarters; other instructors go from the district to the county, town, and primary organizations.

These men are assigned either individually or, to assure fulfillment of important plans, in teams.

The Central Committee of the SED in 1967 included 131 full members and 50 candidates. The Politburo was composed of fifteen members and six candidates. The Secretariat had nine persons who were designated as secretaries, in addition to the first secretary, Walter Ulbricht.

TABLE 22

EAST GERMAN COMMUNIST PARTY (SED) SOCIAL COMPOSITION, 1966

Occupational class	Number of party members	Percent of total membership
Industrial workers	544,410	33.8
White-collar employees and intelligentsia [a]	632,997	39.3
Peasants on collective farms	99,862	6.2
Students	25,771	1.6
Other (housewives, pensioners, etc.)	275,426	17.1
Unaccounted for	32,213	2.0
Total	1,610,679	100.0

SOURCE: U.S. Department of State, Bureau of Intelligence and Research, *World Strength of the Communist Party Organizations* (Washington, D.C., 1967), p. 54.

[a] Intelligentsia members comprise between 6 and 7 percent of the total membership, or about 104,000 persons.

SED BUREAUS AND COMMISSIONS. There are four major bureaus or commissions under the Politburo: the Bureau for Industry and Construction, the Ideological Commission, the Agitation (and propaganda) Commission, and the Agriculture Bureau.[34] With the exception of the Agitation Commission, these are duplicated in the 15 district and 215 county organizations, and are under the supervision of district and county secretariats comprising five or six secretaries.

ORGANS OF CONTROL. Some of the organizations by means of which the communists maintain control over the East German population are unique, while others can be found in one form or another either in the U.S.S.R. or in one or more of the bloc countries. The SED itself is an organ of control, as are the four subordinate political parties already mentioned. The National Front exists in East Germany mostly on paper and is not considered to be very effective.

It is an idea that the Soviets have implemented with varying degrees of success throughout their orbit. In some countries where it attempts to influence those persons not belonging to any organization it plays a more significant role than in East Germany.

The Free German Youth (*Freie Deutsche Jugend*—FDJ) organization is probably the most effective agent of SED control. It has affiliations with its Soviet counterpart, the Komsomol, and with other bloc youth organizations as well as with the World Federation of Democratic Youth. It comprises about one million members, in the age group from thirteen [35] to twenty-five years, many of whom also belong to the Socialist Unity party. Directorates of both organizations interlock. The FDJ secretary, Horst Schumann, is a member of the SED Central Committee. The standard fare of Marxist-Leninist indoctrination is given all FDJ members, as preparation for membership in the communist party. Admission to this organization takes place in a typically military ceremony (introduced in 1966).

Young children, aged six to twelve years, are urged to join the Pioneers (*Die Pionierorganisation*), which corresponds to the Soviet organization with the same name. These youngsters receive ideological indoctrination leading to an atheistic ceremony known as *Jugendweihe* or "youth consecration." It is designed to replace church confirmation. Membership in the FDJ and the Pioneers is promoted by monopolies over sports facilities and education, controlled by the FDJ in cooperation with the trade-unions. All vacations and entertainment, as well as educational scholarships and entrance examinations for universities, are administered by these regime organizations. Nonmembership or even poor performance as a member may deprive the young East German of an opportunity for advancement.

A particularly useful function of the Free German Youth for the SED is its activity in observing and reporting. Every school class has at least one FDJ member who reports on the teacher and on other students. Such informers are used to watch older officials in government agencies, factories, and businesses. Consequently, the FDJ attracts many opportunists and unprincipled young people to its ranks. It is not by any means a popular organization. Many young persons refuse to join, despite the monopoly position mentioned above.

The Fighting Units of the Working Class (*Die Kampfgruppen der*

Arbeiterklasse) are recruited by local SED organizations and are politically responsible to the party.[36] Militarily, they report directly to the Interior ministry's chief administration for the East German "people's police." As members, politically reliable persons working in industry, farming, or administration are sought out. Training is conducted by SED members who are officers in the people's police and by the East German armed forces. The fighting units receive four hours of training per week in light arms, are uniformed, and number about 320,000 men organized into battalions which comprise three or four companies; there are about a hundred "fighters" in each company. One battalion out of four has the heavy equipment allocated to an equivalent army unit of motorized infantry. Toward the end of 1965 there existed 102 such battalions and 27 autonomous mobile companies, all heavily equipped for action outside their own districts in cooperation with the regular armed forces. The purpose of the other fighting units is to combat local disturbances, such as strikes.

The Free German Trade-Union Federation (*Freie Deutsche Gewerkschaftsbund*—FDGB), as is true of labor organizations in all communist countries, has no real bargaining power for improvement of wages or working conditions. It is an instrument of control, supervision, observation, and reporting. About 90 percent of East German workers belong to unions, which now number some 6.4 million members. Most workers are employed in state-owned industries, where organizational control by SED activists is tight and well disciplined.[37] Those employed in the diminishing private sector represent only a very small percentage of the population; here the FDGB has somewhat less influence.

The primary usefulness of a trade-union to the regime is in organizing the labor force to increase productive efforts and fulfill national goals. For these purposes the East Germans have copied the well-known Stakhanovite system from the U.S.S.R. In East Germany, the name of the hero and example for other laborers is Adolf Hennecke, a coal miner. Presumably, this man was not satisfied with his normal output of 6.3 cubic meters during an eight-hour day. He surpassed this quota by about 400 percent and mined 24.4 cubic meters of coal during the same period of time.[38] His achievement and similar efforts in other industries are held before the workers as examples of efficient production.

Such "records" are usually produced under optimum conditions.

Teams of workers have party activists for leaders and challenge one another in "socialist competition." Usually those not engaged in such contests will attempt to hold down the norms by resisting incentives given for overfulfillment. Activists, on the other hand, have the task of obtaining more work out of one or two select squads in order to provide a justification for raising norms. In a typical case the activist is given a project with a team of fresh laborers and the best equipment, to show significantly that a rate of production faster than the norm is possible.

Then, a union meeting is held to honor the team and to vote "voluntarily" for increasing the norm by a certain percentage. At times, this is done in honor of a forthcoming event or even a person. It would be very unwise for a member to speak against an increase, abstain from voting, or vote negatively when one of these proposals comes up at a trade-union meeting. Other methods for increasing production include the payment of wages on the basis of piecework and "volunteering" for extra shifts.

The Democratic League of Women (*Demokratische Frauenbund Deutschlands*) has a membership of somewhat fewer than half of the approximately nine million females in East Germany. It allegedly works for equal rights, as guaranteed by law and under the constitution. These include rights to perform all kinds of manual labor and to provide half of the support for a family. According to official statistics, women comprise almost half (about 3.5 million) of the total East German labor force (about 7.6 million). In families with one child 74.1 percent of the mothers hold jobs; where there are three or more children the proportion is 57 percent.[39]

LEADERSHIP OF THE PARTY. The SED is rigidly controlled by Walter Ulbricht, longest in power among the old-guard communists within the bloc, and a group of men loyal to him. At the Sixth Congress of the party, in 1963, a Central Committee of 121 full members was elected. Seventy-nine had been on the committee previously; the other forty-two were elected for the first time. In general, Ulbricht is supported by a hard-line group that has continually rejected destalinization.[40] At the Sixth Congress the Stalinists reinforced their position of strength by replacing about 30 percent of the Central Committee's membership.

The first secretary, Walter Ulbricht, was born in 1893 at Leipzig.

In the nineteen-twenties and early thirties he worked as a functionary for the German communist party. After emigrating to France
in 1933 he participated in the Spanish civil war. He went to Moscow
in 1940 and worked for the Comintern as the leading German representative. A man who returned with Ulbricht to East Germany
after the war describes him as "innocent of theoretical ideas or personal feelings" though never failing to "carry out the directives transmitted to him by the Soviet authorities with ruthlessness and skill." [41]

IDEOLOGY. The habit of ideological mimicry, which requires
some quick adjustment to keep in step with Moscow's line, has been
followed in East Germany, with few signs of any "polycentric" developments such as have appeared in varying degrees throughout the
rest of the bloc. The party line is coordinated with Moscow, and
embarrassment over mandatory reversals of position seems to have
been minimal.

In East German economic theory, always closely coordinated
with Marxism-Leninism, centralized control and ideological aims
regularly supersede purely economic considerations. Even so, the
theories of the Soviet economist and professor Yevsei Liberman,
whose ideas of "profitability" are very un-Marxist, have begun to
show up in East German writings, though only after experimental
application in the U.S.S.R. At the Sixth Congress of the party Ulbricht even reversed his former position by endorsing the Western
profit concept as well as the law of supply and demand. The first
major statement on the "New System of Planning and Directing the
Economy" was made in September 1964, following the meeting of a
Politburo commission.[42]

DOMESTIC AND FOREIGN POLICIES

The aforementioned June 1964 treaty of friendship between the
Soviet Union and the German Democratic Republic allegedly was
signed on the basis of "full equality, mutual respect for state sovereignty, and noninterference in internal affairs" and of "mutual
advantage and fraternal mutual assistance." [43] It would be difficult,
however, to find instances where East Germany has exercised any
such prerogatives. The country generally is considered to be the most
subservient among those under Soviet influence and, under the lead-

ership of Walter Ulbricht, has echoed every major U.S.S.R. policy since the end of the Second World War.

Paradoxically, only in its reluctance to follow the Soviet lead in the policy of destalinization has East Germany displayed some independence, or so it would appear. In response to Moscow's policy of early June 1953, Ulbricht promised an easing of some restrictions and a greater emphasis on the production of consumers' goods. He failed, however, to modify a decision to increase work norms which had, in effect, brought about a reduction of wages. The result came in the form of an uprising during which the workers demanded economic reforms, free elections, and the release of political prisoners. Disorders spread throughout East Germany, but were put down by Soviet troops. Ulbricht immediately fell back on the tried and trusted remedy of a purge in the party hierarchy and reprisals against leaders of the rebellion.

Again, in 1956, a period of liberalization seemed in order after Khrushchëv's secret denigration of Stalin at the Twentieth Congress of the Soviet party. The response in certain of the satellites was a turn toward national communism and attempts to gain limited freedom from total domination by the Soviet Union. Ulbricht's response came in the form of purges, although he paid lip service to the policy of destalinization and was, indeed, the first among satellite leaders publicly to denounce Stalin. This did not prevent him from continuing to apply the same methods as before.

As political tensions increased over the Berlin question in mid-1961, the number of refugees grew from more than 30,000 during the month of July to more than 40,000 in the first ten days of August. On the night of August 13 the border was sealed on orders of the East German regime. Construction of the Berlin Wall followed. Since then, the flow of refugees has slowed to a comparative trickle and East Germany now stands condemned in the eyes of the world as a police state which retains control over its citizens primarily by physical means.[44]

Like the Soviet Union, the East German regime limits the right of free speech and assembly through its power of licensing. Nothing may be printed without a government permit. No meetings may be held unless official authorization is obtained. These devices are particularly important in the contest between church and state. In matters of religion, primary concern is with the Protestant churches rather than the Roman Catholic Church, which is in a minority. Most East Germans belong to the Evangelical (Lutheran) Church.

After the *de facto* separation of East and West Germany at the end of the 1940's, pressure on the churches in East Germany became increasingly evident. The regime made attempts to censor sermons of pastors and simultaneously to gain the political support of the Evangelical Church. The basic position of the church was stated in a letter to the Soviet military governor, then Marshal V. D. Sokolovskii, by the presiding bishops.[45] According to this document, Christians were obligated to obey the orders of the state as long as these regulations did not contravene moral law. The church claimed the right to support or criticize governmental measures, but only on moral, not political, grounds. This policy was reaffirmed during the summer of 1963 in a statement entitled "Ten Articles on the Church's Freedom and Service."

Church and state consistently have come into conflict also on the issue of education.[46] Although the church accepted removal of religion as a subject from the public school system after the war, it has registered opposition to the use of schools for preaching atheism. The church also has taken a stand against the regime's electoral practices, particularly the wording of referendum questions. It has aroused the anger of state officials by its refusal to grant a blanket endorsement to regime policies by way of a loyalty oath.

Attacks on the church by the government have assumed various forms. Travel and contact between East and West are restricted severely. The church press and its meetings have been controlled through the licensing power.[47] State subsidies have been withdrawn and the right of the church to conduct door-to-door solicitations has been restricted. Church relief agencies have been closed and their leaders arrested. On the other hand, about sixty "progressive" pastors have established a formal organization at Leipzig which is subsidized by the regime.

Probably the most successful mechanism which the state has employed against the church has been its usurpation of rites and ceremonies. There exist now government rituals for such occasions as baptism, marriage, and death. The most successful has been the already-mentioned youth consecration (*Jugendweihe*), akin to the ceremony of church confirmation, wherein young people between the ages of twelve and sixteen years dedicate themselves to socialism rather than to Christianity. Failure to participate in this ceremony often closes the door to further education or favorable employment opportunities.

In early 1965 the East German regime conducted a religious census for the first time. It is estimated that 80 percent of the population, or about 13.6 million out of 17.1 million, belongs to the Evangelical Church, while the number of Roman Catholics is about 1.9 million.[48] The Evangelical Church remains as the one organization that is still formally united on an all-German basis. Attempts to split it between East and West have failed, except for the physical separation.

Life is also difficult on the economic front. In proper communist fashion, the economy has been oriented toward heavy industry at the expense of consumers' goods. Farm policies in East Germany have been just as disastrous as elsewhere in the bloc. Official food rationing was abolished in 1958, but each consumer is required to purchase his butter and meat at a particular store. This in effect continues rationing. Two major reasons can be cited for the inability of the German Democratic Republic to fill its agricultural requirements. Cession of lands east of the Oder and Neisse rivers to Poland resulted in the loss of one-fourth of the arable land possessed by prewar Germany. Probably even more important is the fact that collectivization and communist mismanagement have stifled production.

Collectivization came rather slowly to East Germany. At the end of the war about one-third of the total agricultural land was seized from large landholders and redistributed to individual peasants and to collective farms. By the end of 1959 only half of all farms had been collectivized. Between February and April of 1960, however, the program was pushed through almost to completion in a manner similar to that employed during the early 1930's in the Soviet Union. The results were very much the same. An immediate decrease in grain production took place. Major shortages of meat and of livestock products followed. The farmer is not interested in collective work and devotes as much time as possible to his private garden plot. The only remedial actions taken by the German Democratic Republic have been to increase political controls on farming and to press communist youth groups into emergency service during the busiest times of the year.[49] There has been a grain deficit for several years (see table 23).

Elsewhere the German Democratic Republic displays an economy that is seriously distorted by the demands of the CMEA. East Germany, a founding member of that organization, today specializes in the production of machinery, chemicals, certain consumers' goods, railroad rolling stock, ships, optical goods, and scientific instruments for the bloc. Raw materials are imported mainly from the other East European countries and from the U.S.S.R. Four-fifths of all exports go to communist-dominated countries, the Soviet Union alone absorbing 56.8 percent.[50] East Germany is Russia's largest foreign trading partner and provides half of Soviet machinery imports.

TABLE 23

EAST GERMAN GRAIN DEFICIT, 1958-1964
(In thousands of metric tons)

Production, imports, and consumption	1958	1959	1960	1961	1962	1963	1964
Apparent total grain available for consumption ..	5,484.6	5,636.3	6,063.6	4,547.0	5,248.9	4,885.9	5,586.5
Domestic production ...	3,898.6	3,747.3	3,899.6	2,717.0	2,979.9	3,174.9	3,627.5
Total imports ..	1,786.0	1,889.0	2,164.0	1,830.0	2,269.0	1,711.0	1,959.0
Imports which the Soviet Union provided	1,747.1	1,686	1,848.2	1,787.3	2,185.8	1,552.6	n. a.

SOURCES: Ministerstvo Vneshnei Torgovlii, *Vneshnyaya torgovlya Soyuza SSR: statisticheskii obzor* (Moscow, 1961-1963). [East Germany], Staatliche Verwaltung für Statistik, *Statistisches Jahrbuch der Deutschen Demokratischen Republik* (East Berlin, Staatsverlag der DDR, 1964 and 1965), as cited in Radio Free Europe report (by Dorothy Miller), "East Germany—The USSR's New Mentor," October 31, 1965, p. 4.

NOTE: Total imports were 1,698 tons in 1965. *Statistisches Jahrbuch der Deutschen Demokratischen Republik 1966*, p. 409.

Despite having been looted of some ten to twenty billion dollars' worth of industrial capital goods and production in the years following the Second World War, East Germany by the late 1950's could show a fair measure of economic vitality. It became the world's sixth largest industrial producer and in 1959 adopted a seven-year plan which included the goal of surpassing West Germany by 1961 in per capita production. During 1959 the growth rate was claimed to be 12.4 percent. This admittedly declined to 8 percent in 1960, then to 6.2 percent during 1961, and subsequently became one of the lowest within the bloc. Obviously, the goal of overtaking West Germany could not be achieved.

The seven-year plan with its ambitious goals had to be abandoned in favor of a new one, for 1964-1970. The party's Sixth Congress, January 1963, called for significant changes in the economy. Planning and practice, it was decided, are to be governed more in accordance with economic than with ideological principles.[51] Material interest will be given recognition in the form of wage incentives, bonuses, more realistic pricing, and greater emphasis on profits. The central planning mechanism is to concentrate on the broad outlines, while details will be left to the lower management levels.

These changes are very similar to policies recommended in the Soviet Union. Professional economists also have been admitted to the SED hierarchy by their appointment as candidate members of the Politburo. Determination to maintain political controls was indicated, however, by the establishment in May 1963 of "workers' and peasants' inspectorates" which will watch over the economy to prevent mismanagement and violations of labor discipline.

There are several reasons for the economic difficulties in East Germany. These have included forced industrialization, which resulted in such errors as an expenditure equivalent to $600 million for the construction of a huge steel combine at former Stalinstadt which has been unable to produce anything except crude pig iron.[52] Normal development is hindered also by the requirements of the Soviet Union and the CMEA. Plans for the development of Rostock as a major shipbuilding center and seaport were suspended because of competition with the Polish port of Szczecin. The aircraft industry was abandoned altogether in 1961. Automobile and textile plants have been held back. An industrial complex for uranium mining that employs 140,000 workers is maintained at the Wismuth Aktiengesellschaft works simply to fulfill U.S.S.R. needs. The suicide of the forty-eight-year-old deputy premier and chief economic planner, Dr. Erich Apel, reportedly occurred as a protest against continued exploitation by the U.S.S.R.[53] Despite being on the verge of bankruptcy, East Germany has been forced to extend credits to other bloc states and to underdeveloped countries. An instance was the granting of aid equivalent to $100 million to the United Arab Republic in 1965. There is no evidence that the East German regime has ever resisted CMEA policies, as some of the bloc countries have done rather successfully.

The great foreign policy issue for East Germany is, of course, that of reunification, which naturally would include settlement of the Berlin problem. It appears unquestionable that the population desires reunification, both from national sentiment and as the only opportunity to attain freedom. The self-serving conditions set by the East German regime and the Soviet Union, contrasted with the minimal demands of the West, make it seem extremely doubtful that reunification can be achieved soon. The basic Western position has been that a comprehensive settlement must be based on free elections of an all-German government, to be followed by a peace treaty, and that a united Germany must be allowed to pursue any course in foreign affairs, including alignment with the West.

The basic demand of the East German communists and of the Soviet Union is for Western recognition of the German Democratic Republic as a sovereign state and the conclusion of separate peace treaties with the two Germanys, to be followed by all-German talks on reunification. A unified German government is envisaged as a confederation, in which East and West Germany would enjoy equal representation and the "socialist progress" of the German Democratic Republic would be safeguarded. Elections would come after confederation. The most extreme conditions for reunification were laid down by Walter Ulbricht when he demanded as preliminaries that the Bonn government be replaced by a pro-Soviet regime, all foreign troops be withdrawn from West Germany (but not from East Germany), a European security pact be concluded, and industrial, agricultural, and social "reforms" be instituted in West Germany.[54]

The periodic crises over Berlin obviously are designed to accomplish the first step in this program: recognition of the Soviet Occupation Zone as a sovereign state. In the broad view, it would appear that Ulbricht's objective is to prevent reunification by taking as hard a line as possible.[55] Any reunification plan that provides for free elections or for withdrawal of Soviet troops must inevitably result in his own downfall.

Thus, at the Ninth Plenum of the SED Central Committee, Ulbricht demanded that West Germany pay 120 billion marks (about four to the U.S. dollar at the official exchange rate) as its share in reparations to the U.S.S.R. and for damages caused between

1950 and 1961 by "open borders." In view of the fact that 30 billion marks was announced on several earlier occasions as comprising the amount for damages, it can be surmised that the German Democratic Republic considers 90 billion marks to be Bonn's share of the reparations already paid to the U.S.S.R. by the East German regime.[56]

A second major foreign policy issue, although ostensibly no problem for the East German communists, is that of the eastern frontier. At the wartime Teheran and Yalta conferences there was agreement "in principle" among the Allies that Germany should be dismembered, or at least reduced in size, in order to destroy her military potential, and that the U.S.S.R. would receive territorial concessions from Poland, which in turn would acquire German territory. There was no agreement, however, on the details. The Soviets proposed that Poland should annex all German lands east of the Oder and Neisse rivers, except for the northern and eastern areas of East Prussia, which would become part of the U.S.S.R.

At the Potsdam conference, after the war in Europe had ended, the issue was raised again, but no agreement could be reached. The question ultimately came to be deferred until there should be a peace conference, though it was settled that Poland meanwhile should administer the disputed territory not directly incorporated by the Soviet Union. This is the position maintained by the West today, except by France, whose President Charles de Gaulle indicated at a press conference in 1960 that he thought *de facto* German borders should not be changed. The U.S.S.R., Poland, and East Germany have accepted the Oder-Neisse as a definitive boundary. Confirmation is found even in the constitution of the German Democratic Republic. The territory comprised, before the war, about a fifth of the area of Germany. About eight million German citizens lived there. Owing to flight and expulsion, only about 150,000 of these people remain in the territory, and they have accepted Polish citizenship.

NOTES

1 Stephen D. Kertesz (ed.), *The Fate of East Central Europe* (Notre Dame, Ind., 1956), pp. 160-161.

2 Elmer Plischke, *Contemporary Government of Germany* (Boston, 1961), pp. 182-183, describes the overall economic organization of the zone.

3 Kertesz, *op. cit.,* p. 154.

4 For an official chronology of events from April 1945 to June 1964 see Stefan Dörnberg, *Kurze Geschichte der DDR* (East Berlin, 1964), pp. 513-547.

5 Today five political groupings operate in East Germany. For names of their key members see U.S. Department of State, Bureau of Intelligence and Research, *Directory of East German Officials* (Washington, D.C., 1964), pp. 66-92.

6 [West Germany], Bundesministerium für gesamtdeutsche Fragen, *SBZ von 1945-1954* (Bonn, 1956), pp. 10, 21, 23-27.

7 They took four out of the five *Länder* premierships, the same ratio of key posts in the Interior ministry, three out of five in the Economy ministry, and all five in the Education ministry. Kertesz, *op. cit.,* p. 158.

8 U.S. Office of the High Commissioner for Germany, *Soviet Zone Constitution and Electoral Law* (Washington, D.C., 1951), p. 1.

9 For text with amendments through 1960 see Siegfried Mampel (ed.), *Die volksdemokratische Ordnung in Mitteldeutschland* (Frankfort on the Main, 1963), pp. 56-79.

10 Plischke, *op. cit.,* p. 210.

11 The "basic law" (*Grundgesetz*) of the Federal Republic of Germany specifically states that it is temporary. It makes provision, however, for ratification by other *Länder* and proclaims that it will be terminated only when a "constitution adopted by a free decision of the German people comes into force." See Article 146 in Amos J. Peaslee (ed.), *Constitutions of Nations* (2d ed.; The Hague, 1956), II, 59.

12 For a good analysis see [West Germany], Bundesministerium für gesamtdeutsche Fragen, *Schein und Wirklichkeit: Die Verfassung der Deutschen Demokratischen Republik und Was dahinter Steht* (Bonn, 1964).

13 Plischke, *op. cit.,* p. 90.

14 Bohdan Gruchman and Bolesław Wiewióra (eds.), *Niemiecka Republika Demokratyczna* (Poznań, 1963), p. 215.

15 Arnold J. Heidenheimer, *The Governments of Germany* (2d ed.; New York, 1966), pp. 182-183.

16 For a discussion of the Council of State see I. P. Ilinskii and B. A. Strashun, *Germanskaya Demokraticheskaya Respublika: gosudarstvennyi stroi* (Moscow, 1961), pp. 133-139.

17 Lech Janicki, *Ustrój polityczny Niemieckiej Republiki Demokratycznej* (Poznań, 1964), p. 156.

18 Speech by a Central Committee functionary, quoted in Heidenheimer, *op. cit.,* p. 184.

19 *Pravda,* December 30, 1961.

20 See the 1963 electoral law. It appears in Otto Gotsche, *Wahlen in der DDR* (East Berlin, 1963), pp. 17-21.

21 An analysis of this congress appears in [West Germany], Bundesministerium für gesamtdeutsche Fragen, *Der VI. Parteitag der SED . . . Kommentar, Materialien und Dokumente* (Bonn, 1964).

22 This treaty of friendship, mutual assistance, and cooperation was published in *Krasnaya zvezda* (Moscow) the day after it was signed. Interestingly enough, Article 6 stipulates that "West Berlin is regarded as a separate political unit."

23 L. N. Tolkunov (ed.), *Sotsialisticheskii lager* (Moscow, 1962), p. 163, reveals that 92.4 percent had been collectivized and that another 6.3 percent comprised state farms.

24 Ulbricht's description of the future East German "agricultural city" and the astounding vistas for 1970-1980 appeared in a mammoth speech printed by *Neues Deutschland,* February 29 and March 1, 1964.

25 B. P. Krasnoglazov, *Ekonomicheskoe sotrudnichestvo GDR s sotialisticheskimi stranami* (Moscow, 1965), p. 5, admits this reason for the wall, if only by implication. Figures are from the *New York Times,* August 3, 1966. During 1966, escapees numbered 1,155, including 158 in uniform. *The German Tribune,* April 8, 1967. Refugees totaled 25,180 between the time the wall was built and the end of 1966. *New York Times,* August 13, 1967.

26 *Die Zeit* (Hamburg), March 18, 1966, and *Neues Deutschland,* April 1, 1966, as cited in RFE report (by Dorothy Miller), "Another Chapter in the Case of the Rebellious Professor," April 2, 1966 (7 pp.).

27 For a similar case which ended a decade ago in prison sentences up to ten years each for Professor Wolfgang Harich and his group see the chapter on "The Political Platform of Harich and His Friends" in Hermann Weber (ed.), *Der deutsche Kommunismus: Dokumente* (Cologne, 1963), pp. 598-603.

28 Biographic data on Honecker and Verner appear in [West Germany], Bundesministerium für gesamtdeutsche Fragen, *SBZ-Biographie* (Bonn, 1964), pp. 155, 363. Ulbricht has suffered a mild heart attack, and there is speculation about his retirement. Honecker made the address to the SED Congress in April 1967 on the role of the party, and this speech is customarily given by the heir apparent. His wife became Education Minister in the new government. *New York Times,* July 15, 1967.

29 Ernst Richert, *Das zweite Deutschland: Ein Staat, der nicht darf sein* (Gütersloh, 1964), p. 330, suggests that Ulbricht may be succeeded either by Premier Willi Stoph or else by the SED first secretary for Magdeburg, Alois Pisnik. Their life histories are in *SBZ-Biographie,* pp. 343-344 and 268. See the article on Stoph in *The German Tribune,* August 5, 1967.

30 Theo Sommer, in an article on "The World of the Functionary," *Die Zeit* (Hamburg), May 29, 1964. For a more recent article, entitled "Life Along the Zone Border Is Again Worth Living," see *Die Welt* (Hamburg), airmail ed., October 29, 1966.

31 *Krasnaya zvezda* (Moscow), April 23, 1967.

32 The 25,000-odd professional apparatus workers or "aparatchiki" comprise 15 percent of the total SED membership. [East Germany], Deutsches Institut für Zeitgeschichte, *Handbuch der Deutschen Demokratischen Republik* (East Berlin, 1964), p. 74; hereafter cited as *Handbuch der DDR.*

33 For the statute or party rules adopted at the Sixth Congress of the SED see Mampel (ed.), *op. cit.,* pp. 82-101. This book reprints the statute from *Neues Deutschland,* January 26, 1963.

34 *Line-Up,* p. 12, gives names of incumbents as of July 1967.

35 The admission age was lowered from fourteen to thirteen only recently. *New York Times,* January 19, 1966.

36 A good discussion appears in W. Bader, *Un Ejército para la Guerra Civil* (Mexico City, 1964), p. 128. See also [West Germany], Bundesministerium für gesamtdeutsche Fragen, *SBZ von A-Z* (Bonn, 1966), pp. 233-234, and Armin Hindrichs, *Die Bürgerkriegsarmee* (2d ed.; West Berlin, 1964), pp. 38-40.

37 Hartmut Zimmermann, article on "The FDGB as a Mass Organization and Its Tasks in Implementation of Industrial Economic Plans," in Peter Christian Ludz (ed.), *Studien und Materialien zur Soziologie der DDR* (Cologne, 1964), pp. 115-138.

38 His portrait, photographed at the coal face, appears in *Handbuch der DDR,* p. 57.

39 *New York Times,* August 22, 1965, and November 27, 1966.

40 See the defense of Ulbricht's "personality cult" in *Neues Deutschland,* November 12, 1961, reprinted by Weber (ed.), *op. cit.,* pp. 577-580. This article appeared more than five years after Khrushchëv's secret denunciation of Stalin and even after the public denigration at the Twenty-second Congress of the Soviet party.

41 Wolfgang Leonhard, *Child of the*

Revolution (Chicago, 1958), p. 288; translated from the original German which appeared as *Die Revolution entlässt ihre Kinder* (Cologne, 1955).

42 See RFE report (by Dorothy Miller), "Further Details on the New East German Economic System," November 18, 1964 (7 pp.).

43 Article 1, as given in *Krasnaya zvezda,* June 13, 1964.

44 Since 1949 the East German regime has (in round figures) imprisoned 75,000 persons for alleged political crimes, handed 45,000 over to Soviet "justice," allowed 31,000 to be deported to the U.S.S.R., and collaborated with the U.S.S.R. in the imprisonment of more than 180,000 others in concentration camps, where about one-half have died. "Report on West Germany," *Atlantic,* CCXVI, No. 3 (September 1965), 46. (The report gives no source for these figures. They are uncorroborated, but probably are from the West German government.)

45 Richard W. Solberg, *God and Caesar in East Germany* (New York, 1961), p. 59. See also Friedrich-Georg Hermann, *Der Kampf gegen Religion und Kirche in der Sowjetischen Besatzungszone Deutschlands* (Stuttgart, 1966).

46 For a compilation of laws on education in East Germany see R. Frenzel, *Die sozialistische Schule* (East Berlin, 1960). See also Hans Relmig's article on "Radical Change in SED School Policy" in *Die Welt* (Hamburg), September 3, 1966.

47 For example, the Lutheran World Federation was advised by the East German secretary for church affairs that it could not hold a meeting at Weimar, *New York Times,* July 20, 1966. Churches are being pressured to sever ties with the West. *Ibid.,* March 30, 1967.

48 *Ibid.,* January 10, 1965.

49 West Germany has eased this situation to a certain extent by sending the equivalent of 24 million U.S. dollars in coffee, citrus fruit, butter, fertilizer, etc., as ransom for 2,600 political prisoners held by the German Democratic Republic. *Ibid.,* February 1, 1966.

50 Krasnoglazov, *op. cit.,* p. 110, gives a percentage breakdown of exports and imports between East Germany and ten other communist-ruled countries (excluding Albania and Cuba). Note also figures for 1966-1970, given by the *New York Times,* September 11, 1966.

51 See the discussion of the "New Economic System" in Karl C. Thalheim, *Die Wirtschaft der Sowjetzone in Krise und Umbau* (West Berlin, 1964), pp. 72-90.

52 Carl G. Anthon, "Stalinist Rule in East Germany," *Current History,* XLIV, No. 261 (May 1963), 271.

53 See the excellent analysis of East German foreign trade by Julius Götz in *SBZ Archiv,* XVII, No. 4 (February 1966), 50-59, which provides comprehensive statistics on economic relations with the U.S.S.R.

54 The communist plan is given by M. Vasiliev, *Vneshnyaya politika Germanskoi Demokraticheskoi Respubliki* (Moscow, 1961), pp. 67-72. Ulbricht has been quoted as not discerning any possibility for reunification within the foreseeable future. *Die Welt* (Hamburg), September 24, 1966, airmail edition. See also his response to West German proposals for better relations. *New York Times,* April 23, 1967.

55 This could be seen when regime spokesman Albert Norden scuttled hopes for a scheduled East-West debate by setting impossible conditions, as reported by the East German news bureau Allgemeiner Deutscher Nachrichtendienst (ADN), June 29, 1966, cited in RFE report (by Dorothy Miller), "East Germany Withdraws from Planned SED-SPD Speakers Exchange," June 29, 1966 (3 pp.).

The new West German minister for All-German Affairs, Herbert Wehner, has called for a reconsideration of the Bonn policy of not extending recognition to the East German regime until it has become "democratized." *New York Times,* December 15, 1966.

East Germany has introduced a new citizenship law, proclaiming itself a separate nation. *Ibid.,* February 21, 1967.

56 The speech appeared in *Neues Deutschland,* April 28, 1965. The deduction is made in an RFE report (by Dorothy Miller), "Increased Self-Confidence at the Ninth SED Plenum," April 28, 1965 (7 pp.).

More recently, the regime has demanded credits of 30 billion marks from West Germany as "compensation" for the drain on its manpower up to August 13, 1961, when the wall was built. *Hannoversche Presse,* August 16, 1966, translated in *The German Tribune,* August 27, 1966.

Figures on trade between the two Germanys are given in the *New York Times,* December 9, 1966. During the year 1966, a total of 1,430 East German officials entered West Germany on SED missions. *The German Tribune,* July 15, 1967.

Chapter 5 / HUNGARY:
The Brave Rebel

DURING the "liberation" of Hungary, which lasted from October 1944 to April 1945, and under Soviet tutelage, a provisional government was organized in December 1944 at Budapest while that capital was still occupied by the Germans. A temporary legislature came into being on the basis of five political parties, among which was a small, highly disciplined communist movement.[1] The coalition was led by the Smallholders party, a popular and moderate group. The Provisional Assembly, however, included a plurality of communists, and the police force was wholly communist-manned. Real power, of course, was held by the Red Army occupation forces and specifically by the Soviet chairman of the Allied Control Commission.

Although universal suffrage was adopted and the November 1945 elections for a regular government were to be unencumbered by direct U.S.S.R. pressure, the communists still felt that they would win a plurality. To their surprise, they received only 17 percent of the vote.[2] During the ensuing struggle over allocation of ministries, Soviet influence was successful in placing a communist, Imre Nagy (and shortly afterward László Rajk) in the position of Interior minister. This gave Russian advisers control over the police.

By early 1948 the communists had penetrated every department of the government and actually dominated the Hungarian state apparatus.[3] The tactics used by Mátyás Rákosi, leader of the communist Hungarian Workers' party, during this period have been described as follows:

> With the famous "salami tactics" he first went into a coalition with the Smallholders, Peasant, and Social-Democratic parties

to crush the Conservatives, then annihilated the Smallholders party with the help of the remaining two parties. Then he suborned the Peasant party and absorbed the Social-Democrats, killing off or imprisoning their party leadership. Politicians were bribed, blackmailed, driven to exile, imprisoned, or sentenced to death.[4]

As a prerequisite for complete takeover and promulgation of a new constitution, the "Hungarian People's Front for Independence" came forth with a single list of candidates before the elections of May 1949, after which control was complete.

THE CONSTITUTION OF 1949

The principal feature of the constitution adopted after the takeover in 1949 was the inauguration of a Hungarian people's republic on the Soviet communist pattern. Like all satellite constitutions subsequent to the expulsion of Yugoslavia from the Soviet bloc in June 1948, this one also mentions the prominent role of the Soviet Union in making possible development toward socialism.[5] The Preamble declares:

> The armed forces of the great Soviet Union liberated our country from the yoke of the German fascists, crushed the power of the great landowners and capitalists who were ever hostile to the people, and opened the road of democratic progress to our working people . . . supported by the Soviet Union, our people began to lay down the foundations of socialism and now our country is advancing towards socialism along the road of a people's democracy.[6]

A comparison of the Soviet and Hungarian constitutions shows that most of the latter is inspired by the former. Variations exist, but only where these emanate from the theoretical assumption that the U.S.S.R. has achieved socialism, while Hungary has not. There are a number of instances where this difference is indicated, as in the articles dealing with the status of workers, ownership of the means of production, and citizenship.

The U.S.S.R. is said to be a socialist state, whereas Hungary still unofficially admits the existence of classes other than industrial workers and working peasants. The Hungarian constitution uses the term "working peasant" in Article 7, which guarantees the right of working peasants to the land and thus excludes *kulaks*—those rich peasants who hire farm laborers and who either supposedly have made money by exploiting the poorer class in rural areas or have refused to cooperate with the government. The new intelligentsia is not a distinct class; industrial workers and peasants may become intelligentsia through appropriate education (see table 25).

In Hungary, also, a degree of private ownership is still permitted.[7] Article 8, Section 2, states: "Private property and private enterprise must not be such as to run counter to the public interest." The U.S.S.R. constitution permits private ownership by its citizens "based on their labor and precluding the exploitation of the labor of others," meaning that no one outside the family may be hired. Hungary is still working to "dislodge the capitalist elements," whereas in the U.S.S.R. the capitalist system allegedly has been liquidated already.

Since the U.S.S.R. claims to have achieved the level of socialism in 1936, it is assumed that all persons are instilled with the collectivist spirit. In the Soviet Union a citizen either will work, or he will not eat. Hungary, still being at the lower stage of a people's democracy, has not worded its constitution so strongly in this respect. It is, as is stated clearly in the basic law, only "striving" to apply socialist principles.

In Hungary education was at first guaranteed only to every worker. The right to an education for all citizens, even for those with a "class alien" background (meaning persons who are neither industrial workers nor peasants), was not established until 1963. Faith in the "socialist order"—in other words the regime—continues to be a requirement for all applicants.[8] In the U.S.S.R. each citizen allegedly has the right to an education. Again, the difference can be ascribed to the level of socialist achievement. Hungary admits the existence of classes other than workers. On the other hand, exploiters theoretically have been eliminated from the Soviet Union.

PARLIAMENT. Hungary has a unicameral system, with the parliament designated as the highest organ of state authority. The constitution charges parliament with responsibility of passing laws, determining the state budget, deciding on the national economic plan, electing the Presidential Council and the Council of Ministers, controlling ministries, declaring war and concluding peace, and exercising the prerogative of amnesty. Despite these official duties, this "highest organ" represents a constitutional fiction whose work is carried out by the Central Committee of the Hungarian communist party. For example, the parliamentary session in June 1966 rubber-stamped the economic plan for 1966-1970 that had been approved a month previously by the latter agency.[9]

"Members of parliament are elected by the citizens of the Hungarian People's Republic on the basis of universal, equal, and direct suffrage by secret ballot," says the Hungarian constitution,[10] which like that of the U.S.S.R. provides for the direct election of representatives to all legislative levels. Needless to say, the slate of delegates is controlled by the communist Hungarian Socialist Workers' party.

Parliament meets in regular session twice a year. Its speaker, two deputy speakers, and six recorders are chosen from among the membership. All issues are decided by a simple majority, except for constitutional changes, which require a two-thirds vote. Laws are signed by the chairman and the secretary of the Presidential Council and then are published in the official gazette.

PRESIDENTIAL COUNCIL. At its first sitting, the parliament elects from among its own number a Presidential Council consisting of a chairman, two deputy chairmen, a secretary, and seventeen members. According to the constitution, the competence of the Presidential Council includes calling a general election; convening parliament; initiating legislation; holding plebiscites; concluding treaties, appointing diplomatic representatives, and receiving foreign diplomats; appointing civil servants; and performing the functions of the parliament when it is not in session.

The chairman of the Presidential Council is the nominal chief of state.[11] It is interesting to note that a member of the cabinet, or Council of Ministers, is ineligible for election to the Presidential Council. Article 20 of the constitution gives the Presidential Council authority to dissolve local organs of government if these are "seriously detrimental to the interests of the working people."

COUNCIL OF MINISTERS. The third organ of the central government, referred to in the constitution as the highest organ of state administration, is the Council of Ministers. In 1967 it comprised a chairman, or premier, three deputy premiers, and the heads of twenty-one ministries and four other agencies.[12] Article 24 of the constitution established twenty-six ministries but changes since 1949, primarily through the combining of ministries, have reduced this number. The four agencies are the Planning Board, the Technical Development Committee, the State Office of Religious Affairs, and the National Statistical Office; of these, although their heads are members of the council, only the Planning Board is headed by a minister. The Council of Ministers exercises powers of administration involving the enforcement of parliamentary laws and the decrees of the Presidential Council; fulfillment of economic plans; promulgation of decrees which do not infringe on parliamentary legislation or those issued by the Presidential Council; and supervision over the work of subordinate local organs. Article 27 states that "the Council of Ministers is responsible for its activities to Parliament and must render regular accounts of its work to that body."

LOCAL ORGANS OF STATE POWER. For the purpose of administration Hungary is divided into counties, districts, towns, and boroughs, with some large towns or cities subdivided into precincts. Local organs of state administration include the county council, district council, town council, and precinct council.[13] Members of these councils are elected to four-year terms by voters in the areas which they represent.

Local councils are given the authority to supervise all state organs (except the armed forces) dealing with the maintenance of social, cultural, health, and labor regulations. The civil police organs, although directly under the central government, theoretically are required to submit reports concerning public security conditions to council meetings and their executive committees.

The functions of the councils are essentially the same at all levels, each receiving instructions directly from the central government. This system allegedly makes for an efficient administrative structure, by providing a means to implement directives as they filter down from the central government to the lowest level.[14]

The most important part of any local council is its Executive Committee, elected by the council at the first organizational session. It is presided over by a chairman, who is assisted by one or more deputy chairmen and a secretary. The Executive Committee exercises control over the local administrative apparatus. Its relation to the local council resembles that of the Council of Ministers to the parliament: theoretically subordinate, but actually dominant. On the county and district levels, the Executive Committee is supported in its work by a secretariat and a number of specialized administrative organs. One of the party devices for supervising the work of the Executive Committees involves the establishment of permanent committees. These units report via the communist party chain of command to the central government.

THE JUDICIARY. Justice in Hungary is administered by the Supreme Court, county courts, and district courts. The Supreme Court supervises judicial activities of all other courts. Specifically, according to the constitution, the courts "punish the enemies of the working people, protect and safeguard the state, the social and economic order and the institutions of the people's democracy and the rights of the workers and educate the working people in the observance of the rules governing the life of a socialist commonwealth." [15]

GOVERNMENT IN PRACTICE. Constitutionally, the Presidential Council has a list of functions which appears most impressive. In reality, it does not play a significant policy-making role in government. The fact that István Dobi, the nominal chief of state between 1952 and 1967, was formerly a leader in the Smallholders party was indicative of his subservience to the communists.[16] Since the leading members of the Hungarian communist party are concentrated in the Council of Ministers, and the twenty members of the Presidential Council may not be appointed to ministries, the Presidential Council is composed of people with limited influence.

It is likely that the actual power and influence exercised by the parliament is even less than that of the Presidential Council. In practice, all policies are formulated by the party hierarchy and passed to the Presidential Council for a rubber-stamp approval while the parliament is not in session. Since parliament is rarely in session, and the approval of the Presidential Council is binding, the requirement that all enactments by the council be submitted to the parliament is purely academic.

A list of the members of the Council of Ministers shows that seven of the top positions (those of the premier, the three deputy premiers, the Defense minister, the Culture minister, and the chairman of the

Planning Board) are occupied by members or candidates on the communist party's Politburo. (See table 24.) Constitutionally, the Council of Ministers is subordinate to both the Presidential Council and the parliament, but in practice it is the dominant government organ. This status is derived not from the constitution, but from

TABLE 24

COMMUNIST LEADERSHIP IN HUNGARY, 1967

Political Bureau	Born	Other responsibility	Government posts
FULL MEMBERS			
Apró, Antal	1913	Representative to CMEA	Deputy premier (economy)
Biszku, Béla	1921	Party secretary (cadres)	—
Fehér, Lajos	1917	Chairman, Partisans Association	Deputy premier (agriculture)
Fock, Jenö	1916	—	Premier (industry)
Gáspár, Sándor	1917	Secretary-general, trade-unions	Deputy Chairman, Presidential Council
Kádár, János	1912	Party first secretary	Member, Presidential Council
Kállai, Gyula	1910	Chairman, People's Patriotic Front	Chairman, National Assembly
Komócsin, Zoltán ..	1923	Party secretary (intra-bloc parties)	—
Nemes, Dezsö	1908	Director, Party History Institute	—
Nyers, Rezsö	1923	Party secretary (economy and finance)	—
Szirmai, István	1906	Press and ideology	—
CANDIDATE MEMBERS			
Ajtai, Miklós	1914	—	Deputy premier (planning)
Czinege, Lajos	1924	—	Minister of Defense
Ilku, Pál	1912	Agitation and propaganda	Minister of Culture
Németh, Károly ...	1922	First secretary, Budapest city	—

SOURCES: Radio Free Europe, *Eastern Europe's Communist Leaders* (Munich, June 20, 1966), I, 2-48, and report, "Ninth Hungarian Party Congress Ends with Election of Leading Bodies," December 6, 1966 (9 pp.), pp. 3-6; *New York Times*, April 15, 1967.

NOTE: The national party Secretariat comprises the four men indicated above as secretaries (Biszku, Kádár, Komócsin, and Nyers) and two others: Árpád Pullai, born in 1925, secretary for foreign affairs, and Lajos Cseterki, probably born around 1916, secretary for science and education. Neither of these two men is on the Political Bureau.

the concentration of its leading members in the highest echelons of the Hungarian communist party and from its control over all political, economic, social, and cultural activities.

Some Western observers and analysts see a weakening of communist control over Hungary, or at least a move toward more "liberal" policies. An official planner in Budapest, when questioned about the hoped-for future under communist rule, reportedly gave this description: "That will be when Hungary and all the rest of the bloc can engage in free-enterprise socialism, trading where it profits us to trade, making what it profits us to make, with nobody to ask us, 'Is this really socialism, Comrade?' " [17] The participation of non-party members in responsible positions of the People's Patriotic Front has led some observers to conclude erroneously that this organization will become an opposition party.

János Kádár, the first secretary of the communist party, in a speech before the Front gave some clarification on this point by presenting the official regime policy:

> In the service of determined political purposes the Western bourgeois papers publish quite often articles about the liberalization, the loosening, of the Kádár regime. The writers of such articles and the politicians standing behind them are taking their wish-dreams for reality. . . . They would like to promote and bring about our weakening; this is why they write that the détente of international atmosphere makes possible such a People's Front movement which can lead to the revival of the coalition parties.[18]

HUNGARIAN SOCIALIST WORKERS' PARTY

Béla Kun, the leader of the Hungarian communist party in the aftermath of the First World War, in 1919 tried to establish a communist republic. After the collapse of his regime, the movement almost disappeared. Many of its members fled from Hungary to the U.S.S.R. and continued to work there under Soviet direction. Others stayed behind to engage in subversive activities. Some of the émigrés formed the nucleus for a new communist party of Hungary as the Second World War was approaching its end. Mátyás Rákosi, Ernö Gerö, Imre Nagy, and Mihály Farkas returned to Hungary in 1944 to assume leadership of the party.[19] Meanwhile another group of communists, headed by László Rajk, János Kádár, and Gyula Kállai, had organized a movement at Debrecen, the temporary government capital on "liberated" soil. In February 1945 these two groups merged.

The party was very small at the end of the war. Under the policy of rapid expansion that was then adopted, the usual high degree of selectivity with regard to membership was disregarded in an effort to attract as many people as possible, with the result that the number of members rose from 2,000 in 1944 to more than 1.4 million in 1949.[20] Part of the increase was achieved through a merger with left-wing Social Democrats in 1948, at which time a new name was assumed: the Hungarian Workers' party. Discipline was lax during this period, but was tightened up as the party gained more power.

Mátyás Rákosi's wing of the communist movement, known as the "Muscovites," was supported by the U.S.S.R. and the Red Army.[21] This man controlled the party and ruled over Hungary from 1945 to 1956, although his power was temporarily somewhat lessened between 1953 and 1955 when Imre Nagy held the premiership. Because Rákosi was out of step with the destalinization program, in July 1956 Khrushchëv had him removed. He was succeeded by Ernö Gerö. The Hungarian people, however, associated this man with Rákosi's policies.

No discussion of Hungarian affairs would be complete without at least mentioning the uprising of 1956 and its effect on the people. This event not only left its mark on the participants, but also has colored the nation's internal and external policies. There is no doubt that one of the main causes for the spread of the revolt in Hungary was the brutal intervention by the Soviet army. The seeds of the revolt, however, can be traced back to the Stalinist hard line of Rákosi. Between 1953 and 1955 the Hungarians enjoyed the softer policies of Imre Nagy because Moscow had dictated that Rákosi give up the premiership, although he retained the position of first secretary in the party.[22]

In February 1955 the line shifted, Rákosi returned to full power, and Nagy was expelled from the party. As Rákosi became more and more tyrannical in his rule, the dissident elements (primarily students and intelligentsia) began discussing a return to democracy through open revolt. Although Rákosi was ousted by the Soviet Union in July 1956, as mentioned, by then the Hungarian communist party and the pro-Soviet government had lost control of the country; that is, they could not effectively control the Hungarian population and the armed forces. Notably there was great sympathy among the military for the revolutionary movement. The secret police (AVH) was too weak, alone, to defend the regime.

The uprising of the Hungarians was short-lived and was doomed to failure when its Freedom Fighters were opposed by the troops and the superior military power of the Soviet Union.[23] The leaders of the U.S.S.R., on their part, could not allow one of the satellite countries to defect from the Soviet ideological camp or become neutral, let alone Western-oriented, because of the effect this might have on others, and it is upon such a background that present-day Hungarian policies must be viewed. The details of the rebellion and its suppression are well known.[24] János Kádár, chosen by the U.S.S.R. as the new premier and first secretary of the party, took over both posts on November 4, 1956. The party today is the one that has been shaped by Kádár, and its name, the Hungarian Socialist Workers' party (*Magyar Szocialista Munkáspárt*—MSZMP), is the one which he gave to his new organization.[25]

MEMBERSHIP AND SUPPORT. The only relatively free elections to be held in Hungary since the Second World War took place in November 1945. The communists suffered a defeat, with 83 percent of the votes going to other parties, but obtained representation in the government because of pressure by the Kremlin and the physical presence of Soviet troops in Hungary. In fact, the U.S.S.R. gave permission for the elections only after receiving promises from the noncommunist parties that they would include the communists in the government.[26]

After the 1956 revolt the Kádár regime did not attempt to reconstruct the party along its former lines. The leaders became more selective and allegedly brought into membership only those who really supported the communist movement, hoping thus to develop a hard core. During this period Kádár gradually purged the Rákosi and Gerö elements. Starting with the local and county organizations, and ultimately moving to the top echelon, dogmatic officials were eliminated from responsible positions. In several cases die-hard Stalinists at the highest level even found themselves expelled from the party.

The strength of the Hungarian Socialist Workers' party by the fall of 1962 had risen to more than half a million members.[27] This amounted to about 5 percent of the population. With the passage of time, the composition of the party also has changed. For example, in 1966 it was claimed that 42.5 percent of the membership consisted of workers or former workers (now at desk jobs, presumably) and 37.3 percent of intelligentsia.[28] This would indicate that the educated Hungarians were not boycotting the party. Because the leadership was not satisfied with the number of new members, ideological indoctrination had to be stepped up in order to increase the proportion of white-collar workers in the party (see table 25 for recent figures on the party's social composition). At the same time, the number of industrial workers has dropped. This may reflect the greater opportunism of the former and more disillusionment with the regime on the part of the latter.

TABLE 25

HUNGARIAN SOCIALIST WORKERS' PARTY
SOCIAL COMPOSITION, 1962 AND 1966

Category	Eighth Congress (November 1962)		Ninth Congress (November 1966)	
	Number of members	Percent of total	Number of members	Percent of total
Industrial workers (including farm workers)	301,035	58.8	248,561	42.5
Intelligentsia (white-collar workers)	46,589	9.1	218,149	37.3
Peasants	76,795	15.0	—	—
Armed forces	—	—	46,203	7.9
Pensioners	—	—	54,391	9.3
Students and others	—	—	17,545	3.0
Unaccounted for	87,546	17.1	—	—
Total	511,965	100.0	584,849	100.0

SOURCES: Radio Budapest, November 20, 1962. *Népszabadság*, November 29, 1966.

NOTE: Seven percent of the party members are graduates of a university, and 20 percent are secondary school graduates; the remaining 73 percent presumably have had little or no more formal education than that of the elementary school. *Hazai Tudósítások*, October 1, 1966, cited in RFE report (by William F. Robinson), "On the Eve of the Hungarian Party Congress," November 24, 1966 (13 pp.). In May 1967, party membership reached 626,532. *RFE Situation Report*, June 9, 1967, p. 3 (5 pp.).

Local and factory organizations provide a lower-level course in communist policies and principles, the townships offer intermediate instruction, and the county and major city organs conduct advanced training.[29] In addition to the Socialist Workers' party, mass organizations such as the Women's Association and the Communist Youth League (*Kommunista Ifjusági Szövetség—KISZ*) assist the communists in indoctrination work and control of the population. The KISZ, for instance, has some 743,769 members who can be used by the communist leaders to spread propaganda or to inform on non-members.[30]

PARTY ORGANIZATION. The structure of the communist party is a familiar one which in general emulates the Soviet model. At the bottom of the pyramid are approximately 17,400 primary party organizations.[31] These consist of members in all types of work, organized into cells. On the next level above are the district party organizations in the towns and cities. Members of the primary party organizations send representatives to the district conferences. There is no democracy in this procedure, however, as the representatives are hand-picked by the District Committees. The regional party organizations correspond to the nineteen major political subdivisions of the country and are run by Regional Committees elected at the district conferences.[32]

The national party congress meets every four years (the ninth was held during November 28-December 3, 1966) and elects a Central Committee to carry out policies. It is now composed of 101 full party members. Within the Central Committee is the Politburo, with eleven members and five candidates; its chairman is usually the party leader. The Secretariat of the party, also within the Central Committee, has six members and is responsible for supervising the implementation of Politburo decisions.[33] János Kádár holds the office of first secretary, which befits his role as party leader.

Since the October-November 1956 revolt, the Kádár regime has encouraged the development of a more relaxed political atmosphere. Probably because of this attitude, party organization at the lower levels is rather poor:

> Hungary's rural party organizations are in a sorry state. [A survey in Pest County found that] a fifth of the collective farms in the county had no party organization at all. Those that did had poor discipline. [The] party secretaries were often young and inexperienced.
>
> [In Borsod County] the rural party officials . . . are never around to solve internal problems or to recruit new members.[34]

Vas County also reported a decrease in party influence. One village in 1950 had more than a hundred members and in 1963 had only seven.[35] Some party members attribute this decline to Kádár's policy of denying them special privileges.

The general level of schooling among rural party leaders is very low. Up to 1960 the party was interested, above all, in political reliability and cared little about formal education. Hence the villagers gradually have reached educational levels superior to those of the rural party leaders.[36] Kádár has seen the danger in this development and is now emphasizing the selection of nonparty experts for government work. Knowledge of particular fields is apparently held to be more important than adherence to communist ideology. Some party members have begun to complain about this trend.

PARTY LEADERSHIP. Most of the men who built up the party during 1944 and 1945 by now have died, left the country, or gone into semiretirement because of disfavor. Of those who formally reestablished the movement toward the end of the war, just one (Antal Apró) remains in good standing. The highest posts in the party today are held by a younger group than at any other time. During the years 1945-1956 these men had worked in lower-level party organizations, in mass movements, or within government agencies. Kádár, as first secretary of the party, is assisted by a deputy, Béla Biszku,[37] and four other secretaries. Gyula Kállai is believed to be the heir apparent; in June 1965 he succeeded Kádár as premier, but in turn was replaced by Jenö Fock in April 1967.

POLICIES. At the Eighth Congress of the Hungarian communists, in November 1962, Kádár put emphasis on policies which suggested that the party had broken with its Stalinist past.[38] One of these policies, involving an amnesty for participants of the 1956 revolution, has had international significance. It removed a main obstacle to the acceptance of the Kádár regime by the West in general and the United States in particular.[39]

In speaking of his type of communism, Kádár subsequently stated: "If anybody stands today to the left of the socialist order of the state, the order of building socialism, then he actually stands for nothing but petty bourgeois radicalism and a great many confused ideas." [40] At meetings of East European communist leaders it is Kádár, reportedly, who preaches moderation and urges constant efforts to improve relations between East and West. Domestically, however, a

Politburo member and chief ideologist warned against the West as the "enemy" who plays the old tune "according to which the personality cult"—of Stalinist-type terror—"is the logical product of the socialist system." He added that for many persons, even in Hungary, this conclusion had been "confirmed by the way in which Comrade Khrushchëv was relieved of his duties." [41]

Although the party has liberalized some of its policies, given the population more freedom of action, and even restricted the activities of the secret police, it is still very much in control of Hungary. If the regime considers it necessary, it can and will institute tighter and harsher controls. The party's attitude toward the Hungarian people is displayed in the leaders' statements and acts. Although Kádár has said that "he who is not against us is with us," this does not mean that persons who express themselves openly against the regime will not be punished. The security police is still powerful and ready.[42] Even for Kádár, there is no crossing the ultimate ideological gap and allowing an opposition party to function.

DOMESTIC AND INTRA-ORBITAL AFFAIRS

In Hungary, as in much of Eastern Europe, agriculture was in a state of crisis during the years just before the Second World War. A catastrophic slump in farm prices, coupled with an uneconomic division of the land, had created a chaotic farming situation.[43] In 1945, with the approval of Soviet authorities, Imre Nagy (the Agriculture minister at the time) ordered the expropriation of large landholdings and distribution of small allotments to the peasantry. Collectivization was introduced immediately, because the communist party wanted to assist the "inevitable development" of *kolkhozes*.

AGRICULTURAL POLICIES. The five-year plan during 1950-1954 set extremely ambitious goals for the Hungarians. Statistics reveal that no governmental approach can so mismanage agricultural production as one based on a communist philosophy. Production of bread grain during this period was less than in 1911-1915, while the population to be fed was nearly 25 percent greater.[44] The former breadbasket of Eastern Europe had become an importer of grain.

The headlong rush of the communists to collectivize caused widespread dissatisfaction and antagonism. Agricultural production showed a decline because of mismanagement and attempted coercion on the part of government leaders. The abortive means used to stimu-late production included compulsory deliveries, high taxes, fines for alleged infringement of administrative regulations, and penalties ranging from admonition to death. In table 26, it is significant to note the rapid increase in collective farms in Hungary during a period

TABLE 26

HUNGARIAN COLLECTIVIZATION DRIVE, 1958-1962

Date	Units	Members	Percentage of cultivated land
December 31, 1958	3,507	168,920	14.6
December 31, 1959	4,489	564,568	41.1
October 30, 1960	4,419	881,756	60.6
March 31, 1961	4,572	1,203,904	75.6
September 30, 1962	4,022	1,174,101	79.6

SOURCE: V. A. Kryuchkov in a chapter on the "Building of Socialism in the Hun-garian People's Republic (1957-1962)," in L. N. Nezhinskii (ed.), *Revolyutsionnoe dvizhenie i stroitelstvo sotsializma v Vengrii* (Moscow, 1963), p. 16.

of less than four years (1959-1962),[45] due to the new policy under Kádár, which avoided terror and stressed methods of persuasion and indirect pressure. It is apparent that one criterion for judging the effectiveness of any communist leadership is its ability to promote collectivization, which remains in direct proportion to the amount of pressure applied. Some 97 percent of the cultivated land in 1965 was under collective or state farms.[46] (See table 27.)

The communists themselves have acknowledged that the peasants still have not become adapted to collectivization. In 1964 the private household plots accounted for 23.8 percent of the net agricultural production.[47] One inference that can be drawn is that, despite massive government efforts to promote collectivization, the profit motive still remains an important aspect of peasant psychology. Recent commu-nist pronouncements seem to encourage intensive cultivation of exist-ing private garden plots. The party also appears to recognize the importance of incentives in agriculture. During the years 1966-1970 the employment of young people in farming is supposed to be in-creased by 30 percent over the preceding five-year period.[48] To attain this goal, of course, some means for making rural employment at-tractive to them must be found and applied.

As in other communist countries, the government in Hungary faces the problem of putting into effect impossible agricultural policies. A Budapest newspaper in 1963 reported that 3,719 collective farms had been studied in order to classify them as good, mediocre, or weak. This survey found that 591 (16 percent) were good; 1,677 (18 percent), mediocre; and 1,451 (66 percent), weak.[49] Furthermore, a shortage of meat has existed for years, owing to the lack of incentive for fattening the cattle. Comparative figures released by the regime indicate that Hungary had 1,900,000 cattle in 1935, and 1,990,000 exactly thirty years later.[50]

TABLE 27

HUNGARY'S FARM AREA AND PRODUCTION, 1965

	Total area		Production	Share in national income
Category	Percent	Hectares	(percent)	(percent)
Socialized enterprises [a]	86.0	5,172.4	65	52
Garden plots [b]	10.9	655.6 ⎱		
Private farms	3.1	186.4 ⎰	35 ⎱	48 ⎰
Total	100.0	6,014.4	100	100

SOURCES: *Statisztikai Szemle* (August-September 1965), translated in *Hungarian Press Survey,* October 11, 1965, p. 39. Központi Statisztikai Hivatel, *Statisztikai Évkönyv* (Budapest, 1965), p. 148.

NOTE: More than one million private farms have been replaced with about 3,200 collectives. *Nográd,* September 28, 1966, translated in *Hungarian Press Survey,* October 13, 1966, p. 3. The collectives alone comprise 67.4 percent of the arable land. RFE, *Situation Report,* January 17, 1967.

[a] Collective farms, state farms, and village cooperative enterprises.

[b] Each individual garden plot encompasses 0.3 to 0.6 hectares and is part of the collective farm.

Of course, the goal is to make Hungary self-sufficient in grain, as it was before the war. Kádár's regime has, however, continued agricultural collectivization and the system of state farms despite poor results in grain yields. In addition, during the year 1964 some 40 percent of the state farms and 20 percent of the collectives admittedly operated at a loss.[51] Sharecropping, one of the "evils" of capitalism and its absentee landlord, has been introduced, and sharecropping families earn an average of 1,700 forints (23 to the U.S. dollar) per month, as compared with old men on collectives who earn only 8,000 to 9,000 forints ($350 to $450) per year.[52] The importance of private cultivation in general is shown by the statement of a regime source that private plots furnish "almost 50 percent of the country's horned cattle and pig stocks, 75 percent of the poultry, and from 70 to 80 percent of the milk." [53]

Hungary suffers from a shortage of fertilizer, prevalent throughout the Soviet bloc. Although production has received recently great emphasis and the 1961-1965 five-year plan proposed an increase of 75 percent, the country is still dependent on the U.S.S.R. for many of its agricultural chemicals. Moreover, production alone will not solve the problem. Fertilizers already available have been inefficiently used because of inadequate storage facilities, transportation bottlenecks, and peasant indifference.

The condition of agriculture in Hungary is typical of the vicissitudes which beset bloc agricultural efforts.[54] The doctrinaire approach of communism fails to recognize that among East European peasants there exists a mystical attachment to the land. The soil is viewed by those who work it with a sense of tradition and affinity that cannot be erased by regime decree. The failure of the communists to recognize these psychological attitudes has brought about the paradoxical situation of some peasants being willing to join the party but not to work on the communist-inspired collective farms.

INDUSTRIAL DEVELOPMENT. By March 1948 all large industrial enterprises (having a hundred or more employees) had become nationalized in Hungary. The development of a heavy industry was fostered with even more fanatic zeal than the transformation of agriculture. The first five-year plan, from 1950 to 1954, actually had as its purpose the changing of Hungary first from a mainly agricultural to a balanced agricultural and industrial economy, and then making it into an "iron and steel" country.[55] This attempt at almost overnight transformation took place at the expense of farm production and the manufacture of consumers' goods. The progress that was made toward developing heavy industry was achieved at considerable sacrifice by the population through a lowered standard of living.

Even before the death of Stalin, in 1953, there occurred a slow-down in the rate of industrialization throughout the satellite countries. The slackened pace could be attributed to an unrealistic basis for the attempted industrialization and to the pressure by the people for a decent standard of living. The declining rate of industrial output in the bloc countries during this period is reflected in the following comparisons, where production in the previous year is taken as 100 percent: 1951—130 percent; 1953—111 percent; 1955—108 percent.[56]

As in agriculture, there appeared to be a direct relationship between industrial output and the amount of pressure exerted on the population. After the unsuccessful first five-year plan ended in 1954, a one-year plan was adopted. It stressed an increase of consumers' goods. After the removal of Imre Nagy from the premiership in April 1955 heavy industry again came to be emphasized. These vacillations in the Hungarian economy took their toll in both human motivation and resources.

The effects of the 1956 rebellion and the subsequent Soviet reoccupation exerted an incalculable influence on Hungary. Large credits had to be granted by the Soviet Union [57] and by other satellite countries to aid recovery from the revolt (damage to physical assets, reduced productivity of the workers, and the loss of skilled technicians who had been killed or had fled abroad). Since Hungary is relatively deficient in raw materials but experienced in the manufacture of certain industrial items, the CMEA "division of labor" had great appeal. This organization gave every promise of completely reorienting Hungary's industrial development, which was to become compatible with and complementary to that of the other satellite economies. During the period 1957-1965, however, Hungarian trade with the bloc operated at a foreign exchange deficit of almost 3.5 billion forint.[58]

The industrial development of Hungary suffers from the same problems which beset the Soviet Union and the other East European states. There is widespread popular dissatisfaction with the low standard of living.[59] Hungarian leaders have made it clear, however, that increased investment in industry, the need to repay credits granted by the Soviet Union, and high military expenditures militate against any substantial, rapid increase in consumers' goods or the attainment of a West European standard of living. In Hungary, as in the other Soviet dependencies, politically expedient economic measures (such as the purchase of Cuban sugar at artificially high prices, submission to Moscow's discriminatory price structure, and compulsory aid to underdeveloped countries) limit economic development.[60]

Nationalization encompasses 98 percent of industry. This policy will continue, but certain innovations are being introduced. The government now provides financial assistance to plants that incur additional costs through technological improvements. On the other hand, tax penalties are levied against industries which turn out goods of inferior quality. Enterprises which reduced costs by 1.2 percent during 1964 were authorized to give their workers twelve to thirteen days' pay as a bonus, with an extra day added for each 0.1 percent reduction below the 1.2 percent goal. A new quota bonus has been fixed at 70 percent of that paid the previous year. It can be increased to 100 percent, if the profit plan has been implemented, and even up to 130 percent, depending on the extent of overfulfillment.[61]

Along with other East European countries, Hungary is moving in the direction of economic reform. An enlarged Central Committee plenum met late in May 1966 and adopted resolutions on reform in conjunction with the 1966-1970 five-year plan. The new plan maintains central direction over long-range tasks, but provides for their implementation by the individual enterprises, which will base their schedules on market demand. In the future, each factory will prepare its own plan. The state will apply credit, price, and interest policies to influence the economy indirectly. Even wages are to be established by individual factories within certain limits, which will depend upon profits.[62] The decisive feature of the entire reform program is the new price system, which reportedly will go into effect in January 1968 and will reflect the true value of each article.

CHURCH-STATE RELATIONS. In late 1963 there were some signs that governmental restrictions on clerical activity were being relaxed. Five bishops and one apostolic administrator attended the Vatican Council in Rome and were received by the pope. The leader of the Hungarian delegation, Bishop Endre Hamvas, told the Vatican Council that there were signs of "growing understanding" between Roman Catholics and other Christians in Hungary in the face of "the common danger of atheism." [63] One year later the Vatican signed an agreement with the regime in Budapest, as will be noted below.

Of all the forces at work in a society, there is probably none more annoying to the communists than a well-organized religion. This is particularly true of a church which owes its loyalty to a superior center outside the Soviet bloc. Religion works on the mind, and it is the mind that must be made subservient to the state or neutralized as a center of resistance to communist ideology. In addition, religious influence on the young people must be lessened, just as religious ties abroad must be severed.

Taking exception to any tolerance vis-à-vis the Roman Catholic Church, the initial Hungarian postwar regime under Mátyás Rákosi recognized that religion posed a serious threat to communism. In early 1949 the cardinal-primate of the church, Jozsef Mindszenty, was arrested and, after "confessing" to crimes, sentenced to life imprisonment. Rákosi miscalculated the effect of this move by the government, because Mindszenty became a martyr. The churches filled with both the "religiously" religious and the "politically" religious.[64]

The attempt to control religious groups produced one of the most vexing problems facing the communist regime in Hungary. Priests and other church officials were persecuted and driven from their posts. Government intervention in church activities led to the establishment of a State Office for Religious Affairs, an agency which supervises all denominational activities.[65] Representatives of this office have become known as the "mustached bishops," since they direct all ecclesiastical matters.

Great effort has been expended by the government to reduce Roman Catholic influence. Uncooperative priests were transferred to outlying parishes, monks and nuns expelled from seminaries, and religious orders disbanded. While the Mass and church services were allowed, certain communicants were placed under observation and sermons closely listened to. The oppression of the Catholic Church has received wide publicity, but Protestant churches were also watched and infiltrated by communist-oriented clergymen and lay leaders.

During the 1956 rebellion, churches were among the very first to shed communist restrictions and the regime's control apparatus. By attending church, the people manifested their deep-seated desires for freedom. This new religious tolerance did not, however, last long. After the crushing of the revolt, state control over the churches was reinstituted. Several new government policies toward religion developed, however, and while the regime refused to grant complete freedom to the churches, it did recognize the influence of religion on the population.

In June 1957 the Office for Religious Affairs was dissolved. Late in the year there came a resumption of government subsidy to the

Catholic Church,[66] and the communist-sponsored "peace movement" of priests was disbanded. While these steps indicated the regime's temporary desire to "coexist" with church officials, the state continued to exercise considerable control over the church and its leaders. The partial truce between church and state continued until after the 1958 elections. This balloting apparently caused the government to feel strong enough to drive what it considered to be a lasting wedge between the people and their religion. Catholic and Protestant bishops were required to take humiliating oaths of allegiance to the state, the Office for Religious Affairs was reestablished, and, once again, the government began to exercise open control over all church activities.

In the case of the Catholic Church, the regime will not allow for the primacy of the pope even in religious matters, but it has been unable to divorce the Hungarian Catholics from Rome. The churches have been described as "centers of silent resistance." [67] On September 15, 1964, the Vatican and the regime in Budapest signed an accord. This has given the Catholic Church once again the right to appoint its own bishops. On the other hand, the communist government still requires an oath of allegiance from the bishops. The accord was the first agreement between the Vatican and a communist government.[68]

In conclusion, Hungary has reached a close approximation to the Soviet model state. Collectivization of agriculture and nationalization of industry have changed the country's political, social, and economic appearance. There has occurred also a clever shift in tactics; the strong-arm approach of early collectivization and industrialization has been replaced by more subtle methods. One goal has been to divorce the farmer from his land. The peasant's intricate and traditional social pattern is now being broken. The related attempt to substitute an alien ideology for the traditional agrarian loyalties has not been achieved in full as yet.

In Hungary there remains the feeling that things may yet change for the better,[69] that a future crisis either in the U.S.S.R. or in the West may bring the Hungarian plight to the fore once again. Kádár is trying hard to convince the people that the future of Hungary is unalterably and unequivocally tied to that of the Soviet Union.[70] Barring a major shift in the balance of power, this premise unfortunately may prove valid.

NOTES

1 The five political groupings—Hungarian Workers' (communist), Socialist, Citizens-Democratic, Smallholders, and People's Peasant—were organized into a National Independence Front. See G. V. Barabashev, *Gosudarstvennyi stroi Vengerskoi Narodnoi Respubliki* (Moscow, 1961), p. 4.

2 Admitted by Dezhe Nemesh [Dezsö Nemes], *Vengriya: 1945-1961* (Moscow, 1962), p. 36. The author further states that the communists increased this in the next election (May 15, 1949) to only 23 percent, despite the use of terror.

The spurious People's Front for Independence, established in February 1949, became merged into the so-called People's Patriotic Front for the election itself and has continued to operate in subsequent elections as a tool of the communist party.

3 Ernst C. Helmreich (ed.), *Hungary* (New York, 1957), p. 81.

4 George Pálóczi-Horváth, *The Undefeated* (Boston, 1959), p. 246.

5 Zbigniew K. Brzeziński, *The Soviet Bloc* (rev. ed., New York, 1961), p. 78. Actually, the Third Congress of the Hungarian communist party, in September 1946, already had announced a "people's democracy."

6 Amos J. Peaslee (ed.), *Constitutions of Nations* (2d ed.; The Hague, 1956), II, 185.

7 For example, in the fall of 1961 there were still some 80,000 private entrepreneur-artisans. This figure represented a drop by one-third from the four preceding years. Nemesh, *op. cit.*, p. 65.

8 More than 500 instructors at the university level, nearly 400 in party schools and more than 2,000 propagandists in the public school system are teaching Marxism-Leninism to instill this faith. *Népszabadság*, April 18, 1965, translated in *Hungarian Press Survey*, April 26, 1965; hereafter cited as *HPS*.

9 RFE, *Situation Report,* June 28, 1966, pp. 1-2. The transfer of Gyula

Kállai from premier to chairmanship of parliament in April 1967 may indicate this body will become more active.

10 Article 62, in Peaslee (ed.), *op. cit.*, p. 195.

A new election law passed November 11, 1966, introduces the theoretical possibility of several candidates from each district. All, however, will be selected from the Patriotic Front. RFE, *Situation Report,* November 15, 1966, p. 1. Parliamentary elections have been announced for March 19, 1967. *New York Times,* January 2, 1967.

11 He is Pál Losonczi, who had been Agriculture Minister from 1960 to 1967. *Népszabadság*, April 15, 1967.

12 Listed in *Line-Up,* p. 17.

13 These councils, the equivalent of soviets in the U.S.S.R., are mentioned in an amendment to the constitution. See Law VIII, published in *Magyar Közlöny* (1954), No. 73, translated (Russian) in Y. V. Yakimovich, *Vengerskaya Narodnaya Respublika: gosudarstvennyi stroi* (Moscow, 1960), p. 27.

14 Otto Bihari in an article on "Representative Democracy," *Társadalmi Szemle* (August-September 1965), translated in *HPS,* September 4, 1965, discusses modernization of these bodies along lines desired by him.

15 Article 41, in Peaslee (ed.), *op. cit.*, p. 193. See also *Civil Code of the Hungarian People's Republic* (Budapest, 1960).

16 Helmreich (ed.), *op. cit.*, p. 85.

17 Cited in *U. S. News and World Report,* April 20, 1964, p. 53.

18 Radio Kossuth, March 19, 1964. For an excellent analysis of Kádár see the article by Vincent Savarius in *Osteuropäische Rundschau,* XII, No. 11 (November 1966), 11-15.

19 Paul E. Zinner, *Revolution in Hungary* (New York, 1962), p. 73.

20 For a good study of the communist movement during the early period see Robert Gábor, *Organization and Strategy of the Hungarian Workers'*

(Communist) Party (New York, 1952), especially pp. 1-15.

21 Denis Silagi, *Ungarn* (Hannover, 1964), pp. 83-86.

22 Subsequently, however, Nagy was accused of "left-wing errors" and "revisionism" during this period. M. A. Usievich, *Razvitie sotsialisticheskoi ekonomiki Vengrii* (Moscow, 1962), p. 132.

23 The name Freedom Fighters (*Szabadságharzocosok*) originated in the 1848 insurrection, led by Lajos Kossuth, against Habsburg rule. Tsarist Russian troops put down the insurrection when the Austrians could not do so. The echoes in 1956 are interesting.

For the part allegedly played by the United States in "fomenting" the 1956 revolt see I. I. Orlik, *Vengerskaya Narodnaya Respublika* (Moscow, 1962), pp. 51-53.

24 See Ferenc A. Váli, *Rift and Revolt in Hungary* (Cambridge, Mass., 1961), pp. 243-282.

Reportedly, during the aftermath of the revolt some 63,000 Hungarians were deported to Siberia; as of January 1965 there were 463 participants still in Central Prison at Budapest; and 143 who were under eighteen years of age in 1956 had since been executed. Béla Fábián and the Rev. Imre Kovács, "Kadar's Hungary," letter to the editor, *New York Times Magazine,* January 24, 1965, p. 6.

Kádár commemorated the crushing of the revolt on its tenth anniversary by laying wreaths on the graves of "victims of the counterrevolution." *New York Times,* November 6, 1966.

25 A decision taken allegedly on his own initiative, according to an official biography. Yu. Egorov (ed.), *Yánosh Kádár; izbrannye statii i rechi (1957-1960 gody)* (Moscow, 1960), pp. 622-623.

26 Jozsef Koevágo, "Establishment and Operation of a Communist State Order," in Robert F. Delaney (ed.), *This Is Communist Hungary* (Chicago, 1958), p. 197. By contrast, it is claimed that 98.9 percent of the votes cast during the 1963 elections to parliament went to the single slate pro-posed by the communists. *World Strength,* p. 56.

27 Yánosh Kádár, *Otchëtnyi doklad Tsentralnogo Komiteta Vengerskoi Sotsialisticheskoi Rabochei Partii VIII sezdu partii* (Moscow, 1963), p. 75. It was admitted that some 38 percent of these had joined after May 1957—that is, after the revolt.

Only 300,000 from among 850,000 pre-revolt members reapplied for admission to the reconstituted communist party. *HPS,* August 29, 1966, citing excerpts from Sandor Nogradi's book on "The Start of a New Chapter in History" (Budapest, 1966).

28 *Népszabadság,* November 29, 1966.

29 L. N. Nezhinskii (ed.), *Revolyutsionnoe dvizhenie i stroitelstvo sotsializma v Vengrii* (Moscow, 1963), pp. 44-45.

30 This represents a decline from 800,-000 in 1964 and comprises 40 percent of the 14-26 age group. *Népszabadság,* December 21, 1965. The KISZ is organized into about 21,000 basic units, and 12.3 percent of the membership also belongs to the communist party. *Partelet,* June 1967.

31 Kádár, *op. cit.,* p. 66.

32 For the secretaries of these nineteen committees see U.S. Department of State, Bureau of Intelligence and Research, *Directory of Hungarian Officials* (Washington, D.C., July 1966), pp. 57-75.

33 These figures pertain to organs elected in December 1966 at the party's Ninth Congress. See *Népszabadság,* December 4, 1966, for names of incumbents at that time. Compare *Line-Up,* p. 16, for other identifications as of July 1967.

34 *East Europe,* XII, No. 7 (July 1963), 45.

35 *Ibid.,* XII, No. 11 (November 1963), 42.

36 *Ibid.,* XIII, No. 2 (February 1964), 45.

37 Identified as such in RFE, *Situation Report,* May 3, 1966, p. 2.

38 Kádár, *op. cit.,* pp. 60-62.

39 The United States raised its diplomatic relations with Hungary to ambassadorial level on November 28, 1966. That same day, János Kádár

called for communist unity against "our common enemy" (meaning the United States). James Reston in the *New York Times,* November 30, 1966.

40 Quoted in *East Europe,* XII, No. 4 (April 1964), 42. See also RFE, *Situation Report,* September 30, 1966, p. 3.

41 Reported in an article by István Szirmai ("On Some Timely Ideological Tasks of the Hungarian Socialist Workers' Party"), in *Társadalmi Szemle,* April 1965, translated in *HPS,* April 20, 1965, p. 5.

42 A wave of arrests over several recent months has involved two groups: a Roman Catholic organization, Regnum Marianum, and individuals who participated in the 1956 revolt. *Népszabadság,* February 19, 1966, as cited by the *New York Times,* February 20, 1966.

43 Hubert Ripka, *Eastern Europe in the Post-War World* (New York, 1961), p. 9.

44 Váli, *op. cit.,* p. 87.

45 The communists admit that even in 1957, before the main collectivization drive, there existed no more than three thousand *kulaks* or wealthy peasants who "exploited" the labor of others. Barabashev, *op. cit.,* p. 21, n. 2.

46 State farms in 1965 numbered 214 and encompassed 16.5 percent, or more than one million hectares, of agricultural land. *Statisztikai Szemle,* February 1966, cited in RFE report, "State Farms in Hungary," July 14, 1966 (13 pp.). See table 27.

47 Gyula Varga, "The Household Plot," *New Hungarian Quarterly,* Autumn 1966, p. 10, reproduced in *HPS,* November 14, 1966.

48 *Társadalmi Szemle,* October 1965, as cited in RFE, *Situation Report,* October 19, 1965, p. 1.

49 Cited in "Down on the Collective Farm," *East Europe,* XII, No. 7 (July 1963), 46.

50 *Népszabadság,* December 21, 1965, as cited in RFE, *Situation Report,* December 28, 1965, p. 2.

51 *Népszabadság,* September 17, 1965,

as cited in RFE, *Situation Report,* September 21, 1965.

52 *New York Times,* August 26, 1965. Almost half (41.5 percent) of all collectivized farmers are over sixty years of age, according to a commentary on Radio Budapest, February 7, 1966.

53 Report on a "Round Table Conference on Private Plot Committees," Radio Kossuth, April 24, 1965, translated in *HPS,* April 28, 1965, p. 8.

54 Hungary must import close to 400,-000 tons of bread grain and 500,000 tons of fodder grain during 1967. RFE, *Situation Report,* October 7, 1966, p. 3, and November 25, 1966, p. 3.

55 Váli, *op. cit.,* p. 82.

56 Edward Taborsky, "The 'Old' and the 'New' Course in Satellite Economy," *Journal of Central European Affairs,* XVII, No. 4 (January 1958), 383.

57 The U.S.S.R. reportedly gave Hungary the equivalent of U.S. $320 million in credits during the 1956-1958 period. Lucjan Ciamaga, *Od współpracy do integracji* (Warsaw, 1965), pp. 39-40.

58 Currently some 70 percent of Hungary's foreign trade takes place within the CMEA area and almost half of this is with the U.S.S.R. *Kommunist vooruzhënnykh sil,* XLIV, No. 4 (February 1966), 68. Source for the deficit is RFE report, "Hungary's International Debts," April 18, 1966 (11 pp.), based on official statistical materials.

59 The announcement that food prices would go up, made just before Christmas 1965, was followed by an increase in the cost of fuel averaging 25 percent. Radio Budapest, March 22, 1966. See the excellent RFE report (by J. F. Brown), "Hungary in the Decade Since the Revolution," October 4, 1966 (7 pp.).

60 Ferenc A. Váli, "Hungary Faces the Future," *Current History,* XLIV, No. 261 (May 1963), 292. For the 1967 trade agreement, increasing commercial exchanges by 16 percent over 1966, see RFE, *Situation Report,* November 29, 1966, p. 1.

61 *Népszabadság,* September 17, 1965, as cited in RFE, *Situation Report,*

September 21, 1965, pp. 1-2. The current economic plan is discussed in an RFE report, "Analysis of the Third Five-Year Plan of Hungary (1966-1970)," October 3, 1966 (pamphlet, 30 pp.).

62 *Népszabadság,* May 29, 1966, published the resolutions: cited by RFE, *Situation Report,* May 31, 1966, pp. 1-4. See also the statement by Deputy Premier and Politburo member Jenö Fock in *Társadalmi Szemle,* October 1966, as summarized in RFE, *Situation Report,* October 14, 1966, pp. 2-3, which enumerates six specific measures preparatory to the reform.

63 See "Hungarian Bishops Abroad," *East Europe,* XIII, No. 1 (January 1964), 42.

64 Váli, *Rift and Revolt in Hungary,* p. 65.

65 This office also supervises the Jewish religious community, whose approximately 100,000 persons have only thirty rabbis, according to their chief spokesman, Imre Benoschofsky. *New York Times,* August 9, 1966.

66 This subsidy had been paid by the government to the churches before the revolt. Resumption of payments marked a step in the attempt by the state to regain financial control over the church. See also U.S. Senate, Committee on the Judiciary, *The Church and State Under Communism* (Washington, D.C., 1965), VI, 10-11.

67 Váli, *Rift and Revolt in Hungary,* p. 452.

68 Commentary by Sándor Fekete over Radio Budapest, September 26, 1964.

69 This optimism is tempered in practice by an annual rate of 180,000 induced abortions as against 130,000 live births per year. *Népszabadság,* March 13, 1966, translated in *HPS,* March 23, 1966. Since deaths average about 100,000 per year, there is a net increase of only 30,000 annually —in a population of more than ten million.

70 See his interview with UPI, as published by *Népszabadság,* August 2, 1966, translated in *HPS,* August 18, 1966, p. 21.

Chapter 6 / POLAND:
Captive Eagle

THE U.S.S.R. accomplished a classic operation when it installed a puppet communist regime at Warsaw. All odds were against such a transformation. The countries of Eastern Europe were more receptive to democracy after the Second World War than they had been after the First.[1] The populations had become completely disenchanted with semi-dictatorships and been disgusted by the ruthless Nazi and Soviet occupation forces. The Poles in particular, with their homogeneity and intense nationalism, craved such basic democratic attributes as self-government, freedom of speech, and private ownership. They also sought freedom to practice their Roman Catholic religion, an ideology diametrically opposed to the atheistic communist system that was being imposed upon them from the outside.

Given the foregoing factors, and assuming freedom of choice, Poland would seem to be the East European country least likely to fall under Soviet domination. Yet Poland so fell and remains even today under the control of a communist regime. The governmental structure is patterned, in all important aspects, after that of the U.S.S.R. Although two subordinate political organizations exist, there is no doubt as to who rules in Warsaw: the communist Polish United Workers' party (*Polska Zjednoczona Partia Robotnicza—* PZPR).

Historically, the Russians have maintained the belief that whoever controls the eastern countries holds predominance in all of Europe. A corollary belief is that the power which holds Poland is in a key position throughout Eastern Europe. At the Yalta conference, in February 1945, Stalin agreed to a formula for establishing a Polish government through "free and unfettered elections as soon as possible on the basis of universal suffrage and secret ballot." [2] But the Soviets interpreted the words "free" and "unfettered" in their own totalitarian manner. Their understanding of a government "friendly" to the U.S.S.R., such as the formula also proposed, comprehended only a regime that would act in blind obedience to the Kremlin. They therefore quickly exploited the early postwar situation and pushed ahead with typical Trojan horse tactics. These consisted of infiltration, subversion, purges, and terrorism, all directed toward getting control over communications, elections, and sensitive government positions —particularly the Interior ministry and its security police.

ELECTORAL PROCEDURES

In the years since the Second World War there have been five occasions on which the communist leadership asked the people of Poland to decide on the composition of the government by so-called secret balloting. These were the parliamentary elections. The first, in 1947, came during the intermediate stage in the subjugation of Eastern Europe by the U.S.S.R. The goal was clear: to eliminate, by any means necessary (including violence, deception, and falsified results), all opposition. The campaign was directed primarily against the Polish Peasant party [3] and the Roman Catholic Church. Despite widespread dissatisfaction and disillusionment on the part of the Polish population, the ruthlessly conducted campaign rewarded the communists with success.

By 1952 there was little need to fire bullets or falsify ballots. The communists were in full control. Statutes had been promulgated which made it impossible for an opposition candidate to be considered for election. All of the unopposed 425 United Front "candidates" for the parliament received overwhelming "majorities." As might have been predicted, it was announced that more than fifteen million persons, or 95 percent of the electorate, had voted.

The characteristics which distinguished the 1957 and 1961 elections still prevail in the political scene today and probably will continue during the predictable future. They include (1) an apparent although superficial relaxation of the dictatorial stranglehold on the population, (2) a very real yet subtle and sophisticated communist totalitarianism, and (3) public awareness of the true conditions, resulting in widespread apathy.

In 1957 the elections were somewhat modified by allowing a larger number of candidates than seats available in the parliament (a total of 750 candidates for 459 seats). In view of the fact that all opposition parties had been liquidated in 1947 and none had been allowed to come into existence in the ten years since then, the ruling party presumably considered this to be a safe concession. Even so, the communist leaders had misgivings about the turnout at the polls and the possibility of widespread crossing out of communist names from the ballot by the voters.

To eliminate these doubts, the communist party leader Władysław Gomułka delivered a major speech to the nation shortly before the election. "Deletion of our party's candidates," he warned, "is synonymous with obliterating Poland from the map of Europe." Just prior to the voting he stated: "The point is whether we shall be able to broaden further the democratization of our life or whether we shall be compelled to narrow it." [4] The implication was that, unless support appeared to be overwhelming, Poland might suffer the fate of Hungary. The voters dutifully heeded the warning and advice.

Much the same procedure was followed in 1961, and this time there was noticeably less "overwhelming" support. For example, in Warsaw only 55 percent of the eligible voters bothered to register. The explanation for this, however, probably does not include the resistance and new spirit of independence that some writers have mentioned in their analyses of recent elections. The emotion of the electorate can best be described as apathy. There is no hope for outside help, other than what is provided by Western radio broadcasts. The tragedy in Hungary offered final proof that an uprising would be crushed by Soviet armed forces.

In the 1965 elections there were 617 candidates for 460 seats in the parliament.[5] The formality of voting took place on May 30, with results shown in table 28. In only one way could the population manifest its discontent—by crossing off the names of persons belonging to the communist elite. Among the districts of large population, with several seats out of the total of 460, a candidate whose name was crossed off by numerous voters could still be elected, provided he received more than 50 percent of the ballots, but his ranking within the district would drop below that of other successful candidates, who received a higher percentage of the popular vote. This kind of ranking may serve as a possible basis for judging the public image or popularity of each candidate.

Within the eighty electoral districts, however, only three Politburo members could maintain their top ranking after the election: Gomułka, the party's first secretary; Spychalski, the Defense minister; and Gierek, the chief of the Silesian industrial province.[6] Four of the party leaders dropped to the last possible elected position on their

TABLE 28

POLISH PARLIAMENTARY ELECTIONS, 1965

Party or other group	Seats won	Percentage of total vote
Polish United Workers' party	255	55.5
United Peasant party	117	25.4
Democratic party	39	8.5
Nonparty	36	7.8
Catholic activists	13	2.8
Total	460	100.0

SOURCE: *Trybuna ludu*, June 3, 1965.

NOTE: The Peasant and Democratic parties' representations remained exactly as they had been during the 1961-1964 period. The communist Polish United Workers' party gave up one seat to the "nonparty" group. The Catholics gained two seats from the latter group. Józef Gutt (ed.), *Polska Ludowa; słownik encyklopedyczny* (Warsaw, 1965), p. 329.

respective lists: Kliszko, the unofficial second secretary; Szyr, a deputy premier; Strzelecki, the secretary in charge of police; and Jaszczuk, the secretary for heavy industry. Three others came out just before last in the number of votes for their districts: Cyrankiewicz, the premier; Ochab, the titular president; and Jagielski, the Agriculture minister. Waniołka, a deputy premier, did somewhat better as third from the bottom.

THE 1952 CONSTITUTION

The farce of the Polish "people's" democratic governmental structure extends to its very foundation, namely, the constitution. On the surface, the constitution possesses all elements of a progressive legislative instrument written by representatives of the people to serve the people. In actual fact, it was prepared by a hard core of Russian-trained communist party leaders. In most respects, it derives from the 1936 "Stalin" constitution which is still in force throughout the U.S.S.R.

The preamble to Poland's basic law provides an opening clue to the democratic façade. Unlike its 1921 or 1935 predecessors, this document expresses no religious dependence. References to God have been replaced by expressions of allegiance and gratitude to the almighty Soviet Union. A second clue can be found in the obvious alignment with the U.S.S.R. structure, which until recently claimed to be centered on the proletariat. The Polish constitution of 1952 avowedly relates itself to "the historical experience of the victorious socialist constitution in the U.S.S.R., the first state of workers and peasants." [7]

Following the preamble, the document consists of three principal segments divided into 10 chapters and 91 articles. Opening and closing chapters describe in general terms the political, social, and economic structure of the people's democracy. Aesopian language comes into full play throughout Chapters I-II, with discussions of free elections, social and economic equality, as well as a government operated by and for the peasants and workers. The middle section, Chapters III-VI, deals with the principal state organs: the legislature, executive, and judiciary.

LEGISLATURE. The parliament, or *Sejm,* is designated as the supreme organ of state authority. Its 460 members are elected to four-year terms. Full sessions are held once every six months.[8] Theoretically, the *Sejm* makes laws, controls other state agencies, and appoints and recalls the government. It is also the institution which formally elects the Council of State. In actual practice, this body merely gives official approval to drafts of laws proposed by the executive organs of government. In recent years, however, there has been considerable debate in the *Sejm.* Although regime proposals always pass, some of the deputies have recorded negative votes on legislation.

COUNCIL OF STATE. This body, elected from and by the parliament to four-year terms in office, consists of a chairman who acts as chief of state, four deputy chairmen, a secretary, and eleven other members.[9] The Council possesses authority to call elections, summon parliament, interpret laws, issue decrees, appoint and recall diplomatic representatives, supervise local People's Councils, and legislate during intervals between *Sejm* sessions.

In general, it can be said that the Council performs most of the functions formerly assigned to the presidency. It is not a vitally important policy-making body. The elimination of the presidency and transfer of its functions to the Council of State aligned the governmental structure closer to that of the Soviet Union and other East European countries.

Up to 1952 the post of president was filled by Bolesław Bierut, who also headed the Polish communist party. During the next fourteen years, Aleksander Zawadzki served as chairman of the Council of State. He was reelected twice by the *Sejm,* in 1957 and again in 1961. Since Zawadzki's death in early August 1964, Edward Ochab has been titular chief of state and also a member of the Political Bureau.[10] It was Ochab who stepped down from the leadership of the party during October 1956 in favor of Władysław Gomułka.

COUNCIL OF MINISTERS. This body is defined as representing the highest executive and administrative organ of state authority. Its duties include coordination of the ministries, preparation of the budget and economic plans, supervision over public law and order, control of foreign and defense policies, and direction over the presidia in the People's Councils. In 1967 the Council consisted of twenty-nine members, headed by a chairman or premier.[11]

This instrument of the government supposedly is the key policy-making agency. Just as in the U.S.S.R., however, it serves merely as a legal façade for the party organization. It is interesting that all but four of the ministers are also important members of the communist Polish United Workers' party. The four comprising this small minority belong to either the United Peasant or the Democratic party, both communist-controlled. The Council has been headed since 1954 by Józef Cyrankiewicz, who is thus the premier.[12] A former socialist, he is considered to be a figurehead but a useful one, as was exemplified by his 1965 visit with President de Gaulle in France.

THE PEOPLE'S COUNCILS. These organs are very similar in all respects to the soviets in the U.S.S.R. They are local administrative units existing in each commune (5,238 units), settlement (102), town (784), county (317), city district (39), and province (22). The term of office in the 6,502 councils is four years.[13] Their main functions include adoption of local economic plans and budgets, supervision over local law enforcement, maintaining public services, and, in general, linking local needs to state tasks. Executive organs called presidia are responsible to their closest higher echelon, with the province-level presidia subordinated in turn to the Council of State.

Activities of the People's Councils are defined in a law of January 25, 1958, as having competence over: protection of public order; agriculture; local industry and handicrafts; local building and the development of towns and villages; communal housing management and policy; domestic trade; government purchases; public transportation and the construction and maintenance of roads; management of waterways; education and culture; health, education, and tourism; unemployment; social welfare; and finances. Local budgets in 1963 encompassed 28.4 percent of the total state budget, exactly twice the proportion allocated ten years previously.[14] More than 171,000 councilors were elected in 1965, after a "campaign" that lasted over two months and involved some 60,000 meetings with a reported five million participants. The bulk of the councilors are in the commune or village bodies, whose members total about 120,000.

THE JUDICIAL SYSTEM. This area of government is administered by the Supreme Court for the country as a whole. Province, county, and special courts operate at successively lower levels. Justices on the Supreme Court are elected to five-year terms by the Council of State. Lower-ranking judges receive their appointments from the Justice minister.[15] The makeup of the judicial system shows the absence of any separation of powers. No provision exists for judicial review, and the interpretation of law belongs to the Council of State, which is a body theoretically created by the parliament. A prosecutor general investigates offenses harmful to the safety and independence of the Polish People's Republic. He is assisted by a militia (regular uniformed police) and a secret police.

CONSTITUTIONAL PRACTICE. In any discussion of the governmental structure, it would be a serious error to overlook a concept adopted by the communist hierarchy and known as "constitutional practice." Under this practice, directives are issued which supposedly interpret the real meaning of provisions in the constitution. Changes are made in the content of some provisions, while others are rejected. New regulations or institutions are introduced, not envisioned by the constitution.

There have been many examples of "constitutional practice" since adoption in 1952 of the fundamental law. By passage of an ordinary resolution, for instance, it is always possible for the *Sejm* to expel members. This concept has also enabled members of the parliament to ignore constitutional provisions forbidding them to hold government posts and government officials from holding more than one post simultaneously. In effect, there is no binding constitutional law. The constitution can be manipulated and reinterpreted in any manner that the party sees fit and that will best serve its needs.

DEMOCRATIC CENTRALISM. A key principle in communist governmental methods is designated by the term "democratic centralism," which refers to an organizational theory developed by Lenin and also to a technique first put into practice by him. The principle, in both aspects, arose from Lenin's demand for a tight centralized control which should at the same time allow for flexibility of execution and mass participation in administrative actions. The principle is thus used vertically, in centralized control, and horizontally, in mass participation. This system also has been called "dual subordination."

All policy decisions and directives emanate from the top and filter down vertically to the lowest echelons in the governmental structure. There is little room for interpretation and none for interference or disagreement. At the same time, a horizontal line of activity is carried on by the various territorial units. Each of these performs specific administrative tasks within its own limited sphere. It is apparent that once again the Aesopian language needs interpretation. What the propaganda statements allude to as "local democratic autonomy" is not in fact local, democratic, or autonomous. Such statements merely signify that the implementation of centralized directives is locally administered.[16]

THE COMMUNIST PARTY

The population of Poland is approximately 32 million. Of this number, about two million belong to the ruling political organization. (See table 29.) Similarly to the Communist Party of the Soviet Union, the Polish United Workers' party—the PZPR—maintains a dictatorship in the name of the working class, which itself has only minority representation in the party. How is it possible that a few men in control of a movement having only a minority of the people as members can maintain such regimentation over a nation? The answer lies in the structure of the party and the principle of democratic centralism.

GENERAL ORGANIZATION. The Polish communist party is organized along five distinct levels. Each one of these, with the exception of the primary party organization at the bottom, includes a body of delegates from lower echelons. At the intermediate levels these bodies are called conferences; when assembled on a national scale they form the party congress. Conferences and congresses are too large for handling routine party business. Therefore they form smaller committees for day-to-day activities. The committees then elect bureaus and even smaller organs, secretariats, to handle party affairs.

TABLE 29

GROWTH OF THE POLISH COMMUNIST PARTY, 1942-1967

Date	Number of members	Date	Number of members
1942 (July)	4,000	1954 (March)	1,297,000
1943 (January)	8,000	1956 (January)	1,344,000
1944 (July)[a]	20,000	1959 (March)	1,067,000
1945 (January)	30,000	1961 (July)	1,270,000
1946 (July)	364,000	1963 (January)	1,397,000
1947 (July)	848,000	1964 (June)	1,493,000
1948 (December)[b]	1,500,000	1965 (January)	1,640,000
1950 (December)	1,360,000	1966 (June)	1,848,000
1952 (June)	1,129,000	1967 (May)	2,000,000

SOURCES: Richard F. Staar, *Poland, 1944-1962* (Baton Rouge, 1962), p. 167 (citing various Polish sources for the years 1942-1961). Tadeusz Galiński (ed.), *Rocznik polityczny i gospodarczy 1963* (Warsaw, 1963), p. 98. *Polityka,* June 6, 1964, p. 12. *Trybuna ludu,* October 31, 1965, August 14, 1966 and May 17, 1967.

[a] Some 8,000 of these returned from the U.S.S.R. with the advancing Red Army. *Nowe drogi,* V, No. 11 (January-February 1951), 235.
[b] After the fusion congress with the socialists.

These smaller units and the individual secretaries theoretically are responsible to the parent group on the same level, reporting to it on implementation of tasks.[17] All meetings, committees, organs, and individual secretaries are also sensitive to direction coming from higher-ranking levels and report to them. In this horizontal and vertical responsibility the principle of democratic centralism or dual subordination, manifests itself. The tripartite division of authority at each level (meeting, committee, organ) is in reality a device used to create the feeling among rank-and-file party members that they are involved in decision making. The real authority rests with the holder of the key post at each level, the secretary or first secretary who is the head of the executive organ.

Relationships among the five party levels are governed by a statute issued at the third congress of the Polish communist party, in 1959, and amended by the fourth congress, in 1964. This document defines the principle of democratic centralism. Relations among the levels are guided by the following rules which appear under Chapter II, paragraph 17, of the statute:

> All directing authorities from the lowest to the highest are elected in a democratic manner.
> All party resolutions are passed by a majority vote.
> All party authorities are required to report to the party organizations [which elect them].
> Maintenance of party discipline [is required,] and the minority is subordinate to the resolutions of the majority.
> Resolutions and directives from higher party authorities must be carried out by lower ones.[18]

The five rules comprise a system of checks and controls which allows only one man freedom of action. That man is the first secretary of the party (1943-1948 and since 1956), Władysław Gomułka. An important aspect of this situation for Gomułka is the unknown degree of control that Moscow maintains over him. It is no longer a matter of dictation; this has been replaced by sophisticated techniques.

Theoretically, ultimate control in the party rests with the meetings of members—at the highest level, the congress; at intermediate levels, the conferences; at the bottom, the primary party organization meeting. In actual practice these bodies are little more than rubber-stamp organs whose consent serves to legalize, in the eyes of the rank and file, the actions taken by the party leaders. Almost 68,000 primary party organizations represent the base for this vast façade for the few who actually make decisions in Poland today. There are three types of primary party organizations:

> *Institutional,* for party members working in factories, mines, railroad yards, government agencies, hospitals, or universities.
> *Village,* in rural areas for peasants, artisans, teachers, and doctors.
> *Territorial,* in urban areas for those who work in small shops which do not have a primary party organization or those who—e.g., housewives—are unemployed.[19]

Of the three types, the institutional is normally the largest. If the organization has more than a hundred members, it can be subdivided into brigades, aggregate units, work areas, or shifts, according to the specific production links of the industry involved. General meetings of the primary party organization are being replaced by institutional, village, and territorial conferences of delegates from the smaller units. This sort of conference, by not meeting at the lowest party level, provides for much tighter control over the individual members' participation. Whether it be at the level of the primary party organization, the commune, the county, or the province,[20] all activity and work is handled, theoretically, in accordance with the principle of democratic centralism. Concentration of power in the hands of a small elite is perpetuated through this procedure.

All meetings, conferences, commission sessions, and the like, supposedly expressing the attitudes of Polish United Workers' party members, remain open to influence from above. Itinerant groups from higher authority will attend a meeting to see whether all is proceeding in accordance with the first secretary's wishes. A good example of this principle on an international scale occurred during the eighth plenary session of the Polish party's Central Committee. The meeting had just started when the chairman announced the arrival of Nikita S. Khrushchëv, Vyacheslav Molotov, Lazar Kaganovich, and Anastas Mikoyan, among others. The top hierarchy in Moscow, having learned that standard operating procedures were not being observed in Poland, had come to find out why. This took place in October 1956 and was accompanied by simultaneous Soviet troop movements in the direction of Warsaw.

THE NATIONAL CONGRESS. In December 1945 the Polish communist party's first postwar congress convened.[21] There have been four congresses since that time. The "fusion congress" of 1948 saw the forced merger of the left-wing socialists with the PZPR and for that reason is known as the first. The successive congresses have convened as follows:

> First postwar congress . . . . . December 6-12, 1945
> First PZPR congress . . . . December 15-21, 1948
> Second PZPR congress . . . . . March 10-17, 1954
> Third PZPR congress . . . . . . March 10-19, 1959
> Fourth PZPR congress . . . . . June 15-20, 1964

Party congresses at first were scheduled to meet no less frequently than once every three years. This interval was changed in the new statute adopted at the Third Congress to four years.[22] The meeting in June 1964 was fifteen months overdue. Probably the postponement resulted from uncertainty regarding the control exercised by Gomułka. Extraordinary meetings of the congress may be called by the Central Committee or on application by a majority of the province committees. So far there have been none of this kind.

A total of 1,431 delegates attended the Fourth Congress, in 1964. The number included 1,172 from province conferences and 195 from industrial organizations; the remaining 64 represented the armed forces. About a twelfth of the delegates claimed to be peasants and about a fifth, said to be engaged in production activities, presumably were industrial workers. The remainder came from the intelligentsia stratum of society and were professional government or party functionaries. Nothing ever happens at any of these congresses that has not been arranged in advance down to the smallest detail. Elections are rigged with one candidate for each post, and a rubber-stamp balloting or acclamation places the delegates' approval on the actions of the party leadership.

THE CENTRAL COMMITTEE. This organ is elected by the party congress. Again, only enough names are placed in nomination to fill the total number of seats (162 in 1967). The Central Committee is supposed to meet at least once every four months in plenary session. It has the following functions: to represent the party externally with other communist parties, to establish party institutions and direct their activities, to nominate editorial boards for party newspapers, and to control party cadres that are sent into the field.[23]

When the left-wing socialists merged with the communists in December 1948, only forty-four socialists were added to the Central Committee. Of this original number, just eleven still remained in 1967 at this expanded level of the party apparatus. From the original forty-seven communists elected to the Central Committee in 1945, only nineteen remained there some twenty-two years later. These persons may be considered the hard core of the party. Such a substantial turnover indicates the extent of the permanent purge which operates in all communist-type states.

THE POLITICAL BUREAU. According to the party statute, the

Politburo is elected by the Central Committee from among its own membership and is entrusted with directing the work of that body between plenary sessions. In importance, this agency parallels the position of the Soviet communist party's Political Bureau. It is the most powerful of all organs and represents the summit of the party hierarchy. All of its members can be found on a list of the power elite. (See table 30.)

It is in the Politburo that one sees the principle of interlocking directorates at work. As Politburo members, the hierarchs make policy; as Secretariat members, certain of them see to it that policy is carried out by the party apparatus; as government officials, they legalize policy in the form of laws and decrees which become effective throughout the nation. The internal operations of the Politburo are cloaked in secrecy. The chief of this organ is Gomułka, who is also first secretary of the Central Committee.

Władysław Gomułka was born February 6, 1905, at Krosno in Rzeszów Province.[24] He became a skilled locksmith at an early age. By the time he reached the age of seventeen years, he had become connected with a leftist group. Soon he was elected an official of the chemical industry trade-union, and in 1926 he was arrested and jailed for subversive activities. He saw prison again in 1932-1934, in 1936-1939, and in 1951-1954. The latter confinement was under a communist regime and allegedly for the crime of "nationalist deviation."

Gomułka attended the International Lenin School (of political warfare) in Moscow [25] in the years 1934-1935 and received training in subversive activities. He operated in the Soviet-occupied area of eastern Poland from 1939 to 1941 and remained there after the German attack on the U.S.S.R. Gomułka was elected secretary-general of the Polish communist party in 1943, at a time when there was no radio contact with Moscow. Purged in 1949, he was reinstated in 1956 at a plenary session of the Central Committee and again became party leader.[26]

Gomułka may have a few more years of control ahead of him, if he remains on that narrow line between obedience to Moscow and avoidance of an uprising. His age (sixty-two in 1967) is perhaps no barrier to at least another decade of active life. Judging from his photographs, however, he has not weathered the years so well as some other bloc leaders. The palace *coup d'état* which overthrew

Khrushchëv in mid-October 1964 indicates how insecure the top position may be, even when occupied by a strong leader.

On this topic of age, it may be of interest to examine table 30.

TABLE 30

THE POWER ELITE IN POLAND, 1967

Politburo and Secretariat	Years of age	Government office	Year joined party	Party office (in addition to Politburo where so indicated)
Cyrankiewicz, Józef [a]	56	Premier	1948	—
Gierek, Edward [a]	54	—	1931	Secretary, Katowice Province
Gomułka Władysław [a, c]	62	Member, Council of State	1926	First secretary (leader)
Jędrychowski, Stefan [a]	57	Chairman, Planning Commission	1932	—
Kliszko, Zenon [a, c]	59	Deputy speaker, Parliament	1933	Secretary (deputy leader)
Loga-Sowiński, Ignacy [a]	53	Chairman, Trade-Unions Council	1932	—
Ochab, Edward [a]	61	Chairman, Council of State	1929	—
Rapacki, Adam [a]	58	Foreign Affairs minister	1948	—
Spychalski, Marian [a]	61	Defense minister	1926	—
Strzelecki, Ryszard [a, c]	59	—	1937	Secretary (cadres)
Szyr, Eugeniusz [a]	52	Deputy premier (Economy)	1932	—
Waniołka, Franciszek [a]	53	Deputy premier (Heavy Industry)	1942	—
Jagielski, Mieczysław [b]	43	Agriculture minister	1945	—
Jaroszewicz, Piotr [b]	58	Deputy premier (CMEA representative)	1944	—
Jaszczuk, Bolesław [b, c]	54	—	1933	Secretary (economy)
Jarosiński, Witold [c]	58	—	1932	Secretary (ideology)
Starewicz, Artur [c]	50	—	1932	Secretary (propaganda)
Tejchma, Józef [c]	63	—	1924	Secretary (agriculture)
Wicha, Władysław [c]	54	—	1933	Secretary (security)

SOURCE: Radio Free Europe, *Communist Party-Government Line-Up* (Munich, January 1967), pp. 19-20; (March 1967), pp. 18-19.

[a] Full member, Politburo.

[b] Candidate member, Politburo.

[c] Secretary of the Central Committee.

The youngest member of this elite is forty-three, whereas Gomułka is almost the oldest. It is not a youthful group, nor does it have any substantial young segment which will move into the leadership as the older men die or retire. Most of these people have experienced a difficult life. Many spent several years in prewar and even postwar (that is, communist) prisons. It would seem fairly reasonable to assume that most of them, including the majority of the members of the Politburo and the national Secretariat, will be out of the picture within the next decade.

The Secretariat, considered the hub of party activity, is elected nominally by the Central Committee in plenary session, the same as the Politburo. There are currently eight national secretaries, including Gomułka. Under the direction of these men, sixteen identifiable departments and another sixteen "problem commissions" operate at this top level.[27] The Secretariat maintains a constant check on local party officials throughout the country. It also remains in permanent contact with the Politburo, since four of the eight secretaries are Politburo members or candidates for membership on that policy-making body.

COMPOSITION OF THE PARTY. The social composition of the party is shown in table 31. What does not appear is the quality of the membership. The proportion of intellectuals has risen from below 10 to almost 43 percent within less than a generation, and very probably most of these persons are opportunists. On the other hand, the hard core of the party consists mainly of those members who have been activists and functionaries since the 1920's and early 1930's. There are about eighteen of these left on the current leadership list; fourteen of them appear in table 30. In addition, there are ten ranking military or police officers who can be regarded as part of an extended power elite of Poland.[28] The average age of this group is about ten years under that of the hard core.

Since 1942, when it was reconstituted,[29] the party membership has grown almost steadily (see table 29). Growth, however, has been accompanied by the purging of considerable numbers. The main reasons have been theft, bribery, embezzlement, misuse of official posts, and drunkenness. Table 32 shows the party's losses since 1955. One observer had the following to say about party membership: "If

there is any division in the rank and file of the party, it is only between
those who still believe in communism and those who hang onto their
party cards for more practical reasons." [30]

TABLE 31

POLISH COMMUNIST PARTY SOCIAL COMPOSITION, 1945-1967

Category	December 1945		September 1957		January 1967	
	Number	Percent	Number	Percent	Number	Percent
Industrial workers	130,620	62.2	511,917	39.9	760,039	40.1[a]
Peasants	59,220	28.2	164,224	12.8	224,373	11.8
Intellectuals	20,160	9.6	497,804	38.8	806,620	42.6
Other (artisans, retired, housewives)	—	—	109,055	8.5	103,863	5.5
Total	210,000	100.0	1,283,000	100.0	1,894,895[b]	100.0

SOURCES: *Nowe drogi,* I (January-February 1947), 29, and II (May-June 1948),
30. *Życie Warszawy,* October 25, 1957. *Trybuna ludu,* November 18, 1957. *Nowe
drogi,* XXI, No. 4 (April 1967), 15. Absolute figures computed.

[a] Includes three percent agricultural laborers on state farms.
[b] Includes 199,298 candidates for membership.

TABLE 32

PURGES IN THE POLISH COMMUNIST PARTY, 1955-1966

Year	Number of members purged	Year	Number of members purged
1955	55,000	1959	84,880
1956	48,000	1960	31,177
1957	121,000	1961	37,428
1958	261,000	Total ....(ca.)	638,485

SOURCES: *Nowe drogi,* XII, No. 12 (December 1958), 87. *Trybuna ludu,* January 16 and June 16, 1960, and March 16, 1961.

NOTE: Radio Warsaw on April 15, 1964, claimed that only 400,000 members were
purged between 1956 and 1964, which does not correspond with the information
pieced together above.

Roman Nowak, chairman of the party's Central Control Commission, revealed
that a total of 37,853 members were crossed off the party lists during 1965, including
6,420 for serious misconduct. *Trybuna ludu,* February 26, 1966. During the first
half of 1966 some 22,200 left the party, another 15,411 were crossed off, and 3,000
were purged. *Ibid.,* August 14, 1966.

There has been condemnation by Gomułka of the trend toward
an increasing percentage of intelligentsia in the party. This shift
toward control by the better educated is more than just a trend; it is

in reality a current problem. In 1961 less than 6.3 percent of the proletariat or industrial labor force in Poland were in the party.[31] The goal set by Gomułka reportedly was 90 percent industrial workers and 10 percent "mental" workers. The proportions have developed in reverse, with each of the two groups providing roughly 40 percent of the membership in 1967 (see table 31).

Observations that can be made from a study of the communist party in Poland are rather limited, due to the unstable condition of that organization. The delay in scheduling the Fourth Congress probably showed a lack of confidence on the part of Gomułka. The Central Committee finally announced in July 1963 that the congress would be held during the first half of the following year. Preparations were to be handled by a commission. After numerous protests, apparently from intermediate levels, this group was expanded [32] to include all nineteen first secretaries from the provinces, whether members of the Central Committee or not.

Regardless of any differences among party factions, the winner always will be a communist. The PZPR can be expected to continue to be patterned after its counterpart in the Soviet Union. The goal of the party still remains a "socialist" state, and the maintenance of control over the nation by a self-perpetuating elite is considered a prerequisite. Even the so-called destalinization [33] and "liberalization" have not changed this latter fact of life.

DOMESTIC AND INTRA-ORBITAL RELATIONS

Poland remains unique among the East European countries within the Soviet power bloc. This is not only due to the remarkable success of the communists in fettering the people and establishing a regime, despite seemingly insurmountable socioreligious and political barriers. There are other reasons for uniqueness, among which perhaps the most interesting remains the "deviationist" manner in which Poland's agriculture has been permitted to develop. The unusual modus vivendi between church and state would be another, but it has deteriorated. In the past, however, it permitted such incompatible ideologies as those of the Roman Catholic Church and international communism to coexist within the country.

THE AGRICULTURAL PROGRAM. Even before the cessation of hostilities in the Second World War, radical land reform was introduced by the communist-dominated provisional government. The reform consisted principally in expropriating large landholdings and redistributing them among the peasantry and the new Polish settlers in the so-called Recovered Territories to the west and south of the 1939 Polish-German boundary. Little was done toward the collectivization of agriculture, as the communists were concentrating on consolidation of their control over the government during the early years. This postponement of collectivization represented in Poland, as in some of the other "people's democracies," merely a tactical divergence from the traditional Soviet path toward the ideal socialist state. The deferment was permitted by Moscow during the formative years of the bloc as a temporary means toward the desirable end of solidifying communist control.

By 1947, however, Stalin had decided that the time was ripe for establishing more uniformity within the diverse East European satrapies. Organization of the Cominform [34] in 1947 gave the signal for a beginning of his conformity drive. Gomułka, nominally the leading communist in Poland at that time, reportedly indicated coolness toward the establishment of this international organization and, by implication, objected to forced agricultural collectivization, which had not given the announced "brilliant results" elsewhere. In September 1948 Gomułka was removed as party leader by a plenary session of the Central Committee. By 1949 collectivization patterned after the Soviet model had been launched in Poland.

This forced process was conducted by such coercive devices as compulsory state deliveries, heavy land taxes, and "punitive" visits by party activists and police to farm areas where opposition to the program was encountered. Between late 1949 and the fall of 1956 some 10,600 Polish collectives had come into being in this manner. The resentment of the peasants against abrogation of their property rights mounted. The peasant in Poland not only considers his land as a source of income, but attributes to it also sentimental and traditional values which imbue it with an almost mystical quality.

This growing resentment came finally to be recognized by communist authorities. It was probably this fact more than any other which tempered the degree of force and violence used in Poland to achieve the aims of the program. A much more severe campaign of terror and coercion was applied in the other East European satellites.[35] As a result, collectivization of farms in Poland showed only a 3 percent growth between 1950 and 1958, in contrast with increases of 48 percent in Bulgaria and 52 percent in Czechoslovakia.

Production figures subsequently released indicate that Polish farmland remaining in private hands outproduced agricultural land in the socialist sector (both collective and state farms) by a considerable margin. This led Gomułka, after his return to power in 1956, to suggest the dissolution of unproductive collective farms operating at a deficit.[36] He also announced more liberal regulations pertaining to the formation of production cooperatives, as collective farms are euphemistically called. The reaction to these changes represented a true barometer of the peasant attitude toward collectivization. Taking the speech of Gomułka literally, the peasants began to dissolve the cooperatives. By the summer of 1957 more than 8,500 of the 10,600 cooperatives that had been formed were disbanded.[37] Further liberalization of control over agriculture resulted in reduction of compulsory deliveries to the state, increases in the prices paid for agricultural commodities, and more autonomy within rural areas. (See table 33.)

TABLE 33

AGRICULTURE IN POLAND, 1966

Category	Number of units	Hectares	Percent
Private farms	3,600,000	17,100,000	85.5
State farms	8,826	2,700,000	13.5
Collective farms	1,229	200,000	1.0
Total	3,610,055	20,000,000	100.0

SOURCES: "Small Scale of Socialist Farming?" *Polish Perspectives*, IX, No. 8-9 (August-September 1966), 142. *Dziennik ludowy,* November 11, 1966, translated in *Polish Press Survey,* November 23, 1966.

NOTE: The approximately 6.6 million persons employed in agriculture represent 47 percent of the total labor force in Poland. State farms will acquire a further 300,000 hectares during 1966-1970, according to *Trybuna ludu,* March 17, 1967.

What is the farm picture in Poland today? A review of the results achieved indicates a substantial decline in the production of pork, animal fat, poultry, dairy products and sugar; a drop in total agricultural trade since 1962; and an increase in retail food prices. Furthermore, sizable grain imports annually from the United States, Britain, or France have been found necessary [38] and are continuing.

In order to reverse the downward trend in agricultural production, the so-called agrominium program was adopted in October 1963 by the Council of Ministers. The program involves essentially a set of eight "commandments" for private farmers. The new dicta prescribe agricultural practices with which no enlightened peasant would quarrel. The program itself, however, is disturbing to the rural population. It provides for such sanctions as confiscation of land, in the event that the rules are ignored. Also, it portends a retrogression to stricter and more centralized controls in the future. On the other hand, substantial increases in government payments were announced in the fall of 1965 by Gomułka both for compulsory deliveries and for contract sales.[39] He further revealed that during 1966 the regime would invest 16 billion złotys (4 złotys to the U.S. dollar, officially) in agriculture.

Although this is the only country within the Soviet bloc where collectivization has not been actively pursued since 1956, the communist regime in Poland has not ignored the idea entirely. It instituted the "agricultural circles" to inculcate collectivist attitudes among the peasantry. These state-controlled organizations are designed to favor members over strictly private-entrepreneur farmers in the procurement of agricultural supplies and in arrangements for the distribution and sale of produce.[40] In addition to the introduction of the circles, heavy taxes are being reimposed on individual non-affiliated farms.

Poland's stumbling agricultural economy presents a serious problem to the government, as was admitted by Gomułka at a rally in Budapest: "The growth rate of Polish agriculture does not keep up with that of industry, and this is the main source of the difficulties faced by the national economy." [41] The difficulties have increased since that time.

CHURCH-STATE RELATIONS. The prewar Roman Catholic population of Poland was about twenty-three million out of a total of almost thirty-four million inhabitants. In addition to more than three million Jews (Hebrew religion), the remainder included large Ukrainian (Uniate), German (Lutheran), and Belorussian (Russian Orthodox) minorities. Now, after the Nazi holocaust and the annexation of Polish territory in the east by the U.S.S.R., the minority groups comprise fewer than 500,000 persons, or 1.5 percent, in a total population of thirty-two million,[42] of whom the overwhelming majority adhere at least nominally to the Roman Catholic faith. (See table 34.)

In 1945 the new, communist-dominated Council of Ministers declared null and void the twenty-year-old concordat between Warsaw and the Vatican. This agreement had regulated the activities of the church in Poland. In abrogating the concordat the communist regime claimed that the church had violated its provisions by favoring Germany during the war. From that time on, a slowly intensifying campaign against the church was waged, beginning with press campaigns against the church hierarchy and the teaching of the catechism in public schools. It gradually expanded to include the arrest and trial of clergy and the suppression of Catholic news media.

TABLE 34

MINORITY POPULATIONS IN POLAND, 1965

Name	Approximate number	Percentage of minority total
Ukrainians	180,000	39.74
Belorussians	165,000	36.42
Jews	31,000 [a]	6.84
Slovaks	21,000	4.64
Russians	19,000	4.19
Gypsies	12,000	2.65
Lithuanians	10,000	2.21
Greeks and Macedonians	10,000	2.21
Germans	3,000	0.66
Czechs	2,000	0.44
Total	453,000	100.00

SOURCE: *Polityka,* October 30, 1965, p. 10.

[a] Figures released by the Religious News Service show only 25,000 Jews in Poland. *New York Times,* January 7, 1966.

In January 1949 Archbishop Stefan Wyszyński was appointed primate of Poland. He immediately opened negotiations with regime authorities to clarify the position of the church in relation to the state. These talks became hampered seriously by a Vatican decree ordering the excommunication of all Catholics who actively supported communism. The Polish regime, claiming that this constituted interference in the internal affairs of the country, retaliated by announcing that priests who attempted to enforce the excommunication order would be punished under Polish law.

Despite these difficulties, a *modus vivendi* was signed in April 1950 between the church and the communist regime.[43] In essence, the church agreed to abstain from all political activities and to restrain the clergy from opposition to the regime. The state in turn guaranteed the church freedom of worship, permission for the conduct of religious education in public schools, and noninterference with the Catholic press. The wording of the agreement, however, was flagrantly one-sided and provided the basis for subsequent government interference. In almost every case where specific guarantees of freedom were given, the communist regime carefully qualified the authority with restrictive phrases.

The communists took advantage of this terminology and reverted to their campaign against the church almost immediately. In the years following, state persecution of the church mounted in intensity. The new Polish constitution omitted any mention of safeguards for the church. In September 1953 Cardinal Wyszyński was arrested secretly and forbidden to carry on the functions of his office. Arrests of other clergy followed. The state even went so far as to require and insist on government approval whenever changes in clerical assignments or new appointments were contemplated.

In 1956, immediately after Gomułka's return to power (the so-called October Revolution), Cardinal Wyszyński and other arrested clergymen were released. Persecution of the church temporarily halted, and a new, more liberal church-state agreement was announced whereby religious instruction on a voluntary basis could once again be provided in the schools, government control over certain clerical appointments was relaxed, and other concessions were made to the church.[44] At this time communist control had weakened throughout the country because of the upheaval and there was fear of a revolt.

Subsequent events showed that the new church-state agreement represented more of a political expedient to gain the temporary support of the church than a sincere intention to liberalize former restrictions on church activities. Once the communists had gained sufficient strength, persecution in one form or another followed and, indeed, persists to this day. It is apparent that the communists want not only to separate church and state but also to eliminate religion totally from the lives of the people.[45]

The future of the church in Poland does not look bright. Nevertheless, the large Catholic population is still a powerful factor in domestic politics. The church hierarchy remains well aware of communist desires to rid the country of religion. It continues to fight for religious freedom, despite nearly continuous oppression over the postwar years. In the fall of 1965 Cardinal Wyszyński and Archbishop Antoni Baraniak of Poznań were attacked by regime media for making speeches at the Vatican's Ecumenical Council meeting without mentioning "the avoidance of war, disarmament, and world-wide cooperation by states and peoples on behalf of peace." [46]

Shortly afterward the Cardinal and thirty-five Polish bishops who had participated in the sessions in Rome sent a letter inviting the Catholic bishops in all of Germany to attend the forthcoming 1966 celebration of Poland's millennium at Częstochowa. The letter reviewed relations between the two countries, made a plea for a "dialogue," and offered forgiveness and asked for it in return. The regime in Warsaw reacted vehemently by accusing the church hierarchy of entering into foreign affairs.[47] In January 1966 Cardinal Wyszyński was not allowed to leave for the Vatican, and subsequently all foreigners were refused visas to attend the religious observances of the millennium. Pope Paul VI's intended trip to Poland also was declared to be "inopportune" at the time. Religious demonstrations occurred in cities throughout Poland during the summer. Pessimism about the future has been expressed by an acute observer.[48]

INTRA-BLOC AFFAIRS. Poland belongs to those treaty organizations which are sponsored by the Soviet Union. Among them, the Council for Mutual Economic Assistance (CMEA) is perhaps the most consequential, owing to the effects of its program of economic integration within the bloc.

Involvement in this Soviet-founded group has proven rather expensive to Poland, as it has to several other bloc countries. Large capital investments have been diverted to long-range CMEA economic improvement projects. This capital has been needed badly for shorter-range domestic programs which have remained abortive. Heavy expenditures for construction of the Polish section along the Danube-Oder canal and exploitation of brown coal deposits in the Turoszów area are two examples of such large investments. The best illustration, perhaps, is the "friendship" oil pipeline which crosses Poland from the U.S.S.R. and ends at Schwedt, East Germany. An expensive refinery has been constructed in Płock, Poland, to process this Soviet petroleum. Part of the cost for construction of the pipeline itself has been borne by the Polish government.

Polish economists, however, seem to recognize the problems which long-range investments required by the CMEA are generating in their domestic economy. They apparently no longer follow blindly the dictates of Moscow.[49] For example, on the fifteenth anniversary of the CMEA Deputy Premier Piotr Jaroszewicz admitted that economic differences existed within the organization:

> Even a husband and wife who love each other are not always of the same opinion about investments. It is hard to imagine that eight countries are also of the same opinion. In Comecon [CMEA] the only method is to use persuasion through economic arguments.[50]

It seems likely that Poland's membership in the CMEA has been one of the factors contributing to a faltering economic development. It may be, however, that when the large investments in CMEA projects begin to provide a return the government will be able to invest more funds in the domestic economy. This might conceivably bolster some of the current economic weaknesses that beset the country. One attempt to improve the system involves a cautious change which will somewhat decentralize direction by shifting planning and responsibility down to the intermediate level of industrial unions of similar plants, though not to the level of the individual factory.[51]

Aside from the purely organizational aspects of intra-bloc relations, a geographical issue has loomed large among postwar problems involving Poland and other countries. This issue, still a live question in international politics, concerns the establishment of Poland's western boundary along the line of the Oder and Western Neisse rivers.

THE ODER-NEISSE LINE. The origin of the problem concerning the boundary between Poland and Germany dates back to the latter part of the First World War. Roman Dmowski, chairman of the Polish National Council then recognized by the West as the government of Poland, defended the right to the Oder-Neisse river line as a frontier. Władysław Sikorski, premier of the Polish exile government at London early in the Second World War, suggested the Oder River as the future boundary between the two countries after the war. In 1943 the Polish communists in Moscow echoed this proposal and further indicated that this extension of the boundary to the Oder

River in the west should be considered as compensation to Poland for the territories annexed by Russia in the east (as a result of the 1939 Nazi-Soviet nonaggression pact).

The Big Three discussed Germany's future boundaries in the course of three conferences during and immediately after the war. At Teheran, in November 1943, Stalin proposed the boundary along the Oder River. Both Churchill and Roosevelt agreed in principle, but no firm settlement was reached. Later, at the Yalta meeting during February 1945, the border question was again brought up. The final communiqué after this conference specified that Poland would receive accessions of territory in the north and west, that the Poles themselves were to be consulted prior to a final settlement, and that the ultimate demarcation of borders would be determined at the peace conference after the war.

During the Potsdam conference, in August 1945, the three heads of government agreed that "pending the final determination of Poland's western frontier, the former German territories east of a line running from the Baltic Sea [and] thence along the Oder River to the confluence of the Western Neisse River and along the Western Neisse to the Czechoslovakian frontier [should] be under the administration of the Polish State." [52] There was also an agreed procedure for removal of German citizens from these Recovered Territories (as they have come to be known). This implied that Poland was to repopulate the vacated area.

Despite the provisional nature of the Potsdam agreement, the U.S.S.R. in that same month of August 1945 signed a treaty of friendship with Poland which included an agreement for demarcation of the Polish-Soviet frontier.[53] In June 1950 a Warsaw communiqué issued at the close of negotiations between East Germany and Poland announced agreement over their existing frontiers and established cultural cooperation between the two countries. Finally, the post-Khrushchëv leadership in the Soviet Union traveled to Warsaw in April 1965 and reaffirmed the 1945 pact, signing a twenty-year extension which guarantees inviolability of the Oder-Neisse border.[54]

The Polish regime has consolidated its hold over the Recovered Territories. Besides asserting legal and historical rights to these lands, the Warsaw government has repopulated them with more than eight million Poles. Additionally, reconstruction efforts have been so successful that more than a third of the country's annual gross national product is attributed to production from these former German lands.[55] Many countries apparently regard Poland's hegemony over the territories as a *fait accompli,* although few in the West have given legal recognition to the situation. Even the French refrained from doing so when in September 1965 Premier Cyrankiewicz visited Paris and when President de Gaulle repaid the visit exactly two years later.

In spite of the "revanchist" movement in West Germany, and regardless of the Western stand that Warsaw only administers the territories, it would seem that Poland's sovereignty over the area indeed represents a *fait accompli.* Only a major conflict or a significant shift in the world balance of power could result in a revision of the present boundary between Germany and Poland.[56]

NOTES

1 Hubert Ripka, *Eastern Europe in the Post-War World* (New York, 1961), pp. 28-29. The author, a native of Czechoslovakia, is qualified to make this comment since he lived in the model interwar democracy.

2 U.S. Senate, Committee on Foreign Relations, *A Decade of American Foreign Policy* (Washington, D.C., 1950), p. 30.

3 Other prewar political parties already had been delegalized. For an account of this election by an eyewitness, the leader of the Polish Peasant party, see Stanisław Mikołajczyk, *The Rape of Poland: Pattern of Soviet Aggression* (New York, 1958), pp. 180-202.

4 Władysław Gomułka, *Przemówienia 1956-1957* (Warsaw, 1957), pp. 193, 213.

5 See Jerzy Ptakowski, "Parlamentswahlen in Polen," *Osteuropäische Rundschau*, XI, No. 10 (October 1965), pp. 13-18, esp. 15-18.

6 "The Aftermath of Seym Elections," *Polish Affairs*, XIII, No. 10 (October 1965), p. 15.

7 *Dziennik ustaw*, July 23, 1952.

8 See Vincent C. Chrypiński, "Poland's Parliamentary Committees," *East Europe*, XIV, No. 1 (January 1965), pp. 17-24.

9 *Trybuna ludu*, June 25, 1965, gives the names.

10 See the nomination speech and biographic data given by Gomułka, as reported in *Polityka*, August 22, 1964. Ochab was reelected to this position the following year. *Trybuna ludu*, June 25, 1965.

11 *Line-Up*, p. 19.

12 His biography appears in the *Bolshaya sovetskaya entsiklopediya* (2d ed.; Moscow, 1958), XLVI, 636-637. The new cabinet was listed in *Trybuna ludu*, June 26, 1965.

13 Extended from three years by legislation in December 1963. Tadeusz Galiński (ed.), *Rocznik polityczny i gospodarczy 1964* (Warsaw, 1964), p. 89. The numbers appear in *Nowe drogi*, XIX, No. 8 (August 1965), p. 191.

14 Sylwester Zawadzki, "Decentralization and Democratic Development of the People's Councils in Poland," in Stanisław Ehrlich (ed.), *Social and Political Transformations in Poland* (Warsaw, 1964), p. 170.

15 Eugeniusz Szyr (chief ed.), *Twenty Years of the Polish People's Republic* (Warsaw, 1964), p. 77.

16 Galiński, *op. cit.*, pp. 90-92.

17 For names of incumbents at the national level see Jan Klimek (ed.), *Kalendarz robotniczy 1965* (Warsaw, 1964), pp. 42-43.

18 PZPR, *III Zjazd PZPR* (Warsaw, 1959), p. 751. The amendments did not change these principles. They are discussed by Zenon Kliszko in PZPR, *IV Zjazd PZPR* (Warsaw, 1964), pp. 235-254.

19 Recent figures indicate the number of primary party organizations to have decreased to 67,800. *Nowe drogi*, XXI, No. 4 (April 1967), p. 14.

20 Among the 15,699 PZPR officials at the county, town, and city-district levels, fewer than half (7,027) belonged to the party before 1949. The great majority (9,749) are classified as intelligentsia, with only about one-fifth industrial workers and the rest peasants. Women comprise 10 percent of the total. *Nowe drogi*, XIX, No. 2 (February 1965), p. 19.

21 Władysław Gomułka-Wiesław, *Ku nowej Polsce* (Katowice, 1945), 108 pp., gives Gomułka's four speeches and the final resolution of the congress.

22 PZPR, *III Zjazd PZPR*, p. 753 (Chap. IV, Art. 28, of the statute).

23 *Ibid.*, p. 754 (Chap. IV, Art. 32, of the statute).

24 Hansjakob Stehle, *Nachbar Polen* (Frankfort on the Main, 1963), pp. 36-51, although not always accurate, gives the most comprehensive biographic sketch of Gomułka. A recent official biography appears in *Wielka encyklopedia powszechna* (Warsaw, 1964), IV, pp. 314-315.

25 "Vladislav Gomulka," in *Bolshaya sovetskaya entsiklopediya*, LI, 84.

This is not mentioned in any of the Polish biographies. A German *vita* in Werner Markert (ed.), *Osteuropa-Handbuch: Polen* (Cologne, 1959), pp. 726-727, also states that Gomułka spent the years 1934-1936 in Moscow.

26 The alleged 272-page transcript of this plenum appeared in a special issue of *Nowe drogi,* X, No. 10 (October 1956).

The title of Secretary-General was changed to First Secretary between Gomułka's periods of office.

27 D. L., "The Problem Commissions of the Polish United Workers' Party," *World Marxist Review,* VI, No. 5 (May 1963), pp. 64-68. In 1963 some 2,800 such commissions were functioning under 398 regional committees of the party. Tens of thousands of party members are thus drawn into active PZPR work.

28 Ptakowski, *op. cit.,* p. 14, gives their names.

29 The prewar Polish communist party was dissolved by the Comintern in 1938, and most of its leaders were executed or sent to concentration camps by their Soviet "comrades." Posthumous U.S.S.R. rehabilitation by the Supreme Court came after October 1956. *Polityka,* August 21, 1965, p. 10.

30 Reported by Ptakowski, *op. cit.,* p. 13. This information is corroborated by the fact that 176,000 persons had been admitted into the party as candidates during 1965, amounting to 10 percent of the total membership. *Trybuna ludu,* July 27, 1966.

31 This is not true of the 7,800 key PZPR officials, however, since about 86 percent of them are allegedly of working-class background. (Computed from *Polityka,* June 6, 1964, p. 1.)

32 Ptakowski, *op. cit.* See also his article on "Gomułka and His Party" in *East Europe,* XVI, No. 5 (May 1967), pp. 2-7.

33 See "Destalinization in Eastern Europe: The Polish Model," in Andrew Gyorgy (ed.), *Issues of World Communism* (Princeton, N.J., 1966), pp. 66-85.

34 Eugenio Reale, *Nascita del Cominform* (Rome, 1958), pp. 175, provides an eyewitness account of how the Cominform was founded.

35 Zbigniew K. Brzeziński, *The Soviet Bloc* (Cambridge, Mass., 1960), p. 98.

36 *Nowe drogi,* X, No. 10 (October 1956), pp. 24-25 (complete issue on the Eighth Plenum of the PZPR Central Committee).

37 *Trybuna ludu,* August 28, 1957.

38 Reported in a speech by Gomułka to correspondents of the peasant weekly *Chłopska droga,* broadcast over Radio Warsaw on October 23, 1965.

Trybuna ludu, November 4, 1966, revealed that the U.S.S.R. would supply Poland with one million tons of grain during 1967.

39 Speech to the harvest festival, broadcast by Radio Warsaw on September 5, 1965. Price rebates, tax allowances, and interest-free credit will be given to those farmers who stop purchasing fodder. Gomułka speech on December 8, 1966, as cited in RFE, *Situation Report,* December 12, 1966, p. 2.

40 There exist some 33,000 of these agricultural circles, about one for every two villages. Radio Warsaw, December 7, 1966. In contrast, only 1,200 collective farms are in operation. Radio Warsaw, June 15, 1966.

41 Remarks at a Hungarian-Polish friendship rally, November 22, 1963, cited under "Hungary," in *East Europe,* XIII, No. 1 (January 1964), p. 40.

42 On the other hand, there are about 1.4 million Poles in the U.S.S.R., as follows: Belorussia (539,000), Ukraine (363,000), Lithuania (230,000), the Russian Soviet Federated Socialist Republic (118,000), Latvia (60,000), Kazakhstan (53,000), and other republics (17,000). *Polityka,* October 30, 1965, p. 10.

43 The text of the agreement appears in Henryk Świątkowski (ed.), *Stosunek państwa do kościoła w różnych państwach* (Warsaw, 1952), pp. 132-137.

44 Published in *Trybuna ludu,* December 8, 1956.

45 For efforts in this direction among the peasantry see Józef Kuczyński, *Podstawy światopoglądowe chłopów* (Warsaw, 1961), especially pp. 143-164.

46 An article whose title can be translated as "Pig-headed and Intolerant" appeared in *Życie Warszawy,* October 16, 1965; excerpts were repeated in the party newspaper, *Trybuna ludu.*

47 *Życie Warszawy,* December 10, 1965. The regime in Warsaw has moved to close six of the forty-eight seminaries which train priests. *New York Times,* December 28, 1966.

48 West German commentator Ludwig Zimmerer in a broadcast over the Bavarian state radio, *Bayerischer Rundfunk* (July 4, 1966); paraphrased in RFE, *Situation Report,* July 7, 1966, p. 2. See also Richard F. Staar, "The Hard Line in Poland," *Current History,* LII, No. 308 (April 1967), 209-210.

49 Growing Soviet influence can be seen in the new five-year trade agreement with the U.S.S.R. (1966-1970) which will increase exchange by 63 percent in 1970, reaching 8.2 billion zlotys or more than two billion U.S. dollars. Radio Warsaw, November 18, 1965.

50 Radio Warsaw, as cited by the *New York Times,* April 28, 1964.

51 Report by the PZPR Politburo in *Nowe drogi,* XIX, No. 8 (August 1965), pp. 3-58, and Central Committee resolution on "Changes in the Planning System and Administration of the National Economy during the Years 1966-1970," in *Trybuna ludu,* August 1, 1965.

52 U.S. Senate, Committee on Foreign Relations, "The Berlin (Potsdam) Conference, July 17–August 2, 1945," in *A Decade of American Foreign Policy: Basic Documents, 1941-49* (Washington, D.C., 1950), pp. 43-44.

53 Text in Semyon M. Maiorov (ed.), *Vneshnyaya politika Sovetskogo Soyuza v period Otechestvennoi Voiny* (Moscow, 1947), III, 386-387.

54 Text published in *Trybuna ludu,* April 9, 1965.

55 Kazimierz Secomski, "The Western Territories: 20 Years of Development," *Polish Perspectives,* VIII, No. 9 (September 1965), 3-13. See also the excerpt from a speech by Premier Cyrankiewicz on the twenty-seventh anniversary of the German attack. *Trybuna ludu,* September 4, 1966.

56 For an excellent analysis of Polish attitudes toward the Germans see Jerzy Hauptmann, "Die Wiedervereinigung Deutschlands: Hoffnungen und Befürchtungen," in Alfred Domes (ed.), *Die Politik des Westens und Osteuropa* (Cologne, 1966), pp. 154-167.

Chapter 7 / ROMANIA:
Latin Among Slavs

THE HISTORY of Romania has indelibly affected the makeup of its population. While the communists seek to create a new world in the East European area, the path to their type of "socialism" is no longer the same for all countries. The roots of the past affect not only the attitude of the great masses of the people whom the totalitarian regimes hold captive. This very same past is locked into the attitudes of the current leaders.

These men lay claim to an infallible interpretation of Marxism-Leninism, but what they practice remains far removed from ideological purity. The contemporary Romanian dictatorship may have as firm a hold on the nation as any of its past rulers. Impeding the road to a Soviet variety of socialism and a new world, however, are influences of the past which express themselves in a great variety of ways.

From the background of this land emanates the strong influence of its Latin heritage. Romanians point to this fact with pride today, proclaiming that they are Latins and not Slavs. As proof they cite their language, which has more than 60 percent of its roots in Latin and only 20 percent in Slavic derivatives. Because of this heritage, the views of the people generally have been pro-Western and anti-communist. Perhaps this is the reason why much of the leadership within the communist party of Romania has come from ethnic minorities which felt no compunctions against aligning their goals with Russia and other Slavic groups.[1]

Because of Romania's alignment with the Axis powers during the Second World War, the U.S.S.R. took steps very early to press for a government which would be essentially pro-Soviet. Even so, the provisions on the organization and functioning of central and local agencies contained in the communist-inspired constitutions of 1948, 1952, and 1965 have been applied only when convenient to the rulers. The postwar regime of Romania generally has shown a discrepancy between its professed theory of constitutional government and its actual practice.

In February 1945 the Soviet political representative Andrei Vyshinsky called on King Michael and insisted that the communist-selected front man to head the regime, Dr. Petru Groza, be appointed premier. After assurances and placation of Western fears by Stalin himself, the king complied. The cabinet proposed by Groza included representatives from a number of different political parties. Communists, however, were placed in the key Interior, Justice, and Public Works ministries. After the communists expanded their power from these important positions, elections were falsified. The monarchy remained for two more years, acting as a passive restraint, but was powerless to prevent this consolidation.[2]

The war crimes trial of Romanian leaders responsible for support of the Axis assisted in immobilizing the opposition and prevented the formation of a coalition of liberal and peasant groups to block the communists. In addition, the U.S.S.R.'s seeming to favor Romanian claims to Transylvania fostered some support for the communist program. Opposition parties were withered by the use or threat of violence. From a base of fewer than a thousand members in 1944, through a rapid recruitment up to 217,000 members by September 1945 the communist Romanian Workers' party soon attained the manpower to staff the regime.

During the consolidation period, the essential features of the prewar government were retained. The Grand National Assembly, or parliament, was reinstated in 1946, though as a unicameral body, not bicameral as before. Suffrage was extended to women and the voting age was lowered to eighteen. The parliament underwent a purge of noncommunist members and was sovietized into a rubber-stamp type of legislative body. In December 1947 King Michael was forced to abdicate. Soon afterward the parliament passed Law 393, illegally abolishing the existing constitution of 1923, and called for a constituent assembly to decide on a new basic law. Meanwhile a draft constitution actually appeared before a constituent assembly could be elected; this was published by the People's Democratic Front (the Front, as in other bloc countries, representing the electoral organization for the communist party and its ancillary groups). The new constitution, which introduced the designation "Romanian People's Republic," was adopted in April 1948 and communist control over Romania superficially appeared to have a legitimate basis.[3]

NEW CONSTITUTIONS

The basic law of 1952 was a modification of that adopted four years previously. As with the 1936 Stalin constitution, upon which it is closely patterned, the Romanian document appears to grant all fundamental rights to the people. These rights, however, are subordinated to the interests of socialism. Interpretation of "interests" rests with the ruling party. The Romanian Workers' party gained its official mandate in Article 86, which proclaimed it to be the "vanguard of the working people" and the "leading force of organizations of the working people as well as of the State organs and institutions." [4]

Only the Romanian Workers' party can nominate candidates to the Grand National Assembly. Therefore, as in the U.S.S.R., the party interprets the constitution, makes laws, and maintains complete dictatorial power. Certain judicial prerogatives also transcend constitutional rights. From the standpoint of the individual citizen, since there is no judicial review over the constitutionality of government acts, the sections of the constitution pertaining to basic rights are unenforceable. The constitution prescribes the various organs of government, including ministries, but even these frequently do not correspond to the written outline and are in a constant stage of change.

The subsequent new constitution which was adopted on August 21, 1965, does not substantially change the system.[5] It merely proclaims in Article 1 that Romania is now a socialist republic, meaning that the country has reached the level of development attained in the U.S.S.R. (1936), Yugoslavia (1958), and Czechoslovakia (1960). Whether this document could have been produced in defiance of the Soviet Union is not known, although possibly it was. In keeping with Article 1, the name of the country dropped the reference to a people's republic and became the Socialist Republic of Romania.

GOVERNMENTAL STRUCTURE. The present governmental system is similar, structurally and functionally, to the one established by the 1952 constitution. The fundamental difference is that Article 3 of the 1965 constitution proclaims the entire government to be led by and subordinated to the Romanian communist party.[6] This control is most direct at the administrative level, because party members hold key positions on executive and legislative organs as well as in the judicial arm of the government. Although organizational provisions of the constitution are generally upheld, the composition and action of the various organs are sensitive to direction by the party.

The central government consists of the Grand National Assembly or parliament, the Council of State, the Council of Ministers, and the court system. Functions are not clearly defined, because the communists reject the concept of separation of powers, or checks and balances. The Grand National Assembly is theoretically supreme. It remains essentially a legislative branch, although its function is to provide approval rather than act in a formulative capacity. The Council of State, formerly the presidium of the parliament, plays the role of a collective presidency for the country. The Council of Ministers is the supreme administrative and executive organ.[7] The courts are in charge of administering justice.

GRAND NATIONAL ASSEMBLY. According to Article 43 of the 1965 constitution, the Grand National Assembly has twenty-three specific powers, from adopting and amending the constitution to appointing and recalling the supreme commander. This legislature is elected every four years and has one representative for each 40,000 citizens. The balloting in March 1965 elected 465 deputies, all of whom were candidates of the People's Democratic Front.[8] Laws are adopted by a simple majority and are signed by the president and secretary of the Council of State. The Assembly convenes twice a year for ordinary sessions. Extraordinary meetings may be called when the Council of State or a third of all Assembly members consider it necessary.

The Assembly elects a chairman and four deputy chairmen, to preside over its sessions and guide the flow of business. All members are entitled to address enquiries to the government and to individual members of the Council of Ministers. They are immune to arrest or prosecution and cannot be held legally responsible, without consent of the Grand National Assembly or, between sessions, the Council of State. Such privileges, however, do not alter the fact that the

Grand National Assembly is merely a façade which helps to perpetuate the appearance of democracy. It is unlikely that the new rules
adopted in December 1965 will change this situation, although they
do call for more activity on the part of the members.[9]

STATE COUNCIL. The Council of State consists of nineteen
members, elected by the Grand National Assembly, who from among
themselves elect a chairman and three deputy chairmen. The present
Council of State was elected March 18, 1965. Since the death of
Gheorghe Gheorghiu-Dej on the following day, Chivu Stoica [10] has
been chairman. Theoretically accountable to the Grand National
Assembly under the constitution, the State Council functions along
lines closer to those of a legislature than does the Assembly. It exercises power through decrees, subsequently "approved" by the latter
body. This fact is evident in the small number of laws passed by the
legislature itself and the large number officially enacted only after
having originated with the Council of State. Lawmaking, however,
is a secondary matter. The primary function of both bodies, as in the
case of the Supreme Soviet in the U.S.S.R. and its Presidium, is their
joint role in the ratification of decrees of the government's executive
branch.

At the end of a legislative term, the Council of State orders elections to be held within three months and meanwhile remains in power
until the new Assembly has an opportunity to "elect" another council.
In an emergency the Grand National Assembly may extend the mandate of the council for the duration.

The chairman of the Council of State is *ex officio* the titular head of
state, the president. In 1948 and again in 1952, a chairman who was
not a member of the communist party was elected for tactical reasons.
In 1965 this maneuver did not appear necessary any longer, and a
communist, Chivu Stoica, became chairman. Stoica is also one of
the nine members of the top policy-making Standing Presidium of the
Romanian communist party.[11]

THE EXECUTIVE. Administration of government is centered
where the ruling communist party can best exert its influence and control, in the Council of Ministers. It is significant that there are more
members of the party's Executive Committee in the Council of Ministers than in the Council of State. All the key positions are filled by
trusted communists.

The Council of Ministers is elected by the Grand National Assembly and theoretically is responsible to it and, between sessions, to the Council of State. Decisions of the Council of Ministers are formulated as orders that are binding throughout the country. A good example was the recent decree authorizing public meetings to decide on contributions in money and labor for works of "public interest" such as schools, maternity homes, roads, and bridges.[12] A summary of the council's eleven official prerogatives is given in Article 70 of the new constitution. This document also fully describes the function of the ministries.[13]

The large number of ministers and the agencies under them reflects the specialization as well as the centralized nature of the economy and the extensive administrative apparatus in the hands of government. The exact number of ministries and agencies is in constant flux, with fusion or separation reflecting current needs.

LOCAL GOVERNMENT. The administrative subdivisions of Romania consist of sixteen regions, including the Mureş-Magyar autonomous unit; 150 districts; 183 cities or towns; and 4,259 communes, according to an official yearbook for 1965.[14] The same source gives the total population of about nineteen million as being exactly two-thirds rural and one-third urban.

The local instruments of state power are the People's Councils, which correspond to the soviets in the U.S.S.R. These operate under the principle of democratic centralism, with a downward flow of guidance which limits the initiative of the subordinate units. People's Councils operate at regional, district, town, and commune levels. More important administrative organs within these councils are called executive committees. It is noteworthy that, while the constitution proclaims the supremacy of the councils themselves, the executive committees are packed with trusted communists who exercise real power.

Elections in regions and districts are held every four years, and in towns and communes every other year. Upon expiration of the term, the executive committees retain power pending the election of new councils, in a direct parallel with the Council of State and the Grand National Assembly at the top of the organizational pyramid. The latest elections at the local level coincided with those held nationally in March 1965, and approximately 440,000 deputies were chosen.[15]

Under the electoral provisions in the constitution suffrage is universal for all persons eighteen years of age and older. Candidates for the People's Councils must be at least twenty-three. The right to nominate candidates is reserved to the Romanian communist party and other controlled organizations. Article 25 of the constitution denies suffrage to citizens considered unworthy and unreliable, including "mentally alienated and deficient people." This phrase, of course, can be interpreted to mean any opponent of the regime.

JUDICIAL SYSTEM. The fundamental tasks of the judiciary as defined in the constitution and subsequent laws, include since 1965 defending the regime of "socialism," the rights of the working people, and the interests of state agencies and institutions. The judiciary must insure theoretically the observance of justice and, furthermore, educate the people of the Romanian Socialist Republic in the spirit of devotion to the fatherland and the construction of socialism. Here, as typically in communist regimes, politics becomes the basis for law. All legal rules must be interpreted in the light of the class struggle.[16] Justice is deemed to be the will of the working class.

The task of administering justice is carried out by the "Procuratura" or office of the state prosecutor general, and by regular and special courts. Regular courts, known as people's tribunals, try civil, penal, and any other cases within their competence. Their jurisdiction is graduated in accordance with the various levels of government at which they function. Special courts for railroad, maritime, and fluvial affairs formerly existed; special military courts still operate and presumably have assumed the functions of the others.

In addition to applying the fundamental principles of justice, military courts hear cases and announce penalties provided by the law to punish such enemies of the people as traitors, spies, those sabotaging the construction of socialism or committing "crimes against peace and humanity," warmongers, embezzlers, and those who destroy socialist property, as well as bandits, thieves, hooligans, and like offenders.[17] Regular courts at higher levels hear civil cases regarding the rights and interests of citizens, state agencies, collective farms, and so forth.

Courts in Bucharest and on the regional level hear appeals from the people's tribunals. The Justice minister decides on the number of people's tribunals. The supreme court, theoretically, is entrusted with control over judicial activities of other courts and meets for this purpose at least once every three months. Soviet practices are copied here also, as the supreme court has no power to review the constitutionality of statutes. Judges of all courts are nominated exclusively by the Romanian communist party. People's tribunal judges play a larger role than is specified in the constitution. For example, the Justice minister can assign them from court to court in order to meet exigencies.

The prosecutor general possesses the highest supervisory authority over the observance of law by all central and local governmental organs. Naturally he must be a trusted member of the party. He is "elected" by the Grand National Assembly for a term of five years. He then designates his deputies and prosecutors at lower levels for periods of four years. All prosecutors are independent of local government organs, being responsible formally to the Grand National Assembly or, between sessions, the State Council. The Procuratura is really, however, an organization directed exclusively by the party. It is modeled closely after the corresponding agency in the U.S.S.R. The prosecutor general enjoys a "consultative" vote in the Council of State and the Council of Ministers.[18]

The operations of the Procuratura nullify those sections of the constitution concerning inviolability of the home and person. The agency can arrest any person; it remains independent of the courts; and there is no writ of habeas corpus. Thus the prosecutor general in supervising the administration of justice can, as defender of socialist justice and legality, "supervise" individual citizens and state organs alike. It is almost superfluous to add that he never acts against the party or its leadership.

EDUCATION. The structure of Romanian education is founded on three basic enactments. These are: the educational reform law of August 1948; the joint decree of the party's Central Committee and the Council of Ministers in July 1956, which implemented the resolutions of the party's Second Congress; and the decree of October 1961 transforming into law the resolutions of the Third Congress.[19]

Since 1961 compulsory education has encompassed the first eight grades. This change was made to parallel the system extant in the U.S.S.R. This eight-year period comprises the elementary school, grades one to five, and the *gimnaziu*, grades six through eight. There are four additional grades, from the ninth to the twelfth, providing a complete secondary education. These upper grades are oriented toward either the humanities or the physical and mathematical sciences. If complemented by two years of employment and practical experience, they can lead to a higher education.

Admission to the six universities and some thirty-five other institutions of higher learning [20] in Romania is based both upon successful completion of an entrance examination and upon political reliability, the latter generally being certified by the communist party or youth organization unit at the applicant's place of residence. The aims of the educational system thus include political conformity among the young people. Vocational training is provided at special schools for that purpose. Technicians who teach at these schools have both specialized training and practical experience.

A clear indication of the nature of the Romanian government under the current regime may be found in the treatment of a national minority in the Mureş-Magyar or Hungarian autonomous province. This area in Transylvania was transferred to the Romanians after the Second World War. The peace treaty with the Allies in February 1947 clearly provided that there should be no discrimination against minority groups. Nevertheless, through redemarcation of regions and cities and by resettling Romanians from Bessarabia in the area, the government has gradually reduced the numerical dominance and voice of this Hungarian minority group.

Catholic and Protestant churches in the Mureş-Magyar region were the first to be deprived of their schools. Until 1958, however, a large-scale Hungarian educational system flourished. Such institutions are dwindling in number and being absorbed by Romanian schools.[21] This treatment of the Hungarian minority perpetuates the tradition of oppression which had been prevalent even before the peace treaty. One may expect that all minority groups within the Romanian Socialist Republic will eventually lose their identity, despite the guarantee in Article 22 of the 1965 constitution that minorities shall be permitted the use of their own language.

THE ROMANIAN COMMUNIST PARTY

The communist party of Romania came into existence in 1921, only to be outlawed three years later. The movement continued its agitation underground, but effective government police harassment prevented the maintenance of a viable political organization. Determined action in 1936, which led to the arrest and conviction of nearly all the communist leaders, virtually eliminated the party as a political force. The movement had little or no war record of partisan activity to give it prestige, and in 1944 its reduced leadership consisted mostly of Russian-trained Jews, Ukrainians, and Hungarians.[22]

In August 1944 King Michael forced a change of government and took Romania out of a war that it had been fighting as a German ally. Hitler responded by bombing Bucharest, following which the king formally declared war on Germany and brought in his fifteen divisions on the side of the Red Army.

> Romania's change of front, together with the Teheran decision not to open a front in the Balkans, decided the fate of Central Europe, decided that the Soviet Union should dominate the whole region, that its new order should be a communist new order. Generalissimo Stalin therefore had good reason later to award to King Michael the highest Soviet decoration, the Order of Victory.[23]

In most other countries of the Soviet orbit, communist-dominated "front" governments assumed power immediately after the Red Army invasion. In Romania, however, so-called bourgeois governments were tolerated for a short time. In March 1945 the U.S.S.R. ordered the king to install a People's Democratic Front regime. This government was formed, and the communists received the three ministries they had demanded: Interior (Teohari Georgescu), Justice (Lucretiu Pătrăşcanu), and National Economy (Gheorghe Gheorghiu-Dej).[24] They sought mass support by redistributing confiscated land to peasant smallholders and by promising improved working conditions to laborers. National and local government was controlled by placing trusted personnel in key positions.

In February 1948 the communists and left-wing Social Democrats merged to form the Romanian Workers' party. A new Politburo drew thirteen of its eighteen members from the previous communist organization. This proportion remained intact until 1952, when the communists no longer considered the pretense of any other representation necessary and former Social Democrats were purged. Thus in the period between 1944 and 1952 the initially very small communist party, working with the assistance of Soviet advisers and supported by the presence of U.S.S.R. troops, ousted, destroyed, and replaced all political opposition to make itself sole ruler of Romania.

CENTRAL ORGANIZATION. The supreme organ of the Romanian communists is the party congress, to which delegates are elected by regional party conferences. Congresses are to be called at least every four years, at which time delegates hear and approve reports by central organs, adopt programs, establish policy on basic problems, and elect the Central Committee and the Central Audit Commission, which controls the finances of the party. Congresses perform these functions, then delegate all authority to the Central Committee until the next session.[25]

As the seat of power between congresses, the Central Committee provides a rostrum for publicizing the party program, directs and controls party as well as government organs, and also administers party finances. It has the responsibility for electing the Standing Presidium (formerly called the Political Bureau), Executive Committee, and national Secretariat—though, rather than being elective, these bodies consist of leading party personalities who are chosen by an inner group and then "rubber stamped" by the Central Committee. The new Standing Presidium [26] represents the power core of the party, and the Central Committee is fashioned in such a way as to perform the functions of a consultative body in a subordinate role.

As the foremost consultative body of the party, the Central Committee tends to include the top stratum of the government after the familiar communist model of the interlocking directorate. (See table 35.) Of the forty persons listed as members of the Council of Ministers of Romania in 1967, the majority hold membership or candidate status on the Central Committee of the party. According to an excellent analysis,[27] half of the Central Committee in 1961 was made up of hard-core party professionals, with eighty percent of this half being drawn from the inner circles of government or industry and the remaining twenty percent from lesser positions of power.

As previously mentioned, the locus of party power rests with the Standing Presidium. It functions as the primary policy-making body and also reviews the work of the Secretariat and the Central Collegium (formerly known as the Party Control Commission), which maintains party discipline. The collegium was downgraded in 1965 and now possesses only control and investigative functions.[28] Policy

TABLE 35

ROMANIA'S INTERLOCKING DIRECTORATE, 1967

Executive Committee	Government post	Other party position
FULL MEMBERS (17)		
Apostol, Gheorghe [a]	First deputy premier	
Bîrlădeanu, Alexandru [a] ..	First deputy premier	
Bodnăraş, Emil [a]	First deputy premier	
Ceauşescu, Nicolae [a]		Party secretary-general
Drăghici, Alexandru [a]		Party secretary (cadres)
Maurer, Ion Gheorghe [a] ..	Premier	
Niculescu-Mizil, Paul [a]		Party secretary (deputy leader)
Stoica, Chivu [a]	Chairman, Council of State	
Verdeţ, Ilie [a]	First deputy premier	
Berghianu, Maxim	Chairman, State Planning Committee	
Borilă, Petre	Deputy premier (Consumers Goods)	
Drăgan, Constantin	Chairman, Trade-Unions	
Moghioroş, Alexandru ...	Deputy premier	Party secretary
Rădulescu, Gogu	Deputy premier, CMEA representative	
Răutu, Leonte		Party secretary (Agitprop section chief)
Valcu, Vasile	President, National Union of Agricultural Cooperatives	
Voitec, Stefan	Chairman, Grand National Assembly	
CANDIDATE MEMBERS (9)		
Bank, Iosif	Deputy premier	
Blajovíci, Petre	Deputy premier	
Coliu, Dumitru		Chairman, Central Collegium
Danalache, Florian	Minister of Railroads	
Fazekaş, Ion	Deputy premier	
Gere, Mihai		Party secretary
Lupu, Petre		Party organization section chief
Mănescu, Manea		Party secretary (cultural affairs)
Popa, Dumitru		First party secretary, Bucharest

SOURCES: U.S. Department of State, Bureau of Intelligence and Research, *Directory of Rumanian Officials* (Washington, D.C., August 1966). Radio Free Europe, *Communist Bloc Party-Government Line-Up* (Munich, March 1967), pp. 20-22; Radio Bucharest, January 3, 1967.

[a] Member of the Standing Presidium.

decisions reached by the nine-member Standing Presidium are issued in the name of the Central Committee and of the government. As the implementation of policy at high levels proceeds through the inter- locking directorate, those who make policy are, as often as not, the ones who implement it. The ten-member Secretariat sees to it that policies are executed. Although nominally elected by the Central Committee, it is really appointed by the party leadership and has been a traditional stepping stone to membership on the Executive Com- mittee and Standing Presidium.

Decisions and policies established by the Standing Presidium, and checked by the Secretariat and the Central Collegium, are supposed to be reviewed critically and then approved by plenary sessions of the Central Committee at least four times a year. This procedure, how- ever, merely provides a forum where the party leadership submits to the Central Committee for its rubber-stamp approval the party line as established by the Standing Presidium.

REGIONAL ORGANIZATION. The region and the town or dis- trict are intermediate organizational echelons within the party.[29] The committees of these bodies are near duplicates of the Central Com- mittee at the national level, both organizationally and functionally, although they are smaller in size.

The supreme organ of the region and the town or district is sup- posedly the conference, called to meet by the respective committee every two years. It reviews and approves reports of the committees, debates problems connected with party activities, and elects party committees and delegates to the conference of the next higher party organization or to the national party congress. The conferences are basically sounding boards, and implementation of policies and direc- tives issued by the Central Committee is done by the lower commit- tees and the offices (secretariats) subordinate to them.

The regional committee is supposed to meet every three months. It always remains in contact with the party apparatus at the center through the first secretary of the region, who usually is a member of the Central Committee. The town or district committee meets every two months and represents the immediate superior to the basic party organizations, or cells, which comprise the base of the pyramid.

BASIC PARTY ORGANIZATION. By statute, the party cells constitute the foundation of the party, since they are the ultimate executors of policies and directives issued by the Central Committee. Cells exist in government, industry, agriculture, schools, and military units.[30] Their size can vary from a minimum of three members to a maximum of three hundred. The larger ones are headed by a bureau. If there are fewer than ten members, the leadership comprises a secretary and an alternative secretary. These lowest-ranking organizations (of which there are about 56,000)[31] play a dual role as executors for party and government policies and directives, and as supervisors over the activities of government and other nonparty organs. This is indicative of the manner in which party and government functions overlap and the fact that the party and its organs are placed above the government and its institutions.

PARTY MEMBERSHIP. Probably the most astonishing aspect of the party was its tremendous increase during the postwar years. Membership is estimated to have risen from one thousand [32] in 1944 to almost a million in 1948. Over the next several years the membership fluctuated between 600,000 and 900,000. In 1964, when the party had 1,200,000 members and candidates, about 200,000 of these, or 16 percent, were classified as activists. In 1966 a total of 1,518,000 was reported, representing about 8 percent of the Romanian population.[33]

As with communist parties in the other East European countries, that in Romania has had difficulty in maintaining a proper representation of workers in its ranks. Even with mass recruitment during 1947, the working class component in the membership comprised less than 40 percent, the majority coming from the intelligentsia. This emphasis on worker derivation follows from the glorification of the proletariat in communist doctrine and from the conviction that the leaders within this class—the competitive "Stakhanovite" types with a zeal for surpassing production goals—are generally more reliable, more susceptible to indoctrination, and easier to control. Recruitment procedures were relaxed for this group, and by 1960 the party could claim an increase in the percentage of workers. By 1966, although the worker total was above that of 1960, the percentage had dropped. (See table 36.) Lack of verification of figures and the uncertain definition of just what is a worker make these regime statistics questionable.

MASS ORGANIZATIONS. The Union of Working Youth (*Un-*

iunea Tineretului Muncitor—UTM) was founded in 1948 as a junior branch of the party and comprises a mass organization of some 2.1 million members,[34] patterned after the Soviet komsomol. The UTM is organized similarly to the party, and the party rules indicate that those in the age group of eighteen to twenty years must belong to the UTM in order to be eligible for party membership. Apart from providing the core of future party members and cadres, the UTM has responsibility for carrying out and supervising the execution of party policies as they affect the whole of Romanian youth within its age group and above.

TABLE 36

ROMANIAN COMMUNIST PARTY SOCIAL COMPOSITION, 1960 AND 1966

Category	June 1960		January 1966	
	Number	Percent	Number	Percent
Workers	426,000	51	600,000	39.6
Peasants [a]	186,000	22	480,000	31.8
Intelligentsia [b]	83,000	11	330,000	22.0
Other	131,000	16	99,000	6.6
Total	826,000	100	1,509,000 [c]	100.0

SOURCES: *Scînteia,* July 21, 1965; Radio Bucharest, April 14, 1966.
NOTE: Total membership reached 1,676,000 in 1967. *Scînteia,* May 7, 1967.

[a] This category probably incorporates those on collective, state, and private farms.
[b] Including white-collar employees in 1966 figure.
[c] Some 430,000 women are party members (*Scînteia tineretului,* June 24, 1966, as cited in *Rumanian Press Survey,* June 30, 1966, p. 1).

Until April 1966 the UTM supervised the introductory Pioneers organization for children, whose membership of about 1,300,000 encompasses about 70 percent of the population between the ages of nine and fourteen.[35] The inspiration provided by the similar organization in the Soviet Union can be noted in the Pioneers' former motto: "In the fight for the cause of Lenin and Stalin, forward." They are now under the direct control of the party.

The Central Council of Trade-Unions is one of Romania's largest mass organizations. With a membership of approximately 4.1 million, it covers the complete spectrum of laboring and professional people.[36] Like the party, it is organized according to the principle of democratic centralism. The sixteen component trade-unions have regional and district councils which in turn are superimposed upon some 11,600 basic units. Rather than representing workers, factory committees, and professional groups, the trade-union apparatus has the primary purpose of insuring successful fulfillment of the government's economic plans. It has the added responsibility of raising the cultural level and especially the political consciousness of its members. Indoctrination is generally carried out at the lowest level by party or UTM members who belong to the local trade-union council.

The People's Democratic Front is open to those eligible for membership in other mass organizations. In order to maintain the fiction of representative government, the party has chosen to consider all candidates in parliamentary and local elections as representing the People's Democratic Front. The front accepts the nominees as its own, promotes the election, and presents a political program identical with that of the party. The activities of the front are limited to the election periods occurring every two and four years.

DOMESTIC AND FOREIGN POLICY

The history of the people dates back to the second century, when Roman legions were stationed in what today is Romania. The language, a Romance tongue of Latin origin, can also be traced to this period. Somewhat modified by Slavic, Albanian, Hungarian, Greek, and Turkish influences in the centuries which followed, it still has today a majority of word elements descended from the Latin once spoken in the Eastern Roman Empire. This fact, as noted earlier, continues to be important in the current situation, perhaps as much so as the demographic and geographic features of the country.

Losses of territory occurred in the early part of the Second World War. These comprised Transylvania, Bessarabia, Northern Bukovina, and Southern Dobruja. Transylvania was eventually recovered from Hungary; Bessarabia and Northern Bukovina, however, were transferred in 1940 to the Soviet Union,[37] and Southern Dobruja has been kept by Bulgaria. The several modifications in borders have helped create animosity between Romania and her neighbors, not excepting the U.S.S.R.

When Transylvania was taken back by Romania after the war, some 23,300 square miles of territory were involved, together with the 5,250,000 inhabitants of the area. The 1,500,000 Hungarians included in this transfer still represent the largest minority group in the country. According to the 1966 census, these Magyars comprised in 1966 approximately 8.4 percent of the total population. In recognition of this large minority, a Hungarian autonomous province was created by Articles 19 and 20 of the 1952 constitution. Ethnically, Hungarians comprise 77.3 percent of the population in the province, Romanians a little more than 20 percent, Germans 0.4 percent, Jews 0.4 percent, and Gypsies 1.5 percent.[38] Table 37 shows the ethnic composition of the country together with the extent of change over the 1956-1966 period.

TABLE 37

ETHNIC GROUPS IN ROMANIA, 1956 AND 1966

	1956		1966		
Nationality	Number	Percent of total	Number	Percent of total	Percentage change
Romanians	14,996,114	85.6	16,780,778	87.8	+11.9
Hungarians	1,587,675	9.1	1,602,604	8.4	+ 1.0
Germans	384,708	2.2	376,752	2.0	− 2.0
Other	520,953	3.1	344,922	1.8	—
Total	17,489,450	100.0	19,105,056	100.0	+ 9.2

SOURCE: Radio Bucharest, September 18, 1966.

The 1965 Romanian constitution also makes special provision for minority groups. Article 22 states:

> In the Socialist Republic of Rumania, the coinhabiting national minorities are ensured the free utilization of their native language as well as books, papers, magazines, theatres and education at all levels in their own language. In districts also inhabited by a population of non-Rumanian nationality, all the bodies and institutions use the language of the respective nationality in speech and in writing and appoint officials from its ranks or from the ranks of other citizens who know the language and way of life of the local population.[39]

At one time, there were 2,000 Hungarian elementary schools and 1,000 high schools in the autonomous province.[40] In December 1960, however, the southern part was transferred to the ethnically Romanian province of Braşov. Hungarian archives and libraries have been destroyed here and the buildings torn down to provide stone for new construction. In education, a system of "parallel sections" was introduced which added a Romanian curriculum. After a period of time, the Hungarian curriculum was eliminated.[41]

THE ECONOMY. Romania in the past has been primarily an agricultural country. Approximately two-thirds of the people still remain classified as rural, from a total of just over 19 million. Although the rate of population increase has dropped recently, from 10 per thousand in 1959 to 5.2 per thousand in 1966, it is expected that by 1975 the total will reach more than 21 million.[42] In the years just preceding the Second World War, agriculture and forestry contributed more than half of the national income. By 1962 industry accounted for almost half. Agriculture and forestry contributed a third in 1961, which was a good harvest year.

Investment has been concentrated on industry since the communists gained control. The Soviet communist party's program in 1961 emphasized heavy industry in "creating the material and technical basis for communism," and similarly the leaders in Romania have sought to develop and expand this sector of the economy.[43]

> The consistent Leninist policy of industrializing the country by concentrating on the development of heavy industry, and its main branch, the machine-building industry, has brought about deep changes in the structure of RPR [Romanian People's Republic] exports. Machines and equipment are gaining greater importance in export trade . . .[44]

As a result of primary emphasis on heavy industry, the composition of Romanian exports and imports has changed considerably. Before the war, exports of cereals, oil, timber, livestock, and animal derivatives comprised 90 percent of the total. By 1961, machinery and equipment accounted for 16 percent. In general there has been a change toward an increasing proportion of finished products. Between 1948 and 1958 the proportion of food exports dropped from almost half to 15 percent of the total. The current principal imports —industrial machinery, vehicles, machine tools, iron ore, and coal— also reflect the emphasis on industry.

Economic difficulties resulting from the war and from exploitation by the Soviet Union are still being experienced by the Romanian economy. Although Romania changed sides in August 1944 and fought with the Allies, it was occupied thereafter by Soviet troops.

Many of the Romanian units were disarmed by the Russians at the end of the war. Under armistice agreements with the U.S.S.R., Romania was forced to pay reparations to the equivalent of $300 million in goods at 1938 prices. Over a period of six years, petroleum was delivered to the Soviet Union in considerable amounts for about half the price it would have brought on the world market. The total value of reparations actually obtained by the U.S.S.R. between September 1944 and June 1948 has been estimated at more than $1.7 billion.[45] In order to continue the forced deliveries, several Romanian oil companies were subsidized by the government; even then they failed and had to be taken over by the regime.

The Soviet occupation forces confiscated all property formerly owned by Germans and Italians, including French, Dutch, and Belgian assets expropriated previously by the Germans. (This was in addition to reparations.) Thus in 1946 the U.S.S.R. owned more than a third of all Romania's industrial and financial enterprises. Some of the seized property formed the basis for the Soviet-Romanian joint-stock companies called "Sovroms."

During the 1946-1947 period, about 37.5 percent of Romania's national budget had to be committed for reparations payments. In the next fiscal year the amount rose to 46.6 percent.[46] After 1948 reparations were reduced but not abolished. It was not until 1954 that the Soviet premier, Georgi Malenkov, in an effort to ease the economic situation and increase voluntary political cooperation by Romania, announced the transfer of U.S.S.R. shares in the joint-stock companies to the Bucharest regime. Control, except of "Sovrom-quartz," engaged in mining uranium, was handed over to the Romanian communists during 1954 and 1955.

On the whole, the Romanian economy has had a growth rate higher than that of any other East European country. Between 1950 and 1959, it is claimed, the national income grew annually by 10.3 percent. The officially reported increase was 8 percent in 1960, 10 percent in 1961, 4.5 percent in 1962, and around 10 percent in both 1963 and 1964. The new five-year plan for 1966-1970 envisages an annual 8 percent growth in national income.[47] One of the reasons for this high growth rate is the low level from which it began. There is an admitted disparity between the agricultural and industrial sectors of the economy. Industrial production allegedly has grown at an average rate of 9.7 percent annually over the past several years, while agricultural production increased by only 4.9 percent in the best year during the same period. There are several reasons for this difference.

AGRICULTURE. Approximately two-thirds of the population in Romania still lives in rural areas, as mentioned, yet less than a third of the national income is produced by the agricultural sector of the economy. The reasons for this disparity include opposition of the peasants to collectivization, emphasis on industrial investment and neglect of agriculture,[48] high taxation, inadequate mechanization, continuation of certain backward methods, mismanagement and inefficiency, and droughts. Over the past several years, however, farming has received some increased attention. On the other hand, investment in agriculture is far less than in industry.

The primary crops are corn and wheat. Romania is the only country in the bloc which is self-sufficient in cereals at the present time; in 1963 it even "exported" 400,000 tons of wheat to the U.S.S.R. The year before, complete socialization of agriculture had been announced, two years ahead of schedule.[49] Considering the fact that the Romanian People's Republic was established in December 1947, this represented rather slow progress.

LAND REFORM AND COLLECTIVIZATION. In March 1945, an initial land reform act was passed. On the basis of this legislation, holdings in excess of fifty hectares and all real property belonging to certain categories of individuals, such as war criminals and Germans, was expropriated. Land reform was designed in part to gain peasant support by the granting of small private plots. The major long-term objective, however, was the collectivization of agriculture. Gradual pressure was exerted on the peasants to collectivize. This assumed the form of compulsory delivery quotas, artificially low prices, state ownership of expropriated agricultural machinery, the socializing of credit institutions, mills, and oil presses, and the 1947 monetary reform which practically eliminated peasant savings.

Because of resistance, socialization was carried out gradually and at different levels. The highest of these was the state farm, patterned after the U.S.S.R. *sovkhoz*. In this type of enterprise the agricultural workers do not share in the profits but are paid wages.

Upon joining a collective farm, however, a peasant family turns over to the *kolkhoz* its land, farm implements, draft animals, vehicles, and other equipment. The house and a few head of livestock can be retained. A new member is given a "private" garden plot of land from two-thirds of an acre to one acre in size, depending upon the quality of the soil. After payment of various expenses, delivery of compulsory quotas, and setting aside funds for *kolkhoz* investment, distribution of earnings is made to the collective farmers. This takes place on the basis of the days worked during the year rather than the original contribution of land, animals, or equipment. The number of "standard work days" credited to a member depends upon the type of job performed and can total more or fewer than the actual days worked. Many administrators give themselves several times the number.

> In the district of Dobrudja, for instance, the average number of workdays per *kolkhoz* member annually was 195, while the chairmen of the *kolkhozes* in this district credited themselves with an average of 711 workdays annually.[50]

Because of the strong resistance to collectivization, in 1951 the government introduced the so-called agricultural partnerships. These involve a less rigid form of association. The peasant has a choice of how much he will contribute, and his share of the profits depends upon both the contribution he has made and the amount of work he performs. When the agricultural partnerships tend to become permanent, the higher-level agricultural associations and collective herds are established. In these organizations the cooperation is limited mainly to a pooling of land for plowing, the rest of the work being done by each individual member. In areas where grazing predominates, collective sheep herds and livestock farms have been established.

Collectivization of agriculture at first proceeded slowly. In late 1957 Radio Bucharest announced that 13,065 collective farms existed.[51] These covered less than one-fourth of the arable land. In June 1960, at the Third Congress of the Romanian Workers' party, a new six-year economic plan was adopted. At that time 81 percent of all agriculture was said to be socialized. The largest part consisted of the lowest-level collectives. Only about one-third of the total comprised *kolkhozes*. In early 1962 the goal of 96 percent socialization of agriculture was announced as having been reached.[52] (See, however, table 38, which shows that four years later the officially reported figure was 91 percent.) In attaining this goal, of course, production has been hindered. Because of strict control (some 450,000 communist party members worked in 1966 on collective farms) and a low rate of investment, agricultural growth will probably remain lower than capability.

TABLE 38

TYPES OF FARMS IN ROMANIA, 1966

Type	Area in use (millions of hectares)	Percent of total cultivated area
State agricultural units [a]	4,461.8	30.2
Producer cooperatives [b]	8,993.9	60.8
Agricultural associations	62.8	0.4
Private garden plots	1,272.9	8.6
Total	14,791.4	100.0

SOURCE: [Romania], *Statistical Pocket Book of the Socialist Republic of Romania 1966* (Bucharest, 1966), p. 132.

[a] State farms and experimental stations. The former number 731 on two million hectares, or 14 percent of the land, and during 1966 half of them operated at a loss (combined total) of 380 million lei. Radio Free Europe, *Situation Report*, April 5, 1967.

[b] Collective farms, on which 2.4 million peasants work. RFE, *Situation Report*, January 13, 1967.

INDUSTRY. As in agriculture, nationalization of industry initially lagged. By June 1948, however, most privately owned factories had been taken over by the government. In 1949 the state sector accounted for 85 percent of total industrial production; by 1960 it encompassed 98.8 percent.[53]

As mentioned previously, Romania is concentrating upon heavy industry. Between 1960 and 1965 some 58.8 percent of all national investment was allocated by plan for this sector of the economy.[54] Both imports and exports are oriented toward industry. In order to increase steel production it has been necessary to import large quantities of iron ore, coke, and rolled metals. The trend of imports in machinery and equipment has been toward complete processing plants.

In 1962 Bucharest contracted with West European suppliers to build the largest steel plate mill in the world. A tire factory costing $22 million and two cellulose plants for making paper and related products, obtained from Britain, were set up during the summer of 1963. In 1965 an American company was granted a permit to construct an oil cracking plant. The British are helping set up an ore processing factory at Galați.[55] West Germany, Romania's largest trading partner outside the Soviet bloc, has built an iron and steel mill at Hunedoara in the central part of the country. The French have installed a winery and a processing plant for sugar beets. To pay for this advanced technology and the requisite raw materials Bucharest depends upon exports and credits.

FOREIGN TRADE. Through direct seizure of certain industries, joint-stock companies, and CMEA, the Soviet Union openly exploited the Romanian economy for more than a decade. Since 1954, however, U.S.S.R. control has lessened. The agreement to "sell" Russian interests in industries which were expropriated during the occupation represented a first step in the process of returning stolen property to Bucharest.

The economies of the Soviet Union and Romania are parallel in certain respects. Both countries are engaged in the process of industrialization, although at different levels, and both produce agricultural commodities. Consequently they have similar needs, and these needs are not complementary. The U.S.S.R. probably is reluctant to supply Romania with materials which are in short supply at home. Despite this situation, the largest share of Romania's trade has been with the Soviet Union.[56] (See table 39.)

Bucharest was long deprived of opportunity to obtain foreign exchange, owing to reparations, expropriations, and the arbitrary as well as discriminatory prices established by the U.S.S.R. It is little wonder that the Romanian communists are anxious to trade on a more equitable basis with Western countries. Moreover, Moscow does not protest when Bucharest obtains the latest technology from its enemies.[57]

Importation of coal and iron ore from the Soviet Union has been necessary for continuing the production of steel. During 1963 other sources for iron ore contracts were discussed by Romanian trade missions in the United States, Brazil, India, and Algeria. More recently, emphasis has been placed on the chemical industry [58] because of the availability of oil, methane gas, coal, salt, and other local raw materials. Another reason may be the U.S.S.R.'s twenty-year (1961-1980) fertilizer expansion program and its requirements.

One serious controversy has arisen between the Soviet Union and Romania. This is in connection with the CMEA and economic cooperation. Moscow had wanted Bucharest to concentrate on producing raw materials for industries of the more developed East European countries. The shortage of cereals, particularly wheat, in the Soviet Union and the bloc in general was probably one factor which prompted the U.S.S.R. to press Romania to emphasize agriculture.

TABLE 39

ROMANIAN TRADE WITH THE SOVIET BLOC, 1960-1965
(In millions of lei)

Country	1960	1962	1964	1965	Percentage increase, 1961-1965 over 1956-1960
Soviet Russia	3,329	4,285	5,489	5,067.5 (38.8%)	40
Czechoslovakia ..	759	882	1,030	989.0 (7.6%)	200
East Germany ...	634	613	837	805.4 (6.2%)	50
Poland	264	452	421	492.1 (3.8%)	65
Hungary	406	449	502	399.3 (3.1%)	100
Bulgaria	107	173	125	133.7 (1.0%)	n.a.
Total	5,499	6,854	8,404	7,887.0 (60.5%)	ca. 91

SOURCES: M. Novac, article on "Some Aspects of the RPR's Foreign Economic Relations," *Probleme Economice,* September 1963, as translated in *Rumanian Press Survey,* October 15, 1963, p. 6. I. P. Oleinik, *Pobeda sotsializma v Rumynii* (Moscow, 1962), pp. 202-203. Radio Free Europe report, "Rumanian Foreign Trade in 1964," August 13, 1965, pp. 4-5. *Rumanian Foreign Trade,* No. 3 (1966), as cited in *Rumanian Press Survey,* August 9, 1966. *Die Welt,* September 6, 1966. [Romania], *Statistical Pocket Book of the Socialist Republic of Romania 1966* (Bucharest, 1966), pp. 241-243.
NOTE: Six lei to the U.S. dollar.

Attempts to have this role in the CMEA accepted by Romania were made in person when three high-ranking Soviet officials visited Bucharest. Nikolai Podgorny, then a member of the Soviet party's Presidium and now U.S.S.R. president, came first. Next was the former premier, Khrushchëv, who arrived just before the July 1963 meeting of bloc leaders in East Berlin. (Probably as a result, Gheorghiu-Dej did not attend that meeting.) Khrushchëv was followed by Vasilii V. Kuznetsov, first deputy foreign minister of the U.S.S.R. Accounts of the Bucharest speeches by Podgorny and Gheorghiu-Dej were published in Moscow.

A policy statement issued by the Romanian Central Committee almost a year later, on April 26, 1964, said that Bucharest favored bringing all communist-ruled countries into the CMEA (meaning also Cuba, Albania, and mainland China), but that each bloc state should be completely sovereign over its economic life and must not be forced by any supranational body to take steps it did not wish.[59] Since then Romania seems to have been successful in retaining direction of its economic affairs in this manner.

CHURCH-STATE RELATIONS. In Romania, as in other communist-controlled lands, the churches are allowed to exist temporarily as a necessary evil. Efforts have been made to use them for propaganda purposes, though with only limited success. The mere existence of churches is meant to project the image of religious freedom.

Up to the time that the communists gained control over Romania, religion played a very important part in the life of the people. The Romanian Orthodox Church was the leading and most powerful religious organization in the country before the First World War. It continued afterward to be very active in both local and state government, but its power gradually declined. In 1921 practically all church lands were expropriated. This measure did not affect the Roman Catholic Church as much, because it had always been a minority organization.

The communists assumed control of the churches in 1947 and 1948. This was achieved by taking authority over finances, property, and high-level administration; by placing in key positions clergy considered to be subservient to the regime; and by severing ties with church organizations in foreign countries. As an example, the Bucharest regime in July 1948 abrogated the prewar concordat with the Vatican.

During 1962 the Vatican stated that of the fourteen Catholic archbishops and bishops in Romania, thirteen were under arrest. Three years later it was reported that four of the five Catholic bishops in the country had died in prison.[60] A law since August 4, 1948, has required that all denominations provide the Department of Religious Affairs with inventories of their assets and revenues and that all clergy take an oath of allegiance to the Romanian People's Republic, pledging to obey and help enforce the laws and to defend the state against all enemies.[61] Besides controlling the purse strings and the appointment of personnel in all churches, the Department of

Religious Affairs designates the extent and type of catechism to be taught under church sponsorship.

Apart from these direct techniques, the government uses indirect methods to reduce the influence of churches. Attendance at religious services is not forbidden by law. On the other hand, mass organizations such as the Union of Communist Youth and the Pioneers schedule activities on Sundays and religious holidays (Easter and Christmas are regular working days in Romania) to make church attendance difficult. The general atmosphere created by the communists discourages participation in religious activities by members of the armed forces and those holding government positions. The communists have been successful in reducing the influence of the churches, which no longer poses a significant threat to the government. Although the 1965 constitution (Article 30) guarantees freedom of religion,[62] in practice religion is systematically repressed.

The largest denomination has always been the Romanian Orthodox. This church now has about fourteen million nominal members. Before their forced union with the Romanian Orthodox Church in 1948, the Eastern rite Catholics or Uniates represented the next largest group. The Roman Catholic Church is currently second in size, with about one and three-quarter million members. There are approximately one million Calvinists and some 250,000 communicants of the Lutheran and Jewish faiths.[63] The remaining denominations total fewer than 100,000 members.

FOREIGN POLICY. Romanian foreign policy, since the communists assumed control over the government, has been responsive for the most part to the desires of the Soviet Union. Until the end of 1963 the Romanians always voted with the communist bloc on all questions at the United Nations General Assembly. Although the first two issues on which Romania did not support the bloc were relatively minor,[64] the fact remains that communists pride themselves on unanimity. The Soviets certainly do not welcome this type of divergence in policy.

It was during 1963 that the Romanians began to exercise some independence in their relations with the Soviet Union. While most of the instances have been in the economic sphere, some also involved the cultural area. Romanian trade with capitalist countries in that year already accounted for about a third of the total foreign trade.[65] During 1960 and 1961 Bucharest settled claims by the United States and West European countries. Although the full amounts due were not paid, the settlements probably helped to pave the way for several trade agreements which were signed later.

In 1963 Romania became the first bloc country to resume diplomatic relations with Albania. A summary of Peking's polemical letters to Moscow, published in the Bucharest newspaper *Scînteia* during that year, may have been designed to assist the Romanians in the CMEA dispute which was taking place concurrently. Bucharest probably is alert to the possibilities of increasing trade with mainland China. It has sent delegations to Peking [66] and, although little could be accomplished in mediating the Sino-Soviet dispute, a trade agreement between Romania and China has been signed. Petroleum appeared in it as an export item for the first time. Peking's ambassador to Bucharest, Liu Tang, is a former deputy minister for the petroleum industry.

In a cultural direction, the Institute of Russian Language and Literature has been incorporated by the Slavic Languages department of Bucharest University. In elementary schools Russian has been eliminated as a compulsory language below the eighth grade. In 1965 children down to the fifth grade were given a choice of French, English, German, or Russian.[67] The government also has stopped publishing *Timpuri Noi,* a Soviet periodical printed in the Romanian language, and replaced it with *Lumea,* a foreign affairs magazine which contains a high percentage of reprints from Western publications.

None of this divergence has curtailed Soviet-Romanian trade, which according to a recent agreement [68] will increase some nine percent in 1967. Bucharest's insistence upon exercising sovereignty in economic planning and increasing its trade with the West does not represent a turning from communism. The regime in Romania maintains strict internal control, tighter than in many other East European countries. The fact that Bucharest desires and exercises a certain degree of freedom from Moscow cannot be interpreted as indicating any change from a communist to a democratic ideology.[69]

NOTES

1 D. A. Tomasic, "The Rumanian Communist Leadership," *Slavic Review*, XX. No. 3 (October 1961). 478.

2 Zbigniew K. Brzeziński, *The Soviet Bloc* (rev. ed.; New York, 1962), p. 16.

3 A. B. Mitskevich, *Gosudarstvennyi stroi Rumynskoi Narodnoi Respubliki* (Moscow, 1957), p. 15, discusses the new "people's democracy."

4 "Constitution of the Rumanian People's Republic," in Amos J. Peaslee (ed.), *Constitutions of Nations* (2d ed.; The Hague, 1956), III, 251.

5 [Romania], *Constitution of the Socialist Republic of Rumania* (Bucharest, 1965), p. 34.

6 The party's Ninth Congress, July 19-24, 1965, adopted this name. See the article on "Changes in Romania," *Polityka,* July 24, 1965, p. 10.

7 The 1965 constitution created a permanent Standing Bureau, attached to the Council of Ministers, which comprises an inner cabinet for "collectively settling problems which require an urgent solution." Radio Bucharest, August 20, 1965. It probably includes the premier, the four first deputy premiers, and perhaps all or several of the six deputy premiers.

8 It was claimed that 99.96 per cent of all registered voters had gone to the polls, according to Radio Bucharest, March 9, 1965.

Nicolae Ceauşescu subsequently revealed that 218 deputies were workers, 193 were intellectuals, and 54 were peasants. Speech to the Grand National Assembly, cited in RFE, *Situation Report,* August 25, 1965.

9 See RFE report, "The Rumanian Parliament: Greater Responsibility?", March 4, 1966, p. 1 (5 pp.).

A new electoral law reportedly will allow voters to choose from among several candidates in the future. *New York Times,* December 29, 1966.

10 U.S. Department of State, Bureau of Intelligence and Research, *Directory of Rumanian Officials* (Washington, D.C., August 1966), p. 1, gives the names of the chairman, the three deputies, the secretary, and the 14 other members.

11 For his biography, see RFE, *Eastern Europe's Communist Leaders* (Munich, September 1966), III, 40-43.

12 *România Liberă,* January 13-14, 1966, translated in *Rumanian Press Survey,* February 4, 1966; hereafter cited as *RPS*.

13 As of this writing (1967), there were twenty-four ministries plus five other cabinet offices (Ceremonial, Planning, Agriculture, Culture and Art, and Scientific Research) with the same rank, in addition to a premier, four first deputies, and six deputy premiers. *Line-Up,* pp. 21-22.

14 *Rumanian Statistical Pocket Book 1965* (Bucharest, 1965), table 6, p. 19.

15 Only one candidate was declared not elected; he had obtained less than 50 percent of the vote in his constituency. Radio Bucharest, March 9, 1965.

The People's Councils include some 320,000 workers, 86,000 peasants, and 24,000 intellectuals. Revealed in a speech by Ceauşescu, cited in RFE, *Situation Report,* August 25, 1965, pp. 1-2.

16 Stephen Fischer-Galaţi (ed.), *Romania* (New York, 1957), p. 98.

17 M. A. Gelfer (ed.), *Rumynskaya Narodnaya Respublika; ugolovnyi kodeks 1962* (Moscow, 1962), pp. 143-146.

18 Fischer-Galaţi, *op. cit.,* pp. 96-97.

19 Marin V. Pundeff, "Education for Communism," in Stephen Fischer-Galaţi (ed.), *Eastern Europe in the Sixties* (New York, 1963), pp. 34-35.

20 Randolph L. Braham, *Education in the Rumanian People's Republic* (Washington, D.C., 1963), p. 115. The universities are at Bucharest, Jassy, Cluj, Timisoara, Tirgu Mureş, and, opened in the fall of 1966, Craiova.

21 "The Hungarian Minority Problem in Rumania," *Bulletin of the Inter-*

national Commission of Jurists, No. 17 (December 1963), pp. 35-41.

The population of the Mureş-Magyar region has increased by 50,000 to 818.968 persons over the past decade, *Scînteia*, September 18, 1966.

22 For biographic data to substantiate this point see Tomasic, *op. cit.*, pp. 480-489.

23 Hugh Seton-Watson, *The East European Revolution* (New York, 1956), p. 90.

24 Wayne S. Vucinich, "Soviet Rumania: 1944-1951," *Current History*, XXXII, No. 126 (February 1952), 88.

25 For the most recent, ninth, gathering of 1,564 delegates, at which Nicolae Ceauşescu was elected secretary-general (the same title that Stalin held and one unique in Eastern Europe except for the U.S.S.R. since April 1966), see RFE report (by Herbert Reed), "The Rumanian Party Congress—Round Up," July 30, 1965, p. 6 (11 pp.).

26 This agency (whose members made up the core of the former Political Bureau) as late as 1961 still was not free from external pressure. For security reasons, the maintenance of a system of watchdogs within the Political Bureau was apparently considered necessary to inform Moscow of any threat to its control. Tomasic, *op. cit.*, p. 490.

27 *Ibid.*, p. 492.

28 See RFE report, "The New Rumanian Party Statutes," June 25, 1965, p. 8 (17 pp.).

29 Based on the rules adopted at the second postwar party congress, December 27, 1956.

30 Only those "who do not exploit the labor of others" may become party members and join one of the cells. Yu. Kulyshev (ed.), *III Sezd Rumynskoi Rabochei Partii* (Moscow, 1961), p. 211.

31 An increase of 21,000 since 1960, according to *Scînteia*, July 21, 1965.

32 U.S. Department of State, *Moscow's European Satellites* (Washington, D.C., 1955), p. 12.

33 V. N. Vinogradov (ed.), *Istoriya Ru-*

mynii novogo i noveishego vremeni (Moscow, 1964), p. 382; Radio Bucharest, April 14, 1966.

Romania has abolished the period of candidacy. the first country in Eastern Europe to do this. Radio Bucharest, June 3, 1965.

34 Some 720.000 farmers, 670,000 workers, 600,000 students, and 114,000 young intellectuals (intelligentsia). Speech by Petre Enache, as cited in RFE, *Situation Report*, March 30, 1966, p. 3.

To coincide with the new party designation, the name of this junior partner has been changed to Union of Communist Youth.

35 Radio Bucharest, June 9, 1965; RFE, *Situation Report*, July 13, 1966, pp. 4-5.

A national council of Pioneers' Organizations is to be established. Radio Bucharest, November 11, 1966.

36 RFE report, "The Fifth Congress of Rumanian Trade Unions," June 20, 1966, p. 2 (5 pp.), citing the report by trade-unions' chairman Constantin Drăgan.

37 "On June 28, 1940, following the ultimatum-like demand of the Soviet government, which was accepted by the Rumanian government, Bessarabia and Northern Bukovina became part of the territory of the U.S.S.R." *Lupta de Clasă*, No. 6 (June 1966), translated in *RPS*, July 12, 1966.

38 See "The Hungarian Minority Problem in Rumania," p. 37.

39 [Romania], *Constitution of . . . Rumania*, p. 11.

40 Mitskevich, *op. cit.*, p. 43.

41 "The Hungarian Minority Problem in Rumania," pp. 39-40.

42 RFE, *Situation Report*, June 24, 1966, p. 3; "Demographic Trends in Eastern Europe," *East Europe*, XIII, No. 1 (January 1964), 17.

43 E. D. Karpeshchenko in an article about "Development of a Socialist Economy in the Romanian People's Republic," in V. N. Vinogradov (ed.), *Novaya i noveishaya istoriya Rumynii* (Moscow, 1963), table 3, p. 23.

44 From an article by M. Novac in *Probleme Economice* (Bucharest), Sep-

tember 1963, quoted in *RPS*, October 15, 1963.

See also Karel Holbik's article on investment priorities in Rumania, *Weltwissenschaftliches Archiv*, XCIV, No. 2 (1965), 330-334, for tables.

15 Willard Thorp, U.S. delegate to the 1947 Paris peace conference, as quoted in Alexandre Cretzianu (ed.), *Captive Rumania: A Decade of Soviet Rule* (New York, 1956), p. 51.

46 Brzeziński, *op. cit.*, p. 125.

47 Article by Jerzy Kleer in *Polityka*, July 17, 1965, p. 14. See also RFE, *Situation Report*, June 29, 1966, p. 2, which gives a table with revised targets.

48 During the 1966-1970 five-year plan it is proposed to invest at most 14 percent of the 250 to 260 billion lei (6 lei to the dollar) total in agriculture. Radio Bucharest, June 5, 1965. Revised objectives for 1970 indicate that industry will grow by 73 percent, compared with only 20 percent for agriculture in this five-year period. *New York Times*, July 12, 1966.

49 For an excellent report on developments since that time see RFE, "Rumanian Agriculture since Full Collectivization," April 1965, pp. 4-46 (58 pp.).

50 Wolfgang Oberleitner, "Realities of Agriculture in Rumania," *International Peasant Union Monthly Bulletin*, July-August 1963, p. 19.

51 Cited in *East Europe*, VI, No. 12 (December 1957), 51.

52 The following month, the Grand National Assembly declared collectivization to have been completed. Mikhai Dalya's article on "Socialist Transformation in the Romanian Countryside," in A. Lukovets (ed.), *Narodnaya Rumyniya segodnya, 1944-1964* (Moscow, 1964), p. 18.

53 L. N. Tolkunov (ed.), *Sotsialisticheskii lager* (Moscow, 1962), pp. 293-294.

54 I. P. Oleinik, *Pobeda sotsializma v Rumynii* (Moscow, 1962), p. 110.

55 UPI dispatch, January 3, 1966, cited in RFE, *Situation Report*, January 5, 1966. Britain has also sold Romania a nuclear reactor for research pur-

poses. *New York Times*, September 11, 1966.

56 During the period 1958-1961 about three-fourths of all trade was with the bloc and 40 percent with the U.S.S.R. alone. Valev, *op. cit.*, p. 68. The figure for the bloc trade in 1964 was still 70 percent. Vinogradov, *op. cit.*, p. 386. During that same year the total trade deficit amounted to one billion lei. RFE report, "Implementation of the 1965 Economic Plan," May 13, 1966, p. 8 (14 pp.).

57 Although the United States has sent an official trade mission to Romania, several major problems remain to be solved, such as most-favored-nation treatment, licenses, and credit terms. Agerpres (Romanian press agency) communiqué, May 4, 1966, cited in RFE, *Situation Report*, May 6, 1966.

For 1959 and 1965 figures on trade with capitalist countries see *Probleme Economice*, August 1966, as translated in *RPS*, October 4, 1966, p. 2. Data for 1966 appears in RFE, *Situation Report*, July 12, 1967.

58 Figures showing the substantial increase of chemical production appear in Oleinik, *op. cit.*, table 27, p. 119.

59 Agerpres communiqué, *Statement on the Stand of the Rumanian Workers' Party* (Bucharest, 1964), pp. 27-29. See also the article in *Contimporanul*, No. 31 (1966), translated in *RPS*, August 22, 1966, on the "socialist" nation.

60 Cited by Constantin Vişoianu in U.S. Congress, House of Representatives, Committee on Foreign Affairs, 87th Cong., 2d sess., *Captive European Nations: Hearings* (Washington, D.C., 1962), p. 180. For the names and fates of individual bishops see RFE, *Situation Report*, December 10, 1965, pp. 3-4.

61 Virgiliu Stoicoiu (comp. & transl.), "Church and State in Rumania," in U.S. Senate, Committee on the Judiciary, *The Church and State under Communism* (Washington, D.C., 1965), Vol. II (20 pp.); the oath is given on pp. 4-5.

62 Radio Bucharest, December 29, 1965, claimed that all fifteen recognized denominations operate "without re-

strictions or discrimination." See, however, the testimony of Rev. Richard Wurmbrand on "Communist Exploitation of Religion" in U.S. Senate, Committee on the Judiciary, *Hearings* (Washington, D.C., 1966), pp. 5-25 (42 pp.).

63 According to Chief Rabbi Moses Rosen, Jews number 100,000 and have 250 synagogues as well as smaller temples, but only four rabbis, including himself, and one of these is ninety years old. *New York Times,* August 9, 1966.

64 See "Rumania Splits with Soviets at UN," *East Europe,* XIII, No. 1 (January 1964), 45-46.

65 Soviet "assistance" involves reciprocal arrangements, such as the agreement that Romania will deliver 140 ships to the U.S.S.R. during the 1966-1970 period. Radio Bucharest, March 29, 1965. Some 25 percent of imported machinery, 70 percent of iron ore, and 30 percent of coke is to come from the U.S.S.R. Soviet cotton plays an important role in Romania's light industry. Radio Moscow, May 6, 1965.

66 A visit to Bucharest was made during June 1966 by the Chinese premier, Chou En-lai. See RFE report (by J. F. Brown), "The Failure in Bucharest," June 28, 1966, p. 1 (4 pp.).

67 Ministry of Education program for final examinations, as broadcast by Radio Bucharest, February 7, 1965.

68 Radio Bucharest, November 14,1966.

Romania apparently has given up efforts to strengthen ties with the United States and is concentrating on Western Europe. Note, for example, the establishment of consular relations with Spain. *New York Times,* January 6, 1967.

69 See the statement by Foreign minister Corneliu Mănescu in *Christian Science Monitor,* November 8, 1966. See also RFE report (by J. F. Brown), "Rumania's Situation and Prospects," April 10, 1967 (22 pp.). Note also the reorganization of the secret police into a Council of State Security which experienced observers doubt will bring about any real relaxation "in a regime whose control of its people is one of the tightest in Eastern Europe." *New York Times,* July 21, 1967.

Chapter 8 / YUGOSLAVIA:
Land of Southern Slavs

THE Socialist Federated Republic of Yugoslavia (*Socijalistička Federativna Republika Jugoslavija*) is the only federal state in Eastern Europe and the most heterogeneous country on the continent, except for the U.S.S.R. It has received the following apocryphal description: one political party, two alphabets, three religions, four languages, five nationalities, six republics, and seven bordering states.[1] Even the name Yugoslavia connotes diversity and multiplicity. It means "land of the southern Slavs" and represents a collective designation for all Slavic people in the Balkans, who were present there even before the dawn of recorded history.

GENERAL SURVEY

The establishment of a single country has been the result of Yugoslavia's geographic location. The territory served in the past as a passageway or land route between Western Europe and Asia. This corridor position has influenced the development of the nation both to its advantage and negatively. Predominantly mountainous, with hills covering about 70 percent of the total area, Yugoslavia comprises six federal republics which fall roughly into line with the geographic features. They are Serbia, Croatia, Slovenia, Bosnia-Herzegovina, Macedonia, and Montenegro. The autonomous regions of Voivodina and Kosovo-Metohija (often referred to as Kosmet) are located within Serbia.

Corresponding with this division, ethnic groups can be differentiated as shown in table 40. The total population of Yugoslavia, in the 1961 census, was about 18.6 million. The table shows the fifteen identifiable ethnic groups found in one or more of the federal repub-

215

lics and autonomous areas. None of the divisions of the country are at all homogeneous.

The four basic languages—Serbian, Croatian, Slovene, and Macedonian—are often treated as only three by joining Serbian and Croatian to form the Serbo-Croat language. These basic tongues arose from the slow evolution of dialects from a single language, the Old (Church) Slavonic spoken by the original inhabitants of the Balkan peninsula.

TABLE 40

ETHNIC GROUPS IN YUGOSLAVIA, 1961 CENSUS

Nationality	Number of persons	Percent of total
Serbs	7,806,213	41.8
Croatians	4,293,860	23.0
Slovenes	1,589,192	9.2
Macedonians	1,045,530	5.6
Montenegrins	513,833	2.7
Muslims [a]	972,954	5.2
Yugoslavs [a]	317,125	1.8
Shiptars [b]	914,760	4.9
Hungarians	504,368	2.7
Turks	182,964	1.0
Slovaks	86,433	0.5
Romanians	60,862	0.3
Bulgars	62,624	0.3
Italians	25,615	0.1
Czechs	30,331	0.1
Other and unidentified	142,627	0.8
Total	18,549,291	100.0

SOURCE: [Yugoslavia], *Statistički Godišnjak 1964* (Belgrade, 1964), p. 352.

[a] These consider themselves to be distinct ethnic groups.

[b] Albanians.

Religion is one of the important aspects of the diversity characteristic of Yugoslavia. More than 41 percent of the population is Serbian (Eastern) Orthodox, almost 32 percent Roman Catholic, and more than 12 percent Moslem, with the remaining miscellaneous or not belonging to any church. (See table 41.) It is a significant fact that the Orthodox Church has strongly identified itself with the Serbian nationality, and the Catholic Church with the Croatians and Slovenes. These alignments have influenced and greatly colored nationalistic tendencies and differences which date back to the Middle Ages, when the latter two groups were under the jurisdiction of Rome.

For this reason, the two basic alphabets are Latin and Cyrillic, corresponding to the East-West religious division. The Cyrillic is essentially based on Greek letters, augmented by additional symbols. Generally, it is used by the Serbs and Bulgarians (and also Russians), who comprise in essence the Eastern Orthodox Slavs. The Latin alphabet, on the other hand, supplemented with diacritical marks, is utilized by the Croatians and Slovenes (and also Poles and Czechs), who comprise the Roman Catholic Slavs. Slovenian can be written only with Latin letters, and Macedonian only with Cyrillic. In many newspapers today, both alphabets are found.

TABLE 41

RELIGION IN YUGOSLAVIA, 1953

Church	Nationalities	Number of members	Percent of total population
Serbian (Eastern) Orthodox	Serbs, Montenegrins, Romanians, Bulgars . .	7,000,000	41.5
Roman Catholic	Croats, Slovenes, Hungarians, Slovaks, Italians	5,400,000	31.8
Moslem	Macedonians, Turks, Albanians	2,100,000	12.3
Protestant . . . . Czechs		150,000	0.9
Other denominations		200,000	1.2
None		2,100,000	12.3
Total		16,950,000	100.0

SOURCE: Georg Stadtmüller, article on "The Churches and Denominations of Yugoslavia," in Herbert Ludat (ed.), *Jugoslawien Zwischen West und Ost* (2d ed.; Giessen, 1963), p. 55.

NOTE: For a comparison with 1931 see Roger Portal, *Les Slaves: Peuples et Nations* (Paris, 1965), p. 430.

THE SECOND WORLD WAR. Yugoslavia fell early in 1941 to German invasion. The first guerrilla operations were headed by Colonel (later General) Draža Mihajlović. In June of that year Germany's attack on the Soviet Union provided a signal for all communists to support Moscow. Shortly thereafter, a second resistance movement became active in Yugoslavia. The "Partisans," under the leadership of a mysterious figure known as Tito (Josip Broz, secretary-general of the Yugoslav communist party), began activities against the German occupant, somewhat later than Mihajlović and his London-directed Chetniks. Harsh reprisals became the order of the day. In one case, an entire community of about 7,000 inhabitants was massacred by the Germans.[2] Under Hitler's *Nacht und Nebel* ("night and fog") decree, between fifty and a hundred Yugoslavs were executed for every German wounded or killed.

Proclamation of a *de facto* government by Tito was not carried out until November 1943 and then against the desires of Stalin, who thought the time inopportune and called the decision "a stab in the back of the Soviet Union." The second session of the Anti-Fascist Council for National Liberation of Yugoslavia proclaimed itself at Jajce the supreme representative of the peoples and of the state of Yugoslavia as a whole, divested the royal Yugoslav government-in-exile of its legal rights, forbade King Peter II to return, and decided that the future state should be built on the federalist system.[3]

These moves, combined with British and American favoritism toward the Partisans, led to abandonment of the Chetnik leader Draža Mihajlović and the royal government-in-exile by the West. Concurrently, the small amount of U.S.S.R. military assistance Tito received late in 1944 and the German retreat allowed the communists to seize power. In a typical instance of communist tactics, a provisional coalition government was created.

The coalition provided Tito with twenty-three ministers out of twenty-eight, and he established himself as premier as well as Defense minister. In November 1945 the monarchy was abolished. Establishment of the "Federal People's Republic of Yugoslavia" followed the 1946 promulgation of a U.S.S.R.-type constitution.[4] After a mock trial, the last remnant of the former royalist regime faded from the picture when General Mihajlović was executed.

POSTWAR DEVELOPMENTS. The end of the war saw the Tito resistance movement transformed into a "constitutional" regime. A significant factor has shaped the country, namely, the Yugoslav communists' achieving of political power largely without Soviet assistance. This phenomenon underlies both domestic and foreign relations. It accounts for the early consolidation of the communist regime on a nationalist basis and the subsequent conflict with Moscow.

The standard monolithic totalitarianism featured complete nationalization of industry, centralized economic planning, a single communist front organization, and elimination of all opponents. Thus, during the period 1945-1949, the Federal People's Republic of Yugoslavia was modeled after the U.S.S.R. in both structure and operation.

During the years 1945 and 1946 widespread starvation probably would have resulted except for aid from the United Nations Relief and Rehabilitation Administration. Almost simultaneously, reconstruction and nationalization were set into motion, along with a vigorous campaign to collectivize all peasant holdings into producers' work cooperatives which "ran into passive resistance from the peasantry." [5] The first industrialization drive soon followed.

Planned goals were too high and were prepared by men with little experience. The "big leap" involved the hope for rapid conversion from a basically agrarian to an industrialized economy within the relatively short span of five years (1947-1951). The plan anticipated U.S.S.R. and other East European support in the form of long-term credits for industrial machinery and other equipment. After this economic plan had been set into motion, two basic changes occurred.

First came the slowdown in collectivization, used as a pretext by Stalin for the subsequent break. Moscow demanded firmer agricultural measures, but the leaders in Belgrade relaxed their pressure on the peasants. Next the Communist Information Bureau or Cominform—paradoxically suggested by the Yugoslav communists themselves—was established by Stalin to keep the satellites under control,[6] and this body passed a resolution for the condemnation and expulsion of the Yugoslav communist party, anathematizing it as being outside Moscow's world communist movement. The real reason for the dispute was Stalin's distrust of the leadership in Belgrade.

Tito really had no desire to challenge Stalin, but the traumatic experience produced a degree of unity within the Yugoslav party in spite of and perhaps because of Soviet pressure. The failing condition of the economy and the five-year plan, combined with international isolation, forced Tito reluctantly to turn to the West for aid. The rapprochement with the West surpassed all that Yugoslavia could have anticipated. The net result was "Titoism," which has been defined in various ways, depending upon the point of view and the time.[7]

ECONOMIC PLANNING. Yugoslavia's economic system is complicated, confusing, but socialist. Industry and commerce engage relatively little private enterprise, yet technically there is no state ownership. A varied type of agriculture is carried on by the peasants. The authoritative journal of the world communist movement adhering to Moscow reports the basic principle of the Yugoslav socialist economy to be "planned guidance." [8] The economy is, indeed, planned. The state, however, does not administer the various economic enterprises. Its purposes are accomplished by having them operate allegedly under the management of the workers themselves.

Yugoslav economic planning is unlike that in any other communist-ruled country, primarily because the plan allegedly is not binding. In an interesting but forthright approach, one Soviet writer terms it euphemistically "in the nature of an obligatory guide to all elected bodies." [9] A federal planning bureau is responsible for drawing up the national economic plan. Economic planning takes place simultaneously at all levels, with an attempt at continuous coordination of efforts among republics, districts, communes, individual enterprises, and economic chambers representing groups of enterprises.

WORKER-MANAGEMENT. With the change of policy in the direction of a more decentralized economic system, the concept of worker-management, and specifically the workers' council, had come to the fore. According to the latest constitution,[10] adopted in April 1963, the basis for the system is "free associated labor performed with socially owned means of production and distribution of the social product in working organizations and the community." In theory, the constitution provides that every member of a working organization is "entitled to a personal income proportionate to the results of his work and to the work of his department and of the working organization as a whole." This becomes applicable only after providing out of the profits "means to renew resources expended" and reserves for "expansion of production." [11]

The working organizations, which are in theory independent and autonomous, may include individuals professionally active who form units with the same status as industrial workers. Any such organization includes the following: a workers' council (*radnički savet*), the basic element, consisting of fifteen to 200 members and varying with the size of the enterprise; a management board (*upravni odbor*) usually numbering from three to seventeen persons; and the director or manager of the enterprise, who supervises the business and executes the decisions of the workers' council and other management organs.[12]

All officials are elected from among the employees, with terms being two years for the workers' council and one year for the management board. Although nobody may be elected twice consecutively to the council or more than twice consecutively to the management board, the manager or director may be eligible for additional terms of office. He is nominated by the workers' council, after being proposed by an "appointments commission," and it is through this commission that state and party control is inserted. In theory, however, the new constitution of 1963 states that self-government in working organizations includes the right of workers to manage their respective enterprise directly or by elected bodies, organize production and decide about expansion of the enterprise, distribute income, regulate working conditions, and decide to associate with other enterprises.[13] Workers' councils represent one of the features of the Yugoslav system distinguishing it from all other communist regimes.

ECONOMIC REFORM. After the sixth plenum of the party's Central Committee in March 1964, presided over by Tito,[14] the Yugoslav communist leaders appeared to be torn between restricting the workers' self-management system or making workers' councils a major power in the country. More than a year later, the Central Committee decided to introduce economic reforms which would make each enterprise responsible for itself.

The objective of the new economic measures, as announced at a Central Committee plenum in June 1965, is a decrease in decision-making by the state. Market forces are to determine the distribution of investment funds through a price system including realistic exchange rates. Only those plants which are profitable can survive, in view of the abandonment of subsidies. Voluntary mergers, however, may take place. In order to implement the foregoing, specific measures include a new banking system, devaluation of the dinar, prices determined by unfettered movement on the free market, a different planning system, and a new basis for distribution. Marx is, thus, being used to prove that "a market economy, the law of value, the law of supply and demand, the investment of foreign capital, payment according to work done, and even private ownership" [15] are the essence of socialism and do not imply an adoption of capitalism.

AGRICULTURE. Yugoslavia is traditionally a country of farmers. Agriculture was the most significant branch of the prewar economy. In 1940 the population living on the land amounted to 75 percent of the total, but the proportion has been decreasing rapidly and by 1965 had dropped to 45 percent.[16] Yugoslavia's main goal in agriculture is to increase production. The communists thought at first that this could be attained in part by moving the surplus farm population to the cities. A corollary policy after the war involved the drive to collectivize the peasantry.

Yugoslav economists were intelligent enough to confess the failure of collectivization by force and to abandon this negative policy. A new program in 1953 disbanded most collective farms, the land being returned to private ownership by the peasants. Compulsory delivery quotas were abolished, a free market for agricultural products was introduced, and the private sale and purchase of land was allowed. Farmers could own up to a maximum of ten hectares (24.7 acres) of land for each household.[17] Despite these concessions, agricultural production has not increased substantially, and has even declined in three categories, as shown in table 42.

TABLE 42

YUGOSLAV AGRICULTURAL PRODUCTION, 1959-1964
(In thousands of metric tons)

Commodity	1959	1961	1964
Wheat and rice	4,395	3,360	3,725
Corn (maize)	6,670	4,545	6,960
Sugar beets	2,420	1,745	2,830
Sunflowers	114	117	260
Potatoes	2,760	2,690	2,820
Plums	1,210	1,130	760
Meat	575	670	687
Milk (millions of liters)	2,451	2,415	2,334

SOURCES: P. D. Mineev and V. A. Tokarev, *Yugoslaviya* (Moscow, 1963), p. 32. [Yugoslavia]. *Statistički Godišnjak SFRJ 1965* (Belgrade, 1965), pp. 149-157.

The new approach is oriented toward a gradual socialization of agricultural activities, and increased cooperation between the socialist and private sectors is encouraged in order to achieve the same goal without force. Four basic farm sectors exist today. The private sector predominates, as the peasants themselves own about 89 percent of all agricultural land, on 2.6 million farms. The three nonprivate sectors include Peasant Work Cooperatives which are collective farms, similar to the Soviet *kolkhoz;* state farms, the Yugoslav equivalent of the *sovkhoz;* and General Agricultural Cooperatives, which are the least regimented. (See table 43.) The regime primarily counts on the last two for implementation of its gradual programs of socialization.

TABLE 43

AGRICULTURAL LAND DISTRIBUTION IN YUGOSLAVIA, 1964

Category	Units	Area (hectares)	Percent of total
State farms	314	800,000	5.3
Peasant Work Cooperatives	40	130,000	0.9
General Agricultural Cooperatives	2,424	650,000	4.3
Private farms	2,618,000	13,300,000	88.7
Experimental farms, schools, institutes	471	120,000	0.8
Total	2,621,249	15,000,000	100.0

SOURCES: Radio Free Europe report (by Slobodan Stanković), "State Farms Lose Money in Yugoslavia Also," February 19, 1964 (3 pp.). [Yugoslavia], *Statistical Pocket-Book of Yugoslavia 1965* (Belgrade, March 1965), pp. 43, 48.

NOTE: According to Radio Zagreb, February 6, 1966, some 87 percent of all arable land was still owned privately. The 5½ million peasants comprise 54% of the total labor force.

The Peasant Work Cooperatives are organized, like the nonagricultural enterprises, under worker-management. They are voluntary, with land being community owned and farmed. Only 40 of these exist throughout the country—a drop from 229 in 1959 and 6,625 in 1948—and their role in production is very small. In 1959 there were 4,803 General Agricultural Cooperatives, but in 1964 the number had decreased to some 2,400.[18] The plan to draw the individual peasant into dependence on the state is further strengthened by the fact that all government agricultural investments and subsidies are reserved for state farms and General Agricultural Cooperatives. None go to the private sector.

By and large, however, the Yugoslav regime has failed in its effort to persuade private-entrepreneur farmers to abandon their individual plots and join collectives. The peasants have followed plans of their own, and at the end of 1962 only 8 percent of the land owned by private entrepreneurs remained in voluntary cooperation with the collectives.[19] By means of "sly" one-year contracts, varying annual plowing practices, and adequate fertilization of their land the peasants are able to circumvent the state.

There are many forms of cooperation between the private sector and the General Agricultural Cooperatives, but they fall into three basic categories: "rendering services," usually paid in cash by the private individual for the use of machinery, seed, and chemical fertilizers; "joint production," called a higher form of cooperation, in which socialist and private forces join to share proportionately in productive services and goods; and other forms, such as contracts by a cooperative with a private farmer for his expertise, labor, and products.[20] Between 1959 and 1962 the volume of work performed through socialist cooperation on private farms with respect to plowing almost doubled. Cooperative sowing, cultivation, and harvesting likewise slowly have increased. On the other hand, the land itself and the animals are guarded zealously by the farmer as his own.

One method of comparing results among the private and the other two sectors is to examine the yields per hectare. It would appear from government statistics that the greatest yields come from the state farms (or socialist sector) and the lowest from private farms. Careful analysis, however, shows major discrimination by the government against the private farms. Government investments in the socialist sector run to about six times more per hectare than private entrepreneurs could afford. Even so, yields are only 2.5 times higher in the socialist sector. Private entrepreneurs must pay twice as much for fertilizers as do the others. The socialist and cooperative sectors work the best land and under the most favorable conditions. Additional limitations on the private sector include restricting the owned land to ten hectares, as we have noted, and levying disproportionately heavy taxes.[21]

The main problems in the country's agriculture are, in the private sector, to increase production (so as to remain outside collectives) and, in the socialist sector, to show a profit. The latter amounts to a deficit operation. For example, "the largest state farm in Yugoslavia, called 'Belje,' had a loss of about two billion dinars (approximately 2.7 million dollars) at the end of 1963." [22] This must make Yugoslav communist leaders think, inasmuch as the state farms were created especially to serve as focal points which would attract private farmers, who still cultivate 13.3 million of the 15 million hectares in agricultural land (table 43).

It is evident that the policy of persuasion has not induced peasants to join collective farms. Only under the relative freedom of the individual farmer have there been any broadly positive results. This is significant because nothing goes to the private entrepreneur. Very little is provided even for the General Agricultural Cooperatives. The lion's share has been allocated to the socialist sector, which is failing. In 1965 it was announced that the regime lacked about 100 billion dinars to cover the increased costs of investments in agriculture.[23]

INDUSTRIAL GROWTH AND RESOURCE BASE. The Tito regime has followed Marxist dogma in giving priority to industrialization. Fortunately, the country of Yugoslavia was in a comparatively advantageous position to carry this out. In contrast to agriculture, the means of industrial production were completely nationalized by the state after the war and have remained so. Primary emphasis was placed on heavy industry, mining, electric power, and raw materials in the successive national economic plans. Shifts in policy, however, have prevented Yugoslav industry from developing evenly.

An example of industrial growth is iron and steel production, which has increased to become the largest in the Balkans. Transportation has lagged. The single-track, antiquated railway facilities are being corrected by a plan introduced in 1962 which calls for expansion and modernization. Automatic signaling equipment, new diesel locomotives, and double-track lines are part of the program. The problems of surplus unskilled labor in areas too far removed from the plants and shortages of the skilled are being attacked. Both may be solved by location of "some capacity in areas with plentiful labor" and by training local workers where new plants are being constructed.[24]

Yugoslavia is also fortunate in having substantial raw material reserves to cope with the ambitious plans for economic growth.[25] Mineral resources are abundant, with the exception of coking coal and petroleum products. Despite intensive surveying and drilling over a seven-year period, only half of all petroleum needs in 1963 were supplied from inside the country. The first Yugoslav nuclear plant has been put into operation at Kalva, near the Bulgarian border, utilizing rich deposits of uranium from an active mine.

NATIONALISM. Without any doubt, nationalism represents the most important domestic phenomenon in Yugoslavia. Closely related to this is the problem of the standard of living. On the one hand, there is antagonism between the various "nations" within the country; on the other there is a desire for a better life throughout Yugoslavia. This desire certainly exists in the underdeveloped regions of Macedonia and Montenegro, and in the mountainous parts of Bosnia and Herzegovina, where living conditions have been relatively primitive. One cause for nationalist prejudice appears to be the regime's policy of bringing into better balance the economic development of all regions.

This policy has not been popular, despite the fact that the benefited regions have a more rapidly increasing population, a larger agricultural manpower base, and most of the natural resources. Some 28 percent of all investments in recent years has gone into these areas, which amount comprises twice that allocated to the more developed republic of Slovenia. Moreover, production in Slovenia and Croatia has increased more than twice as much as in the regions favored by generous investments. (See table 44.)

TABLE 44

YUGOSLAVIA'S NATIONAL INCOME, 1964
(Excluding services)

Province	New dinars (billions)	Population (millions)
Bosnia and Herzegovina	6.8	3.5
Croatia	14.6	4.3
Macedonia	3.0	1.5
Montenegro	0.9	0.5
Serbia	21.5	7.9
Slovenia	9.0	1.6
Total	55.8	19.3

SOURCE: "Enterprise and Socialism?" *The Economist,* July 16, 1966, p. 238, air edition.
NOTE: One U.S. dollar equals 12.5 dinars.

This nationalist tendency boiling beneath the surface is connected with measures of centralization, euphemistically called inte-

gration. The liberal intellectuals object to pressures by party apparatus workers. Their resistance in Slovenia and Croatia is directed
against any centralizing measure as a violation of nationality rights.
The old Croat-Serb dispute also remains an issue, with the Croatians
blaming the party (identified mainly with Serbia) for the creeping
increase in prices as adversely affecting their ability to raise the standard of living. Speaking to the fifth congress of his organization, the
secretary of the Slovene League of Communists complained that nationalistic trends among intellectuals "could disturb the healthy
growth of socialist relations" and "do serious damage to the harmony
and unity of the Yugoslav multinational community." [26]

STANDARD OF LIVING. Tourism brought in about 156 mil-
lion dollars during 1966, and contact with the West is relatively free.
With the common desire to be better off, there has developed a trend
toward rising expectations throughout the country. This and the
difficulty of finding employment and housing will have driven some
400,000 Yugoslav workers abroad by the end of 1967, primarily to
West Germany, France, Austria, and Sweden.[27] The reforms announced in July 1965 will result in dismissal of an estimated quarter-
million additional workers. It would be wise for the regime to permit
these unemployed to emigrate on temporary labor permits but retain
their Yugoslav citizenship.

One of the reasons for this heavy migration abroad is that the cost
of living in Yugoslavia today approximates that of Western Europe,
while the wage level is only about one-fourth as high. Industrial workers earn on the average about fifty dollars per month. Prices have
risen as much as 35 percent in a single year. Part of the problem is
related to the fact that various branches of industry have been subsidized by the government up to a total of 400 billion dinars per
year,[28] making the amount of labor expended on a particular product
completely irrelevant to its price.

Yugoslavia's standard of living is, of course, affected by the extent
and availability of education. All children between the ages of seven
and fifteen years are required to attend an eight-year school. The
previously high illiteracy rate has declined to 21.1 percent, though
illiteracy is still "widespread among elderly people and in the villages" and on the average is "three times as high among women as
among the men." According to one estimate, among the adults who

took postwar reading and writing courses about 70 percent, or 1.5 million persons, have reverted to illiteracy. About four-fifths of the population above the age of ten years remains illiterate or has completed only four grades of elementary school.[29]

The working class in Yugoslavia probably is dissatisfied with the limited access to educational opportunities for its children. Owing to the almost prohibitive cost of housing, food, and school supplies, which has been estimated at 10,000 old dinars per month per child, only about one worker's family in four can send its children to a secondary school. In 1963 a weekly youth paper reported that 7 percent of the 33,000 students at Belgrade University were of proletarian extraction.[30]

STRUCTURE OF GOVERNMENT

THE CONSTITUTION. The first postwar constitution was adopted by the Yugoslav government in 1946. Its main feature was the establishment of six constituent republics. This was not a genuine federal arrangement, because the republics were subordinated in most important matters to the central government. The federal principle remained to a great extent theoretical, except that both houses of the so-called parliament had equal powers. There were twenty-four areas of jurisdiction in which the federation possessed exclusive competence, so that the residual powers of the republics had almost no practical meaning.

In 1953 the constitution was drastically modified, so that it became in effect a new one. Eight of its fifteen sections were abrogated.[31] Even in this form it did not cover many important later developments in the political and social system. Hence, in December 1960, the Federal Assembly, or parliament, appointed a constitutional commission to prepare a completely new basic law. A preliminary draft was not ready until almost two years later.

The constitution, as finally adopted in April 1963, lays down a number of principles on which the socialist system in Yugoslavia is founded. It also departs from its predecessor in several fundamental respects. The former people's republic is designated the Socialist Federated Republic of Yugoslavia. The office of the premier (whose official title is president of the Federal Executive Council), abolished the year before, is restored, and a vice-presidency of the republic is introduced. The Federal Assembly now consists of five chambers, instead of the former two. The complicated system of direct and indirect elections is a new feature. Finally, a system of rotation in office has been introduced, whereby members of public bodies may not be reelected to a second consecutive term. Thus, occupancy of the leading political offices is now restricted, except in the case of Tito, who is president of the republic for life.

Another significant feature of the 1963 constitution includes acknowledgment of the League of Communists of Yugoslavia (the party) and the communist-front Socialist Alliance as the only political groups having legal status. Therefore control over the federal government is firmly in the hands of the party, through the president of the republic, who now enjoys enlarged powers.

LEGISLATURE. Corresponding to a Western legislature or parliament is the Federal Assembly, divided into five chambers or councils and having a total of 670 members. The most important chamber is the Federal Council (not to be confused with the Council of Ministers, which is called the Federal Executive Council). It has 120 members, nominated at meetings of voters-at-large in each community under the supervision of the Socialist Alliance and then elected by communal assemblies. This election is "confirmed" by popular referendum. In addition, the Federal Council includes ten delegates from the assembly of each republic and five from each autonomous region who make up the Council of Nationalities, bringing the total to 190 persons. The Council of Nationalities does not function as an upper chamber, and it meets only when matters concerning the equality of the nationalities or the republics and regions are being considered.

The primary task of the Federal Council is to discuss and approve legislation, acting in conjunction with one or another of the four specialized chambers: the Council of the Economy, the Council of Education and Culture, the Council of Social Welfare and Health, and the Political-Administrative Council. Candidates for each of these chambers are selected by and from the appropriate working organizations. They are elected by the communal assemblies. Each chamber consists of 120 members.[32]

The Federal Council is the most important among the chambers because it is responsible for basic policy matters, foreign affairs, and national defense. Vidoje Šmilevski is head of this powerful council, and Milentije Popović is president of the entire 670-member Federal Assembly.[33]

The Federal Assembly, or parliament, is the only body theoretically competent to amend the constitution, pass national laws, adopt federal plans and budgets, call a referendum, ratify international agreements, decide upon questions of war and peace, alter the boundaries of Yugoslavia, lay down the foundation for internal and foreign policy, and supervise the work of the federal executive and administrative bodies.[34] It elects the president and vice-president of the republic, the president of the Federal Executive Council, and members of the federal courts.

As in the British Parliament, the Federal Assembly has a regular question period during which members may obtain information from government officials. In recent years this has been utilized to a somewhat greater extent than heretofore. The resemblance to the similar practice in Britain, however, is more formal than real. Legislative proposals by the Federal Executive Council are rarely amended, except in minor ways, and are, thus, assured favorable Assembly action. Recently, strong objections to having draft laws prepared only by administrative agencies have been publicized.[35]

Certain improvements in the Federal Assembly's ability and prestige have been more pronounced than has any increase of its authority or independence. The establishment of a joint parliamentary committee with broad powers to investigate expenditures and general policies at all levels, of standing committees of the Assembly with some authority over administration, and of the Constitutional Court may have been conceived to permit the Federal Assembly "safely" to act with more independence. Even with all of this, it remains clear that the Yugoslav parliament does not operate like a Western legislative body.

THE EXECUTIVE. This branch of the government is headed by Josip Broz-Tito, president of the Socialist Federated Republic of Yugoslavia. Some important innovations in the presidency appear in the 1963 constitution, but they are likely to have little effect on either the organization of the executive or its practices so long as Tito is chief of state. The new basic law provides a four-year term of office for the president, who may be reelected only once. Tito is exempted from this provision because of his "historic merits" and should remain in his position for life.

The president, who is also commander-in-chief of the armed forces, promulgates federal laws by decree, proposes the election of the judges of the Constitutional Court, appoints ambassadors, grants pardons for criminal offenses, and, if the Federal Assembly is unable to meet, declares war.[36] During a state of hostilities or in the event of an immediate threat of war, the president may pass decrees with the force of law on matters within the Assembly's jurisdiction. These he would submit to the Assembly for approval as soon as it could meet. He supposedly exercises his authority within the restrictions of the constitution and federal law.

The vice-presidency is currently held by Koča Popović, who in July 1966 replaced Aleksandar Ranković. Popović formerly had control over foreign affairs. The vice-presidency is the second most important position in the country. The incumbent is elected by the Federal Assembly and may not be reelected to another consecutive four-year term.[37] The vice-president is not constitutionally designated to succeed the president. If the legal forms of the constitution are complied with, upon the death or retirement of Tito, the president of the parliament will perform the functions of this office until new elections are held.

The Federal Executive Council, being the source of legislative proposals, is the most important governmental body so far as the character of day-to-day government operations is concerned. Its fifty-seven members constitute what is in fact a cabinet.[38] Tito as president of the republic proposes a member of the Federal Assembly as president of the Federal Executive Council; the proposal is then voted on by the Assembly. This officer (at present Mika Špiljak) is automatically the premier. The other members of the council, or cabinet, are elected by the Assembly on recommendation by the premier, one consideration being that the composition of the council shall reflect the various nationalities of the country.

LOCAL GOVERNMENT. Decentralization of both political and economic power, which allegedly represents the basis for Yugoslavia's different approach to communism, is nowhere better illustrated than in local government. The wide administrative authority, the degree of autonomy, and the extent of citizen participation in local government are major factors in the Yugoslav claim to have blended political democracy with socialism. The basic local unit, the *opština* or commune, is claimed to be a genuinely new form of government.

By 1946 the People's Committees were already established as prime movers in political and economic affairs. In 1963 all authority was given to the People's Committees other than that specifically delegated to the federal and the constituent republic and autonomous region governments. People's Committees exist at the level of the *opština,* or subdivision of a district; the *srez,* or district; and the *grad,* or city. At the district and city levels the committees are bicameral. There has been a tendency to reduce the number of districts, and many of them have been abolished.

Since adoption of the 1963 constitution, local government rests on a system of communes. Although in theory a Yugoslav commune is more than a unit of local government, it can best be envisaged as such.[39] As the system is now set up, there exist only two major levels of local government, the commune (*opština*) and the district, which represents a number of communes. Larger cities have the status of districts, and smaller cities are governed by special town councils that operate under district or commune authority.

At present districts hold jurisdiction over broad political matters, such as law enforcement and elections. They are responsible for coordinating activity within their general jurisdiction.[40] But the communes have become the key local units, with three primary concerns. One of these is economic, in connection with planning, investments, internal trade, and supervision over economic enterprises. Another includes municipal services, such as water supply, sewers, streets, and public utilities. A third comprises the whole area of "social management," which means citizen control over public activities.

JUDICIAL SYSTEM. The courts are divided into three categories: regular, economic, and military. The federal Supreme Court (a regular tribunal) is the final appeal for all, including the military tribunals. Economic courts, which do not consider criminal cases, act mostly in arbitration of disputes involving economic enterprises. That the judiciary can be used for political purposes was evident in the recent case of Mihajlov, who was sentenced to twelve months in prison on September 23, 1966, for "spreading false rumors." [41]

There is no jury trial in Yugoslavia. Economic and regular courts of the first instance and at district levels have both professional judges and "lay judges," the latter being legally untrained citizens elected by the People's Committees for limited periods of time. The regular courts on the federal and republic levels have professional judges only. In judicial as in other matters, the autonomous regions are served in the same manner as the republics.

The Constitutional Court, an innovation which started functioning in 1964, decides on conformity of laws and other regulations with the constitution, and of republic with federal law; resolves disputes between sociopolitical committees on the territory of two or more republics; and decides whether any act of a federal agency violates the rights laid down by the constitution.[42]

When the Constitutional Court declares a federal or republic law to be unconstitutional, the competent assembly has six months to bring it into conformity with the basic law. Failure to do so makes the law, or those of its provisions that have been challenged, invalid. A similar procedure applies in a case when republic laws do not conform to federal law. The court also may annul regulations not in conformity with the constitution or with federal law. The president and ten judges of this highest court are elected by the Federal Council for eight-year terms (staggered to avoid election of all at the same time) and may not hold office more than two consecutive terms.

ELECTIONS. The electoral process in the Socialist Federated Republic of Yugoslavia has become almost entirely indirect.[43] Ordinary voters submit names of nominees for commune, district, province, republic, and federal assemblies. This procedure takes place every two years by means of "preelection consultations." The nominees are then presented to voters' meetings which select candidates for half the number of deputies in assemblies at each level. Each deputy serves a four-year term. Ten percent of the registered votes in any electoral unit is sufficient to proclaim a candidate. Hence communist party members attempt to influence the choice and keep down the number of candidates.[44] Once the communal assemblies have been constituted in this manner, they subsequently choose from among the candidates those who will become deputies to the district, province, republic, and federal legislatures.

Only those candidates for the six republic assemblies and the Federal Council are submitted for "confirmation" by secret ballot in a referendum or at times are "elected" in cases where more than one candidate has been chosen by a communal assembly. Amendments to the electoral law have provided that there shall be "no longer any procedural or legal obstacles aimed at preventing two or more persons from becoming candidates for the Federal Council." [45] Deputies for the other four chambers in the federal National Assembly (Economy, Education and Culture, Social Welfare and Health, and Political-Administrative) are chosen by the commune assemblies.

Preelection consultations in 1965 are officially stated to have been attended by several million persons. At voters' meetings during March, unlike previous elections when there were rarely more candidates than posts to be filled, a choice was presented in most communes. Only 21,947 deputies, about half the total serving at this level, received approval. The commune assemblies met in April to select members for the higher-level assemblies. Their choices were rubber-stamped by the electorate two weeks later. An official commentary stated that "one of the characteristics of the completed elections is the use of the most democratic way hitherto for proposing and selecting candidates." [46] The same procedures were laid down for the April 1967 elections.

Despite the above assertion regarding the "democratic way," the fact remains that not even at the level of the presidency has the succession problem been solved. The new constitution seems to have attempted to guarantee an orderly transfer of power when Tito, now in his seventies, passes from the scene. Guaranteeing transfer of power on paper is much simpler than transferring real power in fact. Chaos could easily ensue, though control of the government is still firmly in the hands of the communist party. Some of the important reasons for the strength of the communists are (1) the League of Communists of Yugoslavia and its front organization, the Socialist Alliance, are the only authorized political groups; (2) President Tito proposes the individuals who are elected as judges of the Constitutional Court and as president of the Federal Executive Council, and the latter officer in turn proposes the persons to be elected to that body; (3) all members of the Federal Executive Council are also members of the upper hierarchy within the League of Communists; (4) communists hold the other important positions in the government and use their authority to appoint other communists to positions of power. Thus the party perpetuates its control over the government.

THE RULING PARTY

The communist party of Yugoslavia developed from a fusion between left-wing Social Democratic and communist groups. Known initially as the Socialist Workers' Party of Yugoslavia (Communist), the movement was founded in 1919 at a unification congress.[47] In 1920 the name was changed to the Communist Party of Yugoslavia. The new party joined the Comintern and accepted the principles of revolution, dictatorship of the proletariat, and a Soviet republic as the future form of government.

During the parliamentary elections of November 1920 the communists had the third strongest party in the country and succeeded in winning 58 out of 417 seats. Outlawed the following year because of an attempt on the life of King Alexander and the assassination of the Interior minister, Milorad Drašković, the party lost unity and was beset with factional strife. Eventually it became necessary for the Comintern to intervene actively for the purpose of solving the conflict between left and right elements.

In 1932 the Central Committee of the party was dissolved by the Comintern and Milan Gorkić was appointed leader. Five years later, Stalin began his purge of ranking foreign "comrades" within the Comintern. He wanted to dissolve the party in Yugoslavia, as had been done already in Poland. Dissolution was not carried out, allegedly because of the insistence of one person, Josip Broz-Tito.[48] Gorkić was liquidated, and Tito became head of the party, with orders to reorganize it.

Two events took place in 1941 which set the stage for the communist "liberation" of the Yugoslav people. First came the invasion and occupation of Yugoslavia in April by Germany. The second event was the attack by the Wehrmacht against the U.S.S.R. in June of that year. The communists in Yugoslavia now had a foreign "imperialist" war which they could use as a rallying point for the people and subsequently turn into a "war of national liberation."

Between 1941 and 1945 three wars were being waged in Yugoslavia. One involved the resistance movement against the Germans, Italians, Hungarians, and Bulgarians; another, the religious strife between Croats and Serbs; and the third, the civil war between communist-dominated Partisans and anticommunist Chetniks.[49] All of these conflicts ultimately came out to the advantage of the communists. They were able to destroy their enemies by exploiting the differences among them.

THE COMMUNIST TAKEOVER. An "Anti-Fascist Council for the National Liberation of Yugoslavia" was formed by the communists. Although not organized along the lines of a government, it did function as a central political body, and although created ostensibly for the purpose of uniting various groups, it consisted of delegates drawn solely from communist-dominated Partisan detachments. In November 1943 the council met and declared itself the supreme legislative and executive body of Yugoslavia. It also set up a presidium and a so-called National Liberation Committee to function as a cabinet. Tito was appointed president of the latter organization.

In 1944 an agreement signed by Tito and Premier Šubašić of the exiled royal Yugoslav government included basic provisions that both sides would respect the will of the people in regard to the internal system of the country; that the king would not return until a plebiscite had been held, with a regency council to be established in the meanwhile; and that in a new "coalition" government the communists would be given key positions which included control over the police, army, judiciary, and communications.[50]

The first postwar election, for a constituent assembly, took place in November 1945. The communist-dominated People's Front provided the only candidates, while the registration of voters was managed by so-called People's Committees. As a result, the single list of candidates won 90.48 percent of the vote and all of the seats. This constituent assembly met eighteen days after the election in an unprecedented midnight session and passed a declaration that proclaimed the Federal People's Republic of Yugoslavia. The monarchy was abolished, as had been promised at Jajce in November 1943, and Yugoslavia officially came under communist control.

The Communist Party of Yugoslavia had patterned itself after its Soviet counterpart and wholeheartedly accepted the hegemony of Moscow. No other communist movement adhered more closely to directives from the center than did the Yugoslav.[51] Tito believed that, like the Bolsheviks, he had come to power after a true revolution. The dispute between Moscow and Belgrade, which finally led to the expulsion of the Yugoslav party from the Cominform in June 1948, had many causes. The main ones were of a personal and psychological nature, including an underestimation by Stalin of the Yugoslav leaders and particularly of Josip Broz-Tito.

The statutes adopted at the party's Fifth Congress, in July 1948, in general still followed the rules of the Soviet communist party. By the time the Sixth Congress convened, in 1952, the Yugoslav communists had withstood Stalin's challenge and were stronger than ever before. Party membership had almost doubled. The secret police had purged the party of its pro-Cominform elements. The leaders were convinced that they could pursue communism in their own way, and this meant revisionism to fulfill their new role as deviators from the Soviet model.

Everything possible was done to differentiate the Yugoslav party from its former Soviet model. At the Sixth Congress the party name was changed to the League of Communists of Yugoslavia (*Savez Komunista Jugoslavije*—SKJ). Aside from distinguishing themselves, this action indicated that the Yugoslavs were proclaiming themselves as having advanced into a higher level of development toward the goal of a communist state. The leadership made it clear, however, that the one-party system would be retained in Yugoslavia and that the communist party would continue in its monopoly position. The Seventh Congress reiterated in 1958 this same theme.[52]

PRESENT ORGANIZATION. In spite of its new name and new statute, the SKJ still shows considerable similarity to all other communist organizations. It is operated so as to ensure that a small number of well-disciplined members can carry out major policy decisions and control all aspects of national life. There can be no fundamental criticism of Marxist-Leninist dogma, as interpreted by the party, which adheres to the principles of democratic centralism.[53] The party is similar to a Western political organization only in its efforts to influence public opinion.

A major problem arises from the deployment of a relatively small number of party members throughout the state bureaucracy to maintain the required degree of control. In theory the members are "held together by strict discipline, compulsory allegiance to a rigid political and social dogma, personal advantage, high social status, ego satisfaction, and the pressures of a highly developed secret police system." [54] Although such rewards and restraints exist, in reality there are sharp conflicts within the party, and they are probably related to the distribution of key personnel over a federal state composed of divisive national groups.

The highest organ of the SKJ in theory is the congress, which convenes every four years to pass resolutions, hear reports of the Central Committee and the Audit Commission, adopt the party program and statute, and determine the party's political line. The Eighth Congress, in 1964, was the most recent to be held. Between sessions of the congress, the Central Committee allegedly represents the highest authority. It convenes whenever necessary, but must meet at least twice a year.[55] In practice the Presidium (former Politburo) wields real power.

The three smallest republics, Macedonia, Montenegro, and Slovenia, have the largest number of members on the Presidium in proportion to their percentage of the total population. These small republics have gained at the expense of Serbia, which has the largest percentage of the population. The ethnic representation in the Central Committee is similar. Serbs account for 41.7 percent of the total population, but in 1958 they comprised only a third of the Central Committee members. The current Macedonian, Montenegrin, and Slovene percentages are at least twice the ratio of these groups to total population. One reason may be that Tito, who is a Croat, distrusts the Serbs because they ruled the country up to the Second World War.

Tito has been president of the party since October 1966 and in this capacity also heads the policy-making Presidium (see table 45). The average age of the Presidium members is just under fifty-five years; the average length of time spent in the party runs about thirty-two years. The social make-up of this body when it numbered only fifteen members was nine workers and six intellectuals. Five possessed university degrees; one was a graduate of a teachers' school; and six could claim only to have attended an elementary school; and the rest presumably not even that.[56]

The party chiefs for the six republics belong to the Presidium: Bakarić (Croatia), Crvenkovski (Macedonia), Marinko (Slovenia), Mijatović (Bosnia and Herzegovina), Pajković (Montenegro), and Veselinov (Serbia). Members who are specialists in certain fields include Gošnjak (defense), Humo (science), Jovanovič (judiciary), Kardelj (parliament), Koča Popović (foreign affairs), Stambolić (public administration), and Vlachović (ideology).

The Executive Committee, with eleven members, has a secretary (Todorović) and supervises the daily work of the party organizations. It oversees the implementation of decisions which originate within the Presidium. In addition, five Central Committee commissions were established in October 1966 to deal with the following areas: foreign relations (with other communist parties); sociopolitical relations; socioeconomic relations; political theory, education, science, and culture; interrepublic and internationality relations (see table 46). Only one of these is headed by a member of the Executive Committee.

The financial records of the party are checked by its Central Audit Commission. The ferreting-out of ideological deviations is conducted by the Control Commission.[57] The SKJ structure in the six republics and two autonomous regions is similar to that at the federal level.

MEMBERSHIP. Until 1952, the criteria for membership in the communist party of Yugoslavia were the same as those of its Soviet counterpart. A prospective member was required to be eighteen years of age, have recommendations for membership in writing from two party members (who had been acquainted with him for two years and themselves been members for at least two years), and submit a written biographic statement.

Applications are still reviewed by one of the nearly 35,000 basic party organizations and forwarded to the next higher level. If the prospective member proved acceptable, he used to be placed on probationary status for eighteen months. At the Eighth Congress the requirements were modified to eliminate the written recommendations and the probationary status.[58] It appears that membership can be attained now on nomination by workers who are not necessarily members themselves. The growth of party membership is shown in table 47.

Only a fourth of the 12,000 members in 1941 survived the war.[59] Thus, more than 93 percent of the 1967 membership has joined during the past 26 years. The significant increase in membership between 1948 and 1952 is indicative of how much Stalin underestimated Tito's strength. The drop between 1952 and 1956 can be

TABLE 45

PRESIDIUM, LEAGUE OF COMMUNISTS OF YUGOSLAVIA (SKJ), 1967

Name	Age	Ethnic group	Joined party	Other position
Tito, Josip Broz	75	Croatian	1920	President of Yugoslavia; president SKJ
Bakarić, Vladimir	55	Croatian	1933	Secretary (political), SKJ Croatia
Blažević, Jakov	55	Croatian	1928	Vice-president, Federal Executive Council
Crvenkovski, Krsta	46	Macedonian	1939	Secretary (political), SKJ Macedonia
Dabčević-Kučar, Savka	44	Croatian	1943	Secretary (ideology), SKJ Croatia
Dugonjić, Ratomir	51	Serbian	1938	President, Bosnia-Herzegovina parliament
Gošnjak, Ivan	58	Croatian	1933	Member, Federal Assembly
Hodža, Fadil	60	Albanian	1936	Member, Federal Executive Council
Humo, Avdo	53	Serbian	1939	President, Federal Council for Scientific Research
Jovanović, Blažo	61	Montenegrin	1928	President, Federal Constitutional Court
Karabegović, Osman	56	Moslem	1932	President, Economic Council, Federal Assembly
Kardelj, Edvard	57	Slovene	1928	Professor, Ljubljana University
Kolak, Rudi	49	Croatian	1940	Vice-president, Federal Executive Council
Koliševski, Lazar	53	Macedonian	1933	President, Socialist Alliance
Maček, Ivan	59	Slovene	1938	President, Slovenia parliament
Marinko, Miha	67	Slovene	1924	Secretary (political), SKJ Slovenia
Mijatović, Cvijetin	54	Serbian	1935	Secretary (political), SKJ Bosnia-Herzegovina
Pajković, Djoko	50	Montenegrin	1936	Secretary (political), SKJ Montenegro
Petrović, Dušan	53	Serbian	1936	President, Central Council of Trade Unions

TABLE 45 (continued)

PRESIDIUM, LEAGUE OF COMMUNISTS OF YUGOSLAVIA (SKJ), 1967

Name	Age	Ethnic group	Joined party	Other position
Popović, Koča	59	Serbian	1933	Diplomatic trouble-shooter
Popović, Milentije	54	Serbian	1939	President, Federal Assembly
Popović, Vladimir	53	Montenegrin	1932	Chairman, Foreign Policy Committee, Federal Council of Federal Assembly
Pucar, Djuro	68	Serbian	1922	President, Association of National Liberation Fighters of Yugoslavia
Radosavljević, Dobrivoje	52	Serbian	1933	Secretary, SKJ Serbia
Sekulić, Nikola	56	Serbian	1931	Director, SKJ ideological organ, *Socijalizam*
Šmilevski, Vidoje	52	Macedonian	1940	President, Federal Council
Stambolić, Petar	55	Serbian	1933	Member, Federal Assembly
Šentjurc, Lidija	56	Slovene	1932	Vice-president, Socialist Alliance
Šoti, Pal	51	Hungarian	1939	Member, Federal Conference, Socialist Alliance
Špiljak, Mika	51	Croatian	1938	President, Federal Executive Council
Temelkovski, Borko ...	48	Macedonian	1939	Chairman, Commission for Social Control, Federal Council of Federal Assembly
Veselinov, Jovan	61	Serbian	1923	Secretary (political), SKJ Serbia
Vlachović, Veljko	53	Montenegrin	1935	SKJ ideologist
Vukmanović, Svetozar .	55	Montenegrin	1935	President, Central Council of Trade-Unions *

SOURCES: Radio Belgrade, October 4, 1966. Slavko Janković (ed.), *Ko je ko u Jugoslaviji* (Belgrade, 1957). [Yugoslavia], *Savezna i Republičke Skupštine* (Belgrade, 1964). *Wissenschaftlicher Dienst Südosteuropa*, XV, No. 10 (October 1966), pp. 155-156. Radio Free Europe, *Communist Party-Government Line-Up* (Munich, July 1967), pp. 24-26.

NOTE: Boris Krajger, 53 years old and a vice-president of the Federal Executive Council, had been elected to the SKJ presidium; he was killed in an automobile accident. *New York Times,* January 5, 1967.

* Vukmanović resigned on February 22, 1967, due to the rotating principle under which he held this position for four years. He is now only a member of the Federal Assembly.

attributed to the confusion created by the new doctrine announced at the Sixth Congress and by the Milovan Djilas affair. (See the section below on "Reconciliation with the Kremlin.") Both resulted in purges and disillusionment on the part of many members. From the

TABLE 46

EXECUTIVE COMMITTEE, LEAGUE OF COMMUNISTS OF YUGOSLAVIA (SKJ), 1967

Name	Age	Ethnic group	Joined party	Other position
Albreht, Roman	46	Slovene	1945	Chairman, Committee on Labor Problems, Federal Council
Bijelić, Srečko	37	Croatian	1948	Director, Freight Car Plant, Agram
Cvetković, Marjan	47	Croatian	1938	Secretary (organization), SKJ Croatia
Dizdarević, Nijaz	47	Moslem	1940	Secretary, SKJ Bosnia-Herzegovina
Hadživasilev, Kiro	46	Macedonian	1943	President, Macedonian parliament
Kavčić, Stane	48	Slovene	1941	Secretary (ideology), SKJ Slovenia
Kekić, Danilo	50	Serbian	1939	President, Council of Trade-Unions, Serbia
Miloslavlevski, Slavko .	40	Macedonian	1944	Professor of Law, Skoplje
Pečujlić, Miroslav	39	Serbian	1945	Professor of Law, Belgrade
Šoškić, Budislav	42	Montenegrin	1943	Secretary (organization), SKJ Montenegro
Todorović, Mijalko ...	55	Serbian	1938	Secretary, SKJ Executive Committee

SOURCES: [Yugoslavia] *Savezna i Republičke Skupštine* (Belgrade, 1964). Radio Belgrade, October 4, 1966. *Komunist,* October 6, 1966. *Wissenschaftlicher Dienst Südosteuropa,* XV, No. 10 (October 1966), p. 154. Radio Free Europe, *Communist Party-Government Line-Up* (Munich, July 1967), pp. 24-26.

NOTE: Central Committee Commissions and their heads are foreign relations and international workers' movement (Popović, Vladimir); sociopolitical relations (Minić, Miloš); socioeconomic relations (Krajger, Sergej); political theory, education, science, and culture (Sekulić, Nikola); interrepublic and internationality relations (Hadživasilev, Kiro).

beginning of 1958 through the end of 1964 some 108,236 persons were expelled from the party.[60]

The social composition of the party is shown in table 48. During recent years there has been a constant decline in peasant membership, both in proportion of the total and in absolute numbers. This can be attributed to the typically negative communist approach to agriculture and the emphasis on industry. The peasants have become disenchanted with the party because of the attempts to collectivize the farms. There has been on the other hand a marked increase in the intelligentsia component. This is probably the result of the system, which obliges a person to be an SKJ member if he hopes to acquire an advantageous post after completing higher education.[61]

In Yugoslavia, just as in all other communist-dominated states, control over the youth of the country is of prime importance and also represents a major problem. Supplementing the basic education re-

TABLE 47

YUGOSLAV COMMUNIST PARTY MEMBERSHIP, 1937-1967

Year	Number of members	Year	Number of members
1937	1,500	1956	635,984
1939	3,000	1960	898,300
1940	6,000	1964	1,030,041
1941	12,000	1965	1,031,634
1945	140,000	1966	1,046,202
1948	448,175	1967	1,046,018
1952	779,382		

SOURCE: *Komunist,* October 15, 1964; July 15, 1965; April 28, 1966; April 6, 1967.
NOTE: In 1965 some 178,000 members, or 17.3 percent of the total, were women.

ceived at school, the Pioneer organization provides militant political indoctrination. During holidays or in free time, participation in "volunteer" working brigades is encouraged. Yet the young people themselves have prevented the party from exercising very tight control and have become disenchanted.[62] This does not necessarily produce direct opposition to communism, but it does involve resistance to rigid conformity.

Of the 2,043,520 members in the Union of Yugoslav Youth (*Savez Omladine Jugoslavije*) more than a third of those eligible are neither in the League of Communists nor in the Socialist Alliance front organization. Although this is the sole youth movement allowed, official figures indicate that only 56 percent of the 3.2 million young people between the ages of fourteen and twenty-five years in 1965 were members, and there is dissatisfaction with "insufficient democracy in the elections of leaders." [63]

MASS ORGANIZATIONS. The most important mass movement in Yugoslavia is the Socialist Alliance of Working People (*Socijal-*

istički Savez Radnog Naroda—SSRN), formerly known as the People's Front. It is composed of both organizations and individuals. An individual, to be a member of the SSRN, must enroll in one of its basic organizations. The purpose is to involve as many people as possible in some type of activity over which the party has control.

TABLE 48

YUGOSLAV COMMUNIST PARTY SOCIAL COMPOSITION, 1954-1967

Category	January 1954		January 1959		January 1967	
	Number	Percent	Number	Percent	Number	Percent
Workers (including peasants in collectives)	191,655	27.4	271,100	31.6	355,022	33.9
Peasants (uncollectivized) [a]	189,392	27.1	121,684	14.2	77,134	7.4
Intelligentsia	189,231	27.0	264,629	30.9	408,378	38.8
Other [b]	129,752	18.5	200,124	23.3	96,217	9.5
Pensioners	—	—	—	—	74,610	7.1
Students	—	—	—	—	34,657	3.3
Total	700,030	100.0	857,537	100.0	1,046,018	100.0

SOURCES: *Jugoslovenski pregled*, July-August 1964, pp. 33-35; *Komunist*, April 6, 1967.

[a] This category of peasant in 1946 comprised 49% of the party membership. *Komunist*, May 25, 1967.

[b] Includes housewives, individual artisans, free professions, and members of the armed forces.

The platform of the SSRN has accordingly been designed to be acceptable to practically everyone. A person who has a distaste for the principles of the party may find those of the SSRN more to his liking. The movement has two fundamental purposes, one political and the other economic.[64] Politically, it indoctrinates the masses in Marxism and the general party line, conducts elections, and on special occasions holds political rallies. The economic purpose revolves around assisting in the fulfillment of national economic plans and explaining the need for social change.

The SSRN has an organizational structure similar to that of the League of Communists. It extends from the national level down to the commune and is controlled by the party at all levels. Party members are supposed to influence the SSRN by their own efforts and not through their position in the communist hierarchy. The president of the SSRN, however, is Lazar Koliševski, a member of the Presidium of the party, as is the former secretary-general of this movement, Milentije Popović, who was elected president of the Federal Assembly in May 1967.

The Confederation of Trade-Unions in Yugoslavia (*Savez Sindikata Jugoslavije*—SSJ) is another communist-dominated mass organization.[65] It operates as a means for implementing the party's economic policy. Until 1958 the labor unions had control over the list of candidates for workers' councils. At that time, there were among the 220,656 council members only 60,012 communist party members or 27.2 percent of the total. In individual councils the party membership ranged from 10 to 85 percent. Although the trade-unions no longer control the candidate list, they retain influence within the various industrial enterprises because the party and the government operate the factories with their assistance.

The trade-union movement is completely dominated by the League of Communists. The President of the SSJ central council, Dušan Petrović, is a member of the Presidium of the party. The SSJ secretariat includes Ivan Božicević, a member of the Central Committee of the party, and Pepica Kardelj, wife of Edvard Kardelj (who is on the Presidium of the SKJ).

SUCCESSION. It can be said that there has been at least an attempt by the League of Communists to provide for an orderly succession after Tito, insofar as the new constitution states that the president of the Federal Assembly (at present, Milentije Popović) will become temporarily the head of government, pending the election of a new president. Some danger lies in the lack of a fixed date for elections and the lack of experience in electing anyone as president thus far except Tito. Koča Popović in July 1966 replaced Ranković as vice-president (a post abolished less than a year later), and he and Kardelj might provide the nucleus for a collective leadership if there should not be sufficient support for one person as president. There could be some problems in connection with the purge of the Ranković machine, a faction which was based on the secret police and had distinctly nationalistic Serbian overtones. Tito's departure could revive the old ethnic conflicts and create additional tensions in the party.

Possibly the strongest potential leaders on the scene at present are the Presidium member and Montenegrin Vlachović and the Serb

Todorović (who replaced Ranković and is on the Executive Committee). They rank after Tito and Kardelj in the hierarchy today. Vlachović is a specialist in ideological affairs. Todorović, however, is in charge of cadres besides being secretary of the party's Executive Committee, and his position may allow him to build a machine. His future could be decided in 1968, at the next regular party congress.

It is doubtful that the party will destroy itself through a struggle for power, even though it might become seriously weakened. There is no nonparty individual or organization in Yugoslavia capable of displacing the present Tito regime. The communists long ago liquidated all opposition leaders and organizations they did not control.

FOREIGN RELATIONS

The foreign policy of Yugoslavia has reflected and mainly been determined by the status of that country's relations with the Soviet Union. Until recently, the other bloc leaders have in general mirrored policies set by the U.S.S.R., and Tito, in taking certain exceptions to Soviet policy, was forced at one time to orient himself toward the noncommunist world in order to survive. There can be no question but that Yugoslavia strongly prefers alliance with the Soviet bloc. Despite this preference, it steadfastly refused to become a satellite. While there has been no compromise of this independence, neither has there been any lessening of the Yugoslav government's devotion to communist principles. The importance of this relatively small country has been magnified many times over by its demonstrated ability to defy the bloc between 1948 and 1953 and to obtain Western economic and military aid.

AGGRESSIVE POSTWAR POLICIES. Although provided with extensive wartime military aid from the United States and Britain, and disappointed by the failure of the Soviet Union to contribute substantially, the new postwar government of Tito openly oriented its foreign policies toward the U.S.S.R. and considered the capitalist states as enemies. Backed by an army that had virtually liberated the country alone,[66] communist Yugoslavia attempted to expand its borders. It seems clear that Tito at this time already had visions of a Balkan federation led by himself.

The initial argument was with Italy over the frontier province of Venezia Giulia, which included the port city of Trieste. Populated by a majority of Slavs but ceded to Italy after the First World War, the province had been occupied by the Partisans on the heels of the retreating Germans. The Western Allies subsequently entered the city, but it took nine years to reach a settlement. The Yugoslavs were disappointed in the Soviet failure (1948-1953) to support their claims, and the London agreement in 1954 was concluded without U.S.S.R. participation. It gave the city of Trieste to Italy and the hinterland to Yugoslavia.

In neighboring Albania, representatives of Tito had founded a communist party in 1941 and supported the successful guerrilla struggle against the Italians and Germans in that country. By establishing joint-stock companies and stationing a few army units in Albania, the Yugoslav communists exercised supervision both economically and militarily over their satellite. Imbued with somewhat the same independent spirit as their neighbors, the Albanian communists resisted this domination. Annexation by Yugoslavia never took place (although it had been suggested by Stalin), owing to the Tito regime's 1948 dispute with the Cominform (the Communist Information Bureau created in September 1947 after the dissolution of the Comintern in 1943 and for, not admittedly, continuing its function on a more limited geographic scale).

Another plan for expansion looked toward the Bulgarian and Greek parts of Macedonia, adjoining the similarly named republic in Yugoslavia. The Bulgarian communist party in August 1947 agreed to federation at some future date and permitted immediate cultural penetration by teachers and propagandists from Yugoslavia.[67] Tito also entered the civil war in Greece by reestablishing a Macedonian partisan movement in that country. His plan for consolidating Macedonia was stopped (as in the case of Albania) by the Cominform's expulsion of the Yugoslav communist party in June 1948, together with the termination of the Greek civil war the following year.

THE TITO-STALIN DISPUTE. The Yugoslav communists were completely devoted to Stalin and to the Soviet Union in the early postwar years. This devotion persisted despite several disappointments and differences during the war years and thereafter. Proposals for joint-stock companies, which would have given the U.S.S.R. control over the Yugoslav economy, were opposed. This was precisely the same procedure that Belgrade had contemplated for arranging its own domination over Albania. Soviet military advisers insisted that Partisan units be remodeled after the Red Army, and brazen intelligence activities were conducted by the Russians in Yugoslavia. Spies were recruited in the army, the government, and even the Central Committee of the Yugoslav communist party.

Relations had already been strained when Tito failed to obey Stalin's summons to Moscow in February 1948. In a series of letters the Yugoslavs were accused by the Central Committee of the Soviet communist party not only of deviation, arrogance, and ingratitude, but even of Trotskyism. The charges also reopened the matter of the "insult" to the Red Army which Djilas made in 1945 when he complained because Yugoslav women had been raped by Soviet soldiers. Yugoslav replies were always conciliatory, with pledges of loyalty and suggestions that the Central Committee in Moscow might be the victim of misinformation. They offered time and again to prove their loyalty to the Soviet Union. Tito and his colleagues hoped for reconciliation, almost irrationally and to the very end.[68] Moscow, however, remained adamant and demanded unconditional capitulation.

Refusing to attend a meeting of the Cominform, for he knew that the outcome had been predetermined, Tito protested with a last letter declaring the Yugoslav communist leadership to be unjustly accused and still loyal to Moscow. On June 28, 1948, a resolution of the Cominform declared: "[The Cominform hereby expels the] Yugoslav heretics from its ranks, and openly appeals to the rank and file of the Yugoslav Party to oust its leadership." [69] But Stalin had grossly misjudged the situation in his former satellite.

Failing in the attempt to eliminate Tito with denunciation and by expulsion from the Cominform, Stalin turned to more direct methods of applying pressure economically, politically, and militarily. The minority groups in Yugoslavia were exploited by neighboring states which organized anti-Tito groups, newspapers, and radio stations. Newspapers were smuggled into the country, and radio broadcasts viciously denounced Tito. Agents infiltrated Yugoslavia to incite national minorities, and an economic boycott was established by all other communist-dominated countries. In August 1949 Moscow formally declared that it considered the Yugoslav government to be an enemy. Armed clashes with Soviet satellites along the Yugoslav borders became constant occurrences.

TITO TURNS TO THE WEST. Reluctantly, but without other choice, Tito looked to the West for help. His economy had depended upon trade with East European countries and was now in danger of collapse. The Western response was gradual but positive. American-held Yugoslav assets were released, and a trade agreement was signed in December 1948 with Great Britain. During the following year, negotiations involving trade and a loan from the U.S. Export-Import Bank were completed. In 1950 surplus American grain was sent to alleviate hunger resulting from a serious drought in Yugoslavia.

During the next decade an estimated 3.5 billion dollars' worth of aid was provided by the West. Nearly half of this came from the United States.[70] By July 1962 American economic aid to Yugoslavia amounted to more than 1.5 billion dollars and military assistance to about 719 million dollars. UNRRA's help had totaled nearly a half billion dollars. Another half billion was given by nongovernment charitable institutions such as CARE or came in the form of loans from international banks. This amounted to an annual average of nearly 250 million dollars, which materially assisted in alleviating the foreign trade deficit. (See table 49 for figures on the adverse balance-of-payments problem.)

TABLE 49

YUGOSLAVIA'S FOREIGN TRADE, 1955-1965

Category	1955	1960	1962	1965
		(billions of dinars)		*(millions of dollars)*
Imports	132	248	260	1,287.5
Exports	77	170	207	1,091.5
Total	209	418	473	2,379.0
Adverse balance ...	55	78	59	196.0

SOURCES: V. I. Zolotarev, *Vneshnyaya torgovlya sotsialisticheskikh stran* (Moscow, 1964), p. 136. Radio Zagreb, December 2, 1965. First National City Bank of New York, *Yugoslavia* (New York, 1966), p. 11.

NOTE: Rate of exchange is 1,000 dinars to U.S. $1.33. The figure for 1965 includes a surplus of 67 billion dinars with East European countries and a deficit of 323 billion in trade with the Western, convertible area of the world. Radio Zagreb, December 2, 1965.

One of the hopes of the West had been to bring Yugoslavia indirectly into the North Atlantic Treaty Organization. A step toward this goal was the treaty of friendship and cooperation signed at Ankara in February 1953 by Yugoslavia, Greece, and Turkey. Several months later that same year a military pact was concluded by the three countries. During late 1954 and early 1955, however, Tito toured India and Burma, expounding the principles of "active coexistence," equality of nations, and noninterference in the internal affairs of other countries.[71]

RECONCILIATION WITH THE KREMLIN. After Stalin's death, the first secretary of the Central Committee of the Soviet communist party, Nikita S. Khrushchëv realized that in the anti-Yugoslav policy he had inherited a liability. The earliest sign of a thaw was the establishment of a Romanian-Yugoslav joint commission for administration of their common part of the Danube River, obviously with Soviet permission. Moscow omitted the usual May Day criticism of Tito in 1953 and proposed that the two countries exchange ambassadors. The offer was accepted. The other satellite countries, one by one, adopted an identical course. Border clashes and subversion virtually ceased, and the anti-Tito newspapers and radio stations in neighboring countries closed down.

Two years later, in full realization of the need to heal the breach, Khrushchëv and the Soviet premier, Nikolai Bulganin, journeyed to Yugoslavia. Accepting Soviet responsibility for the break between the two countries, Khrushchëv in a speech at the Belgrade airport blamed the executed secret police chief Lavrenty P. Beria, asked Tito's forgiveness, and proposed renewal of friendly relations between the two governments and communist parties.[72] In a joint declaration Tito and Khrushchëv guaranteed respect for the sovereignty, independence, integrity, and equality of states; accepted the principle of noninterference, based on the premise that differing forms of social development are solely the concern of each individual country; and condemned aggression as well as political and economic domination.

For his part, Tito supported the Soviet Union in the brutal suppression of the 1956 Hungarian revolt. He had opposed the initial interference, while the communists were still in control. After the rebellion got out of hand he considered Soviet intervention to save the country for communism as the lesser of two evils. In 1957 Tito gave diplomatic recognition to East Germany and in an essay published abroad called for the dissolution of NATO, criticizing the West for its negative attitude toward Moscow.[73]

At the same time, no criticism of communism in Yugoslavia or the Soviet Union could be expressed. A good illustration is the *cause célèbre* involving Milovan Djilas. Although earlier he had been considered the heir apparent to Tito, this man resigned from the communist party in 1954 and while in prison wrote *The New Class* (1957). It represents the most devastating and best-known indictment of the communist system. Another book, *Conversations with Stalin* (1962), resulted in his being imprisoned again, for allegedly disclosing "official secrets." After serving part of his sentence Djilas was released December 31, 1966.

THE SECOND SOVIET-YUGOSLAV DISPUTE. Concerned with the unrest in the satellites and beset by differences of opinion at home, Khrushchëv decided it was time to reorganize the Soviet bloc. He had prepared and circulated a resolution on communist unity to be presented and signed at Moscow on the fortieth anniversary of the November 1917 Revolution. The document portrayed the world as two uncompromising blocs and the United States as the "center of world reaction." It defined the socialist bloc in terms of the Warsaw Pact and, in an allusion to the Yugoslavs, declared revisionism to be the greatest danger. Tito was shocked and dismayed. Refusing to attend the anniversary meeting himself, he sent Kardelj and Ranković to Moscow with instructions not to sign the resolution.

During April 1958 the Seventh Congress of the League of Communists, at the Slovene city of Ljubljana, gave Tito the opportunity to present his kind of communism to the world. He circulated drafts of his new party program and in some instances modified it in acquiescence to Soviet objections. The eventual document represented a formal declaration of Yugoslavia's political and ideological independence.[74] Tito's insistence on retaining the main substance of the draft program resulted in a boycott of the congress by the Soviet communist party and its East European adherents. Although ambassadors from these countries attended as observers, all except the Polish representative ostentatiously walked out of the congress.

Moscow's attack on Yugoslav revisionism set the tone and the levels of criticism for its supporters to follow. The rift remained moderate in the beginning. Unexpectedly, however, the Chinese communists launched a vitriolic attack, declaring that the Cominform had been correct in its 1948 expulsion of the Yugoslav party.[75] Moscow announced a five-year postponement of its credit commitment of 285 million dollars to Belgrade, but no economic blockade or disruption of diplomatic relations followed.

TITO AGAIN TURNS WEST. Shortly after the 1958 Seventh Congress at Ljubljana, great friendship for the United States was again declared by the Yugoslavs. This was claimed not to be based on any requirement for assistance, and at the same time the existence of a very real need was admitted. In October 1958 Tito asked for 100 million dollars in aid, and the United States responded with a program encompassing even more.

There were limitations to Tito's Western leanings, as was evidenced by his active support of Castro even to the point of jeopardizing aid from the United States. The renewed friendship with the West did not become as intimate as before, nor was the break with the Soviets as serious as the first one. Belgrade could not be convinced that the schism was irreparable, and Tito privately pictured Khrushchëv as the leader of an anti-Stalinist faction that sincerely sought peace with the West. In the same vein, he criticized the administration in Washington for failing to reach a *détente* with the Soviets.

Tito next attempted to organize the nonaligned nations with "third force" proposals and by calling a conference of these states that met during June 1961 at Belgrade.[76] This effort brought him dangerously close to a rift with the West, for while the neutralists condemned the existence of all "blocs" their policies came close to those of the U.S.S.R. in outspoken support for recognition of East Germany and the seating of Communist China in the United Nations. There was resentment in Washington later that year when Tito supported the Soviet Union during the Berlin crisis in August and failed to denounce Soviet resumption of nuclear testing in September.

THE CYCLE REPEATS ITSELF. With the Sino-Soviet dispute in the open at the Twenty-second Congress of the Soviet communist party, in October 1961, Tito saw a chance to move closer to the U.S.S.R. Despite an amnesty for political prisoners, Milovan Djilas was rearrested in April 1962 because of the imminent publication in English of his book, *Conversations with Stalin,* which was critical of both Stalin and the Soviet leadership during and immediately after the war. Since the U.S.S.R. had split with both Albania and communist China, the Yugoslavs showed by this arrest that they desired closer relations with Moscow.

Commercial agreements provided for the equivalent of some $800 million in exchange between the two countries during the 1961-1965 period.[77] In July 1962 Belgrade announced that trade with the U.S.S.R. would be increased by some 30 percent. The following month it was announced that Yugoslavia had negotiated with Italy for a credit of 12.5 billion lire, thus establishing a solid tie with one of the Common Market countries. In the fall, the U.S. Congress amended the foreign trade bill to remove the most-favored-nation clause from Poland and Yugoslavia, but in 1964 President Lyndon B. Johnson reapplied the most-favored-nation clause to Yugoslavia.[78] Clearly, Tito has been successful in taking from both sides.

Tito has stated that he has no intention of joining the Western bloc. He proclaims neutralism, but his actions contradict this. In a speech at a party conference shortly after the 1958 break with the Soviets and well before the Sino-Soviet split, Tito said flatly that he sided with the Soviet Union on all main problems of foreign policy. At Sverdlovsk in the U.S.S.R. more recently he stated: "We know that there used to be misunderstandings between us, but there was never one single Yugoslav communist who did not think that . . . if hard times should come again . . . we would stand together with the Soviet people and the Soviet communists." [79]

Typical of the whole dilemma of Tito vis-à-vis the free world is the present relationship between Yugoslavia and the Federal Republic of Germany. Belgrade has demanded indemnification for Yugoslav war victims and assailed West Germany for failure to compensate reparations claims.[80] It extended diplomatic recognition to East Germany, as a result of which the Bonn government broke off relations with Belgrade. Still, West Germany is Yugoslavia's current third best economic trading partner, after Italy and the United States. The exchange of ambassadors between Bonn and Bucharest in early 1967 could lead to a resumption of such relations between Bonn and Belgrade.[81]

NOTES

1 U.S. Congress, Senate Committee on the Judiciary, 87th Cong., 1st sess., *Yugoslav Communism: A Critical Study* (Washington, D.C., 1961), p. 3.

2 Dragoljub Durović (ed.), *Narodna vlast i socijalistička demokratija, 1943-1963* (Belgrade, 1964), pp. 22-23.

3 *Ibid.*, p. 56, reproduces the beginning of the proclamation.

4 V. N. Durdenevskii (ed.), *Konstitutsii zarubezhnykh sotsialisticheskikh gosudarstv* (Moscow, 1956), pp. 389-408, gives the text in Russian.

5 Albert Waterston, *Planning in Yugoslavia* (Baltimore, 1962), p. 7.

6 Eugenio Reale, *Nascita del Cominform* (Rome, 1958), pp. 175, provides an eyewitness account of the meeting.

7 For example, Nikita S. Khrushchëv when still in power was quoted as having stated: ". . . on objective laws, on the teachings of Marxism-Leninism, it is impossible to deny that Yugoslavia appears to be a socialist [i.e., communist] country." P. D. Mineev and V. A. Tokarev, *Yugoslaviya* (Moscow, 1963), p. 29.

8 V. Zagladin *et al.*, "Yugoslavia Today," *World Marxist Review*, VII, No. 3 (March 1964), p. 66.

9 *Ibid.* See RFE report (by Zdenko Antič), "Main Characteristics of the Yugoslav 1966-1970 Plan," January 31, 1967 (6 pp.).

10 "Ustav Socijalističke Federativne Republike Jugoslavije," in Durović (ed.), *op. cit.*, pp. iii-xxi, gives the full text in Serbo-Croatian as an appendix.

11 *Ibid.*, pp. iii-iv.

12 Mirko Bošković, *Društveno-politički sistem Jugoslavije* (Zagreb, 1963), pp. 121-126. See also RFE report (by Slobodan Stanković), "More Independence for Trade Unions in Yugoslavia," February 1, 1967 (3 pp.).

13 Durović (ed.), *op. cit.*, p. v.

14 Stipe Dužević (ed.), *VI Plenum Centralnog Komiteta Saveza Komunista Jugoslavije* (Belgrade, 1964), pp. 89.

15 See RFE reports (by Slobodan Stanković), "Political-Ideological Aspects of the Yugoslav Economic Reform," September 23, 1965 (3 pp.) and "Radical Economic Changes Outlined for Yugoslavia," June 22, 1965 (8 pp.).

16 "Enterprise and Socialism?", *The Economist* (London), air edition, July 16, 1966, p. 238.

17 RFE report (by Dušan Pejčić), "Agricultural Cooperation in Yugoslavia," December 12, 1963, Part I, p. 1 (3 pp.).

18 During 1963 losses in socialized agriculture amounted to 13.3 billion dinars (about 180 million U.S. dollars) which was 18 percent higher than the year before. *Jugoslovenski pregled*, July-August 1964, as cited in RFE report (by Slobodan Stanković), "Private Peasant Property," May 13, 1965 (5 pp.).

19 Pejčić, *op. cit.*, Part I, p. 3.

20 *Ibid.*, Part II, p. 2.

21 *Ibid.*, Part III, p. 3.

22 *Borba,* February 18, 1964.

23 Radio Belgrade, November 27, 1965.

24 F. E. I. Hamilton, "Location Factors in the Yugoslav Iron and Steel Industry," *Economic Geography*, XL, No. 1 (January 1964), 53.

25 One way to stimulate this growth would be to exploit "about 2,000 billion dinars of inactive investments . . . plus reserves in unfinished production in the economy worth about 3,150 billion," according to the late deputy premier Boris Krajger. Radio Belgrade, July 10, 1965.

26 Miha Marinko, in *Borba*, March 18, 1965. See also RFE report (by Slobodan Stanković), "What Is Hidden Behind the Language Conflict," April 4, 1967 (7 pp.).

27 According to Svetozar Pepovski, in an article on "Economic Migration," in *Polityka* (Warsaw), May 14, 1966, the workers abroad have sent back as much as the equivalent of $30.5 million in one year. Pepovski is the Yugoslav deputy minister for labor. Unemployment admittedly stood at

309,000 a year later. *Index* (Belgrade), April 1967; cited in RFE report (by Zdenko Antič), "Yugoslav Officials Comment on Economic Reform," April 28, 1967 (4 pp.).

28 Radio Belgrade, June 14, 1965. The following month, a currency devaluation reduced the dinar to 1,250 instead of 750 for the U.S. dollar. Subsequently a new dinar was issued at a parity of 12.5 to the dollar.

29 Quotation and estimate of lapse from Zagladin, *op. cit.*, p. 70. Radio Zagreb, February 12, 1966. Last figures from *New York Times,* September 5, 1965.

30 *Mladost,* October 30, 1963.

31 Durdenevskii, *op. cit.,* gives the text of the 1946 constitution, pp. 389-408, and the modified 1953 version, pp. 409-453.

32 See Jovan Djordjević, *Novi ustavni sistem* (Belgrade, 1964), pp. 356-370.

33 Identified in these positions in RFE report (by Zdenko Antič), "Physiognomy of the New Yugoslav Government," May 19, 1967 (4 pp.).

34 Djordjević, *op. cit.,* pp. 300-307.

35 *Borba,* September 29, 1965. See also RFE report (by Zdenko Antič), "Right to Initiate Bills in Yugoslav Parliament," March 14, 1967 (2 pp.).

36 Gorazd Kušej, *Politični sistem Jugoslavije* (2d ed.; Ljubljana, 1964), pp. 107-109.

37 *Ibid.,* pp. 109-110.

38 For their names see *Line-Up,* pp. 28-30.

39 The Yugoslav commune is completely different from the communist Chinese institution bearing the same name. On its functions see Bošković, *op. cit.,* pp. 266-292.

40 In recommending more initiative on the part of local government, the Federal Assembly chairman (Kardelj) explicitly opposed a weakening or any change in the role of the party or the Socialist Alliance. Radio Belgrade, March 11, 1964.

41 *Komunist* (Belgrade), March 4, 1965, published an attack by Tito himself against Mihajlo Mihajlov, who had allegedly "slandered" the 1917 Russian Revolution in two articles after a trip to the U.S.S.R. On this earlier occasion Mihajlov was arrested and sentenced to nine months in prison, but on appeal the sentence was suspended. He was given an additional four-and-a-half year term for writing against the communist party. *New York Times,* April 20, 1967.

42 See the analysis in RFE report (by Slobodan Stanković), "The Constitutional Court of Yugoslavia," February 11, 1965 (20 pp.).

43 Bošković, *op. cit.,* pp. 170-177. A good discussion appears in RFE report (by Slobodan Stanković), "Organization and Operation of the Yugoslav System of Elections," March 9, 1967 (13 pp.).

44 "Many electorates select wrong candidates . . . and in one case the list had to be changed [by the authorities]." Radio Belgrade, February 25, 1965.

45 *Borba,* November 19, 1964.

46 Radio Belgrade, April 19, 1965. Only a year before (May 31, 1964), the newspaper for Kosovo-Metohija, called *Rilindja,* attacked the same kind of single-list elections in neighboring Albania as "undemocratic." Quoted in RFE report, "Yugoslav Daily Disapproves," June 5, 1964 (3 pp.).

47 See Rodoljub Čolaković (ed.), *Pregled istorije Saveza Komunista Jugoslavije* (Belgrade, 1963), pp. 38-46, on this congress.

48 Tito, a Croatian who in the First World War fought in the Austro-Hungarian army, was captured and sent to Russia as a prisoner of war. After his release he remained there until 1920. Before leaving, he married a Russian woman and became a member of the Soviet communist party. On returning to Yugoslavia he joined the communist movement of his own country. He engaged in party and trade-union work which resulted in frequent arrests and an eventual imprisonment of five years. Upon his release in 1934 he returned to Moscow, where he worked for the Comintern, and directed recruitment of Yugoslav volunteers for the Spanish civil war. U.S. Department of State, Division of Biographic Information,

The Central Leadership of the Union of Communists of Yugoslavia (Washington, D.C., 1958), p. 19; hereafter cited as *Central Leadership.*

49 Alexander Rudziński, "Politics and Political Organizations," in Robert F. Byrnes (ed.), *Yugoslavia* (New York, 1957), pp. 115-116.

50 *Ibid.,* p. 117.

51 Milovan Djilas, *Conversations with Stalin* (New York, 1962), pp. 11-12.

52 Čolaković, *op. cit.,* pp. 548-561, provides a summary of this meeting which was held in April 1958 at Ljubljana.

53 See the new party statute adopted at the Eighth Congress, December 7-13, 1964, and published in Savez Komunista Jugoslavije, *Osmi Kongres SKJ* (Belgrade, 1964), pp. 235-249. Paragraph 3 on page 238 deals with "democratic centralism."

54 Rudziński, in Byrnes (ed.), *op. cit.,* p. 120. The new statute, mentioned above, makes all party members "socially responsible also for the implementation of views and policy of the League of Communists in the agencies of self-management, in sociopolitical organizations, and in political life in general." Radio Belgrade, August 26, 1964, commenting on the draft statute.

55 Paragraph 35 of the statute in *Osmi Kongres SKJ,* p. 246. This statute also includes the provision that any communist proposed for a leading agency must win two-thirds of the votes "or more than half, if the list includes other candidates" and that "all leading agencies must change at least one-fourth of their members" at each election. Radio Belgrade, November 27, 1964, commenting on the draft statute.

56 The social makeup of this body when it numbered only fifteen members was nine workers and six intellectuals. Five possessed university degrees; one was a graduate of a teachers' school; six could claim to have attended only an elementary school and the rest presumably not that.
    Central Leadership, p. 3. This refers to the leadership elected at the

Seventh Congress, held April 22-26, 1958.

57 The twenty-five members of the Control Commission as well as the fifteen on the Central Audit Commission are listed in *Osmi Kongres SKJ,* p. 281.

58 *Komunist,* July 15, 1965; Paragraph 1 of statute, *Osmi Kongres SKJ,* pp. 236-238.

59 Josef Korbel, *Tito's Communism* (Denver, 1951), p. 67.

60 *Osmi Kongres SKJ,* p. 139; *Komunist,* July 15, 1965.

61 Even so, fewer than 20 percent of university students are SKJ members. See the conclusions from twenty youth surveys conducted between 1956 and 1963, which indicate that the "majority of respondents do not really understand Marxist dogma" and show a "preference for individual over collective values." Stanisław Skrzypek, "The Political, Cultural, and Social Views of Yugoslav Youth," *Public Opinion Quarterly,* XXIX, No. 1 (Spring 1965), 104.

62 It was admitted at the Eighth Congress that the percentage of young people in the party up to the age of twenty-five years had dropped from 23.6 percent in 1958 to 13.6 percent in 1964. *Osmi Kongres SKJ,* p. 138. The same percentage was given for 1965 in *Komunist,* July 15, 1965.

63 Radio Belgrade, February 17, 1965; *Statistical Yearbook of Yugoslavia 1966,* p. 71.

64 Bošković, *op. cit.,* pp. 339-347.

65 On the SSJ see, *ibid.,* pp. 347-350. In 1961 it had 6.7 million members, according to Mineev and Tokarev, *op. cit.,* p. 33.

66 Soviet troops only passed through the northeastern part of the country. Djilas, *op. cit.,* pp. 88-89, discussed with Stalin the 121 reported cases of rape (111 of these also involved murder) and 1,204 registered incidents of looting by the Red Army in Yugoslavia. Note that Djilas was released from prison on December 31, 1966.

67 Early in 1948 Stalin turned from his previous opposition and ordered an immediate federation between Bulgaria and Yugoslavia. *Ibid.,* p. 177.

68 Robert Bass and Elizabeth Marbury (eds.), *The Soviet-Yugoslav Controversy, 1948-1958: A Documentary Record* (New York, 1959), pp. 3-39.

69 Quoted, *ibid.*, p. 40.

70 Milorad M. Drachkovitch, *United States Aid to Yugoslavia and Poland: An Analysis of a Controversy* (Washington, D.C., 1963), p. 121.

71 See his speech at Rangoon in Josip Broz Tito, *Selected Speeches and Articles: 1941-1961* (Zagreb, 1963), pp. 172-173.

72 Quoted in Bass and Marbury (eds.), *op. cit.*, pp. 52-54.

73 Josip Broz Tito, "On Certain International Questions," *Foreign Affairs*, XXXVI, No. 1 (October 1957), 70-72.

74 Translated in full in Stoyan Pribechevich (ed. and transl.), *Yugoslavia's Way: The Program of the League of the Communists of Yugoslavia* (New York, 1958), pp. 263.

75 *Jen Min Jih Pao* (Peking), May 5, 1958, translated in Václav Beneš *et al.* (eds.), *The Second Soviet-Yugoslav Dispute* (Bloomington, Ind., 1959), pp. 29-91.

76 See article on "Belgrade Conference of the Non-Aligned" in Marijan Hubeni (ed.), *Atlas svetskih zbivanja* (Belgrade, 1964), pp. 191-192. The speech appears in Tito, *Selected Speeches and Articles*, pp. 388-408.

77 During the three years 1963-1965, trade with the U.S.S.R. increased by 90 percent. N. Stolpov in an article on "Socialist Countries of Europe," in *Kommunist vooruzhënnykh sil*, XLVI, No. 4 (February 1966), Part II, 73. The Soviet Union announced a credit of 160 million dollars to Yugoslavia in 1966. *Neue Zürcher Zeitung*, September 1, 1966. Tito visited Moscow in January-February 1967.

78 During the first eight months of 1965 United States exports to Yugoslavia reached 148 million dollars, compared with only 40 million in imports. Radio Belgrade, October 11, 1965. Then, some 46 million dollars worth of wheat was sold to Belgrade on credit under the U.S. Food for Peace program. *New York Times*, November 23, 1965. Further arrangements of this type had been blocked by Congress in order to prevent such transactions with countries that make shipments to Cuba or North Vietnam. However, the United States sold to Yugoslavia almost 10 million dollars worth of cottonseed and soybean oil on long-term credit. *New York Times*, February 18, 1967.

79 *Borba*, June 23, 1965. The CMEA during 1964 accounted for 30 percent of Yugoslav foreign trade. Hermann Gross in an article on "Economic Systems and Economic Policy of the South-East European States," in Walter Althammer (ed.), *Deutsch-südosteuropäische Wirtschaftsprobleme* (Munich, 1966), p. 7.

80 Nearly two million people, or one in nine, of the Yugoslav population, lost their lives during the Second World War as a result of German or German-allied action. "Report on Yugoslavia," *The Atlantic*, CCXVI, No. 1 (July 1965), 14.

81 *Die Welt*, April 6, 1967.

Chapter 9 / MILITARY INTEGRATION:
The Warsaw Treaty Organization

THE ESTABLISHMENT by the Soviet Union of a multilateral military alliance system in Eastern Europe was announced by Moscow as a response to West German membership in NATO. The true reason for the Warsaw Pact which brought this system into being more probably was the desire of the U.S.S.R. to obtain legal justification for stationing its troops in East-Central Europe. The pact was signed in the capital of Poland on May 14, 1955. One day later the Austrian state treaty was signed in Vienna, restoring sovereignty to Austria and obligating Moscow to evacuate its forces from Hungary and Romania within forty days after the latter agreement had gone into effect.[1] The Warsaw Treaty Organization (WTO) also provided an additional legal basis for the continued presence of Soviet troops in Poland and in the so-called German Democratic Republic, although in the latter case such provision was not at all necessary, owing to the absence of a peace treaty.

A U.S.S.R. government declaration at the height of the Hungarian revolt reaffirmed the right of this presence and added that Soviet forces in Poland had the additional justification of the Potsdam Agreement. This statement claimed that no U.S.S.R. military units existed in any other East European people's democracy—the German Democratic Republic, proclaimed "sovereign" in October 1949, apparently was not considered in this category—and that the Soviet government was ready to discuss the question of its troops abroad with other signatories to the Warsaw Pact.[2]

The subsequently negotiated status-of-forces treaties with Poland (December 1956), East Germany (March 1957), Romania (April

1957), and Hungary (May 1957) all remain in effect today except for the third, which lapsed upon the withdrawal of Soviet troops from Romania in June 1958.[3] These agreements were the first such arrangements to be made known publicly, although secret accords may already have existed. The agreement with East Germany is unique in that it includes a safety clause allowing the U.S.S.R. to interfere if it finds its own security to be endangered. Article 18 of this treaty states:

> In case of a threat to the security of the Soviet forces which are stationed on the territory of the German Democratic Republic [GDR], the High Command of the Soviet forces in the GDR, in appropriate consultation with the GDR Government, and taking into account the actual situation and the measures adopted by GDR state organs, may apply measures for the elimination of such a threat.[4]

This situation has not changed as a result of the bilateral Friendship, Collaboration, and Mutual Assistance Pact signed in 1964 between the two countries.[5]

Apart from the above exception, all the status-of-forces treaties follow a uniform pattern. They deal with the following: [6]

(1) The strength and movement of Soviet forces in the host country.

(2) The jurisdiction over Soviet forces, individual soldiers, members of Soviet military families, and civilian employees while on the territory of the host country.

(3) Soviet control and use of military installations on the territory of the host country.

(4) Jurisdiction of local authorities in civil and criminal matters arising out of, or in conjunction with, the presence of Soviet troops.

(5) Matters subject to the exclusive jurisdiction of Soviet authorities.

(6) Settlement of mutual claims.

The inferior status of the German Democratic Republic can be seen also in certain differences regarding details. For example, the treaties with Poland and Hungary omit the article on the basis of which the GDR guarantees the U.S.S.R. the use of military and nonmilitary facilities, including transport and communications, that were in use on the date the agreement was signed. Further divergencies exist regarding movement of Soviet troops.[7] This can occur in Hungary and Poland only with the consent of the government and by plans made in advance. The GDR agreement provides a general understanding on maneuver areas, but says nothing about troop movements. Again, the treaties with Poland and Hungary require the consent of the governments to changes in the strength of Soviet troops and for the relocation of garrisons, whereas in the GDR only consultation is needed.

The treaty with Hungary is essentially the same as that with Poland, except that the latter is much more elaborate. For example, its Article 5 reads:

> The regulations on entry and exit of Soviet troop units and members of the Soviet armed forces and their families into Poland or from Poland as well as questions concerning types of required documents in connection with their stay on the territory of the People's Republic of Poland will be governed by a special agreement between the contracting parties.[8]

In contrast the Hungarian treaty refers simply to agreement as to the strength of Soviet troops and the places where they will be stationed.

Finally, the treaty with Poland differs from the other two by introducing a statement (Article 15) about a special agreement defining "lines of communication, dates, orders, and compensation conditions for transit of Soviet troops and war material across the territory of the People's Republic of Poland." [9]

A different problem is posed by tiny Albania, which has been outside the bloc since Khrushchëv attacked its leadership in October 1961 at the 22d Congress of the CPSU. Although not expelled from the Warsaw Pact, Albania has refused to attend any sessions of its Political Consultative Committee. Since the ouster of Khrushchëv, two attempts have been made to bring Albania back into active participation, without success. The Albanian communists in January 1965 rejected an invitation, extended by the Polish regime, to attend the seventh meeting of the committee, held in Warsaw later that same month. In January 1966 an invitation from the same source proposed that Tirana send a delegation to a meeting of communist parties from Warsaw Pact and "socialist" countries in Asia to discuss coordination of aid for North Vietnam. The following month the official Albanian news agency published the texts of the short invitation and an extensive refusal.[10]

In September 1965 the CPSU first secretary (since April 1966, secretary-general), Leonid I. Brezhnev, informed the party's Central Committee that changes in the military alliance of the pact countries were under consideration:

> With a view to improving the activity of the Warsaw Treaty Organization, it is necessary to establish within the framework of this pact a permanent and operational mechanism for the evaluation of current problems.
>
> The complex international situation forces us to pay special attention to problems of military collaboration with the [other] countries of socialism. A great effort is taking place according to the following plan: standardization of equipment is being implemented, exchange of combat training experience [has been developed] and joint maneuvers are being conducted.[11]

No further information has been forthcoming on this most intriguing subject of a "permanent and operational mechanism." Indeed, the Political Consultative Committee met at Bucharest in July 1966 without mentioning it in any communiqué.

CHANGES WITHIN THE WTO

Initially established as a highly centralized system, the Warsaw Pact has had only three commanding officers to date. The first, Marshal of the Soviet Union Ivan S. Konev, was succeeded in July 1960 by Andrei A. Grechko, who also holds that highest military rank in the Soviet armed forces and is currently minister of Defense. The present WTO commander is Marshal of the Soviet Union Ivan I. Yakubovskii. There have been three chiefs of staff for the WTO Unified Armed Forces Command, all career Soviet officers: Generals of the Army Aleksei I. Antonov, who died in office; Pavel I. Batov, who succeeded Antonov in October 1962; and, since late 1965, Mikhail I. Kazakov.[12] Batov was a Khrushchëv man who reportedly strove toward a rapid integration of the armed forces of the pact countries along supra-national lines. Kazakov commanded Soviet troops in Hungary for four years after the 1956 rebellion. He has been commanding officer of several U.S.S.R. military districts, most recently at Leningrad. His task may include bringing Eastern Europe into line with the recent Soviet military reorganization.

The Defense ministers of the East European countries are *ex officio* deputy commanding officers of the WTO. (See table 50.) As can be noted from their appointment dates, relatively little change has occurred in top echelon East European military personnel over the past six to ten years. One reason may be that all of these Defense ministers—with the exception of Lomský, who served as an air force pilot before the Second World War, and possibly Ioniţa—have had careers as political commissars and not as professional military officers. This probably makes them more reliable in the eyes of the Soviet leadership and, indeed, more dependent upon their Soviet advisers.

TABLE 50

WARSAW PACT, DEPUTY COMMANDING OFFICERS, 1967

Name	Rank	Country	Appointed Defense Minister
Spychalski, Marian	Marshal	Poland	November 1956
Lomský, Bohumír	General of the Army	Czechoslovakia	April 1956
Hoffman, Karl Heinz	General of the Army	East Germany	July 1960
Ioniţa, Ion	Colonel General	Romania	August 1966
Dzhurov, Dobri Marinov	General of the Army	Bulgaria	March 1962
Czinege, Lajos	Colonel General	Hungary	May 1960
Balluku, Beqir	Lieutenant General	Albania	July 1953

SOURCES: Stavro Skendi (ed.), *Albania* (New York, 1956), p. 324. *Krasnaya zvezda,* October 24, 1965. Jens Hacker, "Der Warschauer Pakt," *Das Parlament,* January 13, 1966, p. 23 of Supplement (for names only). *Neue Zürcher Zeitung,* August 31, 1966. *Krasnaya zvezda,* March 1, March 15, April 6, April 30, June 3, and June 24, 1967.

On the other hand, a definite rotation system can be seen in the U.S.S.R. military commands in pact countries where Soviet forces are stationed. The commanders in East Germany, General of the Army P. K. Koshevoi, and Poland, Colonel General G. V. Baklanov, received their appointments in February and September 1965, respectively; in Hungary, Colonel General K. I. Provalov was appointed in October 1962 and is due for a transfer. These men are not permitted to stay abroad for extended tours of duty, perhaps lest they develop an attachment to the local milieu. The fact that there are no Soviet troops on its territory may have allowed Romania in October 1964 unilaterally and "probably against the wishes of the Warsaw Pact command" [13] to reduce basic military service from twenty-four to sixteen months. To some extent, it would seem to follow, centralized control has decreased.

The true functions of the three U.S.S.R. military commanders, unfortunately, are not known. They do represent a symbol of Soviet power in the three countries involved and no longer seem averse to publicity. Their photographs appear from time to time in Soviet military newspapers, as do also articles by them, and their positions are not concealed. The main contact between the Soviet commanding officer and the regime in Poland, Hungary, and East Germany probably would be the Defense minister. Another channel for control purposes almost certainly is provided by the many high-ranking U.S.S.R. military officers who have adopted the citizenship of these countries and still occupy key positions in the several Defense establishments.

STRATEGIC PLANNING. The WTO was at first devised and regarded by the U.S.S.R. as a defensive alliance, the forward area of which would provide a buffer and absorb the anticipated NATO attack. This attitude, however, has undergone a drastic transformation in the course of the qualitative build-up of the East European armed forces. The change can be seen from the scenario implemented during the most recent quadripartite maneuvers in the German Democratic Republic. Pact Commander Marshal Grechko in an interview granted to Tass stated:

> . . . One must above all note the uniform military doctrine of the socialist countries united in the Warsaw Pact . . . In case of aggression, our armies are ready not to conduct a passive defense but to engage in active military operations, which would be immediately transferred to the territory of the enemy.
>
> The armies of the Warsaw Pact countries also adhere to a uniform tactic of battleground action. As to armament, it has been standardized to a considerable degree . . . Consistently, the methods of army training have been almost identical.[14]

The 1965 maneuvers under the code name "October Storm" (during October 16-22) included Soviet, East German, Czechoslovak, and Polish military units among the 10,000 troops involved and allegedly provided substance for the commander's remarks. "Blue" aggressors crossed the GDR border in the southwest and attacked

"Red" defending forces. Concrete plans for such a NATO blitzkrieg, according to Walter Ulbricht, envisaged a general direction of attack toward

> Eisenach–Erfurt–Karl Marx Stadt [Chemnitz], as far as the upper reaches of the Neisse [River], then swinging north, in order to wrench the GDR out of the socialist camp within 36 to 48 hours. It was argued [by NATO] that if accomplished facts were created so quickly, a world war could be avoided by, as it were, a police action.[15]

During October Storm, however, the Blue offensive was stopped, and the aggressor "like a cornered beast" decided to risk all and use atomic warheads. Responding "in greater numbers and with more powerful calibers of nuclear weapons," the Red side struck at the firing potential and troops of the aggressor.[16] Nearly 1,000 Polish paratroopers were transported by Antonov–22's (air buses) to the drop zone. Their mission was to capture an airfield near Erfurt and subsequently attack the rear of the enemy force.

Red "defenders" advanced on a strategically important bridge, which had been established by reconnaissance as being intact. "In the very last moment, when Blue forces were retreating already, West German workers disarmed a demolition crew and saved the bridge." [17] These war games took place under General of the Army Koshevoi, commanding the Soviet troops in East Germany. Marshal Grechko and all pact Defense ministers were observers. The same high-ranking officers witnessed Operation "Vltava," held in Czechoslovakia during the latter part of September 1966 with Soviet, East German, Hungarian, and Czechoslovak troops.

Although few details have been released on WTO maneuvers up to 1963, there appears to have occurred then a radical change in conduct of these field exercises to reflect the new Soviet military doctrine which, according to an authoritative spokesman, considers that "in a world war, the possibility of a non-nuclear conflict has become an abstraction." [18]

Following this doctrine, the "Quartet" operation of October 1963 in East Germany, the maneuvers of August 1964 in Bulgaria, "October Storm" of 1965 in East Germany, and the exercises of September 1966 in Czechoslovakia all employed large-scale landings from the air which either introduced or took place simultaneously with attacks by armored and motorized rifle units in division strength.[19] These massed forces, moving at a speed of about a hundred kilometers per day, exploit the element of surprise in order to put out of action NATO troops that have survived the initial nuclear strikes.

That this doctrine is of an offensive nature can be seen clearly in a statement by the GDR first deputy minister of Defense which, in essence, repeats the remarks of Marshal Grechko quoted earlier. Writing in Russian for Soviet military readers, the East German said:

> The national mission of the NVA [GDR National People's Army] is to be prepared and able to . . . destroy the aggressor on his own territory by decisive, offensive action together with [other] brotherly socialist armies and to assist progressive forces in West Germany to liquidate the imperialist system [in that country].[20]

The implementation of the U.S.S.R.'s military doctrine and the role of its East European "allies" in its strategy can be seen in the surface-to-surface missiles now standard equipment for all WTO armies and in the fact that the missiles, capable of carrying nuclear warheads, remain under Soviet control. Missiles and rockets are replacing traditional artillery pieces, of which not a single new model has been produced over the past decade. It would seem likely that heavy mortars and recoilless rifles will also be superseded by tactical nuclear-tipped guided missiles.

DECISION MAKING. Only eight meetings of the WTO Political Consultative Committee took place between 1956 and 1966, although twenty-two should have been convened during this period on the basis of two per year set forth in the pact statute. Table 51 gives published data on the topics considered in these sessions.[21] The communiqués issued suggest that the committee meetings serve merely as vehicles for bloc propaganda.

Less is known concerning the sessions attended by the first secretaries of the communist parties of Warsaw Pact countries. Only the one held at Moscow during August 3-5, 1961 has been reported publicly. It apparently approved construction of the Berlin Wall by the East German regime. More important perhaps have been the consultations among Defense ministers of the pact countries at Warsaw in September 1961, at Prague in late January and early February

1962, at Warsaw in February 1963, and at Moscow in May 1966. A special conference of senior commanding personnel including Defense ministers, chiefs of staff, and political indoctrination chiefs met in 1965 for nine days "within the confines of the [U.S.S.R.]

TABLE 51

WARSAW PACT, POLITICAL CONSULTATIVE COMMITTEE MEETINGS,
1956-1966

Place	Date(s)	Proposals and decisions
Prague	January 27-28, 1956	*Approved:* Statute for Unified Military Command; admission of GDR armed forces; establishment of Standing Commission and Secretariat.
Moscow	May 24, 1958	*Proposed:* Nonaggression pact with NATO; summit meeting. *Approved:* Withdrawal of U.S.S.R. troops from Romania.
Moscow	February 4, 1960	*Proposed:* Atom-free zone and cessation of nuclear tests.
Moscow	March 28-29, 1961	*Proposed:* Universal disarmament.
Moscow	June 7, 1962	*Discussed:* Albanian refusal to cooperate with WTO.
Moscow	July 26, 1963	*Discussed:* Status of pact armed forces and coordination of training.
Warsaw	January 19-20, 1965	*Discussed:* Proposed multilateral nuclear force within NATO and "appropriate countermeasures."
Bucharest	July 4-6, 1966	*Proposed:* Reduction of tensions through military détente and a general conference on security in Europe.

SOURCES: U.S. Senate, Committee on Government Operations (89th Cong., 2d sess.), *The Warsaw Pact: Its Role in Soviet Bloc Affairs* (Washington, D.C., 1966), p. 32, for the first seven meetings. *Krasnaya zvezda,* July 8 and 9, 1966, for the eighth meeting.

Sub-Carpathian military district," where tactical exercises were held, new types of arms and material demonstrated, and views on different questions of military development exchanged.[22] From time to time, conferences of the deputy ministers of Defense take place, as in a 1965 two-day session in Warsaw which heard Marshal Grechko discuss combat training, military preparedness, and other measures.[23] Unfortunately, no record of debates or decisions is available.

Apart from positions within their own armed forces, no East European military officer heads any top-level WTO organ or command. Of possible subgroupings within the WTO only one, encompassing the Danubian area, has been reported. All troops in this region allegedly are subordinated to a single high command, the *Oberkommando Donau*.[24] Air defense for all of Eastern Europe has been integrated, but here again under a Soviet commander, in 1964 the U.S.S.R. Chief Marshal of Aviation, Vladimir A. Sudets, who directed the equivalent Soviet armed forces branch, the *Voiska PVO Strany*.[25] Although previously a candidate member of the CPSU's Central Committee, he was not reelected to that body by the Twenty-third Congress, in April 1966, and this was followed by his replacement.

Despite the fact that no high position in the WTO is held by any East European, it is probable that at least the Defense ministers (the great majority of whom are Soviet trained) are given the feeling of participation in decision making. Actually, in certain cases the very opposite is true, where Soviet officers who transferred to satellite armies during and immediately after the war still remain camouflaged in high positions.[26] Some thirty-two former Soviet officers of the rank of general in the Polish army, together with Poland's Defense minister, the former Soviet Marshal Konstantin K. Rokossovsky, returned to Moscow toward the end of 1956 "with the gratitude of the Polish nation." At least three, however, remain in high positions in Poland. They are Lieutenant General Jerzy Bordziłowski, first deputy minister of Defense and chief inspector of training; Major General Józef Urbanowicz, third deputy minister of Defense and chief of political indoctrination for the armed forces; and Vice Admiral Zdisław Studziński, the navy commander.[27] These three positions are among the more sensitive within the military hierarchy of Poland.

Many of the native-born East European officers have attended military schools in the U.S.S.R., and this may provide them with a common experience if nothing else. Integration of commands obviously requires a single language, and here the chosen language is Russian, knowledge of which is a prerequisite for training in the Soviet Union. Bulgarians, Czechoslovaks, and Poles have found Russian easy to learn because of its similarity to their native tongues. It has proved more difficult for East Germans, Hungarians, and Romanians, whose language groups are not related to the Slavic family. Learning has proceeded rapidly, however, since ignorance of Russian presents an obstacle to obtaining higher command positions within the armed forces of the individual satellite military establishments.[28] Russian expressions have penetrated the military vocabularies of most East European countries.

EXECUTION OF DECISIONS. The WTO Unified Command, which has its headquarters in Moscow, theoretically correlates and orders the execution of decisions reached by the representatives of the deputy commanders (that is, of the bloc countries' Defense ministers) who make up the staff of this command.

Under the unification program, certain national contingents have been earmarked for WTO service. Although these have never been openly specified, it is probable that only elite units are assigned, such as the regiment from the 6th Pomeranian Parachute-Assault Division, stationed near Kraków in Poland, which participated in the operation "October Storm." Its commanding officer, at that time thirty-nine-year-old Colonel Edwin Rozłubirski, was the subject of a biographic sketch which appeared, along with his photograph, in the daily newspaper of the Soviet Defense ministry.[29] The Polish 12th Mechanized Division and a brigade of frontier troops reportedly have been assigned specifically to the WTO. On the other hand, all East German troops are at the disposal of the WTO High Command. This situation has not been changed by the June 1964 Soviet-GDR treaty.

Transfer of Soviet troops from the western parts of the U.S.S.R. to any place in Eastern Europe, other than by air, would be difficult owing to the limited number of interchange points for broad-gauge railroad traffic. These reportedly existed in 1960 at Gerdauen, Brest-Terespol, Przemyśl-Medika, Cop-Zahony, Jassy, and Galați only.[30] In the meanwhile the number of such points must have been increased, with a corresponding expansion in machinery for loading and unloading. Construction of secondary railroad links and transmountain lines has been noted. Traffic management has been centralized through the Council for Mutual Economic Assistance (CMEA).

The CMEA is planning a network of automobile expressways which will link the major cities in Eastern Europe with Moscow and Kiev.[31] The CMEA's Permanent Commission for Transportation has the task of coordinating this ambitious scheme. Another project, just completed, involves the 1,900-mile petroleum pipeline which links the Volga-Ural oil fields with Poland, East Germany, Czechoslovakia, and Hungary. During 1963 and 1964 some thirteen million tons of oil went to Eastern Europe through this "Friendship Pipe-line," [32] indicating a considerable dependence on the U.S.S.R. in this respect by all WTO members except Romania.

Oil, of course, remains indispensable for moving modern armies, and oil deliveries have facilitated the organization of joint maneuvers, which did not begin until 1961. Credit for this idea has been claimed by the Polish communists:

> Initiated by our side, joint field exercises by the armies of Warsaw Pact countries have become permanent. Our troops, staffs, and commands annually train on land, on sea, and in the air with troops, staffs, and commands from brotherly armies: the Soviet Army, the Czechoslovak People's Army, and the GDR National People's Army . . .[33]

Actually, these first maneuvers involved only Soviet and East German units. The following spring, the U.S.S.R., Romania, and Hungary conducted joint field exercises.

During the fall of 1963, the code name "Quartet" was assigned to the first set of maneuvers to involve four countries. Tass reported from East Berlin that some 40,000 troops took part, supported by 760 tanks and 350 aircraft, and comprised units from the Soviet Union, Czechoslovakia, the GDR, and Poland.[34] Subsequently it was intimated by the Polish Defense minister that integration and joint command procedures had been improved to the extent that larger formations and more than four countries might participate.

Instead of such a development, however, two separate sets of exercises took place during the following year. One of these included only Soviet and Czechoslovak units. The other brought together Soviet, Romanian, and Bulgarian troops and included the use of paratroopers and the execution of amphibious landings from the Black Sea. Observers representing the other WTO countries could be identified in newspaper photographs. Soviet marines (*morskaya pekhota*) made a landing on the Bulgarian coast.[35] Unfortunately, few details were released.

It is noteworthy that until the September 1966 operation "Vltava" the Hungarians had never trained with the Czechoslovaks. This may be ascribed not only to the events of 1956, but also to the fact that about a million ethnic Hungarians lived in Czechoslovakia between the wars and many still reside there. Nationality differences make for frictions that could lead to outbreaks during joint field exercises. Except for those in Czechoslovakia and Bulgaria, traditionally the East European populations have always been hostile to the Russians, for good historical reasons. Even so, none of the communist sources mention any Soviet dissatisfaction with the performance of troops of the bloc countries in the course of maneuvers.

Ships of East European countries have been utilized for delivery of military equipment to overseas underdeveloped areas. An instance came to light when the captain of the Bulgarian vessel *Veliko Tirnovo* was fined 5.4 million Lebanese pounds (about 1.75 million U.S. dollars) in Beirut for smuggling arms. He and six other persons were detained in connection with the discovery of 1,500 automatic rifles in the ship's cargo, concealed in 75 crates. The official Bulgarian news agency argued that: "It is a well-known fact that the carrier is not held responsible for the content of the commodities shipped and declared in the bill of lading," as if the Navibulgare, owning the ship, were not a state-controlled enterprise.[36]

Although the destination of these rifles (possibly intended for the Kurds) was not revealed, it is known that the Bulgarians have been selling weapons to the royalist forces in Yemen since about 1964. Some twenty-five million dollars in Saudi-Arabian gold reportedly has been paid for these purchases, many of which were channeled through the Bulgarian military attaché in Paris. One such shipment was seized by the French when a chartered transport airplane carrying rifles from Belgium landed at Djibouti in Somaliland.[37] Little information can be found on similar arms shipments during the past decade, although the first known transaction, involving the sale of Czechoslovak weapons to Egypt, occurred as early as 1955. Apart from creating future dependence for spare parts and bringing in foreign exchange, the supplying of arms to insurgents contributes to instability which in turn makes for new communist opportunities to advance the objective of U.S.S.R. control over the underdeveloped countries.

In addition to facilitating the sale of arms clandestinely, military attachés from East European countries also engage in espionage on behalf of the U.S.S.R. Two of these men, Paweł Monat and Władysław Tykociński, defected to the West and have testified about their experiences.[38] After reassignment to Warsaw from abroad, Monat handled reports from all Polish military attachés and forwarded them to Moscow via his office. Tykociński more recently corroborated this fact and disclosed that for a period of time the chief of Polish military intelligence was a Soviet officer.

Another example of espionage is provided by the extensive operations of East European agents in the Federal Republic of Germany. Only the Yugoslav agents no longer may send reports directly to the U.S.S.R., as was their practice until July 1966. During one year more than 1,000 efforts at recruitment of informants was ascertained in West Germany. In consequence 195 persons were convicted of high treason or treasonable relations by the federal court at Karlsruhe and the appellate tribunals in that country. (See table 52.)

TABLE 52

ESPIONAGE IN WEST GERMANY, 1964

Recruitment efforts		Information targets	
Country of agent	Number	Category	Number
East Germany.........	860	Military	1,772
U.S.S.R.	39	Political	408
Czechoslovakia	44	Economic	169
Poland	32	Preparatory and support [a]	1,217
Yugoslavia	12	Total	3,566
Hungary	7		
Romania	4		
Unknown	16		
Total	1,014		

SOURCE: Official figures from [West Germany], Bundesamt für Verfassungsschutz, Bundesinnenministerium (Bonn), as cited in *Soldat und Technik*, IX, No. 2 (February 1966), 99.

[a] Activities involving the acquisition of biographic data on possible contacts and other ancillary activities.

SOVIET FORCES IN EASTERN EUROPE. With the exception of Poland and Czechoslovakia, all the bloc countries have had a so-called Soviet Consultative Group as an element of WTO activity. In 1962 such a Soviet group reportedly operated from the U.S.S.R. embassy in Budapest and thus claimed diplomatic immunity.[39] The rights and privileges of the groups allegedly are concealed in various secret agreements. The effectiveness of the group in Hungary obviously is guaranteed by the presence of U.S.S.R. troops.

The Soviet Consultative Groups function as military advisers. The group in Hungary reportedly controls that country's rear services and armaments industry planning, each headed by a deputy minister of Defense who has as an adviser a Soviet officer with the rank of full colonel. The Defense minister, the deputy ministers, and these highest ranking U.S.S.R. advisers reportedly comprise the "military collegium" in the ministry. The same is said to be true for the general staff. Each section of the latter (operations, intelligence, organization and mobilization, military installations, service regulations, military geography, communications, technology and transportation, air force, anti-air defense, civil defense, training, and logistics) allegedly includes a Soviet staff officer as adviser.[40] To each Weapons Inspectorate—armored and motorized troops, air force, communications troops, artillery, engineers, ABC weapons—there is attached a Soviet colonel or general and two to four other officers as assistants. Similar arrangements allegedly prevail in the military districts and on down into the regimental level. At corps level, one senior Soviet officer is said to control operations and another logistics. It is reported, further, that each of the eleven frontier-guard district commands has a Soviet officer and several aides assigned to it, and that the entire political indoctrination system within the Hungarian armed forces is directed by a high-ranking Soviet officer and six other "advisers." [41]

In Bulgaria, on the other hand, Soviet advisory activities are conducted with considerable restraint. Both the main political administration of the armed forces and the military intelligence section have Soviet "observers." Soviet officers also serve as unit advisers, but mostly at division level, although their network previously extended down into the regiments. Each motorized rifle and armored division allegedly has on its staff a Soviet officer of the rank of lieutenant colonel or major, under whom four or five others function as "instructors." Certain armored regiments and operational squadrons of the Bulgarian air force (possibly those assigned to the WTO) still have Soviet advisers attached to them.

Among the reasons for these differences between Hungary and Bulgaria would be the 1956 rebellion in Budapest, of which there has been nothing comparable in Sofia. Another probably is Bulgarian national pride. Known as the "Prussians of the Balkans," the people would resent any foreign command exercised openly. A third reason amounts to a corollary of the others. Key positions in the military hierarchy are staffed by natives of Bulgaria who were trained as officers in the U.S.S.R. and resumed their original citizenship upon returning home after the war. These officers have included:

> The former Bulgarian defense minister, Army General Ivan Mikhailov.
>
> The former chief of the general staff (about 1950-1959), first deputy Defense minister (1959-1962), and head of the Administrative Organs Department (the cover designation for the Military Department) in the communist party's Central Committee (1962-1965), recently ambassador to East Germany, Colonel General Ivan Bachvarov (killed in an airplane crash at Bratislava in 1966).
>
> The former commander of the navy and former Soviet naval officer, now deputy chief of the general staff, Vice Admiral Branimir Ormanov.
>
> The former commandant of the general staff academy, guerrilla fighter subsequently trained as an officer in the U.S.S.R., and now a deputy Defense minister and air force commander, Colonel General Slavcho Trunski.
>
> The current head of the General Political Department (main political administration) in the armed forces, graduate of both the "Frunze" and the general staff academy in the U.S.S.R., and former commander of the Sofia garrison, Lieutenant General Velko Palin.[42]

In Czechoslovakia the Soviet advisers for the most part control industries which produce weapons and war matériel used by the armed forces of the bloc countries. Use of Soviet personnel in training Czechoslovak forces produced an extensive organization called the "Soviet Satellite Coordination Command" which preceded the 1955 military alliance.[43] This organ may still be operative. References have appeared recently to a Soviet colonel general, Aleksandr M. Kushchev, as representing the Joint Military Command of the Warsaw Pact armies at a two-day conference of communist party members within the Defense ministry of Czechoslovakia and at a Liberation Day reception in Prague.[44]

In Poland it was not necessary to establish a Soviet military mission at all. Some 17,000 Soviet officers directed the Polish armed forces after transferring from the Red Army and accepting citizenship in the country to which they had been detailed. Following the change in communist party leadership at Warsaw in October 1956, many of these men returned to the Soviet Union. The function of those who remain consists of observation, giving advice, and serving as liaison officers as well as securing communications with U.S.S.R. troops in Upper Silesia (Poland) and East Germany.[45]

The situation in East Germany need not be discussed, because this area truly reflects the name used for it by the West Germans: the Soviet Occupation Zone. With approximately twenty U.S.S.R. divisions stationed in the GDR, there is no doubt as to who is in control.

In contrast, Romania probably presents a picture of greater independence of the U.S.S.R. than any other bloc country. In October 1964 military service was reduced to sixteen months, and during the summer of 1965 Bucharest reportedly "balked at sending troops out of the country for additional joint activities."[46] The Soviet military mission is said to number only two or three men today, as against fifteen or sixteen as recently as 1964.[47]

Soviet troops are garrisoned in three Warsaw Pact countries. In Poland, there is the Northern Group of Forces, with headquarters at Legnica in Upper Silesia; in Hungary, the Southern Group of Forces, at Tököl near Budapest; and in the GDR, the Group of Soviet Forces in [East] Germany, with headquarters at Wünsdorf near East Berlin. The generally accepted figures for these forces outside the borders of the Soviet Union are respectively two, four, and twenty divisions.[48] The one-to-one ratio of armored to motorized rifle divisions in these Soviet units shows a considerably heavier concentration on the more powerful type than prevails in the indigenous East European forces. (See table 53.)

In East Germany, the U.S.S.R. troops outnumber those permitted the GDR regime by a ratio of three to one, and in tanks and aircraft the preponderance is even greater. Since 1964, however, the GDR armed forces have been equipped with Frog-4 and Scud-A type ground-to-ground rockets, the latter employing a guided missile. These are being supplied by the U.S.S.R. to East German forces at division levels and are allocated to artillery.[49] These weapons are capable of delivering nuclear warheads over distances up to a hundred miles. It is doubtful that the Soviets would allow the GDR to assume control over such atomic weapons.

According to General Koshevoi, commander of the Soviet forces in East Germany, his troops are in the process of regrouping. Missile and armored units may be increased as other types are reduced.

TABLE 53

WARSAW PACT, ARMED FORCES, 1966-1967

Country	Army personnel	Divisions [a]	Tanks	Security Forces personnel	Navy personnel	Naval craft C [b]	D [c]	S [d]	Air Force personnel	Aircraft
Albania	30,000	2	—	12,500	3,000	—	—	4	6,000	100
Bulgaria	125,000	11(3)	2,500	15,000	7,000	—	2	3	24,000	400
Czechoslovakia	175,000	14(4)	3,200	35,000 [e]	—	—	—	—	45,000	750
East Germany	85,000	6(2)	1,800	70,000	17,000	—	4	—	20,000	400
U.S.S.R.	254,900 [f]	20(10)	7,500	—	(80,000) [g]	(4)	(25)	(75)	—	1,100
Hungary	100,000	6(1)	1,000	35,000	—	—	—	—	9,000	150
U.S.S.R.	55,000	4(4)	1,400	—	—	—	—	—	—	350
Poland	185,000	15(5)	3,000	45,000 [e]	15,000	—	3	8	60,000	950
U.S.S.R.	25,000	2(2)	700	—	—	—	—	—	—	350
Romania	175,000	11(1)	1,500	50,000	8,000	—	2	1	18,000	300
					(50,000) [h]	(3)	(20)	(45)		
Total	1,209,900	91(32)	21,600	262,500	180,000	7	56	146	182,000	4,850

SOURCE: Institute for Strategic Studies, *The Military Balance 1966-1967* (London, September 1966), pp. 2, 5, 6-8.

a Armored divisions, included in total, are indicated in parentheses.
b Cruisers.
c Destroyers.
d Submarines.
e Polish security troops were integrated with the regular armed forces and placed under the Defense ministry in July 1965, according to Radio Warsaw, June 30, 1965. The same move took place in Czechoslovakia, effective January 1966, as reported in *Allgemeine Schweizerische Militärzeitschrift*, CXXXII, No. 2 (February 1966), 93.
f Includes 4,900 in Berlin.
g Figures in parentheses refer to the Soviet Baltic Sea Fleet, estimated allocation.
h Soviet Black Sea Fleet, estimated allocation.

U.S.S.R. antiaircraft defense may be withdrawn completely in the course of gradually transferring this responsibility to the GDR. The main centers of concentration for Soviet troops after reorganization would be the area around Suhl in Thüringen, the province of Brandenburg, and the border territories of the GDR along Czechoslovakia and Poland. Finally, Soviet "instructors" are to be withdrawn from the East German army.[50]

Such regrouping would bring Soviet troops in proximity to Czechoslovakia, where the U.S.S.R. maintains no forces officially and where it is important that the uranium mines at Jachymov, Tepler Hochland, and Przibram be protected, as well as those in adjacent East Germany south of Aue.[51] The output of this strategic raw material goes to the U.S.S.R., in amounts that remain secret. The closer disposition of Soviet troops to Poland would provide for better contact with the two Soviet divisions in Upper Silesia. This would allow for a rapid link-up between forces in the event of another crisis, such as the one in 1956 when Polish troops proved unreliable.

The redeployment of Soviet forces in East Germany may be the result of plans for more flexibility in countering operations, should hostilities break out in Central Europe. The troops formerly were concentrated along the frontier between East and West Germany in several parallel lines from Lübeck in the north to the border with Czechoslovakia at Hof in the south.[52] The new scheme presumably would permit deploying troops in echelons, following an east-west direction, with most of them concentrated along the Oder and Western Neisse rivers.

In Hungary, although indigenous forces number nearly twice those of the U.S.S.R., the latter maintains a preponderance of four to one in armored divisions and more than two to one in aircraft. Besides serving to prevent a repetition of the 1956 rebellion, the Soviet troops ensure delivery of uranium from the Hungarian mines at Fünfkirchen. It should be noted, however, that ground-to-ground missiles were displayed at the April 1965 military parade in Budapest. (The Czechoslovak army's weekly newspaper reported subsequently that all other East European countries except Albania and Yugoslavia have been equipped with these.)[53] In addition, Soviet-built MIG–21 delta-wing fighter intercepters and Ilyushin medium-range bombers flew overhead.

According to the first secretary of the Hungarian communist party,

János Kádár, the presence of Soviet troops is in conformity with domestic as well as international law. Early in 1965, speaking to his pseudo-parliament, he declared:

> [The U.S.S.R. armed forces are] an immense help for our people, because if these troops were not here, we would be forced to keep more soldiers under arms at the expense of the living standard, because the fatherland is more important and stronger than the living standard! [Further,] the presence of Soviet troops in Hungary has no internal reason. It depends on the international situation alone. . . . We are not afraid of the withdrawal of Soviet troops, but we do not support any unilateral withdrawal, and this is in the interest of the international political situation.[54]

Kádár suggested "serious talks which do not mean for any side an important shift in the balance of power geographically." No statement has been made since that time which would indicate any change in the above attitude.

CHANGES IN SOVIET CONTROL

Penetration by Soviet nationals into the East European military establishments definitely has decreased over the past decade. Whereas, for instance, at one time virtually all high positions in the Polish armed forces were held by former Russian officers newly turned Polish citizens and "fulfilling the duties of Poles," only a few of these can be discerned today.

Although it would be difficult to show where their loyalty lies, the case of Konstantin K. Rokossovsky may be illuminating. He came to Poland in November 1949 as Defense minister and remained exactly seven years. After that, he returned to the U.S.S.R. and resumed his rank as Marshal of the Soviet Union. Apparently not losing any seniority, he was made a deputy Defense minister in Moscow, perhaps in reward for services rendered while on detached duty in Warsaw.

SECRET POLICE IN EASTERN EUROPE. Very little information is available on the secret police of the WTO countries. Close cooperation and perhaps even a superior-subordinate relationship between the secret police establishments of the Soviet Union and a satellite was evident in the arrest of British citizen Greville Wynne by the Soviet and Hungarian security services in Budapest and his subsequent trial with U.S.S.R. Colonel Oleg V. Penkovskiy in Moscow in 1963.[55]

An even more significant and an openly admitted role was played by Soviet secret police during the arrests in April 1965 of plotters against the Bulgarian regime. Communist journalists in Sofia were briefed on the conspiracy, which was "uncovered by Soviet intelligence agents in March." [56] One of the ten men involved, Ivan Todorov-Gorunya, had been a member of the Bulgarian party's Central Committee and chairman of the government's directorate for water economy. He committed suicide. In June the others, five army officers and four civilians, were sentenced to prison terms for high treason by the military tribunal of the Bulgarian Supreme Court.

The first announcement of the plot came on April 22 and only three names were mentioned, those of Todorov-Gorunya, Krastev, and Anev. Had Todorov-Gorunya lived, he would have stood trial as the main defendant, since he was a member of the Central Committee. It is probably more than coincidental that all three belonged to the "Gavril Genov" partisan detachment during the Second World War. At least one more of the plotters, Temkov, also fought in a guerrilla unit. The fact that the majority of those tried were high-ranking military officers on active duty indicated strong army involvement in the conspiracy.

A further case of collaboration between Soviet and East European secret police was divulged in connection with the purge in Yugoslavia of Aleksandar Ranković. His subordinates in the security apparatus, which he had controlled on behalf of the Yugoslav communist party, were accused of having "too close links" with the Soviet secret police.[57] Nothing regarding these charges at the July 1966 plenum of the Yugoslav communist party's Central Committee was made public. It should be recalled, however, that Greville Wynne lost in a Belgrade hotel a notebook which later turned up in Moscow during the 1963 trial of Colonel Penkovskiy.

MILITARY PRODUCTION. As a source of war matériel, the most important geographic area in Eastern Europe is the Czechoslovakia-GDR-Poland industrial triangle. The first two countries encompass a human pool of skilled technicians and are provided with precision equipment and modern scientific research facilities, especially in nuclear physics. That the U.S.S.R. does not permit sophisticated military production can be seen from the decision taken at the fourteenth CMEA session, in March 1961, which discontinued East German manufacture of four-engine turbo-jet aircraft already in the testing stage.[58]

On the other hand, Eastern Europe is of great value to the U.S.S.R. as a source of uranium in several countries; bauxite for the production of processed aluminium in Czechoslovakia; basic chemicals, rare metals of particular importance for atomic energy programs, and bismuth mined in association with uranium in East Germany; metallic sodium from a Polish Silesian plant for construction of nuclear-powered reactors; cadmium, used in regulating the speed of nuclear reactions, in both Poland and the GDR; molybdenum for the production of crucially important matériel in Bulgaria and Poland; and titanium used in nuclear technology and graphite required for nuclear reactions in Poland.

PARTY CONTROL OVER THE MILITARY

Political controls by the local communist parties do not appear to have been altered significantly. The primary party organizations, however, do comprise a separate hierarchy, with delegates representing the individual military districts at national party congresses. Criteria for admission to the party are the same for officers and enlisted men of the armed forces as for civilians. The trend seems to be toward absorption of the security forces by the regular military establishment, as took place in Poland in 1965 and Czechoslovakia in 1966. This suggests that the ruling communist parties have more confidence in the regular armies.

Apparently, it remains a prerequisite for attainment of the rank of full colonel that an officer be a party member. In the five countries on which data is available, an average of 82.6 percent of regular officers are party members. (See table 54.) This percentage should not be equated with reliability, which is always difficult to measure.

The only hard figures on defections come from West Germany, and these involve GDR military personnel fleeing west. For example, there are East German battalions of border troops which during 1965 had as many as fifteen successful escape attempts and twenty failures. A total of 1,850 GDR soldiers, including 466 border guards, defected in five years following the building of the Berlin Wall in 1961.[59]

The recent Bulgarian military conspiracy, mentioned earlier, would perhaps indicate dissatisfaction with subordination to the U.S.S.R. in that country. Soviet decision-makers probably would not plan to employ jointly Polish and East German, Czechoslovak and Hungarian, or Romanian and Hungarian troops in actual combat, even though combined maneuvers have taken place.

TABLE 54

MEMBERSHIP OF ARMY OFFICERS IN COMMUNIST PARTIES,
1963-1966

Country	Percent of total officer personnel	Source
Bulgaria	82	*Krasnaya zvezda,* September 23, 1965.
Czechoslovakia	75	*Krasnaya zvezda,* October 6, 1965.
East Germany	96	[East Germany], Deutsches Institut für Zeitgeschichte, *Handbuch der Deutschen Demokratischen Republik* (East Berlin, 1964), p. 289.
Hungary	78	*Krasnaya zvezda,* December 3, 1966.
Poland	70	E. Międzyrzecka and J. Klimek (eds.), *Kalendarz robotniczy 1964* (Warsaw, 1963), p. 136.
Romania	90	*Scînteia,* July 24, 1965.
Average	82	

NOTE: Information not available for army officers of Albania.

CHANGES IN POPULAR SUPPORT

In 1959, researchers at the University of Warsaw polled a representative sample of Warsaw inhabitants on their opinion of the profession of the military officer as a career. The standing of the military probably has risen somewhat since then. Compared with the pre-1939 period, however, when officers in the Polish armed forces stood at or near the top of the career scale, at the time of this poll they ranked fourteenth financially, below lathe operators; sixteenth in job security, below accountants; and twenty-first in social prestige, below office supervisors.[60]

No similar investigation is known from the other East European countries, but apart from this limited indication of changed attitudes it seems likely that generally in the bloc countries the lack of any tradition has reduced the attractiveness of a military career among officers and enlisted men alike and has had a deadening effect. Communist propaganda classifies the pre-1939 armies in Eastern Europe as having been either feudal or fascist. The riots in East Germany during June 1953, the Hungarian rebellion in October-November 1956, and the events in Poland at the time of the Hungarian episode, when local forces in each country took up defensive positions against the threat of Soviet troop intervention, all showed that morale was not high from the communist point of view. It must be remembered, however, that these events took place a decade or more ago.

FUTURE DEVELOPMENTS

Trends and goals remain difficult to project, but it is quite clear that the Warsaw Treaty Organization has changed its emphasis radically from defense to offense. This trend most probably will continue, unless Soviet military doctrine itself undergoes a fundamental transformation.

Over the twelve years from 1955 to 1967 the military equipment and the training of WTO forces have developed consistently in one direction: preparation for a war in which it is unthinkable to the Soviet High Command that nuclear weapons will not be used. Even the previously avowed intention not to be the first to introduce such arms in a conflict is no longer being repeated. The U.S.S.R. military hierarchy would not knowingly allow an opponent endowed with atomic and hydrogen warheads to apply the element of surprise and to initiate hostilities.

Soviet military doctrine probably anticipates a conflict in Central Europe within the next decade involving a confrontation between the main forces of NATO and the Warsaw Treaty Organization. Beginning with U.S.S.R. strategic nuclear strikes, ground operations would be launched simultaneously by massive armored and motorized rifle divisions in conjunction with airborne units employed on a large scale. These movements at speeds of up to 100 kilometers per day would be supported by tactical nuclear weapons.

The role of WTO members in such a war can be seen in broad outline even today. For example, Soviet conflict managers are making a concentrated effort to woo Turkey away from the Western alliance. In mid-August of 1965 the U.S.S.R. extended the equivalent of 150 million U.S. dollars in credits for the construction of dams, cement plants, and factories to that country, the first NATO member to accept Soviet economic aid. In February 1966 the Turks announced that they would revise their bilateral agreements, including the status-of-forces treaty, with the United States.

If Turkey and Greece, where a parallel diplomatic offensive is being carried on by Bulgaria, can be neutralized so as to make ineffective their membership in NATO, the Warsaw Treaty Organization could then concentrate on the main enemy: West Germany. Such WTO members as Romania, Bulgaria, and Hungary (not very powerful and not particularly reliable, except for Bulgaria) could be eliminated from Kremlin calculations.

The Warsaw Pact would then base its military plans on East Germany, Poland, and Czechoslovakia as the main allies of the U.S.S.R. The continuous barrage of anti-West German propaganda, especially in Poland and Czechoslovakia, has the obvious purpose of maintaining a war psychosis fed by the fear of a Nazi resurgence and a new *Drang nach Osten.*

Even so, it is doubtful that Polish or Czechoslovak troops would be allowed to operate independently in any conflict. As part of Soviet fronts (groups of armies), they would fight with units on both flanks and in the rear. The performance of the Warsaw Treaty Organization will depend ultimately on the specific military situation. If NATO should be dissolved, WTO forces would march to the Atlantic with little if any opposition.

NOTES

1 Boris Meissner (ed.), *Der Warschauer Pakt: Dokumentensammlung* (Cologne, 1962), p. 12. A translation of the Warsaw treaty into English appears in Ruth C. Lawson (ed.), *International Regional Organizations* (New York, 1962), pp. 206-210, reprinted from *United Nations Treaty Series*, CCXIX, Part I, p. 24. The stationing of U.S.S.R. troops in Hungary, Poland, and Romania was based until 1955 on the need to secure lines of communication to Germany.

2 Tass communiqué in *Pravda*, October 31, 1956.

3 On the withdrawal of Soviet troops from Romania see Günther Wagenlehner, "Die politische Bedeutung des Warschauer Paktes," *Soldat und Technik*, VIII, No. 3 (March 1965), 115.

4 Meissner, *op. cit.*, p. 128. All status-of-forces treaties are given in German by this source on pp. 117-143.

5 Text in *Krasnaya zvezda*, June 13, 1964.

6 Cited by Kazimierz Grzybowski, *The Socialist Commonwealth of Nations* (New Haven, 1964), p. 205.

7 *Ibid.*

8 Meissner, *op. cit.*, p. 118.

9 *Ibid.*, p. 121.

10 Released by the Albanian Telegraphic Agency in Tirana, February 12, 1966.

11 *Krasnaya zvezda*, September 30, 1965. See also Jens Hacker and Alexander Uschakow, *Die Integration Osteuropas 1961 bis 1965* (Cologne, 1966), pp. 67-94, for documents in German on the Warsaw Treaty Organization.

12 Kazakov's appointment was announced by Tass communiqué, November 23, 1965; reported in *Wehrkunde*, XV, No. 1 (January 1966), 51-52.

13 Raymond L. Garthoff, "Die Armeen der Ostblockstaaten," *Osteuropäische Rundschau*, XI, No. 10 (October 1965), 6.

14 Radio Moscow, February 21, 1966.

15 Cited over Deutschlandsender (East Berlin), October 31, 1965.

16 *Neues Deutschland*, October 23, 1965.

17 Radio Warsaw, October 21, 1965; also reported over Deutschlandsender, October 22, 1965; and in *Neues Deutschland*, October 23, 1965.

For an analysis of the maneuvers in September 1966 see "Pr." (Colonel Erich Pruck), "Erkentnisse aus dem Manöver Moldau," *Wehrkunde*, XV, No. 12 (December 1966), 662.

18 Colonel General Professor N. Lomov (director of instruction, Lenin Academy, Moscow), article on "Influence of Soviet Military Doctrine upon the Development of Military Art," *Kommunist vooruzhёnnykh sil,* XLVI, No. 21 (November 1965), 18.

19 "L'Adaptation des Forces Terrestres Soviétiques a une Guerre Nucléaire," *Revue de Défense Nationale*, XXI, No. 7 (February 1966), 214-215; "Warschaupakt Manöver Moldau," *Soldat und Technik*, IX, No. 12 (December 1966), 632-633.

20 Admiral W.[aldemar] Verner, article on "Ten Years of the GDR National People's Army," *Kommunist vooruzhёnnykh sil,* XLVII, No. 4 (February 1966), 78.

21 The eighth session was at Bucharest in July 1966. A communiqué and two declarations appeared in *Krasnaya zvezda*, July 8 and 9, 1966. See also Fritz Ermarth, "Warschauer Pakt vor der Bukarester Konferenz," *Wehrkunde*, XV, No. 7 (July 1966), 336-340.

22 A TASS communiqué, *Krasnaya zvezda*, May 18, 1965, carried the quotation about this conference.

23 Radio Warsaw, November 23, 1965.

24 Friedrich Wiener, *Die Armeen der Warschauer-Pakt-Staaten* (Vienna, 1965), p. 11.

25 Garthoff, *op. cit.*, p. 13. Joint maneuvers with the participation of GDR, Czechoslovak, and Soviet air forces took place over East Germany, possibly to test defenses. *New York Times*, June 14, 1966.

Sudets was replaced by General of the Army P. F. Batitsky. *Krasnaya zvezda,* October 29, 1966.

26 In Poland, for example, some 17,000 Soviet officers were assigned to that country's armed forces. *Życie i myśl,* No. 10 (October 1964).

27 Joachim Georg Görlich, "Polens Volksarmee," *Wehrkunde,* XV, No. 5 (May 1966), 256. Bordziłowski is the highest ranking officer below the Defense minister, Marshal Marian Spychalski, who holds four-star rank.

28 Hanns von Krannhals, "Leadership Integration in the Warsaw Pact Area," *Military Review,* XLI, No. 5 (May 1961), 47, translated from *Wehrwissenschaftliche Rundschau,* XI, No. 1 (January 1961), 13.

29 Yezhi Lentsut [Jerzy Lencut], article on "The Commander of Airborne Infantry," *Krasnaya zvezda,* August 21, 1965.

30 Von Krannhals, *op. cit.,* pp. 50-51.

31 Stefan C. Stolte, "Comecon's Nineteenth Conference," *Bulletin of the Institute for Study of the USSR,* XII, No. 5 (May 1965), p. 21.

32 *Krasnaya zvezda,* August 11, 1965.

33 Marshal Marian Spychalski, speech at the Fourth Congress of the Polish communist party, *Trybuna ludu,* June 18, 1964.

34 *Krasnaya zvezda,* September 15, 1963.

35 Radio Sofia, September 20, 1964. More recently naval and air units of the U.S.S.R., Poland, and East Germany held joint maneuvers for eight days on and over the Baltic Sea. *Krasnaya zvezda,* July 30, 1966.

36 Radio Sofia, February 2, 1966.

37 *New York Times,* April 10, 1966; source is Bushrod Howard, registered agent in the United States for the royalists.
Note also the clandestine shipment of Czechoslovak weapons to Cyprus. *Ibid.,* December 16, 1966.

38 Paweł Monat, with John Dille, *Spy in the U. S.* (New York, 1962), especially pp. 104-112; U.S. House of Representatives, Committee on Un-American Activities (89th Cong., 2d sess.), *Testimony of Wladyslaw Tykocinski* (Washington, D.C., 1966).

39 Thadaeus Paschta, "Das System der Sowjetischen Militärberater in den Satellitenstaaten," *Wehrkunde,* XI, No. 9 (September 1962), 496, is the source for much of the following information.

40 *Ibid.,* p. 497.

41 *Ibid.,* p. 498.

42 *Ibid.,* p. 499; Radio Sofia, February 15, 1966; U.S. Department of State, Bureau of Intelligence and Research, *Directory of Bulgarian Officials* (Washington, D.C., August 1965), p. 13.

43 Von Krannhals, *op. cit.,* p. 44.

44 *Pravda* (Bratislava), May 10, 1966. See also U.S. Department of State, Bureau of Intelligence and Research, *Directory of Soviet Officials* (Washington, D.C., 1966), I, p. B-11, for names of the other WTO representatives in the different East European capitals.

45 I. I. Barits, *Voennaya kharakteristika sovetskikh satellitov* (New York, 1966), chap. vii, no pagination.

46 Thomas W. Wolfe, *The Evolving Nature of the Warsaw Pact* (Santa Monica, Calif., 1965), p. 20.

47 The new WTO representative at Bucharest, U.S.S.R. Colonel General G. P. Romanov, is one rank higher than his predecessor. Reuters dispatch, May 18, 1966, cited in RFE report, "Grechko's Man in Bucharest," May 20, 1966.

48 Institute for Strategic Studies, *The Military Balance 1966-1967* (London, September 1966), p. 2.

49 *Wehrkunde,* XIV, No. 12 (December 1965), 657. See also Jens Hacker, "Die DDR im Warschauer Pakt," *SBZ Archiv,* XVII, No. 12 (June 1966), 179-182.

50 *Soldat und Technik,* VIII, No. 12 (December 1965), 673. This West German periodical paraphrases Koshevoi's statement but does not provide the original source.

51 *Československi voenski atlas* (Prague, 1965), as cited in *Wehrkunde,* XIV, No. 11 (November 1965), 599.

52 Military attachés from the U.S.S.R., Poland, and East Germany heard the Czechoslovak Defense minister, Bohumír Lomský, address a Warsaw

Pact anniversary friendship rally and state: "For the first time we have a neighbor to the northwest of us [the GDR] on whom we can look with full confidence." *Rudé právo*, May 14, 1966.

53 *Obrana lidu*, May 7, 1965.

54 Radio Kossuth, February 11, 1965. See also his interview with UPI in *Népszabadság*, August 2, 1966, as translated in *Hungarian Press Survey*, August 18, 1966.

55 Oleg Penkovskiy, *The Penkovskiy Papers* (New York, 1965), pp. 373-375.

56 *New York Times*, April 21, 1965.

57 *Ibid.*, July 22, 1966.

58 *Pravda* (Moscow), March 5, 1961.

59 *Soldat und Technik*, IX, No. 4 (April 1966), 202; *New York Times*, August 3, 1966.

60 Adam Sarapata and Włodzimierz Wesołowski, "Evaluation of Occupation by Warsaw Inhabitants," *American Journal of Sociology*, LXVI, No. 6 (May 1961), 583-585.

See also the more recent article by Adam Sarapata, "Social Mobility," *Polish Perspectives*, IX, No. 1 (January 1966), especially table 1, p. 20, regarding prestige of occupations, which also ranks army officers.

Chapter 10 / ECONOMIC INTEGRATION: The CMEA

BEFORE the Second World War most of Eastern Europe could be classified as economically backward. With roughly 80 percent of the population residing in rural areas and more than half of the gainfully employed engaged in agriculture, Eastern Europe was almost completely self-sufficient and there was both a small requirement for and a limited output of manufactured goods. The one exception was Czechoslovakia, where certain lines of industry were highly developed. Elsewhere, the growth of a strong industrial working class and a healthy bourgeoisie in the urban areas was stunted.

The military occupation of certain East European states and the transformation of others into Nazi satellites during the war altered the economies in some areas. Under compulsion to turn out matériel for the Wehrmacht and help supply the domestic needs of Nazi Germany, the industries of Czechoslovakia, Hungary, and what is today East Germany underwent considerable expansion. Romania became primarily a producer of agricultural commodities and petroleum. On the other hand, Bulgaria and Poland were allowed to stagnate. All the countries suffered war damage, but Czechoslovakia emerged with relatively less than the others.[1] All eventually became satellites of the U.S.S.R.

After the war, while Stalin still lived the economies of the satellite states remained under the tight control of Moscow. These countries were even discouraged from developing economic links among themselves. Every major business transaction had to proceed through the Soviet Union. Following the death of Stalin, however, a transformation took place. A meeting in March 1954 of the Council for Mutual

Economic Assistance (CMEA), also known as Comecon, recommended the coordination of national economic plans within the bloc. The CMEA, set up by the U.S.S.R. at the beginning of 1949 as a response to the Marshall Plan, had been dormant until then.

The founding communiqué from Moscow indicated that the six charter members were the U.S.S.R., Bulgaria, Czechoslovakia, Hungary, Poland, and Romania.[2] Subsequently three other countries were admitted: Albania in February 1949, East Germany in September 1950, and Mongolia, the only non-European member, in June 1962.[3] At the council's fifteenth session, in December 1961, Albania's delegate announced that his country would no longer participate in CMEA activities. Since that time, Tirana has refused to pay its dues to the council and also has not been represented at any of the communist party conferences in Moscow.[4] Yugoslavia applied for and received associate status in February 1965 at the nineteenth session of the CMEA council.

The date set for beginning the coordination of economic plans by all CMEA members was January 1956, but the ensuing rebellion in Hungary and related events in Poland during that year disrupted trade and communications over a wide area of the bloc. In the process of reestablishing its control and bolstering the communist regimes throughout Eastern Europe, the Soviet Union claims to have sent considerable emergency credits into the area.[5] (See table 55.) By the end of 1958 industry had recovered, by and large, in both Hungary and Poland.

Soviet credits to the East European regimes are required to be repaid. In addition, the U.S.S.R. seems to have followed a policy of charging higher than world market prices for its exports into the bloc and underpaying for commodities imported from this source. A recent study indicates that over a ten-year period the total loss thus sustained by Eastern Europe amounted to the equivalent of almost 13 billion U.S. dollars. During 1964 alone this type of economic exploitation reached 2.25 billion dollars.[6]

Information regarding Soviet credits is based on official statistics which are now being published annually by East European governments. It is apparent that such figures are subject to manipulation in ways other than straight numerical falsification. State secrets acts [7] and propaganda images still are primary motives for the fabrication of economic results allegedly achieved. Internal misreporting by subordinates contributes to unintentional inaccuracies. Statistical inflation at higher levels magnifies the initial error, especially in agriculture.

TABLE 55

U.S.S.R. CREDITS TO EASTERN EUROPE, 1947-1962
(In millions of U.S. dollars)

Country	Year	Credits	Subtotals
Albania	1957	47.5	
	1958	8.7	
	1959	75.0	131.2
Bulgaria	1947	38.5	
	1948	53.0	
	1949	13.2	
	1950	18.6	
	1951	11.2	
	1956	92.5	
	1957	60.0	
	1958	35.0	
	1960	162.5	484.5
Czechoslovakia	1948	33.0	
	1957	13.5	46.5
East Germany	1953	121.2	
	1956	20.0	
	1957	260.0	
	1958	100.0	
	1962	1,200.0	1,701.2
Poland	1947	27.8	
	1948	450.0	
	1950	100.0	
	1956	300.0	
	1957	120.0	997.8
Romania	1947	30.0	
	1954	50.0	
	1956	67.5	147.5
Hungary	1954	25.7	
	1956	25.0	
	1957	260.0	
	1958	35.0	345.9
Grand total			3,854.4

SOURCE: Lucjan Ciamaga, *Od współpracy do integracji* (Warsaw, 1965), pp. 39-40.

NOTE: The figures do not include credits for military defense purposes. Dollar values in the source presumably are derived from official rates of exchange.

It is true that the rapid expansion of industry has made possible great increases in gross national production in Eastern Europe. In considerable degree, however, the increase has been achieved by deliberately restricting consumption. Rates of gross capital formation have allegedly reached as much as 25 percent of total income. Sustained emphasis on heavy industry, especially for defense purposes, and inadequate investments for agriculture merely accentuated the structural imbalance that had arisen at the expense of the general standard of living.

At the beginning of 1958 there appeared indications that the high rate of gross national production was beginning to decrease. In general, the downward rate of industrial output reflected the trend in the Soviet Union.[8] The various five-year plans in most of the East European countries for the years 1961-1965 finally began to include reduced targets in comparison with previous periods. The average increments of national income were now envisaged at 6 or 7 percent per year except in Bulgaria and Romania, where the rates of growth were to be much higher. Apart from Hungary, the average increase before the new planning was 8 percent annually. Even these more limited targets for 1961-1965 were not attained by most of the countries. (See table 56 for changes.)

TABLE 56

NATIONAL INCOME, EASTERN EUROPE, 1961-1966

Country	Percent of increase or decrease, compared with preceding year					
	1961	1962	1963	1964	1965	1966
Bulgaria	2.8	6.2	8.0	10.0	6.0	11.0 (6.7)
Czechoslovakia	6.5	1.5	—4.0	1.0	2.5	7.0 (2.0)
East Germany	4.0	3.1	—1.0	4.0	4.7	4.5 (3.4)
Hungary	6.2	4.6	5.0	4.0	n.a.	6.0 (4.6)
Poland	7.6	2.8	6.5	7.0	6.0	6.0 (5.9)
Romania	10.0	4.4	9.7	11.0	9.1	7.9 (9.0)
Average	6.2	3.8	4.0	6.2	5.6	7.1 5.3
U.S.S.R.	7.1	5.0	4.3	8.0	6.0	7.5 6.4

SOURCES: Miroslav Polivka, article on "Economy in Comecon Countries in 1965," *Hospodarske noviny* (Prague), April 22, 1966, translated in *Czechoslovak Press Survey,* May 24, 1966. *World Marxist Review*, X, No. 5 (May 1967), p. 39, for 1966 figures and average annual rate in parentheses.

Although they are the most industrialized within the area of Eastern Europe, both the German Democratic Republic and Czechoslovakia have suffered in the first half of the current decade from acute economic problems. During the Sixth Congress of the communist Socialist Unity party in January 1963 at East Berlin, a substitute seven-year plan was unveiled for the 1964-1970 period. The new index figures showed that the preceding plan, scheduled to end in 1965, had been scrapped. The new targets for national income, industrial production, and labor productivity were below those of the unfinished 1959-1965 plan.[9]

A similar situation developed earlier in Czechoslovakia, which announced in mid-1962 that its five-year plan would be abandoned. After a one-year interim period, a seven-year plan, for the years 1964-1970, was introduced, as in East Germany. It is clear that Czechoslovakia, which experienced a 4 percent decrease in national income during 1963 and only a one percent increase in 1964, has not become the "show window" of Eastern Europe.

FORCED INDUSTRIALIZATION

A basic CMEA document, adopted in 1962 at the sixteenth Council session, authoritatively laid down the guidelines for economic integration of industry:

> Socialist industrialization, with the principal emphasis being placed upon heavy industry and its core, engineering, is the main path toward the elimination of technical and economic backwardness.[10]

This belief is fundamental to most communist thinking. Results can be observed in the establishment, at a heavy cost to the populations involved, of modern industries in areas which more often than not remain short on raw materials. Despite the admission of excesses during the early 1950's, heavy industry still leads in investments and, indeed, absorbs the lion's share.

Thus, relatively underdeveloped Bulgaria allocated 38.5 percent of its capital investments for industry in 1949. In 1963 the allocation was 48.3 percent, amounting to more than 726 million leva.[11] In a classic example, the determination by Hungary to pursue "extended reproduction" is seen in the fact that 66 percent of that country's output falls to heavy industry, with the rest being consumers' goods and food. Prominence continues to be given iron and steel facilities as well as the development of engineering projects. Poland plans to triple production at the Nowa Huta metallurgical complex near

Kraków by 1980 to almost 9 million tons of steel, which is approximately what was produced in 1965 by the whole country.[12] Still, Poland will be forced to rely mainly for iron on the Soviet Union, which provides 76 percent of the iron ore used.

Also importing Russian coal, coke, and ore, Romania planned for 1965 a national output of about 3.5 million tons of steel.[13] The Bulgarians, proclaiming the priority of heavy industry in a country without any substantial raw materials base, aimed to achieve some 1.4 million tons of steel by the end of 1964 at the Kremikovtsi combine alone. From these few examples it can be seen that the development of basic industry in each country has not been molded to any great extent by supranational considerations. All of the bloc members want steel mills, but lack a varied or substantial raw materials base for heavy industry. (See table 57.)

TABLE 57

SELECTED CMEA INDICATORS, 1963

Product	Total CMEA output	U.S.S.R. output	U.S.S.R. percent of total	Exported by U.S.S.R. to East Europe
	Million tons			*Million tons*
Petroleum	201.0	186.0	93	13.8
Iron ore	139.0	128.0	92	18.4
Cast iron	71.2	55.3	78	—
Steel	100.5	76.3	76	—
Coal	1,064.0	517.0	49	12.3
Grain	195.0	147.5	76	5.0
	Billion KWH			
Electricity	504.0	369.0	74	—

SOURCE: V. I. Zolotarev, *Vneshnyaya torgovlya sotsialisticheskikh stran* (Moscow, 1964), pp. 366-367.

Still lacking an overall plan, and in most cases distrusting the "international socialist division of labor" principle, the East European states have made only uncertain steps toward commodity specialization despite CMEA efforts along these lines over the past decade.[14] The efforts and the response both have been less than wholehearted. Even bilateral projects are not developing as had been anticipated. Although the basic form of cooperation still remains the all-member method, two other approaches have evolved in practice.

JOINT PROJECTS

The first of the new cooperative techniques theoretically involves the participation of almost all CMEA members. Such activities as the "Friendship" oil pipeline, the "Peace" electric power distribution system, the pooling of railroad freight cars, the contemplated network of expressways, the CMEA bank, and the "Intermetall" steel community are good examples. The very fact that not all East European countries have availed themselves of the opportunity to join these organizations is in itself noteworthy. There appears to be developing within the CMEA a hard core of six members (the U.S.S.R., East Germany, Czechoslovakia, Poland, Hungary, and Bulgaria) which leaves Romania voluntarily on the periphery and Yugoslavia maintaining associate status for the time being.[15]

Much publicity has been given to ambitious schemes sponsored by the CMEA. The pipeline from the Volga-Ural oil fields during 1966 supplied sixteen million tons of petroleum to the several East European petrochemical industries.[16] It extends 1,900 miles from Kuibyshev through Mozyr in the western part of the U.S.S.R. and Płock in Poland to the city of Schwedt in East Germany. A branch runs southwest through Brody and Uzhgorod in the U.S.S.R. and ends at Bratislava in Czechoslovakia, with a spur south to Szászhalombatta in Hungary.[17] Romania, of course, exports petroleum, and neither it nor adjacent Bulgaria has contributed to the cost of constructing the pipeline. The headquarters of the organization is in Moscow, with a Russian director in charge.

Romania and Bulgaria do, however, participate in the CMEA electric power grid which connects with the western Ukraine and specifically the city of Kiev. The coordinating authority is at Prague. About 6.5 billion kilowatt hours of electricity were exchanged during 1966, which is not very impressive when one considers that Romanian production alone in 1964 was 13.8 billion kilowatt hours.[18] The Iron Gates project, agreed upon in December 1963, for construction of a power dam and navigation system along sixty miles of the Danube River, at a cost of about 400 million U.S. dollars, will supply to Romania and CMEA associate member Yugoslavia about 10 billion kilowatt hours of electricity when completed.

Yet another project involves the pooling of railroad freight cars, established in July 1964 with main offices at Prague. In 1967 it had some 103,000 units which transport most of the commodities exchanged within the CMEA area. A network of high-speed expressways, still on paper, ultimately is to connect Moscow, Warsaw, and East Berlin; Warsaw and Prague; Warsaw, Kraków, and Budapest; Kraków and Brno; Moscow, Kiev, Bucharest, and Sofia; Kiev and Brno; East Berlin, Prague, Brno, Budapest, and Bucharest.[19] The council's Permanent Commission for Transport is coordinating this ambitious highway scheme.

A joint operation attempting at least in part to emulate the West's highly successful European Coal and Steel Community, is "Intermetall," established by an agreement signed in July 1965. Although the signing took place at Moscow, the U.S.S.R. was not a charter member, the original signatories being only Poland, Czechoslovakia, and Hungary. Subsequently the U.S.S.R., East Germany, and Bulgaria joined. With head offices at Budapest, this organization has the task of modernizing CMEA steel industries and reducing the time required for production and delivery. A noteworthy provision is that "Intermetall" can pass resolutions binding on all members.[20] Perhaps that is why Romania has not adhered to this agreement, despite the fact that it could profit from membership. Neither does Bucharest participate in the CMEA organization formed earlier, toward the end of 1964, which directs the production of ball bearings and is administered from Warsaw.

Finally, there has been in operation since 1964 the so-called International Bank for Economic Cooperation, headed by Konstantin Nazarkin, former deputy chairman of the Soviet State Bank. The eight participating CMEA countries contributed a total of 300 million rubles. (See table 58.) This capital is in the form of "transferable" rubles, each theoretically containing 0.987412 grams of pure gold. It is this bank which settles commercial accounts among member states; also it grants credits to CMEA countries at 1.5 or 2 percent annual interest. Although the bank reported a profit of only 500,000 rubles during its first year of operation, presumably from loans, it claimed to have had a turnover of 33 billion rubles during that same period.[21]

One of the bank's problems has to do with making the ruble convertible instead of using it merely as an accounting unit to settle the balance of payments among member countries. Although there was a decision to transform 10 percent of the bank's capital into gold and convertible currency, no agreement seems to have been reached on the amounts or shares which each member would contribute.[22] Another problem concerns the manner in which the gold or hard cash might be withdrawn and put to use. Roman Malesa, the Polish member of the bank's board, told Tass in June 1966 that the convertible ruble would be used for CMEA settlements with nonmember countries but gave no other details.

TABLE 58

CONTRIBUTIONS TO THE CMEA BANK, 1964

Country	Capital	Percent of total
	Millions of rubles	
Mongolia	3	1.0
Romania	16	5.4
Bulgaria	17	5.7
Hungary	21	7.0
Poland	27	9.0
Czechoslovakia	45	15.0
East Germany	55	18.2
Soviet Union	116	38.7
Total	300	100.0

SOURCE: Lucjan Ciamaga, *Od współpracy do integracji* (Warsaw, 1965), p. 93.
NOTE: Contribution quotas were based on the volume of reciprocal exports. The official rate of exchange for the ruble is $1.11 in U.S. currency.

BILATERALISM AND FUNCTIONALISM

The other new technique of CMEA collaboration is the financing of projects by one member on the territory of another. As in bloc ventures overseas, the financing member extends medium-term credits repayable at a low rate of interest, and the project becomes the property of the government on whose territory it has been constructed. Repayment is usually in the form of deliveries from the project itself or from other sources. There has been some recognition of the need to distribute the burden of new bilateral investments among more than the two parties immediately involved.

Romanian reed cellulose and Bulgarian copper are good examples of raw materials extracted and processed with the aid of loans from other CMEA members. Poland is developing the extraction of its natural resources for bloc needs, as in the case of coal and sulphur mining. Czechoslovakia has given credits to help Polish mining and also for the expansion of iron ore output from the Krivoi Rog area in the Soviet Union. The reason for this, of course, is that Czechoslovakia's economy remains very sensitive to and depends upon its "outside relations." [23] This euphemism stands for importing practically all necessary raw materials.

An extension of bilateral arrangements involves the so-called interested party or functional approach, which involves projects of immediate concern to several CMEA members. Recent joint agreements between Czechoslovakia, Hungary, and Poland have dealt with the ferrous metallurgical industry. Other joint programs between more than two countries are devoted to the cooperative production of fertilizer and development of basic fuels.[24] In addition, intergovernmental commissions have been introduced for economic and scientific-technical cooperation on a bilateral basis.

Bilateralism can also be illustrated by Polish-Czechoslovak cooperation in manufacturing farm tractors, East German and Polish joint production of high pressure steam boilers, and the Polish-Hungarian joint stock company called "Haldex" which extracts coal from what had been formerly scrapped as waste in Poland's mines. Hungary and Bulgaria also have established mixed companies.[25]

CMEA RELAUNCHED

Soviet leaders belatedly recognized the gathering momentum of West European economic integration and decided to provide CMEA with a new impetus. From the seventeenth session of the council (see chart 1 for organizational structure), held at Bucharest in December 1962, there emerged a variety of recommendations which seemed to portend greater flexibility in bloc economic relations. Since then, multilateral accounting through the International Bank for Economic Cooperation has become the rule for trade between member countries. Also, prices may eventually be placed on a more realistic basis in relation to those used in world trade.[26] Some specialization in production has become evident in national economic plans for 1966-1970 and is indicative of flexibility.

For several years the coordination of long-term planning has been a chief aim of the CMEA. Since the Twenty-second Congress of the Soviet communist party, in October 1961, the perspective has shifted forward to 1980, or a time-span of twenty years. The 1980 date represents the beginning of a transition to communism as promised

CHART 1

CMEA ORGANIZATION, 1967

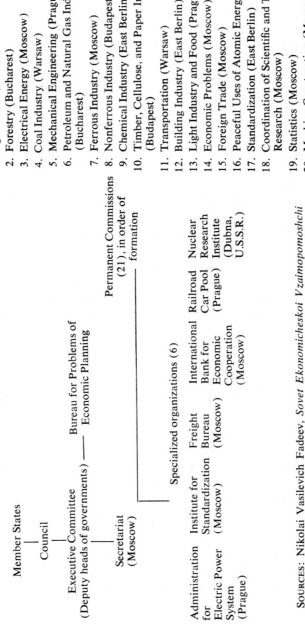

Member States
|
Council
|
Executive Committee ——— Bureau for Problems of
(Deputy heads of governments)   Economic Planning

Secretariat
(Moscow)

Specialized organizations (6)

| Administration for Electric Power System (Prague) | Institute for Standardization (Moscow) | Freight Bureau (Moscow) | International Bank for Economic Cooperation (Moscow) | Railroad Car Pool (Prague) | Nuclear Research Institute (Dubna, U.S.S.R.) |

Permanent Commissions (21), in order of formation

1. Agriculture (Sofia)
2. Forestry (Bucharest)
3. Electrical Energy (Moscow)
4. Coal Industry (Warsaw)
5. Mechanical Engineering (Prague)
6. Petroleum and Natural Gas Industry (Bucharest)
7. Ferrous Industry (Moscow)
8. Nonferrous Industry (Budapest)
9. Chemical Industry (East Berlin)
10. Timber, Cellulose, and Paper Industry (Budapest)
11. Transportation (Warsaw)
12. Building Industry (East Berlin)
13. Light Industry and Food (Prague)
14. Economic Problems (Moscow)
15. Foreign Trade (Moscow)
16. Peaceful Uses of Atomic Energy (Moscow)
17. Standardization (East Berlin)
18. Coordination of Scientific and Technical Research (Moscow)
19. Statistics (Moscow)
20. Machine Construction (Moscow)
21. Foreign Exchange and Financial Problems (Moscow)

Sources: Nikolai Vasilevich Fadeev, *Sovet Ekonomicheskoi Vzaimopomoshchi* (Moscow, 1964), pp. 24-25, insert. Lucjan Ciamaga, *Od współpracy do integracji* (Warsaw, 1965), pp. 76-77. Alexander Uschakow, "Comecon," *Das Parlament*, January 12, 1966, pp. 50-52 of Supplement. *Krasnaya zvezda*, February 26, 1967.

by the former U.S.S.R. leader Khrushchëv. As long ago as March 1961 the CMEA Council noted at its fourteenth session, in East Berlin, that member countries had begun to draw up plans that would reach twenty years into the future.[27] No more than preparatory work on such coordination has, however, been achieved so far.

Assuming that the CMEA does increasingly adopt the character of a general staff for bloc planning, its work is likely to be more effective insofar as it refrains from attempts at drastic interference with national economic goals. Local approaches to industrial development already laid down no longer seem to be challenged. Bulgaria and Romania, for example, are not being asked to remain predominantly agricultural any more. Bulgarian production of some 120,000 automobiles per year in 1980 is being forecast,[28] and this certainly does not fit in with a rational distribution for industry within the CMEA.

The Soviet Union finally has come to realize that it no longer can order the East European countries to do its bidding. The fact seems to have been recognized that not all CMEA members will "fully exploit the possibilities offered by the international socialist division of labor," because some of them,

> though they see the advantages of such cooperation, fear that the interests of the alliance, or the interests of the countries which have a leading position in it, will be predominant over the interests of the smaller countries or of countries economically less developed.[29]

It was only in July 1964 that delegates to the Executive Committee of the CMEA, meeting at Moscow, for the first time exchanged data concerning their broad intentions during the next (1966-1970) five-year planning period.[30]

One country affiliated with the bloc presumably has not gone so far as to reveal its planning to the others. Yugoslavia applied for associate membership in September 1964, at which time a preliminary agreement was initialed. Ratification did not take place until early the next year at the nineteenth session of the council. Associate status allows Yugoslavia to join a number of the Permanent Commissions and to participate in council sessions with an advisory vote. Commissions to which it belongs are Foreign Trade, Foreign Exchange and Financial Problems, Ferrous Industry, Nonferrous Industry, Machine

Construction, Chemical Industry, and Coordination of Scientific and Technical Research.[31]

The status permitted to Yugoslavia might have set a precedent leading to the possibility of admitting Algeria or even the United Arab Republic to the CMEA. What Khrushchëv had in mind in approving the arrangement may never be known, since he was deposed approximately four weeks after the preliminary agreement had been made with Yugoslavia. In the other direction, he had been responsible for the suspension of Albania's participation in CMEA meetings in October 1961. In any case, it is doubtful that the CMEA is "an open organization" and that "adequate forms exist for the participation in its work of any country which would join the basic principles of its activity," as its secretary-general, Nikolai Fadeev, has declared.[32]

The new Brezhnev-Kosygin team in the Kremlin does not appear to be strong enough or perhaps even willing to reverse the trend, evident throughout the bloc, toward what the late Italian communist party chief Palmiro Togliatti had described as "polycentrism." Perhaps the Soviet leaders now consider that the economic facts of life may prove to be sufficiently binding, in view of the fact that between a third and more than half of the intra-bloc trade of each individual East European state (except Yugoslavia and Albania) is with the U.S.S.R. (See table 59.) Dependence on the U.S.S.R. is further underlined by the fact that most of these countries rely on Soviet deliveries of iron ore and coking coal for their steel plants, which are basic to industrial development.

In this polycentric development, all CMEA members to a larger or smaller degree have been adopting capitalist techniques since 1964, even though there exist many obstacles to economic change within the bloc. The slowdown in growth, the warehouses filled with unsold goods of inferior quality, and the tremendous waste which results from central planning have all contributed to the barrage of criticism against the command economy with its regimentation and inefficiency.[33] Although, pragmatically speaking, change is imperative, the vested interest of the plant managers is in maintaining the status quo.

Even in a country like Czechoslovakia, certainly one of the industrially most advanced in Eastern Europe, it was reported in 1964 that about 13 percent of all factory directors had a higher education and only 32 percent had completed more than grade school. About the same time, at the other extreme, it comes as a surprise to find that in one of the less developed countries, Bulgaria, 4,674 or about 21.6 percent of the 21,674 individuals within the category of managerial personnel possessed a higher education.[34] In general, the plant managers are poorly trained party functionaries who want to maintain their posts and, therefore, will make a great effort to prevent any substantive change from taking place.

TABLE 59

CMEA TRADE TURNOVER, 1964

Country	Turnover	Trade within CMEA area	Trade with U.S.S.R. alone	Trans-actions through CMEA
	(Billions of monetary unit)		(Percent)	
Soviet Union	12.1 rubles	70.2	—	—
Poland	14.1 złotys	63.5	32.6	51.0
Czechoslovakia	30.7 crowns	74.2	37.8	51.0
East Germany	3.3 rubles	78.0	49.0	61.5
Hungary	26.4 forints	72.5	38.0	52.0
Romania	10.5 lei	70.0	41.0	59.0
Bulgaria	1.8 leva	82.6	53.0	64.0
Mongolia	2.2 rubles	99.0	(ca.) 75.0	(ca.) 75.0
Average	—	76.3	46.6	59.1

SOURCE: Lucjan Ciamaga, *Od współpracy do integracji* (Warsaw, 1965), p. 179.
NOTE: Official rates of exchange are: 100 Soviet rubles = 111 U.S. dollars; 100 Polish złotys = 22.25 rubles; 100 Czechoslovak crowns = 12.50 rubles; 100 Hungarian forints = 7.67 rubles; 100 Romanian lei = 15 rubles; 100 Bulgarian leva = 76.92 rubles.

Apart from this obstacle there exist others, including (1) the lack of stability regarding the economic plans themselves, as the year 1965 showed; (2) a basic contradiction between the slow growth of agriculture and the promises of a higher standard of living; and (3) problems in drafting specific economic plans for a five-year period.[35] Much of this came out into the open at the CMEA meeting held during early 1965 in Prague. (See table 60 for a listing of CMEA sessions.)

This nineteenth session was unusually long, lasting six days. Some problems were solved tentatively, according to the summary com-

TABLE 60
CMEA Sessions, 1949-1966

Session	Date	Place	Principal discussion or action
1	April 26-28, 1949	Moscow	Organization and plans for 1949
2	August 25-27, 1949	Sofia	Multi-year trade agreements
3	November 24-25, 1950	Moscow	Reports on commercial expansion
4	March 26-27, 1954	Moscow	Coordination with U.S.S.R. economic plans
5	June 24-25, 1954	Moscow	Priorities for coordination
6	December 7-11, 1955	Budapest	Economic development, 1956-1960
7	May 18-25, 1956	East Berlin	Coordination of economic development, 1956-1960
8	June 18-22, 1957	Warsaw	Activation of permanent commissions
9	June 26-30, 1958	Bucharest	International "socialist division of labor"
10	December 11-13, 1958	Prague	Specialization in chemical industry
11	May 13-16, 1959	Tirana	Steel production and 1961-1965 plans
12	December 10-13, 1959	Sofia	Charter approval and 1965-1975 plans
13	July 26-29, 1960	Budapest	Agriculture and 1961-1980 plans
14	February 28–March 3, 1961	East Berlin	Cooperation in chemical industry
15	December 12-15, 1961	Warsaw	"Socialist division of labor," basic principles
16	June 7, 1962	Moscow	Adopted basic principles of division of labor; Executive Committee established
17	December 14-20, 1962	Bucharest	Freight-car pool organized
18	July 25-26, 1963	Moscow	Plan coordination, 1966-1970
19	January 28–February 2, 1965	Prague	Yugoslav associate status approved
20	December 8-10, 1966	Sofia	Agreement on coordination of 1971-1975 plans

Sources: Lucjan Ciamaga, *Od współpracy do integracji* (Warsaw, 1965), pp. 209-237. Radio Warsaw, February 2, 1965. *Życie Warszawy*, December 18-19, 1966.

muniqué. Others could merely be outlined, and the main issues admittedly still remain to be worked out. Regarding specialization and cooperation in production and foreign trade for the period 1966-1970, the Polish representative and deputy premier had the following to say:

> As is known, this work is at a stage in which not all the problems are as yet solved among the [member] countries, not all the questions agreed upon. We tried, through a review of these matters and the determination of problems to which the CMEA organs pay much special attention, to facilitate the further coordination of mutual economic relations over the next five years.[36]

He reported, further, the decision that the CMEA bank will seek to accumulate hard currency and gold. If this decision is implemented extensively, the obvious intent will be to develop trade with the capitalist countries at a more accelerated pace—specifically with Western Europe, to which exports between 1958 and 1965 showed no percentage increase. (See table 61.)

TABLE 61

EXPORTS FROM THE U.S.S.R. AND EASTERN EUROPE, 1938-1965

Year	Total value	Eastern Europe	China [a]	Western Europe	Other
	Millions of U.S. dollars, equivalent		Percentage of total value		
1938	1,960	10	3	68	19
1948	3,170	44	5	37	14
1953	6,850	63	16	15	6
1958	10,340	59	12	20	10
1963	17,242	64	3	19	14
1965	19,945	63	4	20	14

SOURCE: *The Economist,* July 16-22, 1966, p. 273, air edition.

[a] Includes North Korea, North Vietnam, and Mongolia.

The basic reason for the drive toward trade expansion with Western Europe is that all Soviet bloc states require high-grade materials, quality equipment, and technological expertise which remain available only from the outside. In view of the fact that CMEA has proven ineffectual for the most part as a device for obtaining these from the U.S.S.R., it is probable that member countries will continue to go along their separate paths in securing these needs. Even the deep-rooted pyschological antipathy in Poland toward the Germans, for example, has not inhibited the Polish communist regime from negotiating with such West German companies as Krupp and Grundig. About a dozen agreements, reported from Bonn, may provide for joint manufacturing in the future. Trade between West Germany and six of the East European countries in 1966 reached the equivalent of about 853 million U.S. dollars.[37]

The method used by the West Germans is to provide the technological expertise, engineering skills, and capital to start a project. The partner contributes the site, factory buildings, labor, and raw materials. Such an agreement has been reached with Hungary for the joint production of machine tools. Plant ownership remains in the hands of the government on whose territory the plant is situated, as in the case of the new automobile factory in Poland, estimated to cost the equivalent of 40 million U.S. dollars, established with the aid of the Fiat company from Italy.[38] The coordinating committee in charge of NATO members' trade with the communist states recently indicated that it would be legal to sell even nuclear reactors for peaceful purposes to these countries.[39] British industry has been studying this possibility.

The session of the CMEA, which convened for one day in July 1966 at Bucharest, may have discussed some of the foregoing. It was attended by all East European communist party leaders and chiefs of state, with the exception of Albania and Yugoslavia, in the aftermath of the Warsaw Pact deliberations. Apart from listing the participants by name and position, the communiqué merely stated that delegations present had noted the "considerable work accomplished toward coordination of national economic plans, specialization and cooperation of industry, and the expansion on this basis of economic links among CMEA member countries." [40] The meeting took place, as usual, in an atmosphere of "brotherly friendship and full understanding." No other details were revealed.

PROBLEMS IN AGRICULTURE

Although not strictly a CMEA affair, agriculture remains the Achilles' heel of the bloc. Its lack of success adversely affects economic integration. The dogmatic Marxist belief that farming must involve collective activity, controlled through bureaucratic-industrial methods, has led to the collectivization of most peasants in Eastern

Europe. A communiqué issued by the CMEA at its June 1962 meeting in Moscow spoke of the "historic victory" in agriculture by communist countries (except Poland and, not then associated with the CMEA, Yugoslavia). The victory, meaning the completion of the collectivization process, was such in ideology and organization only. In production, the collective system remains a dismal failure. Its destruction of personal responsibility and incentive has, to a large extent, alienated the rural population.

For twenty-five million collectivized farmers and their families, until recently, earnings have been related mainly to the number of labor-days accumulated. This figure is used to calculate each person's share of the farm's net earnings. It is evident that such a system provides little incentive to individual effort. Nor has there been until recently in the majority of countries any minimum level of earnings on the collective farms, such as the state farms provide under their quasi-industrial wage systems. Bulgaria first introduced a scheme for a guaranteed minimum labor-day remuneration in 1963, giving collective farm workers a minimum of 1.8 leva (equivalent to about 1.5 U.S. dollars at the official rate of exchange). The Hungarian regime has the Nadudvár system of monthly payments in cash plus remuneration in kind. Czechoslovakia also makes monthly payments, but without a guaranteed minimum. Romania adheres to a rigid labor-day system, but offers private plot privileges. In Poland the provision of minimum earnings could not make much difference, owing to the small degree of collectivization, and the labor-day remains the rule.

Apart from Poland and Yugoslavia, more than 90 percent of all agricultural land in the bloc countries has been brought into the so-called socialist (collective and state farm) sector. Private plots, although limited in size, retain a disproportionate importance in the economy. Moreover, a surprisingly high percentage of livestock still remains under private ownership, amounting to more than four-fifths in Poland and more than two-thirds in Romania; nowhere is it below one-fifth.[41] A recent Polish communist visitor who traveled throughout the CMEA area wrote that the 4 percent of Hungarian land in garden plots supported 34 percent of all pigs, 36 percent of cattle, and 88 percent of domestic fowl. In Czechoslovakia, the 6.8 percent of farmland in private use accounted for 21 percent of all agricultural production. Bulgaria's 8.7 percent in private ownership accounted for 31.7 percent of the meat, 20 percent of all vegetables and potatoes, some 32 percent of the fruit, and 19.4 percent in total crop production. (See table 62.)

TABLE 62

PRIVATE SECTOR IN AGRICULTURE, 1963-1965

Country	Percent of total production				Percent of arable land	Compulsory deliveries
	Meat	Milk	Eggs	Vegetables		
Soviet Union	46	45	78	45	3.7	No
Hungary	46	60	90	30	4.0	No
Czechoslovakia ..	25	28	56	n. a.	6.8	Yes
Romania	Estimated at 40 percent of total output				5.9	No
Bulgaria	31.7	26	50	20	8.7	No
Albania	Not available				18.0	Yes
Yugoslavia	Not available				82.5	No
Poland	Estimated at 90 percent of total output				85.4	Yes

SOURCES: Radio Free Europe report, "Private Plots to Date," July 15, 1963. Dariusz Fikus, article on "The Garden Plot," *Polityka*, July 3, 1965, p. 11.

NOTE: A distinction must be made between the garden plots of collectivized peasants and the private-entrepreneur farms. Above figures refer to both.

Even mechanization, heralded as the great panacea which would solve all problems, remains far below that of Western Europe. For example, Czechoslovakia and France in 1939 claimed the same ratio of 1.5 tractors per 1,000 hectares of arable land. More than two decades later, the respective figures were 6 and 26. It is claimed that CMEA member states during the year 1966 received a total of 345,700 new tractors. Among the problems in this connection would appear to be the lack of spare parts [42] and even a deficiency in technological culture—the general attitude that if a piece of machinery belongs to the government it belongs to everybody, with the result that no particular care is taken of it.

Most of this equipment has been owned by the government as part of the Machine Tractor Stations (MTS). Once the Soviet Union began to transform its agricultural system by selling the machinery to collective farms, the rest of Eastern Europe or most of it began to do the same. By the end of 1965 all MTS's in Hungary had been converted into Repair Tractor Stations which kept only heavy tractors and special combines. Bulgaria in 1966 had almost completely phased out the MTS except in hilly areas. On the other hand, Czechoslovakia adopted a dual system; collective farms purchase most of the machinery, but MTS's are still operated. Poland abolished the MTS's, converting them to repair stations and selling the machinery to collectives. Only the Romanians have expanded the system, planning to add 56 MTS's by 1970 and making no sales of equipment to farms.[43]

General stagnation has developed in the agricultural output of Eastern Europe during the past several years. The area is no longer self-supporting in food, as it was before the war, and its overall production deficit remains at about 6 to 7 percent. After poor harvests, the deficit is greater and considerably more food is imported. During the accounting year 1965/1966 these countries bought 725 million bushels of wheat from the West.[44] The attempt to solve this problem has been approached in different ways.

Czechoslovakia and East Germany initially took a harsh line, whittling down private plots and the number of livestock allowed and imposing tighter party and state controls over agriculture. Various changes which the U.S.S.R. introduced from time to time in the organization of Soviet collective and state farms were emulated in those two countries. Romania announced a draft proposal for the establishment of cooperative farm unions which would be organized at local, district, and national levels, with supreme authority to be vested in a congress to meet every five years and suggest basic agricultural policy.[45] During 1929-1932 something similar existed in the U.S.S.R. Bulgarian communists have deliberately strengthened producers' incentive at the expense of the consumer by raising both retail and government-paid prices for livestock products. The Polish regime announced late in 1965 a shift toward larger state investment in agriculture.

TRADE BETWEEN CMEA STATES

The CMEA countries do not comprise a free trade area in actual practice. The CMEA organization maintains no common external tariff and apparently does not even aspire to one. The area, therefore, cannot be regarded as a single market. Nevertheless, orthodox communists insist that member states strive to increase trade among themselves in preference to commerce with the "capitalist world." [46] This represents an ideological imperative and, by and large, the whole mechanism of bloc trade is geared to serve this end.

Up to now, trade within the CMEA area has been conducted almost entirely within the framework of bilateral agreements. Khrushchëv had emphasized the need for measures to enhance mutual responsibility within a truly multilateral framework. This has not been achieved. Rational trading practices are further hampered by a reluctance to introduce realistic currency exchange rates. Devaluation of the Soviet ruble in January 1961 and of the Bulgarian lev a year later has not been repeated elsewhere within the bloc itself. On the fringe, however, Yugoslavia devalued its currency in July 1965 by some 66 percent, making the U.S. dollar worth 1,250 instead of the previous 750 dinars.[47] Subsequently it introduced a "strong" dinar by making 12.5 dinars equal to one dollar.

The communiqué issued following the seventeenth council session of the CMEA, in December 1962, indicated that adjustments would be made on the basis of average world prices during the 1957-1961 period. The new base period is 1960-1964, effective as of 1966. The greatest progress toward effective coordination in trade, however, has been brought about by the U.S.S.R. Within the CMEA area commercial exchange more than tripled between 1950 and 1965, an increase comparable with that in the West European Common Market.[48] (See table 63.) Between a third and roughly half of the foreign trade of each East European CMEA member is with the Soviet Union, which in turn does 70 percent of its foreign trade with the bloc (as shown earlier in table 59).

With regard to specialization of production, the East European communist regimes are no more ready than others to surrender their right to engage in particular branches of industry. Nor are the industrially more advanced states necessarily keen to see new industries established by their more backward neighbors. The Soviet Union has proclaimed the prerogative of strengthening all branches of its own economy on the grounds that it is possessed of an international duty to build communism.[49] Thus, all efforts toward a more rational division of labor among the bloc states have been countered by more or less concealed resistance from threatened producers and by the determination of the Soviet Union to proceed along its own path.

Examples of specialization in practice appear to be rather insignificant. Thus, using milling machines as an illustration, the number of different types has been reduced among those manufactured in Poland from 40 to 35, in Czechoslovakia from 62 to 42, in East Germany from 64 to 56, and in Hungary from 20 to 16. The machine-tool industry in 1966 encompassed about 1,800 items. Since Poland alone produces some 300 such items, it is evident that only a small number have been allocated to specific countries as suppliers for the rest.[50]

TABLE 63

TRADE WITHIN THE CMEA AREA, 1950-1970 (PROJECTED)
(In millions of rubles)

Country	1950	1955	1965	1966-1970 (planned)	with U.S.S.R
Soviet Union	2,925	5,840	8,470	59,718	—
East Germany	788	2,206	3,673	16,872	13,000
Czechoslovakia	1,280	2,040	3,284	12,210	10,000
Poland	1,170	1,660	2,489	10,434	8,500
Hungary	580	1,040	1,762	6,993	5,700
Romania	405	790	1,189	4,662	3,800
Bulgaria	275	380	1,564	8,547	7,200
Total	7,423	13,956	22,431	119,436 [a]	48,200

SOURCES: V. I. Zolotarev, *Vneshnyaya torgovlya sotsialisticheskikh stran* (Moscow, 1964), p. 165, and, for 1966-1970 five-year trade agreements, recomputed into rubles, *New York Times,* January 21, 1966. Radio Liberty, "Soviet Foreign Trade Agreements," March 22, 1967 (2 pp.), which gives original sources as footnotes. *Życie gospodarcze,* May 21, 1967.

[a] An official source claims that trade within the CMEA area during 1961-1965 amounted to 100 billion rubles and that agreements already signed for 1966-1970 total 150 billion rubles. S. Zavolzhsky and L. Lukin, "Bourgeois Criticism of Socialist Economic Co-operation," *International Affairs* (Moscow), XIII, No. 1 (January 1967), p. 8.

The nature of the CMEA's organization also has militated against effective supranational planning. The central council of the CMEA, an advisory body which issues recommendations to member governments, had to wait until the middle of 1962 before it acquired an executive committee. Six months later, Khrushchëv spoke out plainly to a Central Committee plenary session of the Soviet communist party on the need to establish a joint planning body "empowered to formulate common plans." [51] Developments since that time suggest that Soviet pressure has not managed as yet to advance this politically delicate matter beyond the level of strengthening various subordinate commissions such as those for statistics and foreign trade. The supranational planning office, in effect, has been dropped.

One of the principal supporters, Poland, recently has altered its attitude toward the future of the CMEA. The new Polish proposals can be summarized as follows: (1) no more support for complete specialization of production; (2) stress on international coproduction of subassemblies on a specialized basis; (3) retention of the CMEA as an advisory body, with the recommendations of its council to be implemented through bilateral agreements and only optionally; (4) the principle of at least two producers for any given product in the bloc; (5) more participation in world trade through purchase of Western licenses; and (6) quality and prices to be tested against capitalist standards.[52]

Poland, thus, appears to be following in the footsteps of Romania by favoring looser ties with the CMEA. The acquisition of licenses to produce machinery now being manufactured only in the West obviously would be to the advantage of the entire Soviet bloc. Since it has been difficult for the U.S.S.R. to achieve unanimity within CMEA council meetings, the suggestion of optional implementation is not really so revolutionary as it might seem. The proposals emanating from Warsaw are possibly even supported by the current leaders in the Soviet Union.[53]

NOTES

1 In 1945, however, Czechoslovak industry was producing at only 50 percent of its 1937 level. V. I. Morozov, *Sovet Ekonom·cheskoi Vzaimopomoshchi; soyuz ravnykh* (Moscow, 1964), pp. 80-81.

2 Text in Alexander Uschakow, *Der Rat für gegenseitige Wirtschaftshilfe* (Cologne, 1962), p. 86.

3 Gotthold Rhode, article on "Political and Social Problems of Integration in the Eastern Bloc Countries of Central-Eastern Europe," in Erik Böttcher (ed.), *Ostblock, EWG und Entwicklungsländer* (Stuttgart, 1963), pp. 29-30.

   For the 1960 CMEA charter, translated into English, see Michael Kaser, *Comecon* (London, 1965), pp. 181-187.

4 Lucjan Ciamaga, *Od współpracy do integracji* (Warsaw, 1965), p. 17, n. 2.

5 Poland allegedly received the equivalent of $420 million (mainly in rubles) and Hungary about $285 million during the 1956-1957 period. *Ibid.,* pp. 39-40.

6 Aleksander Kutt, *Prices and the Balance Sheet in 10 Years of Soviet-Captive Countries Trade, 1955-1964* (New York, 1966), pp. 5-7.

   Note that the official monthly magazine of the U.S.S.R. Foreign Trade ministry, *Vneshnyaya torgovlya,* November 1966, claims that the Soviet Union was underpaid on 2.5 billion rubles' worth of goods exported to "Socialist" countries. Cited in RFE report, "USSR Exploited by Comecon?", January 18, 1967.

7 See the discussion of such a law by the Interior minister, Josef Kudrna, in an article on "The National Security Corps [secret police] in the Fight against Crime," *Rudé právo,* June 26, 1965, translated in *Czechoslovak Press Survey,* July 6, 1965.

8 During 1958-1963 it dropped to an average of 4.5 percent annually. U.S. Congress, Joint Economic Committee, *Current Economic Indicators for the USSR* (Washington, D.C., 1965),

table I-1, p. 12. For later data see Joint Economic Committee, *New Directions in the Soviet Economy* (Washington, D.C., 1966), Part II-A, table 1, p. 104. The growth rate for the rest of Eastern Europe decreased from 13 percent in 1955 to 8 percent in 1963, according to Radio Belgrade, December 20, 1965.

9 Plans for 1966 called for increasing industrial production by 5 percent to the equivalent of about 33 billion U.S. dollars. Investment targets totaled $4.7 billion. *New York Times,* January 23, 1966.

10 See the article on "Fundamental Principles of the International Socialist Division of Labor," *Pravda,* June 17, 1962.

11 [Bulgaria], Central Board of Statistics, *Statistical Manual of the People's Republic of Bulgaria* (Sofia, 1965), tables 4 and 5, pp. 93-94. The official rate of exchange is 1.17 leva to the U.S. dollar.

12 [Poland], *Mały rocznik statystyczny 1966* (Warsaw, 1966), table 7, p. 64.

13 The steel output for 1964 was slightly more than 3 million tons. [Romania], *Rumanian Statistical Pocket-Book 1965* (Bucharest, 1965), table 53, pp. 88-89.

14 From a total of about 1,600 recommendations concerning specialized machine building adopted by CMEA, only 250 have been implemented. *Népszabadság,* September 2, 1966. It is claimed that all specialization agreements cover nearly 2,300 types of engineering output. *Pravda,* July 16, 1967.

15 Stefan C. Stolte, "Comecon's Nineteenth Conference," *Bulletin of the Institute for Study of the USSR,* XII, No. 5 (May 1965), p. 21. See also RFE report (by Harry Trend), "Soviet Economic Relations With Comecon Members," October 24, 1966 (8 pp.).

16 *World Marxist Review,* X, No. 5 (May 1967), p. 40.

17 It is possible that the U.S.S.R. will use the pipeline also from its closest

point to Austria for export of oil to Western Europe—specifically to Italy, which in one year bought 5.5 million tons of Soviet petroleum. Marijan Hubeni *et al., Atlas svetskikh zbivanja* (Belgrade, 1964), p. 26.

18 *Rumanian Statistical Pocket-Book 1965*, table 54, p. 100. *World Marxist Review*, X, No. 5 (May 1967), p. 40.

19 Stolte, *op. cit.*, p. 20.

20 "Intermetal" exchanged 950,000 tons of steel products during 1965 and 1.3 million in 1966. Nikolai Syomin, "Council for Mutual Economic Assistance: Cooperation of Equals," *Soviet Life*, XI, No. 12 (December 1966), p. 24.

21 Victor Veselovsky and Edward Tserkover, "International Socialist Bank," *ibid.*, IX, No. 9 (September 1965), 13.

22 Piotr Jaroszewicz, article on "A United Effort," *Trybuna ludu*, December 31, 1965–January 1, 1966. See also, *ibid.*, October 8, 1966, which indicated that the decision on convertibility had not been implemented.

23 Radio Prague, January 4, 1966. For example, 80 percent of the iron ore and 98 percent of the petroleum used in Czechoslovakia comes from the U.S.S.R. Gerhard Wolfrum, "Comecon," *Soldat und Technik*, VIII, No. 5 (May 1965), 244.

During 1966-1970 the Soviet Union will supply Czechoslovakia with 19 million tons of coal, 40 million tons of petroleum, and 50 million tons of iron ore. Josef Holeček, "Soviet-Czechoslovak Economic Co-operation," *International Affairs* (Moscow), XII, No. 9 (September 1966), 125.

24 *Népszabadság*, March 13, 1964, cited in RFE report (by Harry Trend), "Recent Developments in Comecon," March 14, 1964, pp. 1-2. For other examples see *New York Times*, November 27, 1966.

25 S. Pomazanov, article on "Friendship, Cooperation, and Mutual Assistance," *Krasnaya zvezda*, August 11, 1965, p. 3. The writer is a senior research associate at the Institute on the World Economy of the Socialist System in Moscow. See also Syomin, *op. cit.*, pp. 25-26.

26 György Tallos, article on "Price Modifications in Comecon," *Figyelö*, December 15, 1965, translated in *Hungarian Press Survey*, December 22, 1965.

27 Stanisław Skrzypek, "Soviet-Satellite Economic Developments: New Trends toward Supranational Planning," *Polish Review*, VI, No. 4 (Autumn 1961), 109.

28 [Bulgaria], *Directives of the Eighth Congress of the Bulgarian Communist Party for the Development of the People's Republic of Bulgaria in the Period of 1961-1980* (Sofia, 1963), p. 36.

29 Stanisław Kuziński, article on "Problems of International Specialization in the World System of Socialism," *Problemy mira i sotsializma*, VII, No. 6 (June 1964), cited by Radio Prague, June 16, 1964.

30 Piotr Jaroszewicz, the Polish representative on the CMEA executive committee, over Radio Warsaw, July 16, 1964.

31 Ciamaga, *op. cit.*, p. 10. Repeated over Radio Zagreb, December 26, 1965.

32 Interview in Belgrade's *Journal Export*, quoted by Radio Zagreb, December 26, 1965.

33 "Obstacles to Economic Change in East Europe," *Special Information Note*, January 15, 1965, p. 1.

34 *Pravda* (Bratislava), November 25, 1964; *Rabotnichesko delo*, November 11, 1964.

35 Secretariat chief for the Committee on Economic and Scientific-Technological Cooperation, Jaroslav Kořalka, over Radio Prague, January 24, 1965.

36 Piotr Jaroszewicz, over Radio Warsaw, February 2, 1965.

37 *New York Times*, January 21 and June 27, 1966. See also article on "Socialist Camp Fraternizes with Capitalism," *Die Zeit* (Hamburg), February 3, 1967, for other details.

38 Bruno Steiner, article on "Hard Words," *Svet motoru* (Prague), No. 22 (November 1966), translated in *Czechoslovak Press Survey*, Novem-

ber 14, 1966, gives other examples in East Germany, Hungary, and Romania.

39 See Mose L. Harvey, *East-West Trade and United States Policy* (New York, 1966), esp. pp. 97-105.

40 *Krasnaya zvezda,* July 9, 1966. This was an *ad hoc* meeting which did not represent a session of the CMEA council.

41 Bolesław Strużek, *Rolnictwo europejskich krajów socjalistycznych* (Warsaw, 1963), p. 258.

42 When the total tractors available numbered 1.9 million, almost 1.5 million were in the U.S.S.R. Morozov, *op. cit.,* p. 52. In Hungary, "there are not enough machines and equipment to repair them. And even those relatively few tractors are not under a roof, because there are not enough sheds." Radio Budapest, December 27, 1965. *World Marxist Review,* X, No. 5 (May 1967), p. 38 provides 1966 figures.

43 RFE report, "The Decline of the MTS, a Stalinist Relic," March 8, 1966, p. 3, gives a table.

44 *New York Times,* July 18, 1966. A permanent CMEA agricultural commission has been seeking since 1962 to solve this problem.

45 RFE report, "Cooperative Farm Unions," January 23, 1966, citing *Scînteia,* December 19, 1965.

46 Trade between CMEA members and capitalist countries quadrupled from 1950 through 1961. Morozov, *op. cit.,* p. 83. The problem, of course, is that communist countries have lit-

tle to sell and already have drawn about 2 billion dollars in credits from the West. *New York Times,* May 23, 1966.

47 Wages were to go up 22 percent, but the cost of living had already increased some 72 percent since the beginning of the year in Yugoslavia. *New York Times,* August 1, 1965.

48 A. Polienko, article on "Trade among Comecon Countries at a New Stage," *Vneshnyaya torgovlya,* XLII, No. 1 (January 1963), 9-13, provides statistics by country for U.S.S.R.-bloc trade turnover. The volume of commercial exchange within CMEA during 1961-1965 reached 99 billion rubles, according to *Pravda,* September 22, 1966.

49 See *1961 Programme of the Communist Party of the Soviet Union* (Moscow, 1961), quoted in Jan F. Triska (ed.), *Soviet Communism: Programs and Rules* (San Francisco, 1962), p. 122.

50 V. Khalipov, article on "Growing Unity among Countries of Socialism," *Krasnaya zvezda,* July 29, 1966, pp. 2-3; *World Marxist Review,* X, No. 5 (May 1967), p. 40.

51 See "The Council for Mutual Economic Assistance: Its Many Troubles," *Special Information Note,* June 11, 1963, p. 7.

52 *Życie Warszawy,* March 12, 1966, and *Życie gospodarcze,* March 13, 1966, both translated in *Polish Press Survey,* March 23, 1966.

53 *New York Times,* January 15, 1967.

Chapter 11 / POLYCENTRISM,
Or Unity in Diversity

THE EXPERIMENT of maintaining a single organization, the Communist Information Bureau or Cominform, to control Eastern Europe politically from Moscow existed less than nine years. It is doubtful that this instrument could have been used at all after the death of Stalin. The only eyewitness account of the Cominform's establishment tells how Andrei Zhdanov proposed that its weekly newspaper be called *For a Lasting Peace, For a People's Democracy*. This political slogan was treated as a joke, especially by the Italians and the French. Only after Zhdanov had explained that he was voicing Comrade Stalin's suggestion did the laughter cease.[1]

This organizational meeting took place during September 22-27, 1947, at Szklarska Poręba (the former Bad Schreiberhau) in that part of Silesia which Poland had annexed with Soviet support at the end of the Second World War. Representing the host country's communist party was Władysław Gomułka, who signed the original Cominform manifesto denouncing the Marshall Plan and condemning the United States as "an arsenal of counterrevolutionary tactical weapons."[2] The other delegates came from the remaining East European parties and from those in Italy and France, where it was assumed the communists would be in power shortly.

The second meeting took place at the beginning of 1948 in Belgrade, where Cominform headquarters functioned for a brief period. The next, at Bucharest, on June 28, 1948, issued the communiqué excluding the Yugoslav communist party from the organization. A fourth meeting, at Budapest toward the end of 1949, devoted its time to planning a world drive for signatures to a so-called peace manifesto.[3] After that, little was accomplished and the Cominform was all but forgotten until April 1956, when it was dissolved, apparently as part of the price for reconciliation between Belgrade and Moscow.

Abolition of the Cominform, the existence of which had manifested itself during the last few years only by publication of the weekly newspaper, left a vacuum in the Soviet bloc. Coinciding with what has become known as destalinization, this act seems to have had a further purpose of helping transform the image of East European leaders, so that they would appear not as Moscow agents but as respectable "national communists" à la Tito. Nikita S. Khrushchëv had launched the process with his secret speech in February 1956 to the Twentieth Congress of the CPSU.[4] Apart from denigration of Stalin, this elite gathering also heard the formula of different roads to socialism enunciated.

Whatever may have motivated Khrushchëv to repeat his denunciation of Stalin publicly at the Twenty-second Congress, in October 1961,[5] sweeping changes in Eastern Europe had to be avoided at all cost. The simple fact of the matter is that even today many regimes would fall if destalinization were implemented. Most of the leaders in power (as of 1967) at one time or another have been ardent supporters of Stalinist techniques, and some might even yet like to revert to them. Hence, by and large, destalinization was restricted to changing the names of streets and cities, taking down statues of Stalin, including the five-ton one in Prague made from a solid piece of marble, and removing mummies from mausoleums. Nothing has come, however, of Khrushchëv's proposal to "erect a monument in Moscow to perpetuate the memory of comrades who fell victims to arbitrary rule," [6] either in the U.S.S.R. or elsewhere.

EAST EUROPE'S LEADERS

The men controlling communist regimes within the Soviet bloc, even those in Albania and Yugoslavia, share many characteristics. They are all hard-core apparatus workers, professional revolutionaries who reached the top post after having served in less responsible work when their parties were banned by the prewar governments. They have all proven themselves to be dedicated communists, some of them in "capitalist" prisons and even in their own postwar jails. (See table 64.)

TABLE 64

EAST EUROPE'S COMMUNIST LEADERS, 1967

Country	Leader's name and party position	Year of birth	Father's occupation	Joined communist party	Profession	Years in jail	Spent Second World War	Years in U.S.S.R.	Government post	Became member of party Politburo
Albania	Hoxha, Enver; First secretary, 1941—	1908	Small landholder	1941	Teacher	1939 (briefly)	Albania	None	None	1941
Bulgaria	Zhivkov, Todor; First secretary, 1954—	1911	Peasant	1932	Printer	None	Bulgaria	1936-41?	Premier	1951
Czechoslovakia	Novotný, Antonín; First secretary, 1953—	1904	Brick-layer	1921	Locksmith	1941-45	Germany	None	President	1951
East Germany	Ulbricht, Walter; First secretary, 1950—	1893	Tailor	1919	Carpenter	1918; 1930-32	U.S.S.R.	1933-45	Chairman, Council of State	1934
Hungary	Kádár, János; First secretary, 1956—	1914	Peasant	1932	None	1933-35; 1951-54	Hungary	None	Member, Presidential Council	1956
Poland	Gomułka, Władysław; Secretary-general, 1943-1948; First secretary, 1956—	1905	Oil-field worker	1926	Blacksmith	1932-34; 1936-39; 1951-54	Poland	1934-36	Member, Council of State	1943
Romania	Ceaușescu, Nicolae; Secretary-general, 1965—	1918	Poor peasant	1936	None	1936-39; 1940-44	Romania	None	Member, Council of State	1954
Yugoslavia	Tito, Josip Broz; Secretary-general, 1937-1966; President, 1966—	1892	Peasant	1920	Metal-worker	1915-17; 1928-34	Yugoslavia	1915-20; 1934-36	President (for life)	1934

SOURCE: Radio Free Europe, *Eastern Europe's Communist Leaders* (5 vols.; Munich, 1966), with 1967 identifications from the press.

Enver Hoxha [7] is the best educated among these eight communist leaders in Eastern Europe. Definitely of "bourgeois" origin, he attended the French secondary school at Korçë and after graduation studied one year at the University of Montpellier in France. Back in Albania after working in Paris and Brussels over a period of five years, he taught the French language at a secondary school up to the Italian occupation. Hoxha became first secretary of the Albanian communist party when it was founded and has directed the movement ever since. After his Yugoslav mentors were expelled from the Cominform in 1948, he took advantage of this development to become a most favored protégé of the U.S.S.R. Another turn in his fortunes came at the Twenty-second Congress of the CPSU, when the Albanian communists were read out of the world movement loyal to the Soviet Union. Hoxha had already shifted his allegiance to Peking, much farther away geographically.

Bulgaria's leader Todor Zhivkov [8] spent the war years in his own country, like Hoxha, as one of the communist partisans. Here, however, the resemblance ends. Born into a peasant family, Zhivkov completed only a few years of elementary school. Between 1936 and 1941 he may have been in Moscow undergoing training; there is a gap in this period of his biography. In 1952 Zhivkov succeeded the notorious "Little Stalin," Vulko Chervenkov, as a member of the new collective leadership in Bulgaria. He has never deviated from the Moscow line and rivals his East German and Czechoslovak colleagues in this respect.

The leader in Czechoslovakia is Antonín Novotný,[9] who joined the communist movement in his country as a founding member. He worked in the capacity of a party functionary and during four years just preceding the German occupation supervised regional communist affairs at Prague. Arrested by the Gestapo in 1941, he spent the rest of the war in the Mauthausen concentration camp. Novotný became party leader on the death of Klement Gottwald, which followed soon after that of Stalin, and has had the support of Moscow ever since. This man rarely deviates from the policies established by the U.S.S.R. Prague remains headquarters for the monthly *World Marxist Review,* successor to the long defunct Cominform weekly newspaper—certainly an indication of confidence on the part of the Kremlin.

Of all East European leaders, Walter Ulbricht [10] in the so-called

German Democratic Republic is perhaps the most submissive in his relations with the Soviet Union. A member of the Spartakus Bund, he joined the German communist party when it was founded and even represented it in the Reichstag. Ulbricht served as an international Comintern agent as far back as 1924 and worked for the Soviet secret police (NKVD) during the Spanish Civil War. He has been Moscow's viceroy in East Germany ever since he returned to East Berlin in the uniform of a Red Army colonel at the end of the Second World War. In 1963 Ulbricht became a "Hero of the Soviet Union" for services rendered.

Another man who has also spent his entire adult life in the service of communism is János Kádár [11] in Hungary. Although he remained in his native country during the war (and thus did not receive training in Moscow), by 1948 he had become deputy secretary-general of the Hungarian party. The following year Kádár betrayed his best friend, Interior minister László Rajk, who was executed. Regardless of this, he was swept up in the purge of suspected Titoists and spent thirty-two months in prison. Kádár next turned traitor to the Imre Nagy government, of which he had been a member without portfolio, by clandestinely establishing a counter-regime at Uzhgorod in Soviet-occupied Sub-Carpathian Ruthenia and calling on the U.S.S.R. in early November 1956 to suppress the Hungarian freedom fighters. Two years later, Nagy was executed. Since the Hungarian rebellion, Kádár has always been sensitive to Moscow's advice.

Like his counterpart at Budapest, Władysław Gomułka [12] of Poland spent the war in his native country and was a victim of the anti-Titoist purge. As secretary-general of the Polish party in the early postwar period, he proved just as adept in employing Stalinist techniques against the opponents of communism as any other East European leader. Although not apprised that Gomułka would become the first secretary in October 1956, the U.S.S.R. accepted this decision after a lengthy confrontation. Since that time, and perhaps because Gomułka was a student of political warfare at the International Lenin School in Moscow during the mid-1930's, relations between the Polish and Soviet communist parties have been excellent.

The youngest leader in the bloc is Nicolae Ceaușescu [13] of Romania. Like several others, he underwent imprisonment by the pre-communist government of his country. Always advancing to more important party positions, Ceaușescu spent the war in Romania and most of this time in prison. His contacts with the Soviet Union have included repeated visits ever since 1957, when he represented the Romanian communist party at the fortieth anniversary celebrations of the Bolshevik Revolution. Even so, no delegation from Bucharest went to Moscow for the March 1-5, 1965, meeting of communist parties intended as a preliminary to a world conference. The Albanians and the Chinese also refused to attend. On the other hand, Ceauşescu was host to the Warsaw Pact and Council for Mutual Economic Aid sessions during July 1966 in Romania.

Finally, a man unique in Eastern Europe is Josip Broz-Tito,[14] whose relationship with the Soviet Union goes back to 1917 and membership in a Red Guards unit at Omsk, Siberia. He returned to Yugoslavia but left again for Moscow, where he taught in the mid-1930's at the International Lenin School, while Gomułka was one of the students. In 1937 Moscow appointed Tito secretary-general of his party and sent him back to Yugoslavia. There he spent the war and emerged as leader of the country, only to have his party expelled from the Cominform by Stalin. The rapprochement which started with Khrushchëv has continued under the new Soviet leadership.

UNITY IN DIVERSITY. As can be seen from the foregoing, the backgrounds of these eight communist leaders would suggest that they might be difficult for the U.S.S.R. to manipulate. Oddly enough, it was a communist from outside the bloc who contributed more to the development of so-called polycentrism than anybody else.[15] Palmiro Togliatti, secretary-general of the Italian communist party, is credited with having used this term in 1956. While Stalin was still alive, this man had been among the most obedient of foreign communist leaders. In 1964, however, during a vacation at Yalta in the U.S.S.R., he wrote a memorandum intended to represent the basis for discussions with Khrushchëv. These never took place because Togliatti died. His body and the memorandum were removed to Italy.

Leonid I. Brezhnev, today secretary-general of the Soviet communist party, represented Moscow at Togliatti's funeral in Rome. He first learned of the memorandum there and attempted to have it suppressed. Although it never would have appeared if Togliatti had lived, the new Italian communist leaders under Luigi Longo eventually decided to publish it.[16] After its issuance in Italy early in September 1964, *Pravda* carried a translation five days later, but without any comment. Subsequently the press of most other East European communist parties also printed the memorandum. Many of its ideas, of course, had appeared already in one way or another.

Togliatti maintained that the Soviet bloc had been developing a "centrifugal tendency." That is, the individual parties were moving away from centralized control exercised by Moscow. He went on to express opposition to any proposal for creating once again any organizations like the Comintern (1919-1943) or Cominform (1947-1956). Togliatti rebuked the U.S.S.R. and the communist-ruled states in Eastern Europe for their slowness and resistance in "overcoming the regime of restrictions and suppression of democratic and personal freedom introduced by Stalin." Finally, he asserted: ". . . one must consider that the unity one ought to establish and maintain lies in the diversity and full autonomy of the individual countries." [17] Togliatti proposed, in brief, an Eastern Europe based on polycentrism.

If Khrushchëv had permitted translation and publication of the Togliatti memorandum, it would have been because his policy toward Eastern Europe included an effort to eliminate the master-servant relationship existing under Stalin. His goal appeared to be the introduction of more flexible contacts with the various communist parties, whereby common policies might be reached by means of discussion, although the U.S.S.R. would still maintain the decisive voice due to its power position. This grand design failed for various reasons, including the half measures which Khrushchëv allowed, the unexpected strength of nationalism, the effects of incomplete destalinization, and the impact of the Soviet dispute with China.

Ever since the dissolution of the Cominform, the day-to-day business of handling relations among the various bloc communist parties has been conducted through special units within the Central Committee apparatus of each organization. (See table 65.) Mikhail Suslov, chief ideologist for the CPSU, indicated early in 1964 that international discipline no longer involves orders "from above" and that it is, instead, voluntary.[18] The most that he and Khrushchëv seem to have regarded as obtainable among the communist countries was an international system of "democratic centralism" in foreign policy, wherein the minority would accept the decisions of the majority.

FALL OF KHRUSHCHËV AND AFTER

Togliatti had dealt with the lack of freedom in communist-ruled states, and the manner in which Khrushchëv was dismissed enhanced the impact of his memorandum. The nuances of the slogan "unity in diversity" can be observed very well in the various reactions to the *Pravda* editorial explaining the change in leadership at Moscow.[19]

TABLE 65

FOREIGN DEPARTMENTS OF COMMUNIST PARTIES IN BLOC
COUNTRIES, 1966-1967

Country	Director of department	Unit designation
Albania (1)	Bita, Piro	Department of International Relations
Bulgaria (2)	Tellakov, Konstantin [a]	Foreign Policy and International Relations Department
Czechoslovakia (3)	Kaderka, Oldřich [b]	International Department
East Germany (4)	Florin, Peter [a]	Foreign Policy and International Relations Department
Hungary (5)	Puja, Frigyes [a]	Department of Foreign Relations
Poland (6)	Czesak, Józef [a]	Commission on Foreign Affairs
Romania (7)	Vlad, Vasile [b]	Foreign Relations Section
Soviet Union (8)	Rusakov, Konstantin [c] (First deputy and Acting)	Section for Liaison with Communist and Workers' Parties of Socialist Countries
Yugoslavia (9)	Popović, Vladimir [a]	Commission for International Relations

SOURCES: (1) Radio Free Europe report, "Sino-Albanian Position on the International Communist Movement," May 3, 1966, p. 1. (2) Bulgarian Telegraphic Agency (BTA), May 30, 1967. (3) Radio Prague, February 3, 1967. (4) Werner Leimbach (comp.), *Der Parteiapparat der SBZ* (Bonn, 1966), p. 10. (5) *Népszabadság,* April 13, 1967. (6) Radio Warsaw, December 30, 1966. (7) Radio Bucharest, January 30, 1967. (8) *Krasnaya Zrezda,* July 27, 1967. (9) *Wissenschaftlicher Dienst Südosteuropa,* XV, No. 10 (October 1966), 156.

[a] Member of Central Committee.
[b] Candidate member of Central Committee.
[c] Member of Central Audit Commission.

Even the most obedient among the East European regimes finally had come to the realization that it did have some bargaining power vis-à-vis the Kremlin. Nowhere was this more true than in Romania.

Bucharest published a summary of the Soviet editorial but gave a full translation of the paragraph describing Khrushchëv's deficiencies.[20] This probably was meant to indicate dissatisfaction with the deposed leader, who had attempted to pressure the Romanians into giving up certain of their more independent policies. In the cases of Hungary, Czechoslovakia, and Poland irritation could be discerned, since Khrushchëv had only recently visited these countries. Here, communist spokesmen all praised him.

Kádár, who had been placed in power by Khrushchëv, returned from a visit to Warsaw and in a broadcast speech admitted that the change in Moscow had caught him by surprise. In this same speech he declared:

> I am of the opinion that Comrade Khrushchëv had very great merits in the struggle against the Stalin personality cult. . . . The hundreds of thousands of Hungarians who not long ago this year, here in our country, were able to greet Comrade Khrushchëv and did so wholeheartedly . . . did well to do so and have nothing to reflect on subsequently.[21]

The following day, the principal Czechoslovak communist newspaper printed a full translation of the *Pravda* editorial. Three days later, the party's Presidium issued a statement which remarked that "the news of the decision by the CPSU Central Committee on relieving Comrade Khrushchëv was received by our whole party and the public with surprise and emotion," and then went on to repeat Kádár's praise of him.[22] This marked the first time that an official pronouncement in Prague deviated from the Moscow line. Khrushchëv had toured Czechoslovakia in late August and early September, endorsing the Novotný leadership.

Only in one case, that of Poland, did the new Soviet duumvirate travel outside the U.S.S.R. to explain in person why they had deposed Khrushchëv. Gomułka, in a speech praising Khrushchëv, admitted that the dismissal had taken him by surprise. He may have been concerned about the forthcoming extension of the April 1945 twenty-year friendship treaty with the U.S.S.R., which Khrushchëv had promised would include a specific guarantee of the Oder-Neisse boundary line. At any rate, the meeting of Brezhnev, Aleksei Kosygin, Gomułka, and the Polish premier, Józef Cyrankiewicz, took place, in the Białowieża Forest near Białystok. The brief announcement merely stated that the talks had been conducted in an atmosphere of "friendship, cordiality, and complete identity of views." [23]

It was the East German communists, and specifically Ulbricht, who showed most apprehension over events in the Kremlin. Apart from the Politburo statement, mentioning the "profound stir" that Khrushchëv's departure had caused in East Germany, a rally of all political parties and mass organizations "unanimously consented" to the Soviet changes. These groups pledged themselves to "activate" the U.S.S.R.–East German friendship treaty.[24] This reference to the June 12, 1964, pact probably indicated a real fear concerning future Kremlin policy in Germany.

Bulgaria alone made no comment about Khrushchëv himself. All newspapers carried photographs of the new leaders, Brezhnev and Kosygin, with factual information about the changes. Zhivkov's telegram of congratulations and their biographic sketches appeared together with the *Pravda* editorial on front pages. The same day, a Central Committee meeting pledged support for the CPSU line and promised to "march side-by-side in unflinching unity with the great party of Lenin." [25] Only the Albanian communists sent no congratulatory message, in contrast even to the Chinese.

On the other hand, the first authoritative comment from Yugoslavia reflected the anxiety of Belgrade at what had occurred in Moscow:

> The situation in the international workers' movement today requires a thorough analysis, and the changes in Moscow cannot be isolated from this situation. . . . The changes are of special importance in view of the role played by the international workers' movement and the prominent role played by Comrade Khrushchëv, together with other Soviet party and government leaders, in eradicating the Stalinist heritage, not only in the Soviet Union, but also in the international workers' movement, and particularly in relations between the Soviet Union and other socialist countries and Yugoslavia.[26]

The day before this appeared in print, Foreign Secretariat spokesman Dušan Blagojević indicated that the events in Moscow were the internal affair of the Soviet Union, and that the Yugoslav government had found significant the affirmation by the U.S.S.R. of its policies based on decisions of the Twentieth and Twenty-second Congresses of the CPSU.

Thus, in general, the fall of Khrushchëv at first caused bewilderment over almost the whole of Eastern Europe. Whereas previous changes of this kind had been accepted without hesitation by all communists, there was now comment that included questioning and, in many cases, even criticism. Demands for more detailed explanations as to why Khrushchëv had been deposed continued, and the new Soviet leadership found itself compelled to state its case in Moscow to delegations from a number of communist parties. Some of this could be taken care of during the traditional anniversary celebrations of the Bolshevik Revolution in November. It is not known from the communiqués issued at various times whether the delegations were satisfied with the results of these talks.

THE POST-KHRUSHCHËV ERA. Khrushchëv had scheduled a preparatory conference of 26 communist parties to be held at Moscow on December 15, 1964. The conference was to draw up the agenda for a world congress of representatives from the international communist movement. A high-level Chinese delegation, headed by Chou En-lai, attended the anniversary celebrations in the U.S.S.R. during the preceding month and probably influenced the new Soviet leaders to postpone the preparatory conference until the following spring. Finally, it was scheduled definitely for March 1-5, 1965.

Only eighteen of the parties invited sent delegations, plus an observer from an additional one, and the gathering became merely a "consultative meeting," which meant that it could make no decisions binding upon the absent communist parties. The Albanians, like the Chinese, refused to attend. Aside from them, the only other East European communist party that decided not to send any representatives was the Romanian. The communiqué on the meeting, issued five days after it was over, for the time being and for all practical purposes dropped the idea of holding a world congress, but left open the possibility of a congress sometime in the future, providing conditions changed.[27]

Previously the Albanians had been invited by the Polish hosts to the seventh session of the Warsaw Pact's political consultative committee. They refused to come, even though reconciliation between Tirana and Moscow would have involved the new Soviet leadership. Perhaps there existed a suspicion that the gathering might be used as a vehicle for establishing a more binding political relationship, rather than being restricted to purely military affairs. Albania also did not participate in the eighth session, at Bucharest, and may not have been asked to come this time.[28]

In is interesting that the Romanian communists were hosts for this session. The fact that they were suggests that the country's desire and hope for withdrawal from the Warsaw Treaty Organization have been undermined. Economic nationalism, however, is another matter. On April 26, 1964, the Central Committee of the Romanian communist party issued a declaration which included the following:

> During the development of the relations of cooperation among the socialist countries which are CMEA members, ways and means have been suggested, such as a joint plan and a single planning body for all member countries, interstate technical-productive branch unions, enterprises jointly owned by several countries and interstate economic complexes . . . [But] these measures are not in keeping with the principles which underlie relations among sovereign states. . . . Transmitting such levers to the competence of superstate or extrastate bodies would make of sovereignty an idea without content.[29]

The U.S.S.R. under Khrushchëv and his successors has been unable to supply Romania's needs in full and, thus, cannot respond satisfactorily with economic pressure to that country's defiance.

The struggle for economic independence is closely related to the process of removing Soviet political influence. For a brief period Bucharest even suspended publication of the *World Marxist Review* in the Romanian language. When resumed, the journal came out with reduced contents and specific deletion of articles that might embarrass Bucharest's neutrality in the Sino-Soviet dispute or contradict its position on other political and economic matters.[30] At the communist-front World Federation of Trade Unions meeting in Warsaw during October 1965, Romania went so far as to support China against the U.S.S.R.

Some of the East European leaders are, to a certain extent, exploiting feelings of nationalism in order to obtain some identification with the people. In the case of Romania, this has led to an overtly anti-Soviet attitude. On the other hand, Gomułka in Poland has had to discourage the deep feelings of hostility against Russians in general and Soviet communists in particular. His nationalism has become diluted as the years have passed.[31] Only recently have the Bulgarians begun to pay lip service to nationalism, and the East German regime, of course, is in no position to do even that.

Except for Bulgaria and Czechoslovakia, in all East European countries the people (in contrast with their rulers) for good historical reasons have been traditionally antagonistic toward the colossus in the east. Germans fought against Russians in both World Wars. The same is true of the Hungarians, even though many of them may have done so reluctantly. During the Second World War, Romania ceded Northern Bukovina and Bessarabia to the U.S.S.R. under a direct threat of force. The people of Poland, steeped as they are in history, remember that Russia (tsarist and communist) participated in all six dismemberments of their country: 1772, 1793, 1795, 1939, and 1945. Neither have they forgotten the suppression of revolts in the nineteenth century, the mass deportations that followed the Hitler-Stalin pact, the massacre of prisoners of war in Katyn Forest, and the failure of the Red Army to assist the 1944 Warsaw uprising against the Germans.[32] No sweeping generalization could cover isolated Albania and multinational Yugoslavia, but popular feeling here has hardly ever risen above distrust or indifference toward the Soviet Union.

CONFLICTS WITHIN EASTERN EUROPE

Apart from negative attitudes toward the Soviet Union, the East European countries have many traditional enmities among themselves.[33] The image of East Germany is affected by the others' painful memories of Nazi occupation or domination. Although the communist regimes attempt to divert these feelings westward toward the German Federal Republic, much of the wartime hatred of all Germans still remains, some of it going back to before the war. It has been, understandably, especially prevalent in Czechoslovakia since the Munich crisis of September 1938 and in Poland from the time of the tension of March-September 1939. These two countries might be much friendlier toward each other as a consequence, were it not for the memory of the seizure of Cieszyn (Tešin) by the Prague government in 1920 during the Polish-Soviet war and its recovery in 1938 by the use of an ultimatum at the time of Munich.

MINORITY PROBLEMS. The most important potential area of bloc conflict involves the Hungarians in the territory of Transylvania that was acquired by Romania. Forcible assimilation of these people was intensified after the 1956 uprising in Hungary, when the possibility of contagion seemed imminent. Budapest has made no public effort to intercede in their behalf. It is probable, however, that Hungarians even within the communist party feel strongly about the repression of their kinsmen across the border. There is also the fact that some former parts of Hungary distinct from Transylvania, like the city of Oradea Mare (Nagyvárad), are currently in Romania.

Czechoslovakia too has its Hungarian minority and is pursuing a process of assimilation. For example, in 1961 the Slovak communist party weekly stated that the "participation of workers and collective farmers of Hungarian nationality in the country's economic upsurge will depend on the extent to which they can master Czech and Slovak technical literature as well as on their expertise in their respective fields." [34] It is noteworthy that bus lines between Czechoslovakia and Hungary were not opened until 1964 and that the bridge over the Danube between the two countries at Esztergom was still not rebuilt more than twenty years after being destroyed at the end of the Second World War.

The best illustration of minority problems can be found in Yugoslavia, with its many nationalities. Bulgaria has alleged from time to time that the Bulgars in the Macedonian region of Yugoslavia are being persecuted. These charges became particularly vociferous in 1958 during the second Soviet-Yugoslav dispute. Even six years later the main communist party newspaper in Belgrade printed a list of current anti-Yugoslav speeches and articles still referring to Macedonia as ethnically Bulgarian.[35] Officially, however, friendship is proclaimed between the two countries. There are also some 900,000 Albanians living in Yugoslavia, and a steady stream of denunciation comes from across the border.[36]

INTERNAL NATIONALITY PROBLEMS. Two of the East European countries, Czechoslovakia and Yugoslavia, are faced with the question of how to foster and preserve unity among their different ethnic groups and yet not erase national identities. The two states have not existed long enough to change the fundamental individualism of their minority components. Slovaks remember their brief separate statehood during the Second World War, and even the communists are proud of the 1944 uprising against the Germans in Slovakia. After the war, local autonomy was granted, but resentment flared in 1960 when the Slovak Board of Commissioners, symbolizing that self-rule, was dissolved under the new "socialist" constitution.

The dismissal during 1963 of two notorious Stalinists of Slovak extraction, Karol Bacílek from headship of the communist party of Slovakia and Viliam Široký from the premiership of the entire country, only contributed to further demands for restoration of autonomy. The fact that the new premier, Josef Lenárt, was formerly president of the Slovak National Council suggests that the government wished to appear to have made a concession. The powers of the Slovak National Council were increased the following year.[37] Its primary task, however, is still to help in the achievement of the state economic plan. The Slovaks will continue to strive for more freedom, although certainly they have no future as an independent entity under communism.

The problems in Yugoslavia are more complex. After the final reconciliation between Khrushchëv and Tito at the end of 1962, a general domestic relaxation led to a revival of nationalism within the individual republics which must have worried the communist leaders in Belgrade. Tito complained about this revival in his 1963 address to the congress of the Union of Yugoslav Youth, attacking unnamed persons who, he said, confused the nation with the state. Economic overtones also appear to be significant, especially in connection with subsidies given by more developed Croatia and Slovenia in the north to the southern republics of Serbia and Montenegro. This was intimated in an article in a Zagreb weekly by the secretary of the city's communist party committee, Mika Tripalo, who observed that

> when the greater part of the investment funds is centralized and thus is outside of any influence that might be exercised by the direct producers . . . there will always be discontent. Since we are a country of several republics and nations, this discontent can assume a national character.[38]

Opening the Eighth Congress of the Yugoslav communist party, Tito warned against wanting to "create something new and artificial —one unified Yugoslav nation, which is not unlike . . . centralism" and against "chauvinism": in Yugoslav "socialist integration," all nationalities would find their individual interest.[39] Nationality, however, most assuredly will play a part in the leadership succession. The fact that Tito is a Croatian may be insignificant, but this will not be the case with regard to his successor. Aleksandar Ranković is a Serb and his replacement as vice-president in July 1966 was of that same nationality,[40] indicating that the ethnic balance is important.

CONFLICTS WITHIN COMMUNISM. The communist system was imposed upon the countries of Eastern Europe against the wishes of the vast majority of the populations involved. This basic conflict between the people and their rulers exploded during 1953 into riots at Plzen and East Berlin as well as demonstrations during 1956 at Poznań and Warsaw, culminating in full-scale revolt at Budapest.[41] Other conflicts on the interstate level have involved Yugoslavia twice and Albania once with the U.S.S.R. since 1948 and 1961, respectively. These two countries broke away completely from the Soviet bloc, although Yugoslavia again is a member in good standing. The most recent case in which independence is being asserted concerns Romania and overtly dates back only to 1964. On the whole, differences in both politics and economics exist among the East European regimes themselves which in turn affect their relations with the U.S.S.R.

Although intervention by Soviet armed forces crushed the rebellion in Hungary, apart from the initial post-revolt terror there has been no return to the Stalinist type of government which had precipitated the uprising. János Kádár soon demonstrated firmly the impossibility of an alternative to the communist regime, and it seems that the population has indeed come to terms with reality. This situation is reinforced by the presence of some 50,000 Soviet troops permanently garrisoned in Hungary. Although these forces pose a sensitive problem, Kádár has indicated openly that they will remain as long as they are needed.[42]

No U.S.S.R. troops have been stationed in Romania since 1958, and it is perhaps because of this omission that the communist leadership in Bucharest has dared to exploit nationalist sentiments domestically. There has been a deliberate attempt to underemphasize the role the Red Army played at the end of the war in establishing the present system throughout Romania. Compulsory study of the Russian language has been discontinued in secondary schools, Soviet names of streets in Bucharest have been changed, and even the anniversary of the Romanian-Soviet friendship treaty was celebrated in 1965 on a much smaller scale than before. This trend reached a high point with the publication of previously unknown manuscripts by Karl Marx on Romanian history of the late eighteenth and early nineteenth centuries which indicted Tsarist Russian policies. Further, a party journal has published a study of the early period of the communist movement in Romania which discusses Comintern interference in 1920 with appointments to the party leadership.[43]

As these developments have been taking place in various East European countries, bringing some internal relaxation and even attempts at asserting some degree of independence vis-à-vis the Soviet Union, one of the bloc states has remained locked in the vise of Stalinism. East Germany's position will continue to be unique, due to the fact that it is part of a divided country. Ulbricht must counter all polycentrist tendencies and prevent domestic relaxation, in order to avoid ferment and agitation for union with the much larger and wealthier Federal Republic of Germany. This is also the reason behind his drive for recognition of the German Democratic Republic as a sovereign state in its own right.

The agreements to establish West German trade offices in Poland, Romania, Hungary, Bulgaria, and Czechoslovakia have made Ulbricht uneasy.[44] Negotiations by the Krupp combine for economic cooperation and joint enterprises in Eastern Europe have political as well as economic overtones. Obviously, a growing trade with Bonn will make the other bloc partners less sensitive to the needs of Pankow. That is why East German propaganda has been stressing the danger of subversive activities by the trade missions and raising the specter of economic blackmail by the West.

On the other hand, Yugoslavia has supported East Germany and extended official recognition to the Ulbricht regime despite the sanctions applied by West Germany under the Hallstein Doctrine, whereby Bonn claims to speak for all Germans and until early 1967 would not exchange ambassadors with any government recognizing the GDR. There are no longer any diplomatic relations between Bonn and Belgrade. Attitudes by the bloc toward Yugoslavia have varied, depending upon the behavior of Moscow. During two periods, 1948-1955 and 1958-1962, Tito found himself ostracized.[45] By December 1962, however, when he visited the U.S.S.R., it was conceded by Khrushchëv that Yugoslavia was indeed a socialist country. The following month, a Yugoslav communist delegation traveled to East Berlin to attend another bloc party's congress for the first time since 1948.

At the interstate level also, in January 1965 the Yugoslav foreign minister at that time, Koča Popović, paid a visit to Bulgaria, the first such trip by a cabinet member since November 1947, when Tito went to Sofia. Ulbricht and Novotný paid visits to Belgrade during September 1964. There existed no special difficulty in reaching reconciliation with Poland and Hungary, since both Gomułka and Kádár had been imprisoned as "Titoists." Romania staged no trial for nationalist-deviation, and even during the second Yugoslav-Soviet dispute in 1958 maintained its attacks at a low level. All but one of the East European parties and governments now accept Yugoslavia as a member of the socialist camp. Only little Albania continues to denounce its communist neighbor.[46]

The reasons for this continued hostility include the fear of annexation and the presence of a sizeable Albanian minority in Yugoslavia whose number equals nearly half the total population inside the borders of Albania itself. Toward the end of 1960, at the conference of eighty-one communist parties in Moscow, Enver Hoxha attacked the Soviet Union and accused it of attempting to starve Albania into submission. During the spring of 1961 the U.S.S.R. and Czechoslovakia stopped aid to Tirana, which over the preceding thirteen years had amounted to the equivalent of 600 million U.S. dollars; by the end of the summer all bloc experts and technicians in Albania had left for home.

At the Twenty-second Congress of the CPSU, in the fall of 1961, Khrushchëv openly attacked the Albanian leadership for "resorting to force and arbitrary repression." [47] Diplomatic relations between the two countries were severed in December at the instigation of Moscow. Since that time, Albania has not sent representatives to any Warsaw Pact or CMEA meetings, although not officially expelled from either organization. The other bloc countries reduced their ranking diplomatic representatives to the level of chargé d'affaires. Only the Romanians have kept on friendly terms with Tirana. Bucharest even sent a delegation to the Fifth Congress of Albania's communist party in November 1966, perhaps as an indication of its neutrality in the Sino-Soviet conflict.

SINO-SOVIET DISPUTE. Besides the conflicts between the U.S.S.R. and individual countries within Eastern Europe, as well as among the latter states themselves, the Sino-Soviet dispute has made an impact on the bloc due to the differing attitudes toward this rift. Ideologically, of course, the communist parties of all these countries except Albania give their support to Moscow. Yet they are not in unanimous agreement about the manner in which the dispute has been handled by the CPSU. Besides proclaiming its neutrality, Romania attempted to mediate the quarrel in 1964 with the dispatch of a delegation to Peking. Bucharest is definitely against any excommunication of China and remains opposed to a world conference that might precipitate such a move. Romania refused to attend even the 1965 "consultative" conference in Moscow for this reason.

The leaders of East Germany, Bulgaria, and Czechoslovakia support the Soviet position as being correct both doctrinally and in the tactics used to handle the differences.[48] Spokesmen for the regime in Poland have indicated their hesitation at giving the CPSU full backing, and these statements make it apparent that the communist leadership at Warsaw is not very enthusiastic about a permanent schism. At any rate, other regimes in Eastern Europe may follow the Romanian example and try to exploit the Sino-Soviet dispute for their own ends.

It would have seemed natural for the Romanians to utilize the arrival of Chou En-lai in June 1966 for another demonstration of independence. At the same time, the Chinese premier undoubtedly chose to make his visit just three weeks before the bloc summit meeting of Warsaw Pact members with the purpose of influencing this session by exploiting the strained relations between Romania and the Soviet Union. Chou praised his hosts for "fighting against all attempts at control or interference from the outside." [49] He added that by standing up for their sovereignty they were defending the correct basis for relations between communist parties and states.

At a banquet Chou attacked the CPSU leaders as "modern revisionists," but the reference was deleted from reports of his speech by Romanian censorship, and he apparently desisted from any further criticism of the U.S.S.R. during the one-week visit. Although nothing is known about the private talks which took place with Ceauşescu, there could not have been much agreement on substantive matters. Even the farewell rally had to be delayed some two hours, probably indicating a clash regarding Chou's parting remarks. The final joint statement had little to say about the exchange of views, except that these had "led to increased knowledge." [50]

If this visit diminished Chinese prestige—and it was in Bucharest, at the Romanian communist party congress in 1960, that China first attacked the Soviet Union openly—there still remained one country in Eastern Europe where Chou could receive full support for his views. Arriving in Tirana, he saw portraits of Stalin and Mao Tse-tung together with those of Marx and Lenin. Here the spokesman for China denounced the "treachery and collusion" of Soviet and United States leaders, whose alleged plans to dissolve NATO and the Warsaw Pact he explained as a plot to encircle China.[51] The Albanian premier, Mehmet Shehu, echoed the visitor's charges at a mass rally in Durrës.

THE LIMITS OF RELAXATION

It would seem logical that the attainment of some freedom from Soviet control throughout Eastern Europe should be connected with a loosening of the totalitarian control exercised by each regime upon the population concerned.[52] That this is not necessarily true can be seen from the example of Albania, which has been *de facto* outside the bloc since the end of 1961, when the U.S.S.R. severed all relations with that country. The leadership in Tirana continues its harsh rule and, hence, will not be treated in this section.

Among the other bloc countries, three have long delayed an internal détente because the leaders do not seem able to overcome their Stalinist background. In Czechoslovakia, the nationalism of the Slovaks and the general intellectual ferment have forced Novotný to make some concessions, but he will not allow the détente to proceed beyond manageable proportions. East Germany has had no relaxation to speak of and recently "celebrated" the sixth anniversary of the Berlin Wall.[53] The domestic "thaw" in Romania has been gradual and maintained under strict control, in sharp contrast to assertions of independence within the CMEA and the Warsaw Pact.

In two countries which played principal roles in the attempts at defiance of the Soviet Union in 1956, major differences can be seen. Kádár, who was put in power in Hungary by the U.S.S.R. and served its interest by betraying the government of Imre Nagy, has tried to obtain the support of the population and, by and large, has relaxed domestic conditions. Gomułka, conversely, on whom so much hope was placed in Poland, has pursued a constant policy of retrogression, so that today the country stagnates politically and economically.[54] Restrictions on freedom of speech and a violent campaign against the Catholic Church have been undertaken, and only the most cautious economic reforms.

Bulgaria has become a pioneer in economics, with more than half of its key industrial plants introducing experimental reforms. Finally, Yugoslavia holds a certain fascinating interest because of the changes that are proposed in its communist party organization.

Despite some changes, the communist regimes in Eastern Europe remain more similar than they are different. Not one of them has indicated an intention to abandon one-party rule or the centrally planned economy. Regardless of wishful thinking engendered by some of its behavior, even Romania will not leave the CMEA or the Warsaw Treaty Organization. It is true that the secret police are less in evidence throughout the bloc, but detailed card files on persons suspected of anti-regime feelings are most certainly being maintained.[55] Last but not least, the ouster of Khrushchëv has served to remind the average citizen that change in the top leadership may come suddenly in Eastern Europe.

The relaxations that have occurred do not seem to have affected the numerical strength of the various communist parties. If anything, membership has increased. Czechoslovakia claims the highest proportion of party members (11.4 percent) to the total population.[56] In other bloc countries this ranges from 5 to 10 percent. Drives to increase membership alternate with purges so that, despite the apparent size of the communist movement in each country, the party can no longer guarantee effective administration of the government. Thus a trend has developed, beginning in Hungary and spreading throughout Eastern Europe, toward professional qualifications rather than party service as the basis for determining who shall occupy certain positions in the economy and public administration.[57] The resulting conflict between the young, by and large nonpolitical cadres and the old party members without any training in management is becoming acute.

The need for economic reform is closely connected with this trend and the differing attitudes of the young managerial elite and the party apparatus workers. Most countries in the bloc now realize that progress cannot be achieved without a more realistic pricing system, at least some decentralization, and appropriate incentives for workers. This should not be confused with a return to capitalism, because all measures are to remain within the framework of central planning. Economic reforms were begun in Yugoslavia during 1949-1950, but it was eight years before another East European country made a few steps in the same direction, and in that country, Poland, opposition in 1957-1958 stymied any progress for a full year.

Impetus did not come until after the publication of the article by Professor Yevsei Liberman, of Kharkhov, on proposed reforms in the Soviet economy.[58] His ideas affected East Germany, where they have been introduced. They also led to a study in Czechoslovakia, after the negative performance of that country's economy in 1962-1963, and to the subsequent reform.[59] The regime in Hungary announced during November 1965 that fundamental changes were required but would be introduced gradually.[60] After some experimentation, the Politburo in Bulgaria in December 1965 released its "Theses" according to which the individual factory will be self-supporting while remaining under central control and within the program of the five-year plan. Yugoslavia has proceeded farther than any other bloc regime by withdrawing subsidies from enterprises that do not make a profit.[61]

Recently there has appeared also a trend toward allowing the small remaining amount of private enterprise to develop. Data which show higher production by the small garden plots in comparison with the socialized sectors in agriculture may have contributed to this. All the bloc countries except Yugoslavia and Poland have announced the victory of collectivization. (See table 66.) Yet incentives are being provided to maintain the private plots. East Germany, Hungary, and Poland even allow craftsmen to operate on their own within certain limits. Recently, similar regulations in Czechoslovakia and Bulgaria permit a limited degree of private enterprise in the service trades, which should make life somewhat easier.

These developments have been accompanied by more contacts with the West, even in the case of regimes which have maintained the tightest control over their own populations. Although tourism is recognized as a major source of foreign exchange,[62] Western visitors are still considered to represent a danger from the ideological point of view. In the opposite direction, only Romania and Bulgaria have

TABLE 66

EASTERN EUROPE, BASIC DATA, 1966-1967

| Country | Area (sq. km.) | Population (millions) | Communist party members (millions) | Socialized sector (percent of total) | | Trade | | Gross national production |
				Industry	Agricultural land	Wholesale	Retail	
Albania	28,700	1.8	0.066	99.5	82.0	100.0	92.9	90.5
Bulgaria	110,900	8.2	0.611	99.5	98.1	100.0	99.9	99.5
Czechoslovakia	127,900	14.1	1.700	100.0	93.6	100.0	100.0	95.0
East Germany	108,800	17.0	1.770	89.0	94.0	100.0	77.0	83.0
Hungary	93,000	10.1	0.627	98.0	95.2	100.0	98.8	96.6
Poland	312,500	31.6	2.000	99.6	14.6	100.0	98.5	76.9
Romania	237,500	19.0	1.676	99.6	94.1	100.0	100.0	95.7
Yugoslavia	255,800	19.7	1.046	100.0	17.5	100.0	99.0	n. a.
Average	—	—	—	ca. 98.2	ca. 73.6	100.0	ca. 95.1	ca. 91.0
Total	1,275,100	121.5	9,496	—	—	—	—	—

SOURCES: *Kommunist vooruzhënnykh sil*, XLVI, No. 3 and 4 (February 1966), Parts I and II, pp. 71-78 and 67-74. *Hospodarske noviny* (Prague), December 2, 1966, p. 10. *World Strength* (1967), pp. 49-62.

NOTE: The validity of certain data remains questionable, especially in the agricultural column. Unfortunately, the sources do not always define terms used.

an almost complete ban on foreign travel by their citizens. East Germany, of course, is unique in that none of the West European countries recognize it; GDR citizens find it difficult to obtain visas from these countries. Currency restrictions probably are the reason why it is difficult for Hungarians and Czechoslovaks to obtain passports.

Perhaps the threat of Western ideological corruption has also caused the reimposition of strict controls on cultural life in Eastern Europe. Throughout the area, it seemed that 1962 and 1963 represented the beginning of greater freedom for writers.[63] This could be observed in Czechoslovakia, Hungary, Poland, and, even, Yugoslavia. Since that time, journals have been closed down, editorial boards changed, and some individuals indicted. The well-publicized cases of the Polish philosophy professor Leszek Kołakowski and the Yugoslav university instructor Mihajlo Mihajlov are especially pertinent; the one has been expelled from the Polish communist party, and the other is serving a one-year prison term.[64]

Although a certain degree of relaxation has taken place in Eastern Europe during the past several years, it is strictly limited and subject to sudden reversal. If developments in the Soviet Union may serve as a rough model, one should anticipate a struggle for power within the communist parties of the individual countries as soon as or even before the current leaders pass from the scene. It is not unlikely that one or more of these key individuals may follow in the footsteps of Khrushchëv and be overthrown by a palace *coup d'état*. The attempt during 1965 to oust Todor Zhivkov in Bulgaria may serve as a lesson on how not to organize a conspiracy.[65]

Any détente in Eastern Europe must be limited because of the common desire on the part of the communist regimes to remain in power, which position they do not and never have held by the will of the people they rule. This, then, is the broad framework within which the communist systems operate: they cannot permit freedom of expression, and their choice of policies is limited by the ideological straitjacket of Marxism-Leninism. Perhaps the only hope for Eastern Europe should be sought in the laws governing the development of human society, which in fact represent communism's invincible enemy.[66]

NOTES

1 Eugenio Reale, *Nascita del Cominform* (Rome, 1958), p. 51.
2 *For a Lasting Peace, For a People's Democracy,* November 10, 1947.

See also Günther Nollau, *Die Internationale: Wurzeln und Erscheinungsformen des proletarischen Internationalismus* (Cologne, 1959), pp. 193-196.
3 *For a Lasting Peace, For a People's Democracy,* July 1, 1948, and November 29, 1949.
4 *Speech of Nikita Khrushchev before a Closed Session of the XXth Congress of the Communist Party of the Soviet Union on February 25, 1956* (U.S. Senate, Committee on the Judiciary, 85th Cong., 1st sess. [Washington, D.C.: Government Printing Office, 1957]), 66 pp.
5 Translation in Charlotte Saikowski and Leo Gruliow (eds.), *Current Soviet Policies IV: The Documentary Record of the 22nd Congress of the Communist Party of the Soviet Union* (New York, 1962).
6 *Pravda,* October 29, 1961.
7 See U.S. House of Representatives, Committee on Un-American Activities, *Who Are They?* (Washington, D.C.: Government Printing Office, 1958), Part 9, pp. 3-7.
8 See Radio Free Europe, *Eastern Europe's Communist Leaders: Bulgaria* (5 vols.; Munich, 1966), V, 34-37.
9 See, *ibid., Czechoslovakia,* IV, 21-23.
10 See [West Germany], Bundesministerium für gesamtdeutsche Fragen, *SBZ-Biographie* (Bonn, 1964), p. 360.
11 See Radio Free Europe, *op. cit., Hungary,* I, 27-33.
12 See Charles Malamuth, "Gomulka: Head of People's Poland," *Communist Affairs,* III, No. 5 (September-October 1965), 19-30, and No. 6 (November-December 1965), 17-26.
13 See Radio Free Europe, *op. cit., Rumania,* III, 19-22.
14 Biography in *Krasnaya zvezda,* June 18, 1965. See also chap. viii, n. 48.
15 Even the Yugoslavs have adopted this term, as seen from a lecture by Milenko Marković, of the Institute for Study of Workers' Movements, over Radio Belgrade, February 5, 1965.
16 *Renascita,* September 5, 1964.
17 *Ibid.,* Points 33, 34.
18 *Pravda,* April 3, 1964.
19 Issue of October 17, 1964.
20 *Scînteia,* October 18, 1964, as translated in "Eastern Europe and the Fall of Khrushchev," *Special Information Note,* October 29, 1964, p. 1.
21 Radio Budapest, October 18, 1964.
22 *Rudé právo,* October 19, 1964; Radio Prague, October 22, 1964.
23 Tass, October 25, 1964.
24 *Special Information Note,* October 29, 1964, p. 3.
25 *Ibid.* See also *Rabotnichesko delo,* October 19, 1964.
26 *Borba,* October 23, 1964.
27 *Krasnaya zvezda,* March 10, 1965.
28 For names and identifications of participants, see, *ibid.,* July 5 and 6, 1966.
29 As quoted in "Rumania—The Successful Rebel," *Special Information Note,* October 14, 1964, pp. 1-2.

The full declaration appeared in an Agerpres pamphlet, *Statement on the Stand of the Rumanian Workers' Party* (Bucharest: Rumanian News Agency, 1964); excerpts in "A Rumanian Manifesto," *East Europe,* XIII, No. 6 (June 1964), 25-30.
30 *Special Information Note,* October 14, 1964, p. 3.
31 RFE report (by James F. Brown), "Eastern Europe and the USSR since Khrushchev," October 15, 1965, p. 2.
32 See Hanns von Krannhals, *Der Warschauer Aufstand 1944* (Frankfort on the Main, 1962).
33 Much of this section is based on a pamphlet entitled *Conflicts of Interest in Eastern Europe* (London, May 1965), p. 34.
34 *Predvoj,* January 19, 1961, as quoted in *Conflicts of Interest . . .,* p. 9.
35 *Borba,* April 2, 1964.
36 On alleged mass deportations of Albanian workers from Kosovo see *Zëri i popullit,* June 5, 1964, and *Conflicts of Interest . . .,* p. 10.

37 Resolution on the Slovak National Council by the Central Committees of the Czechoslovak and Slovak communist parties, *Rudé právo,* May 22, 1964.

38 *Vjesnik u srijedu,* October 14, 1964, as quoted in *Conflicts of Interest . . .,* p. 13.

39 Speaking over Radio Zagreb, December 7, 1964.

40 Koča Popović, whose biography appeared in the *New York Times,* July 15, 1966, upon his appointment as Vice President.

41 See Ferenc A. Váli, *Rift and Revolt in Hungary: Nationalism versus Communism* (Cambridge, Mass., 1961).

42 Radio Kossuth, February 11, 1965.

43 Unc Gheorghe and Dan Mihaela, article on "Documents Concerning the Struggle for the Creation of the Rumanian Communist Party, 1916-1921," *Lupta de clasă,* No. 6 (1966), as reported in *Rumanian Press Survey,* July 28, 1966.

44 See articles in *Neues Deutschland,* May 18, 19, and 20, 1965.
   The recent agreement to exchange ambassadors between Bonn and Bucharest is discussed in the *New York Times,* February 14, 1967.

45 Robert Bass and Elizabeth Marbury (eds.), *The Soviet-Yugoslav Controversy, 1948-1958: A Documentary Record* (New York, 1959), and Václav Beneš *et al.* (eds.), *The Second Soviet-Yugoslav Dispute: Full Text of Main Documents, April-June 1958* (Bloomington, Ind., 1959).

46 "The attitude of the Tito clique toward the struggle of the Vietnamese people has unmasked it long since as an agency of American imperialism and its close collaborator." Radio Tirana, February 24, 1966.

47 Radio Moscow, October 28, 1961.

48 All of the East European communist parties which sent delegates to the Hungarian congress, with the exception of the Romanian, have lined up with the Soviet party regarding the necessity to hold a world conference during 1967. *Die Welt* (Hamburg), December 2, 1966.

49 See the article, "Each for Himself in Eastern Europe," *Interpreter,* July 1966, p. 8.

50 *Ibid.,* p. 9.

51 *Ibid.* See also "Chou among Friends," *East Europe,* XV, No. 8 (August 1966), 35-37.

52 Much of this section is based on a pamphlet entitled *The "Thaw" in Eastern Europe* (London, June 1966), pp. 40.

53 "East Germany: With Flowers All over Their Guns," *The Economist,* CCXX, No. 6417 (August 20-26, 1966), p. 722, air edition.

54 See Richard F. Staar, "Hard Line in Poland," *Current History,* LII, No. 308 (April 1967), pp. 208-213, 244.

55 A good example of this close relationship between the Soviet KGB and East European secret police services was the arrest in Czechoslovakia of an American citizen, Vladimir Kazan-Komarek, whose nonstop Moscow-to-Paris flight via Aeroflot on October 31, 1966, was diverted to Prague for this purpose. After considerable U.S. pressure, he was released. *New York Times,* February 5, 1967.

56 *Rudé právo,* July 12, 1966, gave the total party membership as 1,698,002 (including 59,307 candidates).

57 See, however, regulations in the Sofia journal of laws, *Darzhaven vestnik,* July 8, 1966, which give priority in appointments to "active fighters against fascism and capitalism," regardless of their education. Cited in RFE, *Situation Report,* July 19, 1966, p. 2.
   Another problem is that of the new generation. For a discussion see Fritz Schenk, "Die Enkel der Revolution: Probleme des Generationswechsels," *SBZ Archiv,* XVII, No. 23 (December 1966), 357-359.

58 *Pravda,* September 9, 1962.

59 To be introduced in 1967, according to Josef Toman's article on "Socialist Planning," *Nová mysl,* July 12, 1966, noted in *Czechoslovak Press Survey,* July 28, 1966.

60 This reform is to begin in 1968. *Társadelmi Szemle,* July-August 1966, noted in *Hungarian Press Survey,* July 19, 1966.

61 See the discussion by Alojz Volf of "The Yugoslav Reform," *Predvoj,* July 14, 1966, noted in *Czechoslovak Press Survey,* August 1, 1966.

62 Yugoslavia, for example, expected to earn about $140 million in foreign exchange during 1966 from tourism. During the first six months of that year the total of 920,000 visitors represented an increase of 30 percent over the same period in 1965. *New York Times,* August 21, 1966.

63 See Jerzy Mond and Robert Richter, "Writers and Journalists as a Pressure Group in Eastern Europe," *The Polish Review,* XI, No. 1 (Winter 1966), 92-108.

64 *New York Times,* November 13, 1966.

65 Radio Free Europe, *Colonel Tykocinski's Revelations* (Munich, 1966), 44-45.

66 *The "Thaw" in Eastern Europe,* p. 40.

Chapter 12 / EPILOGUE

ALBANIA in 1967 was well into the second phase of its Chinese-inspired cultural revolution. Although some 15,000 party and government officials had been sent "back to the masses," which is to say, into production work, Enver Hoxha called for reducing the bureaucracies further, to a bare minimum. A Red Guard movement began the use of wall posters, called "flash bulletins," and these quickly spread throughout the country. *Zëri i popullit* announced that more than 500 mountain farms, comprising 10 percent of all arable land, had been collectivized during the first quarter of 1967. Since the figure for 1966 was 89 percent, this means in effect total collectivization. A joint Central Committee and Council of Ministers declaration "On Further Development and Intensification of the Revolutionary Movement and the Working Masses' Creative Initiative" appeared April 30, 1967, calling for cuts of 50 to 66 percent in the size of private garden plots on collective farms, lowering of wages in general, and transfer of the entire intelligentsia to production work for thirty days each year. A decrease in prices of certain consumers' goods allegedly will balance these austerity measures.

One of the problems faced by the communist regime in Albania is that of the younger generation and its indifference to the ruling party. The "voluntary" campaign to open up new farmland in the mountains involves 20,000 youths; another 150,000 are building the Rogozhine-Fier railroad and a major highway; thousands have gone to old collective farms for one- to five-year periods (*Zëri i popullit*, May 19). These figures, if true, would include the entire age group from fourteen to twenty-six years. The same source, however, complained that about 70 percent within this age bracket had not joined the official youth organization in the districts of Berat and Shkoder. The League of Albanian Working Youth opened its fifth congress on June 26, but it is doubtful that the apolitical attitude of the younger generation can be changed. This situation does not augur well for the future of communism in Albania.

BULGARIA, which among the East European countries ranks second only to Albania as an agriculturally oriented economy, held a conference of delegates from its 920 collective farms, which cover 84.5 percent of its arable land. Meeting at Sofia in late March 1967, the conference approved a new model statute. This was followed a month later by a congress of the communist-dominated Bulgarian Agrarian Union, used as a tool by the ruling party to influence the peasantry. The union claims 120,000 members—no increase over the past decade. All but one sixth of the membership is employed on collective farms. Deterioration in agriculture would be assumed from the 1967 agreement with Canada for the purchase of more than a half million tons of wheat over the next three years, with an option to increase the amount. Even so, Radio Sofia on June 6 announced prospects of a rich harvest in bread grains for the third consecutive year. Perhaps some of the imported wheat will go to the U.S.S.R., trade with which should increase by 1970 to about 60 percent of the total (compared with 51.8 percent in 1965).

In domestic affairs, there are complaints that religion still influences the population, especially women, Turks, and gypsies. The secretariat of the communist party has called for a more intensive atheistic indoctrination of the Bulgarian people in all spheres of life. The sixth congress of the Fatherland Front, the communist-sponsored mass organization, convened during mid-May 1967. Its membership totals almost 3.8 million persons, or 65 percent of the electorate. Resolutions were adopted condemning the "United States' aggressive war in Vietnam" and also "West German imperialism and revanchism, supported by American imperialists" as a "danger to European security and world peace."

CZECHOSLOVAKIA is also concerned about growing more food. To the government's District Agricultural Associations (replacing the Production Boards) there have been added cooperative "Councils of Collective and State Farm Representatives." The government hopes to bring both types of farms closer together, intensify agricultural production, lower grain imports, stabilize manpower, and simplify administration. A tightening can also be observed in price and wage policy, as envisaged until 1970. Wholesale prices were to be increased by 25 percent during 1967 as compared with the previous year. Wages are to rise between 3.2 and 3.4 percent during the current five-year plan, provided labor productivity increases at an even higher rate. A Central Committee plenum decided to speed up the growth of national income from a total of 23 to 29 percent during the 1966-1970 period (*Rudé právo*, May 5, 1967). As in agriculture, it is the worker who will be squeezed to obtain capital.

In foreign trade, exports during 1966 surpassed imports by 814 million crowns. On the other hand, Czechoslovakia remains heavily dependent upon the U.S.S.R., and during 1966-1970 is to buy from the U.S.S.R. 39 million tons of crude oil, 50 million tons of iron ore, half of all cotton needs, and 40 percent of cereal requirements. A natural-gas pipeline from the Soviet Union opened in 1967 and by 1970 should deliver one billion cubic meters per year, or more than half of what the country uses. In return, the U.S.S.R. will receive almost 1,000 electric and 880 diesel locomotives, about 150,000 tons of rolling equipment, and 3,850 heavy-duty machine tools, 120 million pairs of shoes, and 250,000 motorcycles.

The key to providing these exports is the New Economic Model, based on decentralization. Apathy exists, however, regarding the feasibility of loosening the administrative superstructure. It has not been possible to introduce a new system of prices which would eliminate subsidies, but this is promised for 1967. Enterprises now finance 15 percent of capital investments from their own resources. Steps have been taken also to allow industrial enterprises a direct relationship with foreign markets, although as yet on a limited scale. This may help in solving other economic problems.

EAST GERMANY also looks toward economic reform as the means for reversing a decreasing annual GNP that has declined from 11.4 percent in 1951-1955 to 7.1 in 1956-1960 and 3.4 in 1961-1965. (Among the states of the Soviet bloc, the so-called German Democratic Republic [GDR] at one time had the highest per capita standard of living and industrial production; it is now at the bottom in growth.) In 1967, however, no more than 30 percent of the GDR's enterprises had been placed under the new economic reform system. Although experimentation continues, no integrated system has been achieved as yet. Plans are more realistic than before, yet nobody appears to know how existing fixed prices can be adjusted to changing conditions.

A worker-and-peasant inspectorate operating in industrial branches, districts, enterprise commissions, and people's control committees employs on a part-time basis more than 120,000 persons from labor unions and the Free German Youth. The inspectors watch over activities, export contracts, investment projects, and agriculture. In this last area, imports of wheat have averaged 1.2 million tons per year, or half the total requirements. Even potatoes, a traditional export, are being brought from Poland in exchange for automobiles. Much of the food comes from the Federal Republic of [West] Germany, trade with which increased during 1966 by 20 percent over the previous year.

Relations between the two parts of Germany appeared to be headed toward improvement when, before the seventh SED congress, Chancellor Kurt Georg Kiesinger announced a sixteen-point program in human, cultural, and economic areas. Walter Ulbricht's response came in a speech (fourteen full pages in *Neues Deutschland*, April 18, 1967) which demanded diplomatic recognition for his regime, alteration in the status of West Berlin, renunciation of atomic weapons by West Germany, acknowledgment of present borders, and reduction in defense expenditures by the Bonn government. Members of the Free German Youth at a rally in mid-May 1967 at Karl-Marx-Stadt (Chemnitz) proclaimed hatred for West Germany, paraded before effigies of Kiesinger and All-German Affairs minister Herbert Wehner, and then threw the papier-mâché figures into a wagon labeled "The Garbage Heap of History."

Elections were held on July 2 to the Volkskammer, or parliament, and 538 candidates were allowed to run for 434 seats. Voters had the theoretical possibility of striking names off the ballot. In practice, the entire lists were returned, and those at the bottom became alternates. The new Volkskammer has plans to approve a new constitution which will replace the one adopted in 1949 and, presumably, make the split between the two parts of Germany even more rigid than it is today.

HUNGARY'S first congress of agricultural cooperatives met during late April 1967 at Budapest. A resolution called for enterprise-type management and a gradual transfer of privately owned but collectively used land to cooperative ownership. Legislation will provide each collectivized farmer in good standing between 0.27 and 0.57 hectares of land as his private garden plot, and, from 1968 on, a guaranteed 80 percent of anticipated profits in wages (*Népszabadság,* April 21, 1967). The problem here is that among the one million members of collectives, nearly 40 percent are women and 650,000 are more than fifty years of age; of the latter, about 201,000 are in their seventies. Between 1960 and 1965 some 250,000 members became too old to work, and only 80,000 young persons entered the collective farm labor force. Between 1961 and 1964 about 150,000 young persons left rural areas for jobs outside agriculture.

Two candidates were allowed to compete against each other in eight of the 349 constituencies during the March 1967 elections to parliament. The transfer of Gyula Kállai from premier to chairman (speaker) of the National Assembly just four weeks later indicated that a "more firm and expert management of economic policy had become necessary," according to Radio Budapest on April 15. The new premier, Jenö Fock, is knowledgeable regarding production and enterprise problems. Economic development in Hungary had come to a standstill, apparently due to lack of incentive. The "new economic mechanism" is to be implemented during 1968. It will be up to the current leadership, including presidential council chairman Pál Losonczi, who is a farming expert, to solve these problems. The first step was taken in a resolution, passed by the Economic Committee, on the new system of economic planning.

The new system will go into effect on January 1, 1968. It is based on two principles: "(1) the economic plan still remains the main device for the execution of economic policy and the basis for central economic management; and (2) the implementation of the economic plan will not be carried out through a detailed breakdown for each successively smaller unit, but will be decisively [based] on the system of economic regulations." (RFE, *Situation Report,* June

13, quoting from *Magyar Nemzet.*) Individual enterprises will draw up their own plans. Central direction will be maintained through short-term (one year), medium-range (five years), and long-term (fifteen years) economic planning.

POLAND continues to build up Soviet economic power. Another 170 merchant ships, in addition to almost 400 already delivered, will be built for the U.S.S.R. during 1966-1970, which amounts to 80 percent of Polish production. In return, Poland will receive 90,000 tons of cotton and eleven million tons of crude oil annually until 1975. The United States, on the other hand, is trying to help Poland's adverse balance of payments and ease the $485 million debt by extending repayment time as well as instituting a joint program for English-language teachers in lieu of $9.5 million due in 1967. This will aid in paying $140 million for the 1966-1967 import of two millions tons of grain. Radio Warsaw on June 10, 1967, admitted a total foreign trade deficit of 888 million exchange złotys ($222 million) during 1966. This was double the deficit for the previous year.

Despite the fiasco of collectivization, which was all but abandoned in 1957, the regime in Poland intends to resume the process and use agricultural circles as a first step. There were 32,616 circles in 1967, with 1.9 million members in 35,000 villages, or 86 percent of the total. According to the official economic affairs weekly, *Życie gospodarcze* (April 9, 1967), "there are three stages in the transformation of privately owned farms into cooperatives: agricultural circles, collective farms, and state farms." That this policy will eventually succeed can be seen from the fact that some 842,000 (or 23.3 percent) of the private holdings under two hectares in size are being farmed by persons sixty years of age or older. As the owners die off, the government will take over their property.

Another problem for the regime involves the Catholic Church and its hold on the population. The communist party makes a distinction between the "reactionary" part of the church hierarchy and the Vatican. On May 29, 1967, Pope Paul VI appointed Archbishop Karol Wojtyła of Kraków as Poland's second cardinal. At the age of forty-seven years, he is probably more flexible than the sixty-five-year-old Stefan Cardinal Wyszyński. Shortly before the nomination,

Monsignor Agostino Casaroli had made a fact-finding visit to Poland and interviewed various bishops in their dioceses. It may be that a new agreement can be worked out between church and state. A first step in this direction was the appointment of four Polish bishops in the Oder-Neisse territories as apostolic administrators *ad nutum sanctae sedis,* who are now directly responsible to the Pope rather than to Cardinal Wyszyński.

The eighth plenum of the central committee for the first time since 1963 discussed intraparty politics rather than economic affairs. Based on excerpts from the thirty-two speeches in *Trybuna ludu* (May 18, 1967), it can be seen that the communist party is divided into three main factions: the partisan group under the Interior minister, General Mieczysław Moczar, which has penetrated key positions in the party, government, armed forces, and culture and youth organizations; the so-called revisionist "liberal" group, comprising writers and intellectuals as well as university students and other party members in Warsaw, which is being attacked most viciously by the partisans; and the underground Natolin or Stalinist group, now distributing anti-Gomułka brochures and leaflets in Poland. Headed by Kazimierz Mijał, currently residing in Albania, it has established a clandestine Communist Party of Poland, according to Radio Tirana (May 13, 1967). The first two groups are already jockeying for position in the power struggle for Gomułka's mantle.

Romania, despite its relatively good economic position with regard to raw materials (oil, timber, wheat), expects a "planned" foreign trade deficit of 2.5 billion lei during 1966-1970. In the year 1967, it exchanged consular and trade missions with Spain, established full diplomatic relations with the Federal Republic of Germany and with Canada, increased its trade with Mainland China by at least a third over the preceding two years, and signed a commercial agreement with Israel. In the case of West Germany, certainly this occurred contrary to the wishes of the Soviet Union. Trade with the Federal Republic now approaches $200 million per year and is second only to that with the U.S.S.R., which still accounts for 39 percent. The percentage with all "socialist" countries is 59.6 and with "capitalist" states about 34 percent, according to Radio

Bucharest (June 4, 1967). The remaining 6.4 percent presumably involves trade with the underdeveloped countries, not belonging to either camp.

Regardless of this economic influence of the Soviet Union, party leader Nicolae Ceauşescu in an article on the forty-sixth anniversary of the Romanian communist movement gave three preconditions for bloc unity: interparty relations based on bilateral ties, national distinctiveness for each country's development of socialism, and monolithic unity in every communist party. This last element referred to an attempt by "another party" to establish direct ties with individual members of the Romanian Communist Party (*Scînteia,* May 7, 1967). Only the Communist Party of the Soviet Union has ever promoted this type of subversive effort in the past, vis-à-vis the Yugoslav, Albanian, and Chinese movements.

The communist leadership in Romania continues its relatively independent course, especially in foreign affairs. This could be seen in the announcement that Constantin Oancea had been appointed ambassador to Bonn and arrived there July 10, 1967. Bucharest also refrained from breaking off diplomatic relations with Israel, and Premier Ion Gheorghe Maurer called for a negotiated settlement in the Middle East during his speech at the United Nations. Subsequently, he met President Lyndon B. Johnson in Washington, D.C., and their talks may have precipitated his unpublicized trip to Peking (reported in the *New York Times* on July 5, 1967).

YUGOSLAVIA, among all the East European states, appears headed toward the most exciting change. First of all, the official youth federation and its two million members will no longer represent merely a "transmission belt" for the League of Yugoslav Communists (SKJ). A complete reorganization should take place at its November 1967 congress. The youth federation president, Tomislav Badovinač, has declared that interference by the party must cease. In his words, the new organization "will reflect the interests and discuss the problems of its own membership," according to *Borba* (March 9, 1967), and will focus on education, scholarships, and employment for youth. The party has suffered from a declining percentage of young persons within its ranks.

Another problem involves the language conflict. Many Croatian intellectuals in the party consider that Serbian is being imposed upon them. A declaration signed by nineteen cultural institutions requested that the Croatian tongue be recognized as a separate and equal literary language with Serbian, Macedonian, or Slovenian and that the 1963 constitution be amended to this effect. In reply, forty-five Serbian writers published a counterdeclaration, demanding that the 650,000 Serbs in Croatia be taught in the Serbian language and the Cyrillic alphabet. A crackdown has followed this exchange, with many expulsions from the SKJ.

The ruling party also faces a reorganization. It will allegedly retain primacy but no longer command. Josip Broz-Tito, reelected president in mid-May 1967, has stated that the SKJ will not wither away and that the forthcoming change "does not mean the creation of an organization which would not be based on the principles of Marxism-Leninism, and neither does the reorganization support the idea that the party is outdated," according to Radio Belgrade (April 17, 1967). Ten days later, *Draft Theses* on the reorganization of the SKJ were published (text in *Osteuropäische Rundschau*, XIII, No. 6 [June 1967], 37-40). They are to serve as the basis for a discussion of party reforms. Moscow had warned previously that "any limitation on the role of the party, any restriction of its function to ideology, is totally unacceptable and damaging to the cause of socialism" (*Pravda*, February 20, 1967).

On the government side, the April 1967 elections provided a limited choice, as follows: Federal Chamber, 81 candidates for 60 seats; republic chambers, 428 candidates for 325 seats; communal assemblies, 40,000 candidates for more than 20,000 seats. In actual practice, communists competed against communists. Although several instances where the party intervened were recorded, in 30 percent of the contested electoral districts at the republic level (78 seats), party favorites were defeated (23). Despite the fact that these elections were indirect and certainly not free, it can be anticipated that more choice will be provided in 1969, when the other half of the deputies to all assemblies are to be chosen.

The federal parliament has passed six amendments to the constitution. In effect, the Albanian or Hungarian representatives can henceforth convene the Chamber of Nationalities. Also, the Federal Executive will be limited in allocation of resources to the various republics. The vice-presidency has been abolished, and the speaker of the National Assembly (Milentije Popović, elected in May 1967 to replace Edvard Kardelj) will perform the functions of the chief executive in case of Tito's death or incapacity. Elimination of the deputy commander in chief separates the authority of the armed forces' commander from the administrative functions of the National Defense secretary. Finally, the republics have been given more competence in security matters and even foreign policy, which may portend the development of Yugoslavia toward a confederation.

The WARSAW PACT has held two sets of maneuvers in anticipated preparation for large-scale war games such as have occurred during every fall since 1961. The first exercise took place May 27-June 2, 1967, on the territory of the so-called German Democratic Republic (GDR), with the participation of Polish, Soviet, and GDR troops under the command of Poland's Defense minister, Marshal Marian Spychalski. The second exercise was held June 14-19, in Hungary. It included U.S.S.R., Czechoslovak, and Hungarian units which were directed by Marshal of the Soviet Union Ivan I. Yakubovskii. Both maneuvers tested operational problems at the staff level and were reported in *Krasnaya zvezda* (June 7, 21).

It had seemed very possible that Yakubovskii would be appointed commander in chief of the Warsaw Treaty Organization (WTO) because his promotion to the highest Soviet military rank from general of the army bypassed the two intermediate levels: marshal of type forces and chief marshal. Simultaneously, he was made U.S.S.R. first deputy Defense minister, at the age of fifty-four. This was the position held by the WTO commanding officer, Marshal of the Soviet Union Andrei A. Grechko, prior to the announcement by Tass on April 12, 1967, that he had become U.S.S.R. Defense minister. The same agency announced on July 7 Yakubovskii's appointment as WTO commander.

Yakubovskii joined the Soviet communist party in 1937 during the great purge of the Red Army. He attended the General Staff Academy and was graduated in 1948, sixteen years after entering the armed forces and becoming a tank specialist. Yakubovskii served with U.S.S.R. troops in East Germany during 1957-1960 as deputy to the commanding officer and subsequently until 1965 as commander. His most recent assignment, in charge of the military district of Kiev, also brought him into close contact with the WTO, for which he provided assault troops, reinforcements, and logistics support. It is, thus, considerable experience that Yakubovskii will bring to the Warsaw Treaty Organization.

The CMEA or COUNCIL FOR MUTUAL ECONOMIC ASSISTANCE represents another organization, in addition to WTO, which binds the East European countries closely to the U.S.S.R. At the twentieth CMEA session, in Sofia (December 1966), coordination of national economic plans for 1966-1970 was completed in principle, a full year after these had gone into effect. Trade agreements have been signed for this period of time by all member states with one another, including Romania. Even so, the rate of increase for commercial exchange has been declining steadily, from 85 percent in 1955 (over 1950) and 71 percent in 1960 (over 1955) to 55 percent in 1965 (over 1960). The figures for 1970 (over 1965) will show a further decrease.

The fact that bilateral and multilateral agreements are contracted at high administrative levels represents one reason for the decline. Individual plants or industrial associations might stimulate trade within the CMEA area, if allowed to consult their counterparts directly. More specialization and cooperation in producing finished goods would also help to stimulate trade exchange. It is, however, admitted by East European sources that autarchic tendencies characterize some of the economic cadres. Not all these countries perceive cooperation through CMEA as being to their national interest. On the other hand, some do conduct the bulk of their trade with other "socialist" countries, as in the case of Czechoslovakia (68.9 percent), Bulgaria (72.7 percent), and East Germany (almost 75 percent).

At the Bucharest meeting in July 1966 it had already been agreed that universality could not be enforced in CMEA projects. According to the principle of individual interest, not all members even coordinate their investments. Otherwise, only plans are being synchronized—at least in terms of time span—but there is extensive cooperation in certain branches of industry (electric power, railroads, ball bearings, ferrous metallurgy) and in the operation of petroleum and natural gas pipelines. Figures are given in *World Marxist Review*, May 1967 (p. 40).

The CMEA is now faced with the coordination of economic plans for the 1971-1975 period. A proposal by Poland envisages specialization in the production of subassemblies rather than final products only. This would extend the international division of labor and perhaps make it more effective. Another problem involves the establishment of more realistic prices for goods exchanged. These have been corrected twice, most recently on the basis of the world market for the 1960-1964 period. On the other hand, items have been appearing in Soviet periodicals to the effect that the U.S.S.R. is losing money on its raw materials deliveries to the East European countries. (See *Voprosy ekonomiki,* March 1967.) Now that the bloc countries are so heavily dependent upon their "benefactor," these notices may presage further economic exploitation.

POLYCENTRISM, which is obviously developing, has not even been mentioned by the Soviet Union, which continues to project the image of fraternal relations with all East European states in its sphere of influence. Two multilateral political conferences were, nevertheless, held during the first half of 1967. The first convened at Karlovy Vary, Czechoslovakia, April 24-26, and attempted to project a united front regarding European peace and security. Albania, Romania, and Yugoslavia refused to send delegates. Albania, of course, has not attended any bloc conference since October 1961. The other two also will not recognize Moscow as coordinator of policies for Eastern Europe, much less for the world communist movement. The declaration issued at Karlovy Vary by representatives of twenty-five communist parties from both East and West Europe attacked the United States and the Federal Republic of Germany. Among other matters, it called for: acceptance of existing borders, especially the Oder-Neisse line; diplomatic recognition of both German governments; a ban on nuclear weapons for the West Germans; acknowledgment of the 1938 Munich agreement as void *ab initio*; and simultaneous dissolution of NATO and the WTO.

Agitation for the last-named objective will increase as 1969 and the term of the Atlantic alliance approaches. Even if the two military blocs were to be dissolved, however, the system of bilateral pacts in Eastern Europe would still remain in force. These friendship and mutual assistance treaties, originally signed for periods of twenty years, are being extended currently for similar lengths of time. Between the months of March and September 1967, a series of bilateral treaties have been entered into by the GDR on the one hand and Poland, Czechoslovakia, Hungary, and Bulgaria on the other. This has brought the GDR into bilateral alliance with all the East European states except Albania, Romania, and Yugoslavia. It will be of interest to note whether similar Romanian agreements, due to expire in January and February 1968, will be renewed.

The other conference took place on June 9 in Moscow and was attended by all East European communist party chiefs except the Albanian leader. Even the Yugoslavs were represented, by Tito and the head of the international workers' movement commission, Vladimir Popovič. All except the Romanians signed a party-government declaration attacking Israeli "aggression," which was represented as a plot by "imperialist forces, and first of all the United States, against the Arab states." (Text in *Krasnaya zvezda,* June 11.) The signatories subsequently broke off diplomatic relations with Israel. At a secret two-day meeting at Budapest July 11-12, bloc leaders pledged long-term economic assistance to the Arab countries, especially to Egypt. Romania apparently had not been invited to attend this conference.

In conclusion, the traditional role played by the communist parties, both as policy makers and as executors of their own decisions, may come to be modified—but only gradually—under the impetus of changing conditions. In many of the East European countries it is the old, hard-core apparatus workers who block initiative. They lack education, compared with the young technical intelligentsia, and they resent any change, be it economic or political. As mentioned already, Yugoslavia appears to be taking the lead by modifying in principle the role of the party to one of limited supervision. Practice is another matter, of course.

Whether this example is followed in other bloc countries will depend to a great extent upon developments within the U.S.S.R. and upon the degree of influence exercised by the U.S.S.R. over each of the East European states. The current Soviet leadership will not consider any meaningful evolution of its political system. It did suggest at the recent twenty-third party congress that the Supreme Soviet should be given more authority, and this has been emulated in other bloc parliaments. The latter have gone beyond the U.S.S.R. example by allowing a limited choice in elections.

Regardless of the signs indicating certain evolutionary tendencies, it can be predicted with some assurance that most of the contemporary East European leaders feel insecure and will not allow their communist parties to become merely ideological guides and abdicate rule by fiat. The authoritative attitude remains that as society becomes more complex, the party must increase its role. As long as democratic centralism and "scientific" infallibility are considered dogma, there can be little hope for true freedom in Eastern Europe.

BIBLIOGRAPHY

BOOKS AND PAMPHLETS

Agerpres communiqué. *Statement on the Stand of the Rumanian Workers' Party*. Bucharest: Rumanian News Agency, 1964. 51 pp.

[Albania]. *Vjetari Statistikor i Republika Popullore e Shqipërisë 1965*. Tirana: Drejtoria e Statistikes, 1965. 487 pp.

————. *Twenty Years of Socialism in Albania*. Tirana: The "Naim Frashëri" State Publishing House, 1964. 127 pp.

Albanien und Seine "Protektoren." Munich: Presseausschnitte und Radioberichte aus den Osteuropaeischen Laendern, August 1966. 22 pp.

Althammer, Walter (ed.). *Deutsch-Südosteuropäische Wirtschaftsprobleme*. Munich: Südosteuropa Verlagsgesellschaft m.b.H., 1966. 113 pp., 25 tables.

Aperyan, V. *Narodnaya Respublika Bolgariya*. Moscow: Izdatelstvo Instituta Mezhdunarodnykh Otnoshenii, 1963. 86 pp.

Back, Harry, Cirullies, Horst, and Marquard, Günter. *POLEC: Dictionary of Politics and Economics*. West Berlin: Walter de Gruyter and Company, 1964. 961 pp.

Bader, W. *Un Ejército para la Guerra Civil: Los Grupos de Combate del Partido Comunista en la Alemania Oriental*. Mexico City: Impresiones Modernas, S.A., 1964. 128 pp.

Balloukou, Beqir. *Discours Prononcé a la Réunion Solennelle Consacrée au 20ᵉ Anniversaire de la Fondation de l'Armée Populaire*. Tirana: Entreprise d'Editions de l'Etat "Naim Frashëri," 1963. 52 pp.

Banovič, Ranko. *Posleratni razvoj privrede u Albaniji*. Belgrade: Institut za Medunarodnu Politiku i Privredu, 1959. 98 pp. Mimeographed.

Barabashev, Georgi Vasilevich. *Gosudarstvennyi stroi Vengerskoi Narodnoi Respubliki*. Moscow: Gosyurizdat, 1961. 94 pp.

Barits, Iosef I. *Voennaya kharakteristika sovetskikh satellitov.* New York, 1966. No pagination. Mimeographed.

Basiński, Euzebiusz. *Bastion pokoju między Odrą i Łabą: powstanie i rozwój NRD.* Warsaw: Ludowa Spółdzielnia Wydawnicza, 1963. 346 pp.

Bass, Robert, and Marbury, Elizabeth (eds.). *The Soviet-Yugoslav Controversy, 1948-1958: A Documentary Record.* New York: Prospect Books, 1959. 225 pp.

Beneš, Edward. *Memoirs of Dr. Edward Beneš.* Translated by Godfrey Lias. London: George Allen and Unwin, Ltd., 1954. 364 pp.

Beneš, Vaclav, Byrnes, Robert F., and Spulber, Nicolas. *The Second Soviet-Yugoslav Dispute: Full Text of Main Documents, April-June, 1958.* Bloomington, Ind.: Indiana University Publications, 1959. 272 pp.

Bidinskaya, L. (ed.). *Istoriya Bolgarskoi Kommunisticheskoi Partii.* Moscow: Gospolitizdat, 1960. 392 pp. Translated into Russian from Bulgarian.

Boettcher, Erik (ed.). *Ostblock, EWG und Entwicklungsländer.* Stuttgart: W. Kohlhammer Verlag, 1963. 173 pp.

Bošković, Mirko. *Društveno-politički sistem Jugoslavije.* Zagreb: Naprijed, 1963. 365 pp.

Braham, Randolph L. *Education in the Rumanian People's Republic.* Washington, D.C.: U.S. Department of Health, Education and Welfare, 1963. 229 pp.

Brzezinski, Zbigniew K. *The Soviet Bloc.* Cambridge, Mass.: Harvard University Press, 1960; rev. ed., New York: Praeger, 1961. 467 pp.

[Bulgaria]. Central Board of Statistics. *Statistical Manual of the People's Republic of Bulgaria 1964.* Sofia: Foreign Languages Press, 1965. 168 pp.

⸻. *Constitution of the People's Republic of Bulgaria.* Sofia: Foreign Languages Press, 1964. 33 pp.

⸻, *Statistichesky Godishnik na Narodna Republika Bulgariya 1965.* Sofia: Tsentralno Statistichesko Upravlenie, 1965. 558 pp.

Bulgarian Communist Party. *Directives of the Eighth Congress of the Bulgarian Communist Party for the Development of the People's Republic of Bulgaria in the Period of 1961-1980.* Sofia: Foreign Languages Press, 1963. 72 pp.

―――. *VIII Zjazd Bułgarskiej Partii Komunistycznej.* Warsaw: Kriążka i Wiedza, 1963. 295 pp. Translated into Polish from Bulgarian.

―――. *Osmi Kongres na Bulgarskata Komunisticheska Partiya (5–14 Noemuri 1962); stenografski protokol.* Sofia: Izdatelstvo na BKP, 1963. 1,064 pp.

―――. *Ustav (s nyakoi izmeneniya vneseni ot VII Kongres na Partiyata).* Sofia: Izdatelstvo na BKP, 1962. 63 pp.

Byrnes, Robert F. (ed.). *Yugoslavia.* New York: Praeger, 1957. 488 pp.

Bystrzhina, Ivan. *Narodnaya demokratiya v Chekhoslovakii.* Moscow: Gosudarstvennoe Izdatelstvo Yuridicheskoi Literatury, 1961. 265 pp. Translated into Russian from the Czech, *Lidová Demokracie.*

Černy, Jan, and Cervenka, Václav (comps.). *Státní občanství ČSSR.* Prague: Orbis, 1963. 196 pp.

Chalupa, V. *The National Front in Czechoslovakia.* Chicago: Czechoslovak Foreign Institute in Exile, 1958. 70 pp. Mimeographed.

Chistyakov, Mikhail Aleksandrovich. *Chekhoslovatskaya Sotsialisticheskaya Respublika: Ekonomika i vneshnyaya torgovlya.* Moscow: Vneshtorgizdat, 1964. 194 pp.

Chung Il Yung. *Legal Problems Involved in the Corfu Channel Incident.* Geneva: E. Droz, 1959. 287 pp.

Ciamaga, Lucjan. *Od współpracy do integracji: zarys organizacji działalności RWPG w latach 1949-1964.* Warsaw: Książka i Wiedza, 1965. 250 pp.

Čolaković, Rodoljub (ed.). *Pregled istorije Saveza Komunista Jugoslavije.* Belgrade: Institut za Izučavanje Radničkog Pokreta, 1963. 571 pp.

Cretzianu, Alexandre (ed.). *Captive Rumania: A Decade of Soviet Rule.* New York: Praeger, 1956. 424 pp.

Czechoslovak Communist Party. *XII. Sjazd Komunistickej Strany Československa.* Bratislava: Vydal Ústredný Výbor KSČ, 1962. 151 pp.

[Czechoslovakia]. *The Constitution of the Czechoslovak Socialist Repub-lic*. Prague: Orbis, 1964. 70 pp.

————. *Czechoslovak Statistical Abstract 1963*. Prague: Orbis, 1963. 167 pp.

————. *Statistická Ročenka ČSSR 1965*. Prague: Státní Nakladatelství Technicke Literatury, 1965. 612 pp.

Dedijer, Vladimir. *Jugoslovensko-Albanski odnoši, 1939-1948*. Belgrade: Borba, 1949. 227 pp.

Delaney, Robert F. (ed.). *This Is Communist Hungary*. Chicago: Henry Regnery Co., 1958. 260 pp.

Dellin, L. A. D. (ed.). *Bulgaria*. New York: Praeger, 1957. 457 pp.

Dilo, Jani I. *The Communist Party Leadership in Albania*. Washington, D.C.: Institute of Ethnic Studies at Georgetown University, 1961. 20 pp.

Djilas, Milovan. *Conversations with Stalin*. Translated by M. B. Petro-vich. New York: Harcourt, Brace and World, Inc., 1962. 211 pp.

Djordjević, Jovan. *Novi ustavni sistem*. Belgrade: Savremena Adminis-tracija, 1964. 1,046 pp.

Doernberg, Stefan. *Kurze Geschichte der DDR*. East Berlin: Dietz Ver-lag, 1964. 558 pp.

Domes, Alfred (ed.). *Die Politik des Westens und Osteuropa*. Cologne: Verlag Wissenschaft und Politik, 1966. 238 pp.

Drachkovitch, Milorad M. *United States Aid to Yugoslavia and Poland: Analysis of a Controversy*. Washington, D.C.: American Enterprise Institute for Public Policy Research, 1963. 124 pp.

Durdenevskii, V. N. (ed.). *Konstitutsii evropeiskikh stran narodnoi demo-kratii*. Moscow: Gosudarstvennoe Izdatelstvo Yuridicheskoi Litera-tury, 1954. 183 pp.

————. *Konstitutsii zarubezhnykh sotsialisticheskikh gosudarstv*. Mos-cow: Gosudarstvennoe Izdatelstvo Yuridicheskoi Literatury, 1956. 460 pp.

Durović, Dragoljub (ed.). *Narodna vlast i socijalistička demokratija, 1943-1963*. Belgrade: Novinsko Izdavačko Preduzeči "Mladost," 1964. 212 pp.

Dužević, Stipe (ed.). *VI Plenum Centralnog Komiteta Saveza Komunista Jugoslavije*. Belgrade: Edition "Komunist," 1964. 89 pp.

[East Germany]. Deutsches Institut für Zeitgeschichte. *Handbuch der Deutschen Demokratischen Republik*. East Berlin: Staatsverlag der DDR, 1964. 910 pp.

――――. *Statistisches Jahrbuch der Deutschen Demokratischen Republik*. Volume XI. East Berlin: Staatliche Zentralverwaltung für Statistik, 1966. 608 + 88 pp.

Egorov, Yu. (ed.). *Kadar, Yanosh; Izbrannye statii i rechi (1957-1960 gody)*. Moscow: Gosudarstvennoe Izdatelstvo Politicheskoi Literatury, 1960. 643 pp.

Ehrlich, Stanisław (ed.). *Social and Political Transformations in Poland*. Warsaw: PWN–Polish Scientific Publishers, 1964. 329 pp.

Epifanov, M. P. (ed.). *15 let svobodnoi Chekhoslovakii*. Moscow: Izdatelstvo IMO, 1960. 191 pp.

Evans, Stanley George. *A Short History of Bulgaria*. London: Lawrence and Wishart, 1960. 254 pp.

Faddeev, Nikolai Vasilevich. *Sovet Ekonomicheskoi Vzaimopomoshchi*. Moscow: Izdatelstvo "Ekonomika," 1964. 168 pp.

First National City Bank of New York. *Yugoslavia: Rocky Road to a Freer Economy*. New York, 1966. 16 pp.

Fischer-Galaţi, Stephen (ed.). *Romania*. New York: Praeger, 1957. 399 pp.

――――. *Eastern Europe in the Sixties*. New York: Praeger, 1963. 239 pp.

Free Europe Committee, Inc. *A Chronology of Events in Albania, 1944-1952*. New York: Free Europe Press, 1955. 150 pp. Mimeographed.

――――. *Communist Party Leaders from Eastern Europe*. New York: [Free Europe Press], September 1960. 16 pp. Mimeographed.

Frenzel, R. (comp.). *Die sozialistische Schule: Eine Zusammenstellung der wichtigsten gesetzlichen Bestimmungen und Dokumente*. East Berlin: VEB Deutscher Zentralverlag, 1960. 494 pp.

Gábor, Robert. *Organization and Strategy of the Hungarian Workers' (Communist) Party*. New York: National Committee for a Free Europe, 1952. 84 pp.

Galiński, Tadeusz (ed.). *Rocznik polityczny i gospodarczy 1963*. Warsaw: Państwowe Wydawnictwo Ekonomiczne, 1963. 735 pp.

――――. *Rocznik polityczny i gospodarczy 1964*. Warsaw: Państwowe Wydawnictwo Ekonomiczne, 1964. 782 pp.

Gegaj, Athanas, and Krasniqi, Rexhep. *Albania*. New York: Assembly of Captive European Nations, 1964. 48 pp.

Gelfer, M. A. (ed.). *Narodnaya Respublika Albaniya*. Moscow: Gosudarstvennoe Izdatelstvo Yuridicheskoi Literatury, 1961. 159 pp.

――――. *Narodnaya Respublika Bolgariya*. Moscow: Gosudarstvennoe Izdatelstvo Yuridicheskoi Literatury, 1961. 192 pp.

――――. *Rumynskaya Narodnaya Respublika; ugolovnyi kodeks 1962*. Moscow: Gosudarstvennoe Izdatelstvo Yuridicheskoi Literatury, 1962. 345 pp.

Gomułka-Wiesław, Władysław. *Ku nowej Polsce*. Katowice: Wydawnictwo "Literatura Polska," 1945. 109 pp.

――――. *Przemówienia: pazdziernik 1956–wrzesień 1957*. Warsaw: Książka i Wiedza, 1957. 481 pp.

Gotsche, Otto. *Wahlen in der DDR: Ausdruck echter Selbstbestimmung des Volkes*. East Berlin: Schriftenreihe des Staatsrates der DDR, 1963. 59 pp.

Gruchman, Bohdan, and Wiewióra, Bolesław (eds.). *Niemiecka Republika Demokratyczna*. Poznań: Instytut Zachodni, 1963. 449 pp.

Grzybowski, Kazimierz. *The Socialist Commonwealth of Nations*. New Haven: Yale University Press, 1964. 300 pp.

Gutt, Józef (ed.). *Polska Ludowa; słownik encyklopedyczny*. Warsaw: Wiedza Powszechna, 1965. 483 pp.

Gyorgy, Andrew (ed.). *Issues of World Communism*. Princeton, N.J.: D. Van Nostrand Co., Inc., 1966. 264 pp.

Hacker, Jens and Alexander Uschakow. *Die Integration Osteuropas, 1961 bis 1965*. Cologne: Verlag Wissenschaft und Politik, 1966. 328 pp.

Halasz, Nicholas. *In the Shadow of Russia*. New York: Ronald Press, 1959. 390 pp.

Hamel, Hannelore. *Das Sowjetische Herrschaftsprinzip des demokratischen Zentralismus in der Wirtschaftsordnung Mitteldeutschlands.* West Berlin: Duncker & Humblot, 1966. 210 pp.

Hamm, Harry. *Albania: China's Beachhead in Europe.* London: Weidenfeld and Nicolson, 1963. 176 pp.

Harvey, Mose L. *East-West Trade and United States Policy.* New York: National Association of Manufacturers, 1966. 175 pp.

Hegar, Milan (comp.). *Usnesení a dokumenty ÚV KSČ.* 2 vols. Prague: Nakladatelství Politické Literatury, 1962.

Heidenheimer, Arnold J. *The Governments of Germany.* 2d ed. New York: Thomas Y. Crowell Co., 1966. 254 pp.

Helmreich, Ernst C. (ed.). *Hungary.* New York: Praeger, 1957. 466 pp.

Herrmann, Friedrich-Georg. *Der Kampf gegen Religion und Kirche in der Sowjetischen Besatzungszone Deutschlands.* Stuttgart: Quell-Verlag, 1966. 142 pp.

Hindrichs, Armin. *Die Bürgerkriegsarmee: Die militanten Kampfgruppen des deutschen Kommunismus.* 2d ed. West Berlin: Arani Verlags-GmbH, 1964. 174 pp.

Hubeni, Marijan *et al.* (eds.). *Atlas svetskih zbivanja.* Belgrade: "Sedma Sila," 1964. 211 pp.

[Hungary]. *Civil Code of the Hungarian People's Republic.* Translated by Pál Lamberg. Budapest: University Printing House, 1960. 200 pp.

————. *Statistical Pocket Book of Hungary.* Budapest: Publishing House for Economics and Law, 1965. 197 pp.

————. *Statisztikai Évkönyv 1965.* Budapest: Központi Statisztikai Hivatel, 1965. 363 pp.

Ilinskii, Igor Pavlovich, and Strashun, Boris Aleksandrovich. *Germanskaya Demokraticheskaya Respublika: gosudarstvennyi stroi.* Moscow: Izdatelstvo IMO, 1961. 205 pp.

Institute for Strategic Studies. *The Military Balance 1966-1967.* London: September 1966. 50 pp.

Janicki, Lech. *Ustrój polityczny Niemieckiej Republiki Demokratycznej.* Poznań: Instytut Zachodni, 1964. 361 pp.

Janković, Slavko (ed.). *Ko je ko u Jugoslaviji (Biografski podaći o Jugoslavenskim savremenicima)*. Belgrade: Izdanje Sedme Sile, 1957. 810 pp.

Kadar, Yanosh [János]. *Otchëtnyi doklad Tsentralnogo Komiteta Vengerskoi Sotsialisticheskoi Rabochei Partii na VIII sezdu Partii*. Moscow: Gospolitizdat, 1964. 78 pp. Translated into Russian from Hungarian.

Kapsa, Lothar (comp.). *Zusammenstellung der von der DDR seit deren Gründung abgeschlossenen internationalen Verträge und Vereinbarungen*. 4th ed. Bonn: Archiv für gesamtdeutsche Fragen, 1965. 221 pp.

Karłowicz, Edward. *Wolność przyszła z gór*. Warsaw: Wydawnictwo Ministerstwa Obrony Narodowej, 1956. 181 pp.

Kaser, Michael. *Comecon: Integration Problems of the Planned Economies*. London: Oxford University Press, 1965. 215 pp.

Kazantsev, N. D. (ed.). *Agrarnoe zakonodatelstvo zarubezhnykh sotsialisticheskikh stran*. Moscow: Gosudarstvennoe Izdatelstvo Yuridicheskoi Literatury, 1958. 238 pp.

―――――. *Osnovnye zakonodatelnye akty po agrarnym preobrazovaniyam v zarubezhnykh sotsialisticheskikh stranakh*. 4th ed. Moscow: Gosudarstvennoe Izdatelstvo Yuridicheskoi Literatury, 1958. 239 pp.

Kertesz, Stephen P. (ed.). *The Fate of East Central Europe*. Notre Dame, Ind.: University of Notre Dame Press, 1956. 463 pp.

Khadzhinikolov, Veselin (ed.). *Materiali po osnovi na nauchniya ateizm*. Sofia: BKP Izdatelstvo, 1965. 374 pp.

Klimek, Jan (ed.). *Kalendarz robotniczy 1965*. Warsaw: Książka i Wiedza, December 1964. 479 pp.

Korbel, Josef. *The Communist Subversion of Czechoslovakia: 1938-1948*. Princeton, N.J.: Princeton University Press, 1959. 258 pp.

―――――. *Tito's Communism*. Denver: University of Denver Press, 1951. 368 pp.

Kostov, Pavel, Trifonova, Minka, and Dimitrov, Mircho St. (eds.). *Materiali po istoriya na Bulgarskata Komunisticheska Partiya (1944-1960 g.)*. Sofia: Izdatelstvo na Bulgarskata Komunisticheska Partiya, 1961. 195 pp.

Kovács, Imre (ed.). *Facts About Hungary: The Fight for Freedom.* New York: The Hungarian Committee, October 1966. 382 pp.

Krannhals, Hanns von. *Der Warschauer Aufstand 1944.* Frankfort on the Main: Bernard & Graefe Verlag für Wehrwesen, 1962. 445 pp.

Krasnoglazov, Boris Petrovich. *Ekonomicheskoe sotrudnichestvo GDR s sotsialisticheskimi stranami.* Moscow: Ekonomika, 1965. 135 pp.

Krechler, Vladimír (ed.). *Příruční slovník k dějinám KSČ.* 2 vols. Prague: Nakladatelství Politické Literatury, 1964. 598 & 1,050 pp.

Kuczyński, Józef. *Podstawy światopoglądowe chłopów.* Warsaw: Wiedza Powszechna, 1961. 183 pp.

Kuhn, Heinrich. *Der Kommunismus in der Tschechoslowakei.* Cologne: Verlag Wissenschaft und Politik, 1965. 304 pp.

Kulyshev, Yu. (ed.). *III Sezd Rumynskoi Rabochei Partii.* Moscow: Gosudarstvennoe Izdatelstvo Politicheskoi Literatury, 1961. 240 pp.

Kurpits, N. Ya (ed.). *Konstitutsiya i osnovnye zakonodatelnye akty Narodnoi Respubliki Albanii.* Moscow: Izdatelstvo Inostrannoi Literatury, 1951. 291 pp.

Kušej, Gorazd. *Politični sistem Jugoslavije: idejne i organizacijske osnove političnega sistema SFRJ.* 2d ed. Ljubljana: Knižnica "Delavska Univerza," 1964. 129 pp.

Kutt, Alexander. *East-West Trade and Industrial Trends in the Soviet Area.* New York: Assembly of Captive European Nations, August 1965. 26 pp.

————. *Prices and Balance Sheet in 10 Years of Soviet-Captive Countries Trade.* New York: Assembly of Captive European Nations, March 1966. 27 pp.

Lawson, Ruth C. (ed.). *International Regional Organizations.* New York: Praeger, 1962. 387 pp.

Lazarov, Kiril. *Ekonomicheskoe razvitie Narodnoi Respubliki Bolgarii.* Moscow: Izdatelstvo Inostrannoi Literatury, 1963. 279 pp. Translated into Russian from Bulgarian.

League of Communists of Yugoslavia. *Yugoslavia's Way: The Program of the League of the Communists of Yugoslavia.* Translated by Stoyan Pribechevich. New York: All Nations Press, 1958. 263 pp.

League of Communists of Yugoslavia. *Osmi Kongres SKJ: 7-13 Decembra 1964.* Belgrade: Kultura, 1964. 286 pp.

Lebedev, M. P. (comp.). *Chekhoslovatskaya Sotsialisticheskaya Respublika: konstitutsiya i zakonodatelnye akty.* Moscow: Izdatelstvo IMO, 1962. 404 pp.

Leimbach, Werner (comp.). *Der Parteiapparat der SBZ.* Bonn: Archiv für gesamtdeutsche Fragen, 1966. 44 pp.

Leonhard, Wolfgang. *Child of the Revolution.* Chicago: Henry Regnery Co., 1958. 447 pp. Translated by C. M. Woodhouse from the German, *Die Revolution entlässt ihre Kinder* (1955).

Le Procès de Espions Parachutés en Albanie. Preface by Georges Fournial. Paris: Éditions Sociales, 1950. 201 pp.

Liess, Otto Rudolf. *Rumänien zwischen Ost und West.* Hannover: Niedersächsische Landeszentrale für Politische Bildung, 1965. 73 pp.

Ludat, Herbert (ed.). *Jugoslawien zwischen West und Ost: Probleme seiner Geschichte, Wirtschaft und Politik.* 2d ed. Giessen: Wilhelm Schmitz Verlag, 1963. 173 pp.

Ludz, Peter Christian. *Studien und Materialien zur Soziologie der DDR.* Cologne: Westdeutscher Verlag, 1964. 540 pp.

Lukovets, A. (ed.). *Narodnaya Rumyniya segodnya, 1944-1964.* Moscow: Izdatelstvo "Pravda," 1964. 231 pp.

Maiorov, Semyon M. (ed.). *Vneshnyaya politika Sovetskogo Soyuza v period Otechestvennoi Voiny.* 6 vols. Moscow: Gosudarstvennoe Izdatelstvo Politicheskoi Literatury, 1947-1950.

Mampel, Siegfried. *Die volksdemokratische Ordnung im Mitteldeutschland: Text zur verfassungsrechtlichen Situation mit einer Einleitung.* Frankfort on the Main, A. Metzner, 1963. 155 pp.

Markert, Werner (ed.). *Osteuropa-Handbuch: Polen.* Cologne: Böhlau Verlag, 1959. 829 pp.

Meissner, Boris (ed.). *Der Warschauer Pakt: Dokumentensammlung.* Cologne: Verlag Wissenschaft und Politik, 1962. 204 pp.

Międzyrzecka, Ernestyna, and Klimek, Jan (eds.). *Kalendarz robotniczy 1964.* Warsaw: Książka i Wiedza, December 1963. 511 pp.

Mikołajczyk, Stanisław. *The Rape of Poland: Pattern of Soviet Aggression.* New York: McGraw-Hill, 1948. 309 pp.

Mineev, Pëtr Danilovich, and Tokarev, Viktor Andreevich. *Yugoslaviya.* Moscow: Izdatelstvo "Znanie," 1963. 48 pp.

Mitskevich, Aleksei Valentinovich. *Gosudarstvennyi stroi Rumynskoi Narodnoi Respubliki.* Moscow: Gosudarstvennoe Izdatelstvo Yuridicheskoi Literatury, 1957. 94 pp.

Monat, Paweł, with John Dille. *Spy in the U.S.* New York: Harper and Row, 1962. 208 pp.

Morozov, Vasilii Ivanovich. *Sovet Ekonomicheskoi Vzaimopomoshchi; soyuz ravnykh.* Moscow: Izdatelstvo "Mezhdunarodnye Otnosheniya," 1964. 128 pp.

Nemesh, Dezhe [Nemes, Dezsö]. *Vengriya; 1945-1961.* Moscow: Gosudarstvennoe Izdatelstvo Politicheskoi Literatury, 1962. 87 pp. Translated into Russian from Hungarian.

Nezhinskii, L. N. (ed.). *Revolyutsionnoe dvizhenie i stroitelstvo sotsializma v Vengrii (sbornik statei).* Moscow: Izdatelstvo Akademii Nauk SSSR, 1963. 276 pp.

Nollau, Günther. *Die Internationale: Wurzeln und Erscheinungsformen des proletarischen Internationalismus.* Cologne: Verlag für Wirtschaft und Politik, 1959. 344 pp.

Oleinik, Ivan Prokofevich. *Pobeda sotsializma v Rumynii.* Moscow: Izdatelstvo Ekonomicheskoi Literatury, 1962. 216 pp.

Orlik, Igor Ivanovich. *Vengerskaya Narodnaya Respublika: vneshnyaya politika i mezhdunarodnye otnosheniya.* Moscow: Izdatelstvo IMO, 1962. 87 pp.

Oshavkov, Zhivko *et al.* (eds.). *Izgrazhdane i razvitie na sotsialisticheskoto obshchestvo v Bulgariya.* Sofia: Izdatelstvo na Bulgarskata Akademiya na Naukite, 1962. 488 pp.

Paloczi-Horvath, György. *The Undefeated.* Boston: Little, Brown and Co., 1959. 305 pp.

Papajorgji, Harilla. *The Development of Socialist Industry and Its Prospects in the People's Republic of Albania.* Tirana, 1964. 147 pp.

Peaslee, Amos J. (ed.). *Constitutions of Nations.* 2 vols. Concord, N.H.: The Rumford Press, 1950.

―――. *Constitutions of Nations.* 3 vols. 2d ed. The Hague: Martinus Nijhoff, 1956.

Penkovskiy, Oleg. *The Penkovskiy Papers*. New York: Doubleday and Co., 1965. 411 pp.

Plischke, Elmer. *Contemporary Government of Germany*. Boston: Houghton Mifflin Co., 1961. 248 pp.

[Poland]. *Mały rocznik statystyczny 1966*. Warsaw: Nakładem Głównego Urzędu Statystycznego, 1966. 334 pp.

————. *Rocznik statystyczny 1965*. Warsaw: Nakładem Głównego Urzędu Statystycznego, 1965. 656 pp.

————. *Wielka encyklopedia powszechna*. 6 vols. Warsaw: Państwowe Wydawnictwo Naukowe, 1964.

Polish Communist Party. *See* Polish United Workers' Party.

Polish United Workers' Party. *III Zjazd PZPR*. Warsaw: Książka i Wiedza, 1959. 730 pp.

————. *IV Zjazd PZPR*. Warsaw: Książka i Wiedza, 1964. 382 pp.

Portal, Roger. *Les Slaves: Peuples et Nations*. Paris: Armand Colin, 1965. 519 pp.

Radio Free Europe. *Colonel Tykociński's Revelations*. Munich, 1966. 65 pp.

————. *Communist Party-Government Line-Up*. Munich, July 1967. 26 pp.

————. *Eastern Europe's Communist Leaders*. 5 vols. Munich, June-September 1966.

Reale, Eugenio. *Nascita del Cominform*. Rome: Arnoldo Mondadori Editore, 1958. 175 pp.

Reiman, Pavel (ed.). *Dějiny Komunistické Strany Československa*. Prague: Státní Nakladatelstvi Politické Literatury, 1961. 710 pp.

Reisky de Dubnic, Vladimir. *Communist Propaganda Methods: A Case Study on Czechoslovakia*. New York: Praeger, 1960. 287 pp.

Richert, Ernst. *Das zweite Deutschland: Ein Staat, der nicht sein darf*. Gütersloh: Sigbert Mohn Verlag, 1964. 341 pp.

Ripka, Hubert. *Eastern Europe in the Post-War World*. New York: Praeger, 1961. 266 pp.

[Romania]. *Constitution of the Socialist Republic of Rumania.* Bucharest: Meridiane Publishing House, 1965. 35 pp.

——. *Rumanian Statistical Pocket Book 1965.* Bucharest: Central Statistical Board, 1965. 294 pp.

——. *Statistical Pocket Book of the Socialist Republic of Romania 1966.* Bucharest: Central Statistical Board, 1966. 316 pp.

Saikowski, Charlotte, and Gruliow, Leo (eds.). *Current Soviet Policies IV: The Documentary Record of the 22nd Congress of the Communist Party of the Soviet Union.* New York: Columbia University Press, 1962. 248 pp.

Schechtman, Joseph B. *Postwar Population Transfers in Europe, 1945-1955.* Philadelphia: University of Pennsylvania Press, 1962. 417 pp.

Sergeev, Sergei Dmitrievich, and Dobrokhotov, Andrei Fedorovich. *Narodnaya Respublika Bolgariya: ekonomika i vneshnyaya torgovlya.* Moscow: Vneshtorgizdat, 1962. 272 pp.

Seton-Watson, Hugh. *The East European Revolution.* New York: Praeger, 1956. 406 pp.

Shedivyi, Yaroslav, and Korzhalkova, Kveta. *Vneshnyaya politika Chekhoslovatskoi sotsialisticheskoi Respubliki v 1945-1960 gg.* Moscow: Izdatelstvo Sotsialno-Ekonomicheskoi Literatury, 1960. 171 pp. Translated into Russian from Czech, *Zahranični politika ČSSR v letech 1945-1960.*

Siegert, Heinz. *Bulgarien Heute: Rotes Land am Schwarzen Meer.* Vienna: Econ-Verlag, 1964. 269 pp.

Silagi, Denis. *Ungarn.* Hannover: Verlag für Literatur und Zeitgeschichte GmbH, 1964. 149 pp.

Silin, Mikhail Aleksandrovich. *Chekhoslovatskaya Sotsialisticheskaya Respublika: perekhodnyi period i zavershenie stroitelstva sotsializma, 1945-1961 gg.* Moscow: Izdatelstvo IMO, 1963. 267 pp.

Skendi, Stavro (ed.). *Albania.* New York: Praeger, 1956. 389 pp.

Smirnova, N. D. *Obrazovanie Narodnoi Respubliki Albanii.* Moscow: Izdatelstvo Akademii Nauk SSSR, 1960. 195 pp.

Solberg, Richard W. *God and Caesar in East Germany: The Conflicts of Church and State in East Germany Since 1945.* New York: Macmillan, 1961. 294 pp.

Spasov, Boris, and Angelov, A. *Gosudarstvennoe pravo Narodnoi Respubliki Bolgarii.* Moscow: Izdatelstvo Inostrannoi Literatury, 1962. 607 pp.

Staar, Richard F. *Poland, 1944-1962: The Sovietization of a Captive People.* Baton Rouge: Louisiana State University Press, 1962. 318 pp.

Stehle, Hansjakob. *Nachbar Polen.* Frankfort on the Main: S. Fischer Verlag, 1963. 416 pp.

Strużek, Bolesław. *Rolnictwo europejskich krajów socjalistycznych.* Warsaw: Państwowe Wydawnictwo Rolnicze i Leśne, 1963. 267 pp.

Świątkowski, Henryk (ed.). *Stosunek państwa do kościoła w różnych krajach.* Warsaw: Książka i Wiedza, 1952. 177 pp.

Szyr, Eugeniusz (chief ed.). *Twenty Years of the Polish People's Republic.* Warsaw: Państwowe Wydawnictwo Ekonomiczne, 1964. 319 pp.

Taborsky, Edward. *Communism in Czechoslovakia, 1948-1960.* Princeton, N.J.: Princeton University Press, 1961. 628 pp.

Tang, Peter S. H. *The Twenty-second Congress of the Communist Party of the Soviet Union and Moscow-Tirana-Peking Relations.* Washington, D.C.: Research Institute on the Sino-Soviet Bloc, 1962. 141 pp.

Thalheim, Karl C. *Die Wirtschaft der Sowjetzone in Krise und Umbau.* West Berlin: Duncker & Humblot, 1964. 190 pp.

Thomas, Stephan (ed.). *Das Programm der SED.* Cologne: Verlag Wissenschaft und Politik, 1963. 160 pp.

Tito, Josip Broz. *Selected Speeches and Articles, 1941-1961.* Zagreb: Naprijed, 1963. 460 pp.

Tolkunov, Lev Nikolaevich (ed.). *Sotsialisticheskii lager; kratkii illyustrovannyi politiko-ekonomicheskii spravochnik.* Moscow: Gospolitizdat, 1962. 430 pp.

Tomasic, Dinko A. *The Communist Leadership and Nationalism in Czechoslovakia.* Washington, D.C.: Institute of Ethnic Studies at Georgetown University, 1960. 15 pp.

Triska, Jan F. (ed.). *Soviet Communism: Programs and Rules.* San Francisco: Chandler Publishing Co., 1962. 196 pp.

Tsvetkovski, Nikola D. (ed.). *Nakazatelen kodeks: tekst, literatura, sudebna praktika.* Sofia: Derzhavno Izdatelstvo "Nauka i Izkustvo," 1961. 732 pp.

Tyagunenko, L. V. *Development of the Albanian Economy.* Washington, D.C.: U.S. Joint Publications Research Service, 1961. 75 pp. Translation from Russian, *Razvitiye ekonomiki Narodnoi Respubliki Albanii* (1960).

U.S. Congress, House Committee on Foreign Affairs, 87th Cong., 2d sess. *Captive European Nations: Hearings.* Washington, D.C.: Government Printing Office, 1962. 377 pp.

————, House Committee on Un-American Activities, 87th Cong., 1st sess. *The New Role of National Legislative Bodies in the Communist Conspiracy.* Washington, D.C.: Government Printing Office, 1962. 47 pp.

————, ————, 89th Cong., 2d sess. *Testimony of Wladyslaw Tykocinski.* Washington, D.C., 1966. 52 pp.

————, ————. *Who Are They?* 9 parts. Washington, D.C., 1957-1958.

————. Joint Economic Committee, 89th Cong., 1st sess. *Current Economic Indicators for the USSR.* Washington, D.C.: Government Printing Office, 1965. 220 pp.

————, ————, 89th Cong., 2d sess. *New Directions in the Soviet Economy* (1966). Part II A, 337 pp.

————, Senate Committee on Foreign Relations, 81st Cong., 1st sess. *A Decade of American Foreign Policy.* Senate Document 123. Washington, D.C.: Government Printing Office, 1950. 1,381 pp.

————, Senate Committee on Government Operations, 89th Cong., 2d sess. *The Warsaw Pact: Its Role in Soviet Bloc Affairs.* Washington, D.C.: Government Printing Office, 1966. 49 pp.

————, Senate Committee on the Judiciary, 89th Cong., 2d sess. *A Study of the Anatomy of Communist Takeovers.* Washington, D.C.: Government Printing Office, 1966. 70 pp.

————, ————, ————. *A Study of the Communist Party and Coalition Governments in the Soviet Union and in Eastern European Countries.* Washington, D.C., 1966. 33 pp.

————, ————, ————. *Communist Exploitation of Religion.* Washington, D.C., 1966. 42 pp.

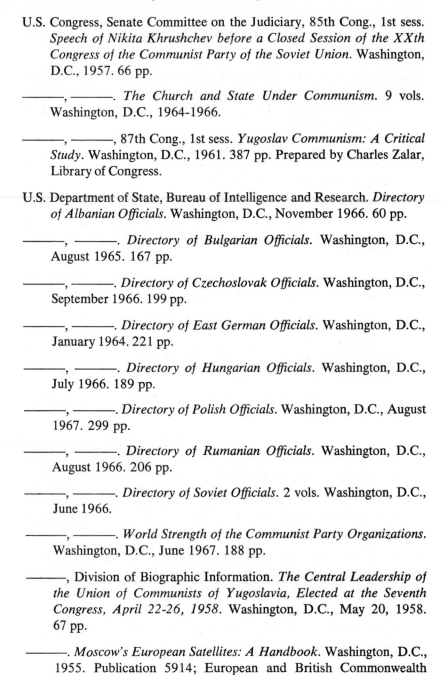

U.S. Congress, Senate Committee on the Judiciary, 85th Cong., 1st sess. *Speech of Nikita Khrushchev before a Closed Session of the XXth Congress of the Communist Party of the Soviet Union.* Washington, D.C., 1957. 66 pp.

————, ————. *The Church and State Under Communism.* 9 vols. Washington, D.C., 1964-1966.

————, ————, 87th Cong., 1st sess. *Yugoslav Communism: A Critical Study.* Washington, D.C., 1961. 387 pp. Prepared by Charles Zalar, Library of Congress.

U.S. Department of State, Bureau of Intelligence and Research. *Directory of Albanian Officials.* Washington, D.C., November 1966. 60 pp.

————, ————. *Directory of Bulgarian Officials.* Washington, D.C., August 1965. 167 pp.

————, ————. *Directory of Czechoslovak Officials.* Washington, D.C., September 1966. 199 pp.

————, ————. *Directory of East German Officials.* Washington, D.C., January 1964. 221 pp.

————, ————. *Directory of Hungarian Officials.* Washington, D.C., July 1966. 189 pp.

————, ————. *Directory of Polish Officials.* Washington, D.C., August 1967. 299 pp.

————, ————. *Directory of Rumanian Officials.* Washington, D.C., August 1966. 206 pp.

————, ————. *Directory of Soviet Officials.* 2 vols. Washington, D.C., June 1966.

————, ————. *World Strength of the Communist Party Organizations.* Washington, D.C., June 1967. 188 pp.

————, Division of Biographic Information. *The Central Leadership of the Union of Communists of Yugoslavia, Elected at the Seventh Congress, April 22-26, 1958.* Washington, D.C., May 20, 1958. 67 pp.

————. *Moscow's European Satellites: A Handbook.* Washington, D.C., 1955. Publication 5914; European and British Commonwealth Series 48. 52 pp.

U.S. Office of the High Commissioner for Germany. *Soviet Zone Constitution and Electoral Law*. Washington, D.C.: Government Printing Office, 1951. 107 pp.

Uschakow, Alexander. *Der Rat für gegenseitige Wirtschaftshilfe (COMECON)*. Cologne: Verlag Wissenschaft und Politik, 1962. 199 pp.

Usievich, Marina Aleksandrovna. *Razvitie sotsialisticheskoi ekonomiki Vengrii*. Moscow: Izdatelstvo Akademii Nauk SSSR, 1962. 216 pp.

Valev, E. B. *Albaniya*. Moscow: Gosudarstvennoe Izdatelstvo Geograficheskoi Literatury, 1960. 88 pp.

————. *Rumyniya: ekonomiko-geograficheskii ocherk*. Moscow: Gosudarstvennoe Izdatelstvo Geograficheskoi Literatury, 1963. 110 pp.

Váli, Ferenc A. *Rift and Revolt in Hungary: Nationalism versus Communism*. Cambridge, Mass.: Harvard University Press, 1961. 590 pp.

Vasilev, M. *Vneshnyaya politika Germanskoi Demokraticheskoi Respubliki*. Moscow: Izdatelstvo IMO, 1961. 88 pp.

Verbitskii, G. (ed.). *20 let SEPG: Dokumenty Sotsialisticheskoi edinoi partii Germanii*. Moscow: Izdatelstvo Politicheskoi Literatury, 1966. 291 pp.

Vesely, I. *Osnovanie Kommunisticheskoi Partii Chekhoslovakii*. Moscow: Izdatelstvo Inostrannoi Literatury, 1956. 234 pp.

Vinogradov, V. N. (ed.). *Istoriya Rumynii novogo i noveishego vremeni*. Moscow: Izdatelstvo "Nauka," 1964. 408 pp.

————. *Novaya i noveishaya istoriya Rumynii*. Moscow: Izdatelstvo Akademii Nauk SSSR, 1963. 288 pp.

Vodenicharov, Tinko (comp.). *Spravochnik na aktivista*. Sofia: Izdatelstvo na BKP, 1961. 1,052 pp.

Vvedenskii, B. A. (chief ed.). *Bolshaya sovetskaya entsiklopediya*. 51 vols. 2d ed. Moscow: Gosudarstvennoe Nauchnoe Izdatelstvo, 1949-1958.

Waterston, Albert. *Planning in Yugoslavia: Organization and Implementation*. Baltimore: The Johns Hopkins Press, 1962. 109 pp.

Weber, Hermann (ed.). *Der deutsche Kommunismus: Dokumente*. Cologne: Kiepenheuer & Witsch, 1963. 679 pp.

[West Germany]. Bundesministerium für gesamtdeutsche Fragen. *Der VI. Parteitag der SED vom 15. bis 21. Januar 1963: Kommentar, Materialien und Dokumente.* Bonn, 1964. 148 pp.

————, ————. *Schein und Wirklichkeit: Die Verfassung der "Deutschen Demokratischen Republik."* Bonn, 1964. 87 pp.

————, ————. *SBZ Biographie.* Bonn, 1964. 406 pp.

————, ————. *SBZ von 1945 bis 1954.* 3d ed. Bonn, 1961. 324 pp.

————, ————. *SBZ von 1955 bis 1958.* Bonn, 1961. 594 pp.

————, ————. *SBZ von 1959-1960.* Bonn, 1964. 317 pp.

————, ————. *SBZ von A bis Z.* 10th ed. Bonn, 1966. 605 pp.

Wiener, Friedrich. *Die Armeen der Warschauer-Pakt-Staaten.* Vienna: Verlag Carl Überreuter, 1965. 176 pp.

Wolfe, Thomas W. *The Evolving Nature of the Warsaw Pact.* Memorandum RM-4835-PR. Santa Monica, Calif.: The Rand Corporation, December 1965. 45 pp.

Yakimovich, Yadviga Vladimirovna. *Vengerskaya Narodnaya Respublika (gosudarstvennyi stroi).* Moscow: Izdatelstvo IMO, 1960. 169 pp.

Yugoslav Communist Party. *See* League of Communists of Yugoslavia.

[Yugoslavia]. *Savezna i Republičke Skupštine.* Belgrade: "Sedma Sila," 1964. 311 pp.

————. *Statistical Pocket-Book of Yugoslavia 1965.* Belgrade: Federal Institute of Statistics, March 1965. 255 pp.

————. *Statistički godišnjak SFRJ 1964.* Belgrade: Savezni zavod za Statistiku, 1964. 730 pp.

————. *Statistički godišnjak SFRJ 1965.* Belgrade: Savezni zavod za Statistiku, 1965. 730 pp.

Zhivkov, Todor. *Otchëtnyi doklad Tsentralnogo Komiteta Bolgarskoi Kommunisticheskoi Partii VIII Sezdu Partii.* Moscow: Gospolitizdat, 1963. 192 pp. Translated into Russian from Bulgarian.

Zinner, Paul E. *Communist Strategy and Tactics in Czechoslovakia.* New York: Praeger, 1962. 264 pp.

———. *Revolution in Hungary.* New York: Praeger, 1962. 380 pp.

Zolotarev, Vladimir Ivanovich. *Vneshnyaya torgovlya sotsialisticheskikh stran.* Moscow: Vneshtorgizdat, 1964. 390 pp.

PERIODICALS

ACEN News. Bimonthly. Assembly of Captive European Nations, New York.

ACEN Survey of Developments in the Captive Countries. Semiannual.

Allgemeine Schweizerische Militärzeitschrift. Monthly. Swiss Officers' Association, Aargau, Switzerland.

American Journal of Sociology. Bimonthly. Chicago.

Atlantic. Monthly. Boston.

British Survey. Monthly. British Society for International Understanding, London.

Bulgarian Press Survey. Irregular. Radio Free Europe, Munich.

Bulletin of the Institute for Study of the USSR. Monthly. Munich.

Bulletin of the International Commission of Jurists. Quarterly. Geneva.

Canadian Journal of Economics and Political Science. Quarterly. Canadian Political Science Association, Toronto.

Communist Affairs. Bimonthly. University of Southern California, Los Angeles.

Current History. Monthly. Philadelphia.

Czechoslovak Press Survey. Irregular. Radio Free Europe, Munich.

Deutsche Aussenpolitik. Monthly. Society for Dissemination of Scientific Knowledge, East Berlin.

Dziennik ustaw. Irregular. Polish People's Republic, Warsaw. Journal of laws.

East Europe. Monthly. Free Europe Committee, Inc., New York.

Economic Geography. Monthly. Concord, N.H.

Ekonomia popullare. Bimonthly. Tirana. Official organ.

Est & Ouest. Bimonthly. Association for Studies and International Political Information, Paris.

Foreign Affairs. Quarterly. New York.

Hungarian Press Survey. Irregular. Radio Free Europe, Munich.

International Affairs. Monthly. All-Union Society, "Knowledge," Moscow.

International Peasant Union Monthly Bulletin. New York.

Interpreter. Monthly. London.

Journal of Central European Affairs. Quarterly. University of Colorado, Boulder. Defunct since January 1964.

Journal of Politics. Quarterly. Southern Political Science Association, University of Florida, Gainesville.

Jugoslovenski pregled. Monthly. Belgrade. Official organ.

Komunist. Weekly. League of Communists of Yugoslavia, Belgrade.

Kommunist vooruzhënnykh sil. Bimonthly. Main Political Administration of the Soviet Army and Navy, Moscow.

Lupta de claša. Monthly. Bucharest. Theoretical organ of the Romanian Communist Party.

Military Review. Monthly. U.S. Command and Staff College, Fort Leavenworth, Kansas.

Norsk Militaert Tidsskrift. Monthly. Oslo.

Nova myśl. Monthly. Prague. Theoretical organ of the Czechoslovak Communist Party.

Novo vreme. Monthly. Sofia. Theoretical organ of the Bulgarian Communist Party.

Nowe drogi. Monthly. Warsaw. Theoretical organ of the Polish United Workers' Party.

Osteuropäische Rundschau. Monthly. Free Europe Committee, Inc., Munich.

Partelet. Monthly. Budapest. Organizational journal of the Hungarian Socialist Workers' Party.

Partiyen zhivot. Monthly. Sofia. Organizational journal of the Bulgarian Communist Party.

Polish Affairs. Monthly. Executive Committee, Polish Council of National Unity (in exile), London.

Polish Perspectives. Monthly. Warsaw. Official review.

Polish Press Survey. Irregular. Radio Free Europe, Munich.

Polish Review. Quarterly. The Polish Institute of Arts and Sciences in America, New York.

Public Opinion Quarterly. Princeton, N.J.

Revue de Défense Nationale. Monthly. Paris. Official.

Revue Militaire Générale. Monthly. Paris.

Rruga e partisë. Monthly. Tirana. Theoretical organ of the Albanian Workers' Party.

Rumanian Press Survey. Irregular. Radio Free Europe, Munich.

SBZ Archiv. Bimonthly. Publishing House for Politics and Economics, Cologne.

Situation Report. Irregular. Radio Free Europe, Research Departments, Munich.

Slavic Review. Quarterly. University of Illinois, Urbana.

Soldat und Technik. Monthly. Frankfort on the Main. Published in collaboration with the Defense Ministry, Federal Republic of Germany.

Soviet Life. Monthly. Moscow. Official U.S.S.R. organ, sold in the United States by reciprocal agreement.

Special Information Notes. Irregular. Washington, D.C.

Társadalme Szemle. Monthly. Budapest. Theoretical organ of the Hungarian Socialist Workers' Party.

U. S. News and World Report. Weekly. Washington, D.C.

Voprosi istorii KPSS. Monthly. Moscow. Official organ of the Institute for Marxism-Leninism at the Central Committee, CPSU.

Wehrkunde. Monthly. Association for Military Science, Munich.

Weltwirtschaftliches Archiv. Quarterly. Institute for Navigation and the World Economy, University of Kiel.

Wissenschaftlicher Dienst Südosteuropas. Monthly. South-East Institute, Munich.

World Marxist Review. Monthly. Toronto. North American edition of *Problems of Peace and Socialism (Problemy mira i sotsializma)*.

Život strany. Bimonthly. Prague. Organizational journal of the Czechoslovak Communist Party.

Życie i myśl. Bimonthly. Wrocław. Pro-regime Catholic organ.

NEWSPAPERS

Bashkimi. Daily. Democratic Front, Tirana.

Borba. Daily. League of Communists of Yugoslavia, Belgrade.

Chłopska droga. Biweekly. United Peasant Party, Warsaw.

Christian Science Monitor. Daily. Boston.

Cominform Journal. See *For a Lasting Peace, For a People's Democracy*.

Economist. Weekly. Air edition, London.

For a Lasting Peace, For a People's Democracy. Weekly. Communist Information Bureau, Belgrade (1947-1948), and subsequently Bucharest (1948-1956); defunct.

German Tribune. Weekly. Air edition, Hamburg. Translations from the West German press, made by *Die Welt* publishing house.

Hospodarske noviny. Weekly. Prague. Government organ on economics.

Izvestiya. Daily. Moscow. Official organ of the U.S.S.R. government.

Krasnaya zvezda. Daily. Moscow. U.S.S.R. Defense Ministry official organ.

Mladá fronta. Daily. Union of Czechoslovak Youth, Prague.

Mladost. Weekly. Union of Yugoslav Youth, Belgrade.

Népszabadság. Daily. Hungarian Socialist Workers' Party, Budapest.

Neue Zürcher Zeitung. Daily. Zurich.

Neues Deutschland. Daily. Socialist Unity Party, East Berlin.

New York Times. Daily. New York.

Obrana lidu. Daily. Defense Ministry of Czechoslovakia, Prague.

Otechestven zov. Weekly. Vratsa. Bulgarian Communist Party district organ.

Parlament. Weekly. Bonn. Federal Center for Service to the Country.

Politika. Daily. League of Communists of Yugoslavia, Belgrade.

Polityka. Weekly. Polish United Workers' Party, Warsaw.

Práce. Daily. Revolutionary Trade-Union Movement, Prague.

Pravda. Daily. Communist Party of Slovakia, Bratislava.

Pravda. Daily. Communist Party of the Soviet Union, Moscow.

Rabotnichesko delo. Daily. Bulgarian Communist Party, Sofia.

Renascita. Weekly. Italian Communist Party, Rome.

Rudé právo. Daily. Communist Party of Czechoslovakia, Prague.

Scînteia. Daily. Romanian Communist Party, Bucharest.

Smena. Daily. Slovak Central Committee of the Czechoslovak Youth Union, Bratislava.

Süddeutsche Zeitung. Daily. Munich.

Svobodné slovo. Daily. Czechoslovak Socialist Party, Prague.

Trybuna ludu. Daily. Polish United Workers' Party, Warsaw.

Vneshnyaya torgovlya. Weekly. U.S.S.R. Foreign Trade Ministry, Moscow.

Die Welt. Daily. Hamburg.

Die Zeit. Daily. Hamburg.

Zëri i popullit. Daily. Albanian Workers' Party, Tirana.

Życie gospodarcze. Daily. Warsaw. Government organ on economics.

Życie Warszawy. Daily. Warsaw. Official government newspaper.

Index

Albania: 1–28; communist take-over, 1–2; relations with Soviet Union, 2–3, 14, 16–18, 20–25, 26 (nn. 5, 18), 316, 325, 328, 330; constitution, 3, 6–7, 9; government structure, 6–9; elections, 7–9; private property and enterprise, 7, 28 (n. 42), 304–305, 341; judiciary, 9, 27 (n. 29); economy, 9–12, 15–17; industry, 11, 16–18, 20, 23; social classes, 11–12, 18–20; peasants, 11–12, 18–19; church-state relations, 12–13; education, 12–14, 27 (n. 25); intelligentsia, 13, 341; dissidence, 13–15, 19–20, 27 (nn. 27, 28); police, 14–15, 27 (n. 23); foreign trade, 16–17, 24–25; CMEA, 16, 25, 288, 290, 293, 299, 330; Stalinism, 17, 20, 22–23, 28 (n. 45); agriculture and collectivization, 18–20, 28 (n. 39), 341; planning, 17–18, 27 (nn. 33, 35, 37); youth, 20, 341–342; armed forces, 20–21, 276 (table); foreign relations with countries other than Soviet Union, 21–25, 209, 326, 330; national minorities, 22, 28 (n. 57); WTO, 25, 28 (n. 59), 261, 276, 330; Albanian minorities abroad, 216–217 (tables), 326; basic data, 335 (table)

Albanian communist party. *See* Albanian Workers' Party

Albanian Workers' Party: 2–16, 21–23, 247, 316, 320 (table); structure, 3–5; composition, 5–6;

"interlocking directorate" with government, 9, 10 (table); controls, 11–15

Apel, Erich, 120

Apró, Antal, 133, 139

Armed forces. *See* individual countries; Warsaw Treaty Organization

Armenians, 50 (table)

Bacílek, Karol, 69, 81, 327

Badovinać, Tomislav, 348

Baraniak, Antoni (Archbishop), 175

Belishova, Liri, 22

Belorussians, 173 (table)

Beneš, Eduard, 57–58, 60, 71, 74

Beran, Josef (Cardinal), 89, 95 (n. 81)

Berlin. *See* East Germany

Bierut, Bolesław, 158

Biszku, Béla, 133, 139

Blagoyev, Dimitar, 35

Brezhnev, Leonid I., 262, 318

Bulgaria: 29–56; prewar history, 29–30; national minorities, 29, 46, 49–50, 55 (n. 63); relations with Soviet Union, 30, 32, 37–39, 41, 44, 47–49, 316, 322, 324; constitution, 30–32, 35; communist takeover, 31, 35–36; Fatherland Front, 31–33, 35–36, 40, 53 (n. 8), 342; dissidence, 31, 35–38, 40, 44, 46–47, 53 (n. 10), 54 (n. 25); government structure, 32–33; private property and enterprise, 32, 41, 51, 305, 334; judiciary, 33, 54 (n. 34); peasants,

DATE DUE

GAYLORD			PRINTED IN U.S.A.